Reforming Liberalism

Reforming Liberalism

J. S. Mill's Use of Ancient, Religious,

Liberal, and Romantic Moralities

Robert Devigne

Yale University Press

New Haven & London

Set in Adobe Garamond and Stone Sans types by The Composing Room of
Michigan, Inc.
Printed in the United States of America.

Library of Congress Cataloging-in-Publication Data

Devigne, Robert.
    Reforming liberalism : J. S. Mill's use of ancient, religious, liberal, and romantic
    moralities / Robert Devigne. — 1st ed.
        p. cm.
    Includes bibliographical references and index.
    ISBN-13: 978-0-300-11242-9 (alk. paper)
    ISBN-10: 0-300-11242-4 (alk. paper)
    1. Mill, John Stuart, 1806–1873.   2. Liberalism.   3. Liberty.   4. Ethics.
5. Plato.   I. Title.
B1608 .L5D48 2006
192—dc22

                                                                    2005032281

A catalogue record for this book is available from the British Library.

The paper in this book meets the guidelines for permanence and durability
of the Committee on Production Guidelines for Book Longevity of the
Council on Library Resources.

10 9 8 7 6 5 4 3 2 1

To my family:
Kathleen, Michael, & Jacqueline

Contents

Acknowledgments

I have benefited from the assistance of many persons and institutions while writing this book. First mention must be made of Joseph Hamburger, who introduced me to the complexity of Mill's thought. Hamburger's challenge—the view that Mill's thought is characterized by polarized positions—forced me to recognize that the discovery of the meaning of Mill's liberalism required working one's way through apparent contradictions. It is with profound regret that I note the passing of Joseph Hamburger, a scholar, teacher, and friend.

It is a fond pleasure to thank Vickie Sullivan and Malik Mufti, my colleagues at Tufts University, for their friendship, conversation, and advice. Vickie read all of my drafts, and I am grateful for her criticisms and wise counsel. Malik corrected mistakes in the manuscript on many occasions and consistently offered insightful commentary.

Many other colleagues and friends have given me the benefit of their learning, their criticisms, and their encouragement. Clifford Orwin and Nathan Tarcov provided invaluable direction at different stages of this project. Over the years, conversations and correspondence with Peter Berkowitz, Eldon Eisenach, Stanley Kurtz, Michael

Mosher, Thomas Pangle, Linda Rabieh, Alan Ryan, Andy Sabl, Barry Shain, Allan Silver, Steven Smith, and Michelle Tolman-Clarke have been very helpful to me in the preparation of this book. Among the friends from whom I have learned, I must single out John Ransom, who in the early stages of this project spent countless hours helping me to think out more clearly the issues discussed here.

I also owe a great deal to Tufts University, which has given me a home and a wonderfully congenial work atmosphere. I have experienced nothing but kindness and encouragement from colleagues and students alike. I had the benefit of a talented Tufts student, Justin Race, who was an invaluable researcher, reader, and critic. Nina Cherny and Tal Rabinowitz were excellent research assistants. The students in my classes on "Liberalism and Its Philosophic Critics" and "Liberty, Morality, and Virtue" contributed to my understanding of the themes and issues of this book far more than they probably realize. Tufts University also provided me with access to Harvard University's Widener Library. I also wish to acknowledge the general encouragement of two other members of my department, Tony Smith and Jeffrey Berry.

A draft of chapter 2 was presented at a political theory seminar at the University of Toronto. A draft of chapter 3 was delivered at a political theory seminar at Boston College. Portions of chapters 3 and 7 were presented at the political theory workshop at Yale University. I am grateful to these various audiences for their criticisms and comments. I also am thankful to the National Endowment for the Humanities, the Mellon Foundation, and the Faculty Research Awards Committee at Tufts for financial support. Finally, I am grateful to John Kulka and Mary Traester of Yale University Press. Thanks also to Lawrence Kenney of Yale University Press for his expert copy editing.

The dedication of this book expresses my appreciation to the members of my family. All of them have invigorated me in many ways during this project. The debt that I owe my wife, Kathleen, is beyond measure. Her support and spiritedness have been unfailing. I wrote this book in the years when our children, Michael and Jacqueline, have been growing up. All of them have had the burdens and opportunities of life to shoulder and seize during these years; they did it—and are doing it—with grace and character. A book is a modest statement of gratitude to all of them.

Introduction

Because both supporters and critics of liberalism view John Stuart Mill as formulating many of its key theoretical underpinnings, a truly comprehensive assessment of his thought is essential to any evaluation of liberalism itself. Such an assessment has proved to be elusive. It is evident, of course, that Mill contributes to liberalism by defending free speech and arguing for the liberation of women. But precisely because this aspect of his writing speaks so forcefully and persuasively on matters of intimate and immediate concern to us, it has tended to blot out sections of Mill's thought he himself considered crucial to his overall scheme. Thus, he attached importance not only to the generic individual and his rights, but also to the cultivation of persons who realized freedom through the power of self-command, including exceptional individuals, or geniuses, as well as to the forging of bonds that would cultivate a just moral conscience and higher forms of social unity. Not all of these additional elements are recognizably liberal. Indeed, some can be viewed as bringing tension to bear from either the Left or the Right on liberalism and its focus on free human conduct. In pursuit of such diverse goals, Mill drew not only from classic liberalism, but also from ancient thought, religious practices, and romanticism, proposing a new moral outlook that built upon the strengths and overcame the weaknesses of each of these currents in Western culture. This book, then, seeks to reopen the debate regarding the genesis and development of John Stuart Mill's political and moral thought.

The centrality of Mill's position in Western political philosophy cannot be overemphasized, though it has been frequently misconstrued and, frankly, oversimplified by critics and admirers alike. Mill's education was classical. He was not only familiar with, but to certain extent in love with, the political and ethical world of the Greeks. The intellectual world of his youth combined openness to radicalism in the form of Jeremy Bentham's extreme variant of empiricism—an uncompromising brief on behalf of the utilitarian principle—with a suspicion bred by his contact with the ancients that not every idea of the good is reducible to gross pleasures. During the latter stages of his formative years, Samuel Taylor Coleridge introduced Mill to German romanticism's critique of empiricism. Standing at the crossroads of the fundamental divisions in Western political thought, Mill set out to integrate the insights of the ancients and empiricism's critics into the liberal mainstream.

"So far as I have any *general* object at all," Mill writes in a private correspondence while reformulating his political philosophy, it is to "do most to forward that alliance among advanced intellects and characters of the age, which is the only general object I have in literature or philosophy."[1] His goal was announced publicly in the preface to *The System of Logic Rationative and Deductive:* "To cement together the detached fragments of [philosophizing], never yet treated as a whole; to harmonize the true portions of discordant theories, by supplying the links of thought necessary to connect them, and by disentangling them from the errors with which they are always more or less interwoven."[2] How much richer and deeper our understanding of the liberal political tradition would be if we took seriously such an important and overlooked element of Mill's corpus. Can the older, virtue-centered tradition of the ancients be made to mesh with the modern political, jurisprudential, and economic focus on human equality and freedom? Can empiricism's grounding of human freedom in the natural right of every individual to secure his or her self-preservation and self-interest be reconciled with Immanuel Kant's grounding of freedom in the capacity of human beings to act out of respect for the rational moral law? Mill thought so, and his work as a whole attests to the ambition and comprehensiveness of such a task. His thought challenges the position that the ancients and modern suffered an irreconcilable breach and that the foundational assumptions of German romanticism are at loggerheads with its supposed counterpart, British empiricism.[3]

The most original feature of my interpretation in this book is that it presents a Mill who argues that the Anglo-Scottish liberalism established by Thomas Hobbes, John Locke, David Hume, and Adam Smith was capable of being reformed so as to incorporate the insights of the ancients and romantics, thereby developing more robust ideas of liberty, morality, and human excellence. Mill argues that the positive conception of freedom as a self-directed, radically self-defined moral existence is not as opposed to the classic liberal tradition as originally thought. Instead, he used ancient thought to help negotiate the differences between empiricist and romantic currents of modern political theory. He adopted and modified the ancients as he rallied traditional liberalism to meet and incorporate romanticism's challenges: developing a conception of liberty that centers on self-legislation and self-determination, establishing justice as an ethical outlook and not mere adherence to rules, and embracing the tasks of cultivating human perfection and general moral development. In a word, Mill drew from ancient and romantic thought to reconcile conflicts and antinomies that were confusing and hobbling classic liberalism—liberty and virtue, self-interest and morality, equality and human excellence.[4]

Unfortunately, contemporary political theory has not been fully equipped to investigate this feature of Mill's political philosophy. For most of the postwar era, academic liberals and many of their best-known critics formed an unwitting alliance, promulgating the view that liberal political theory, on the one hand, and theories of politics that dealt with moral development, better and worse ways of life, and human perfection, on the other, represented rival and incompatible frameworks. Classic liberalism for these academic commentators is in direct opposition to the cultivation of virtue typical of ancient philosophy, the moral outlook needed to live in conformity with universal norms,[5] and the self-developed, self-realized individuality that characterizes romanticism.[6] To this alliance of advocates as well as critics, classic liberalism offered merely the articles of a peace treaty among individuals with diverse conceptions of the good but common interests in self-preservation and prosperity; the good liberal society required no more than the proper configuration of rational self-interested activity.

In recent years, influential commentators on political thought have begun to question the adequacy of this depiction of liberalism. Some scholars are returning to the fountainheads of liberal thought to ask to what extent liberalism might be able to respond to these criticisms within its own tradition. Some analysts are discovering, for example, that seminal liberal thinkers recognized that our desires can mislead us and hold back our moral agency. Certain character traits were necessary for what they considered higher types of desires.[7] Other theorists are revising the prevailing view of liberalism by identifying the reconciliation of putatively competing traditions in surprising ways. For example, the combination of liberalism and republicanism, which until very recently would have been considered an implausible, if not impossible, combination, has begun to affect and invigorate the study of American political thought.[8]

This book contributes to the scholarship that reexamines liberalism's content and claims. I argue that the older predominant understanding of liberalism's distinct aims that places it in fundamental conflict with those of ancient, religious, and romantic outlooks has been dramatically overemphasized—so much so that the influence of these perspectives on Mill's political philosophy has either been written off altogether or at best given a superficial glance.[9] For instance, I contend that contemporary theory's focus on empiricism's emphasis on the freedom to pursue one's private passions—most notably, for private property—combined with its concentration on Jean-Jacques Rousseau's and Kant's proposition that the free individual transcends subjection to the natural mechanism of desire and inclination contributes to commentators' overlooking Mill's position that his reconciliation project bridged the gap between the empiricist and romantic wings of modern political philosophy.

In short, most contemporary commentaries on Mill are one-sided. They tend to concentrate only on a part of Mill's thought: the many circumstances in which free choice is to be permitted and the fewer instances in which it might be limited.[10] The damage that results has to do not only with the broad range of Mill's contributions, but even with those elements of Mill's thought that are emphasized, namely, the assessments of utilitarianism and the character of liberty. If one read many of Mill's expositors, one would never know that Mill was deeply concerned with reconciling the ancient and modern conceptions of liberty and justice, consistently attentive to the problem that English liberalism had not sufficiently broken with Christianity, and persistently focused on closing the political differences between Enlightenment liberalism and its romantic critics. Of course, we can hear echoes of these concerns in his better-known works, *On Liberty* and *Utilitarianism,* in which references to the personalities, events, and teachings of the ancient, medieval, and Continental worlds are frequent. But a full understanding of the role these references play in Mill's teachings requires that we turn our attention to a wider range of material produced by Mill than commentators have included in their treatments thus far.[11]

Such a broadening—which would have to include Mill's assessments of Plato (chapters 2 and 3), Athens and Sparta (chapter 3), the ancient and modern conceptions of justice (chapters 3 and 6), empiricism's and romanticism's competing conceptions of liberty (chapter 3), Hume's and Smith's theory of moral sympathy (chapter 2), Kant's conception of the moral conscience (chapter 2), revealed Christianity and the Enlightenment's natural religion (chapters 4 and 5)—discloses that the full meaning of *On Liberty* is not revealed unless one takes into account integral themes of the Mill corpus. It reveals that Mill's *On Liberty* is not primarily directed at Christianity's hold on the Victorian mind or the hold of a monolithic opinion of any kind.[12] A broader reading of Mill reveals that *On Liberty*'s concern about these limitations on freedom is an integral part of Mill's fundamental goal to reform English liberalism and the one-sided or distorted moral development of the West, which has pitted the goal of developing and perfecting the individual against the aim of ensuring the equality and moral development of the general public (chapter 4). For instance, by taking into account Mill's posthumous publications on Christianity, we learn that the fundamental point of Mill's discussion of freedom of thought in chapter 2 of *On Liberty* is the Anglo-Scottish Enlightenment's failure to break with the Christian tradition of obedience and fear of the creative will (chapters 4 and 5). According to Mill, if English society is to generate a comprehensive morality for the future, the Anglo-Scottish Enlightenment's universal rules of justice and reformed Christianity, or natural religion, must be augmented by civil practices and values that support high ambitions, the pursuit of distinctiveness, and the self-respect that engenders human conduct that rises above narrow self-interested activities.

Situating *On Liberty* in the context of the Mill corpus also shows that his goal in chapter 3 of that work is to establish a quality which characterized ancient thought but is noticeably absent in modern thought: an idea of the best life, or *summum bonum*. I show that Mill's envisioned highest type of individual is a step to overcoming the problems stemming from the one-sided divisions in Western morality and to harmonizing and synthesizing the constituent elements of a morality that cultivates the complete human character: creative individuality and just conduct. This book explains that *On Liberty* considers two different standards of this highest type of individual. On the one hand, Mill puts forth an ideal that synthesizes ancient and modern conceptions of liberty, encouraging strong desires and wills toward goals that serve the public good, while also protecting the freedom and security of all citizens. On the other hand, Mill establishes a romantic-expressive idea of the best life that is characterized by spontaneity, struggle, and self-development, with the individual experiencing conflict between himself and the prevailing norms and practices of society. I examine both visions of human development—showing what they invoke, what qualities they exemplify, how they are similar, how they are different, how they both stood in opposition to English liberalism, and why, in Mill's view, the romantic-expressive conception of human development is ultimately preferable. I explain how Mill integrated this expressive conception of liberty with the dialectics of Coleridge and the German Romantics to introduce a new conception of *Bildung,* or culture, into English liberalism that synthesizes what an individual uniquely contributes to society and what the values of the society make him or her, a back and forth that leads to higher forms of individuality and greater social and political unity.

What my book shows, then, is that Mill both acknowledges and attempts to integrate the fundamental divisions in Western political and moral thought. He touches and transforms almost all significant currents of thought as his assessment of their advantages and disadvantages directly contributes to his envisioned morality of the future. The book also provides insights into our contemporary intellectual landscape. It shows that, by incorporating the insights of the ancients and the romantics within the liberal mainstream, Mill worked to tame the Continental opposition to traditional liberalism while purging the latter of its emphasis on prosaic and bourgeois aims. Today we see liberalism's opponents on the Left and Right spinning their wheels attempting to offer alternatives to liberalism—reconstituted republicanism, revised critical theories, and revaluated outlooks centered on human excellence.[13] Mill's thought raises the possibility that these so-called alternatives are rooted in liberalism itself through its absorption of the criticisms of its former opponents.

This book emphasizes and assesses Mill's appropriation of various schools in the history of political and moral thought, so I should clarify what I mean by *ancients, religious, classic liberal,* and *romantic.* By ancients, I am primarily referring to the political philosophy of Plato and the political practice of Athens in the Periclean Age. Mill studied and evaluated Plato's effort to join different ends: the cultivation of wise, creative individuals liberated from society's constricting norms and the development of common ethical bonds. He studied Athens to discover the qualities of character and practices that led to an explosion of creative energy and human agency.

By religion, I am referring to Mill's assessment of the advantages and disadvantages of Christianity, the natural religion of the Enlightenment, and his proposed Religion of Humanity as moral outlooks. Mill approached religion as a source of morality with two questions in mind: Is belief in the gods necessary to establish an object of the good by reference to which all of our conduct is to be judged? Is religion necessary for establishing an imaginative picture of human perfection? The relation between philosophy and religion is also of crucial interest to Mill, as he believes both to be the key creators of the values that animate society.

By classic liberal, I am referring to Anglo-Scottish philosophers—Hobbes, Locke, Hume, and Smith, among others—whose thinking contributed to the protections of freedoms of religion, speech, representation, and the accumulation and protection of property in the United Kingdom and much of the West. Mill's critical engagement with this school, of which he was a part, centered on two key themes: Does empiricism's negative notion of liberty, with its focus on what cannot be done to the individual, fail to cultivate a truly free will and thus undermine human agency, which is necessary for progress and the protection of liberty itself? Does empiricism's position that our general ideas simply reflect the particular features of the experiences from which they originate render it incapable of explaining universal moral norms and so of refuting the charges of egoism and immorality?[14]

Finally, by romanticism I am referring to the revolution in philosophy, literature, and criticism that originated with Rousseau, flowered during the so-called Sturm und Drang period in late eighteenth-century Germany, spread to the English poets Coleridge, Percy Bysshe Shelley, and others, included Kant, and deeply influenced G. W. F. Hegel. Mill's thinking was spurred by a variety of the romantics' critiques of early modern liberalism: freedom could never simply mean the untrammeled pursuit of one's empirical desires; morality could not be so deeply interconnected with utilitarian calculations of pleasure and pain; a psychology of mind could not be based on a subject-object duality which depends on a mind separate from the rest of the world. In Germany (and to a lesser extent in England) the Romantic movement had two interrelated, yet competing, currents of thought, expressivism and moral idealism, and Mill consistently engaged both. The dual focus in expressivist thinking, as most fully represented by Friedrich Schiller, Friedrich Schelling, and Friedrich Hölderlin, was the cultivation of the individual's unique capabilities and the Imagination's or the Artist's synthesizing of the distinct contributions of these individuals into deeper modes of social and political unity. Moral idealists—most notably, Kant and Johann Fichte—claimed that humans' ability to transcend impulses and desires as well as choose for themselves distinguishes us from other animals and makes moral conduct possible and that moral freedom required transcending all desires for the good of the morally right.[15]

Throughout the book, I also examine the most serious challenges to Mill's project to reconcile the putatively alternative currents in Western political thought. For instance, like Mill, Friedrich Nietzsche claims that the central disputes of the Western philosophic and cultural tradition are of secondary importance and that modern democracy has the potential to reconcile these differences. But to Nietzsche, the unifying theme of Western values has been the centuries-long taming of the will characteristic of Platonism, Christianity, the Enlightenment, and German idealism; a tradition that is united in elevating the weak over the strong. He argues that, unlike the ancient Greeks and Romans, moderns confront the lack of transhistorical values with a weak will and heavy conscience. Thus while Nietzsche values the promotion of the strong will and creative spirit, he argues that regenerating excellent individuals requires going beyond integrating either ancient virtues or romantic self-development with liberal democracy. In his view, such reconciliation projects will accelerate mass homogeneity because they reflect the Western tradition's decay and reveal, "to what extent the judgment of the exhausted had penetrated the world of values."[16]

I also examine Alexis de Tocqueville's differences with Mill's project. Tocqueville, unlike Mill, sees modern and premodern regimes as fundamentally distinct and opposed social states. He rejects Mill's vision of a democracy in which creative individuals originate alternative experiences that allow people to discover the best life and have the opportunity to gain more control over their mental and moral faculties. Tocqueville maintains that the substantive outlooks of exceptional individuals and the mass in modern democracy are fundamentally the same and that the public is primarily focused on improving its material well-being and has little concern for alternative ideas and social practices.[17]

Finally, the book explains how the prevailing interpretations of Mill in the academy contribute to a restricted conception of liberalism. The dominant view of Mill, notably articulated by Isaiah Berlin, recognizes the competing emphases in Mill's thinking regarding liberty, moral integration, and human excellence. But Berlin is unable to discover coherence among these different aims and so concludes by suggesting that the central tenet of liberalism is choice, a claim based on Mill's confusion concerning political philosophy's proper goals. Revisionist interpreters of Mill, such as Alan Ryan, identify a coherent doctrine in Mill's thinking but neglect most of his ethical and moral concerns in favor of a focus on when behavior infringes on the rights of others. As a result, the debate on Mill in the academy has centered on a traditional interpretation of a confused Mill unable to reconcile conflicting views and a revisionist portrayal of an incomplete, prosaic Mill.[18] Given these interpretations, it is not surprising that in recent decades the predominant view of liberalism became synonymous with indifference to substantive moral concerns, hostility to human bonds that hold societies together, and antagonism to human excellence. Is it any wonder that many deem Mill a boring political philosopher?

Recent scholarship on Hegel and republicanism has begun reconsideration of the conflict between theories of individual liberty and community.[19] A reevaluation of Mill's liberalism gives us a deeper understanding of the largely untapped middle ground between these two alternatives. This book shows that a seminal writer in the liberal tradition critiqued liberalism's weaknesses—its abstract individualist methodology, its lack of universal aims, its failure to cultivate a positive conception of the human good—with a forcefulness that is usually associated with critics of liberalism. A close analysis of Mill's thought will make it possible for us to see that liberalism is not necessarily as restricted an outlook as many of its critics and defenders believe.

Chapter 1 The Moderns and Plato

Late twentieth-century analyses of Plato highlight how the many paradoxes, tensions, and dramatic settings in which the Platonic dialogues occur often seem to undermine the substance of Plato's foundational and doctrinal assertions—the doctrine of ideas, the pure spirit, philosopher-kings, among others. These commentaries reopen questions that were shut down in the wake of the midcentury totalitarian verdict dealt to Plato by R. H. S. Crossman, Karl Popper, and others.[1] This closed view of Plato as a monolithic dogmatist had limited analysts' ability to understand modern, as well as ancient, political thought.

John Stuart Mill, for instance, considered Plato the most significant influence on his "mental culture," claiming no modern thinker had been influenced by Plato as much as he had.[2] In many of Mill's works there are numerous accounts, some quite specific and comprehensive, of Socrates and Plato. Nonetheless, the commentators on Mill who enjoyed the greatest influence in the last half of the twentieth century simply rejected the possibility that Mill appropriated aspects of Plato's thought. Whereas Plato, Isaiah Berlin insists, founded the belief in immutable, undivided truths, the importance of Mill lies in his complete rejection of this teaching. Alan Ryan, upon identifying a Platonic strain in Mill's thought, dismisses any further investigation of this point because "Mill's age had not learned to see Plato as a totalitarian."[3] Part of the damage from this void in Mill commentaries is the fact that it ignores the broad range of Mill's contributions to political philosophy, for example, his position on Plato and his project to reconcile the competing currents in Western morality. Yet it not only limits key elements in his thought while overemphasizing others, but also misses the fuller, richer idea of liberty he intended.[4]

MILL AND PLATO

While all of Mill's major writings refer heavily to Socrates and Plato, Mill was determined to develop and publish a comprehensive position that dealt solely with Plato. This desire is dramatically expressed in letters to his wife and in *Diary* entries he wrote in the winter of 1854, when coughing fits and blood-ridden phlegm convinced Mill he was suffering from tuberculosis, the same disease that killed his father. Confronting the possibility of an early death, Mill felt a great impetus to produce a series of essays on the most important questions, "which thinkers . . . after us may nourish themselves with & then dilute for other people." Most are not surprised to find on Mill's agenda the themes published in *On Liberty, The Subjection of Women,* and the *Three Essays on Religion,* but few expect to find Plato.[5]

In 1865, Mill used the opportunity of reviewing George Grote's *Plato, and the Other Companions of Sokrates* as a venue to publish his comprehensive position on Plato. He reread all of the Platonic dialogues, in the original Greek, while alone in southern France as he worked on the essay. "The chief occupation of this year," Mill wrote to Grote at the end of 1865, "has been with Plato, Socrates, and you: and there could not have been to me, a pleasanter one." In this letter, Mill immodestly states that no single essay discusses Plato as thoroughly as the one he was then completing.[6]

Mill had also published works regarding Plato during the 1830s, the period when he was reevaluating empiricism's positions that reason is exclusively the instrument of the passions and that our general ideas simply reflect the particular features of the experiences from which they originate. In 1834–35, Mill published translations with commentaries of four Platonic dialogues for the *Monthly Repository.* The series proved to be popular. Indeed, in the *Autobiography* Mill notes that in the late 1830s he was surprised to discover that these dialogues and commentaries had been read and "their authorship known, by more people than were aware of anything else which I had written up to that time." Mill was set to publish work on five more dialogues when the editor, W. J. Fox, decided to move the journal toward a different intellectual orientation for practical considerations.[7]

In his introduction to the volume of Mill's *Collected Works* that houses the nine translated dialogues and commentaries, F. E. Sparshott reflects the trend by contemporary analysts to dismiss Mill's interest in Plato. Sparshott asks, Why is Mill interested in the Platonic dialogues? Unable to answer his own question, he guesses that Mill chose to translate the following dialogues— *Protagoras, Phaedrus, Gorgias, Apology, Charmides, Euthyphro, Laches, Lysis,* and *Parmenides*—to support Friedrich Schleiermacher, who contributed to the Platonic revival in Germany during the 1820s and 1830s. Mill, Sparshott conjectures, set out to reinforce Schleiermacher's goal of founding a popular Platonic canon.[8]

Indeed, Mill is in accord with Schleiermacher's position that Socrates' primary contribution to philosophy consists not in the specific truths he proposed, "but in the improved views which he originated respecting the mode in which truth should be *sought*."[9] However, it is unlikely Sparshott's conjecture that Mill was reinforcing Schleiermacher's project to establish a Platonic canon is right, as Schleiermacher considered the *Gorgias* and *Apology* irrelevant, possibly fraudulent, dialogues.[10] Mill also barely recognized Schleiermacher's work; and he opposed the positions held by Schleiermacher (among other commentators on Plato) which dismissed dialogues that did not contribute to a coherent Platonic outlook and held that Plato's positive assertions—such as the doctrine of Ideas and the Myth of Er—were direct outgrowths of Plato's dialectical investigations. Finally, Mill opposed the position held by Schleiermacher and others that Plato was a prophet of Christianity and transcendental philosophy.[11]

A more promising avenue of inquiry for discovering Mill's intent in translating and commenting on Plato's dialogues is provided by the anonymous ancient commentator, who suggested that studying Plato enables us to contemplate Plato's teachings and discover our own assumptions and questions about the world. This commentator reports the myth that "Plato himself, shortly before his death, had a dream of himself as a swan, darting from tree to tree, causing great trouble to the bird catchers, who were unable to catch him. When Simmias the Socratic heard this dream, he explained that all men would endeavor to grasp Plato's meaning, none, however, would succeed, but each would interpret him according to his own views, whether in a theological or a physical or any other sense."[12] From this perspective, the reader of Plato must confront contradictory teachings, myths, irony, and dialogues in which the author never speaks for himself, so any commentary on Plato teaches as much about the assumptions and concerns of the commentator as it does about Plato himself.

Mill's actual analysis of the dialogues focuses on themes that are central to both Plato's and Mill's political philosophies. In Mill's account, the *Charmides, Laches, Euthyphro,* and *Lysis* show how dialectical investigations are the key method of overcoming the greatest human problem, what Socrates calls our common ignorance in thinking that we know when we do not. This theme is central to Mill's *On Liberty:* "Where there is tacit convention that principles are not to be disputed, where the discussion of the greatest questions which can occupy humanity is considered to be closed, we cannot hope to find that generally high scale of mental activity which has made some periods of history so remarkable."[13] Mill's commentaries and analyses of the *Protagoras* and *Gorgias* examine Plato's positions on the relation between individual happiness and virtue. Accordingly, Mill opens *Utilitarianism* with the statement that the relation between virtue and happiness has bedeviled political philosophy "since the youth Socrates listened to the old Protagoras, and asserted . . . the theory of utilitarianism against the popular morality of the so-called Sophist."[14] Finally, Mill's attention to the *Phaedrus* and *Parmenides* is devoted to the proper relation between philosophy and poetry, philosophy and faith: namely, the philosophical quest to discover the truth and the creation of ennobling religious and poetical teachings. These concerns are central to the *Three Essays on Religion,* in which Mill examines and explores the "most painful position to a conscientious and cultivated mind, to be drawn in two contrary directions by the noblest objects of all pursuits, truth, and the general good."[15] In short, studying Mill's evaluation of Plato provides insights into the political philosophies of both Plato and Mill himself.

Mill's interest in Plato—and in classical political thought and practice more generally—should not come as a surprise. He began to study the works of Homer, Herodotus, Thucydides, Xenophon, Plato, and Aristotle as a child.[16] As early as 1840, in commenting on Tocqueville's thesis that modern democracy distorts intellectual thought, Mill argued that it was "incumbent upon those who had the power to do the utmost towards preventing" the decline of classical studies.[17] Friend and foe alike criticized Mill for placing such high value on the study of Plato and the ancients and for calling for a reconciliation in "that age old conflict between the ancients and the moderns."[18] In response to Herbert Spencer's criticism that his vision of higher education placed too much emphasis on the ancients, Mill wrote, "In regard to classical instruction, I do not altogether agree with you that the side favourable to it is too strong; for I think there is a growing reaction to the opposite extreme, producing a danger on that side which being the side most in harmony with modern tendencies has the best chance of being ultimately the stronger."[19] Mill also was a central figure in the debate among mid-Victorian intellectuals on the significance of the art, religion, and politics of ancient Greece. As his friend and biographer Alexander Bain pronounces, Mill "was a . . . Greece-intoxicated man,"[20] and to ignore as much is to do Mill's legacy a great injustice.

THE PLATONIC REVIVAL

Mill was not alone in his philosophical engagements with Plato. A crucial moment in Western intellectual history began at the start of the nineteenth century, when philosophers, poets, and historians throughout the West turned to Plato for help in understanding the sources of and cures for the materialism and disunity of the age. This Platonic revival, which originated in Germany decades earlier and spread to England during the early Victorian period, did not produce a unified view of Plato. On the contrary, the treatment of Plato by one writer often came in reaction to another, and soon there were Romantic, but also Hegelian and even Empiricist Platos, and some thinkers, such as Mill, developed positions on Plato that reflected the views of the different schools of thought. The significance of this discussion and its continued reverberations in modern thought has been too little appreciated by contemporary commentators on political theory.[21]

Here I will briefly review the competing appropriations of Plato by various schools in the cultural and philosophical spectrum of Europe in the nineteenth century. Several conclusions emerge from such a review. First, on an abstract plane, one learns that the supposed mutual incomprehensibility of intellectual traditions originating on the Continent as compared to the putatively more sensible kinds in Great Britain is a modern myth. The cultural unity of Europe among the higher echelons of the elite was still a factor in the nineteenth century, and these elites were still required to learn something of ancient Greek history, language, culture, and politics. Thus, when Schiller and Hölderlin wrote about ancient Greek dramatists and philosophers, they were quite comprehensible to Shelley and Coleridge across the channel.[22] In turn, philosophers and classicists on the Continent closely studied and debated Grote's works on Plato and the ancients. Nietzsche, for instance, cites Grote's works repeatedly in his lectures on ancient philosophy in the 1870s, particularly noting Grote's position that Socrates orchestrated his death in order to help found philosophy as a way of life; Nietzsche himself eventually put forward that view in *The Twilight of the Idols*.[23]

But it is not only that the philosophers, poets, and classicists talked to and understood one another. To think that the foundational assumptions of German romanticism were at loggerheads with its supposed counterpart, British empiricism, would be equally erroneous. This capacity, displayed by some members of the European intellectual elite—most notably, Mill[24]—leads to a second discovery: Mill used Plato to help negotiate the disputes between both empiricism and romanticism and the ancients and moderns as part of his project to overcome the one-sided development of Western morality. Mill learned distinct lessons, positive and negative, from Plato, the romantics, and the empiricists and formulated a new outlook that built upon the strengths and overcame the weaknesses of each.[25]

For instance, seminal thinkers from the Anglo-Scottish liberal tradition, including Hobbes, Locke, and Hume, saw liberty in terms of removal of constraints on individual action. This negative notion of liberty focuses on what cannot be done to the individual. Mill was aware of and impressed by the criticism of this vision provided by the Continental thinkers such as Kant: that if our understanding of liberty is restricted to what others cannot do to the individual by the exercise of their wills, society will ignore the task of cultivating self-mastery and thus truly free individuals.

In offering a response to this criticism on behalf of empiricism, Mill believed it was necessary to include the insights of Plato as well as of the romantics. He concluded that Plato also had a deep understanding of what was required—what qualities had to be encouraged—if societies were to arrive at an ethics capable of fostering developed forms of individuality and human agency. And it was precisely the seriousness with which Plato, Coleridge, Fichte, and other ancients and romantics pursued this question that convinced Mill that the dominant "individualist" theories of his own school of empiricism were weak in comparison: both the ancients and the romantics help us recognize that individuals have the capacity to shape and master their own character.

But Mill was also aware that both the ancient and romantic conceptions of liberty involved risks. Despite his happiness at finding in Plato and romantic sources a serious consideration of what was involved in perfecting the individual, he recognized that they offered no protection against the emergence of overly willful and tyrannical types like Alcibiades or Napoleon, individuals who strive to overcome conventional norms in order to attain private gain at the public expense. This recognition of the potential dangers posed by human creativity spurred Mill to develop an entirely new moral theory for empiricism, which was already withering from Kant's and romanticism's criticisms.

In short, it turns out that Mill directly engaged Plato and took very seriously the nineteenth-century debate between empiricism and romanticism on the character of liberty, morality, and human perfection. In that context, Mill worked very hard to incorporate the insights of Plato, Coleridge, Kant, and other ancient and romantic sources to develop a liberal political philosophy that would reform an English liberalism that refused to take responsibility for developing the motives and practices that lead to self-mastery and the exertion of human energy. As John Skorupski puts it, "[Mill's] chosen role is to educate the serious-minded; his philosophical stance is numbingly comprehensive, lucid, and systematic. . . . If Bacon wrote philosophy like a Lord Chancellor, Mill all too often writes like a self-appointed Royal Commission."[26] The result is a version of liberalism that has a richer, fuller notion of the individual: not just as a bearer of a limited number of rights, but also as a person who can and should be cultivated in a particular direction, including the ability to amend oneself.

PLATO AS POET

The mystical and poetical Plato of the English Romantics—Shelley, Coleridge, William Blake, among others—predominated among the writers who read Plato seriously in England during the first third of the nineteenth century. Placing dialogues such as the *Symposium* and the *Phaedo* at the forefront of the Platonic corpus, the romantic poets viewed Plato as a dramatist and author of inspiring myths whose whole approach to the world was the antithesis to the materialism and utilitarianism that in their view debased the contemporary age. To these poets, Plato cultivated the moral sensibilities of humanity by painting pictures of a more pervasive beauty that lay beyond the civilized world: the doctrine of recollection indicated how civilization's norms enervated humanity, and the immortal soul told how real life began when the soul was freed from bodily appetites. Ignoring Plato's argument that poets merely imitate the tastes and passions of the audience that have been shaped by conventions,[27] Shelley, William Wordsworth, John Keats, and many other romantics were inspired by Plato to find individual perfection, the beautiful itself, and their own souls through poetry that returned the individual to nature.[28]

The key contemporary intellectual influence on the English poets was the expressive current of the German romantics—Johann Herder, Schiller, Hölderlin, to name a few—who called for liberation from the modern outlook of *Aufklärung,* materialism and utility, which stood in contrast to the ancient Greek ethos of wholeness and harmony.[29] Typically, the German romantics' view of history begins with the description of the unconscious, undifferentiated unity of the ancients, then moves into a period of sustained estrangement between thought and action, subjective will and objective good. These divisions, in turn, drive a historical process back toward unity at a higher level of coherence and awareness. Among the ancient Greeks whom they idealized and in the future for which they held such high hopes, the German romantics saw images of the harmoniousness for which they so ardently yearned. As Schiller put it, "What single modern steps forth, man to man, to strive for the prize of humanity with a single Athenian? Whence then, with every advantage of the race, this disadvantageous relation of individuals? In what consisted the qualifications of a single Grecian to represent his time, and why may not a single modern attempt the same? Because all-uniting nature had imparted her forms to the former, and all-dividing intellect her own to the latter."[30]

Schiller blamed the spiritual deadness of his age on science and a fragmented civil society—on the physicists and astronomers who taught that the sun is merely a ball of fire and the society of specialization that truncated our faculties and restricted social intercourse. He lamented what was sloughed off as the necessary price for progress, in society and science alike. Overwhelming indifference had permeated social interactions, charged Hölderlin, and was causing social and political atrophy. Only culture would enable people to regain mutual regard in their interpersonal encounters and to forge bonds of solidarity and trust in the rules and institutions that govern meaningful connections between people. It was therefore crucial that artistic and educative energies be activated in an attempt to reestablish binding values of coexistence. The culture that the romantic-expressivists imagined had the doubly imposing tasks of liberating individuals from the constraints of custom and convention, allowing them to realize their unique nature in the full, while also synthesizing the highest contributions of individuals into new values and deeper social and political integration.[31]

It was the general view of the German Romantics that Plato, standing at the dawn of humanity's divisions, recognized the role of the artist as a vital cultivator of wholeness and unity.[32] Plato's art itself reflected his understanding of the proper relation between the parts and the whole. Plato was "able, with much dexterity, but in a natural way, to produce a dialogue, to distribute the subject matter appropriately among the persons carrying on the discussion, to have each person think in character and allow him to speak occasionally, and yet to keep sight of the whole. The unity of the ultimate purpose joined the manifold parts to each other so fortuitously that the thread of the conversation could be followed without confusion, and that the subject mastered remained in sight."[33] The German Romantics embraced many of Plato's specific moral teachings as well. They saw Plato's teaching regarding the One and the Many as a forebear of their own belief in an absolute unity and harmony behind the many-colored, ever-shifting mass of phenomena. The *Phaedrus* and the *Symposium,* which expound Plato's philosophy of love, were seen as an anticipation of the romantics' conception of *eros*—the universal, eternally creative, and generating force which operates through an infinite chain of conflicts, giving unity and continuity to finite, divided forms of being.[34]

To be sure, the British Romantics were far less united in regard to the implications of Plato's and their own art.[35] In Wordsworth's view, Plato's Doctrine of Recollection—whereby the "path of recollection" starts from an experience of perplexity and the discovery of one's ignorance—expresses the poets' goal to disengage the self from the distorting thoughts and experiences of society, allowing the individual to rediscover his most natural sentiments and feelings. Through this conflict between the natural and social selves, the individual returns to nature at a higher level as the conflict engenders range, depth, and sensitivity in one's self-awareness.[36]

The poet, in Wordsworth's account, recognizes that the human mind has the potential to be excited, beautiful, and dignified, and that one era is elevated above another in proportion as the mind is so cultivated. "To endeavour to produce or enlarge this capability [of the mind] is one of the best services in which, at any period, a Writer can be engaged, but this service, excellent at all times, is especially so at the present day. For a multitude of causes, unknown to former times, are now acting with a combined force to blunt the discriminatory powers of the mind, and unfitting it for all voluntary exertion to reduce it to a state of almost savage torpor." The goal of poetry is to create "excitement in co-existence with an overbalance of pleasure"; its aim is to regenerate humanity's feelings, to extend their sympathies, and enlarge the capacity "of being excited without the application of gross and violent stimulants." The poet considers humanity and nature "as essentially adapted to each other, and the mind of man as naturally the mirror of the fairest and most interesting qualities of nature." Ancient poets like Plato, Lucretius, and Catullus were more aware of poetry's task than contemporary poets, asserts Wordsworth. Writing at the time civilization was founded, they recognized the tension between nature and artifice, using language that was daring and figurative to identify the primary laws of nature.[37]

Coleridge, like the German Romantics, identified a more politically constructive, form-making role for the poet than Wordsworth did. The poet did not merely present ordinary things in unusual and uplifting ways; rather, the imagination of the poet was to embrace every facet of life, shaping and transforming it into one harmonious, beautiful entity. "The poet, described in *ideal perfection,* brings the whole soul of man into activity, with the subordination of its faculties to each other, according to their relative worth and dignity."[38] In true Platonic fashion, Coleridge argued it is illuminating to evaluate all particular phenomena—most notably, the state—in light of the true, universal "idea." It is "that conception of a thing which is not abstracted from any particular state, form or mode in which they may happen to exist at this or that time," states Coleridge. "Nor yet generalized from any number or succession of such forms or modes; that which is given by the knowledge of *its ultimate aim.*[39] Coleridge makes the argument for a political order in which a constitutional monarchy maintains a dynamic equilibrium between the traditionalism of the aristocracy and the innovation of the commercial and intellectual classes. Coleridge, who praised the philosopher-kings, the perfected individual, and the perfect state of Plato's *Republic,* envisaged a new church, or "clerisy" as he named it: a caste of higher-type men who mediated and synthesized the contributions of the two great classes and devoted attention to the development of a national culture. Coleridge identified moral cultivation as "the harmonious development of those qualities and faculties that characterize our humanity," and it was on this type of education that he placed his highest hopes.[40]

Shelley did not draw lessons about hierarchy and philosopher-kings from Plato. Not that Plato failed to politically inspire Shelley. One of Shelley's greatest poems, *Prometheus Unbound,* derives from his reading of Plato and Aeschylus; its theme is the never-ending battle between good and evil that is found in Plato's *Statesman* and Aeschylus's *Prometheus Bound.* Plato inspired Shelley on two levels. The Platonic dialogues featuring the skeptical questioning of dogmatism encouraged Shelley to compose essays such as "Refutation of Deism," which assessed the advantages and disadvantages of faith and atheism. The dialogues featuring Plato's imaginative powers, which posited that education and virtue could overcome corruption, emboldened Shelley to proclaim that the poet is someone "divine" who can apprehend the good and teach his readers. After rereading chapter six of the *Republic*, Shelley commented that "if ever the world is to be arranged upon another system than that of the several members of it destroying & tormenting one another for the sake of the pleasures of the senses, or from the force of habit and imitation; it must start from" the principles of moral education in the *Republic*.[41]

In Shelley's account, the imaginative powers of Plato and all poets require not only the ability to combine diverse elements into a coherent, harmonious whole; they also must have a mediating power that apprehends a superior reality, creating a link between the known world and the transcendental realm. The objects initiated by the great poet are the eternal Forms discerned through the veil of fact and particularity. The poet "strips the veil of familiarity from the world, and lays bare the naked and sleeping beauty, which is the spirit of its forms." This poetry is particularly important in periods such as the present when, "the excess of the selfish and calculating principle, the accumulation of the materials of external life exceed the quantity of the power of assimilating them to the laws of nature. The body has become too unwieldy for that which animates it."[42]

Shelley often borrowed Plato's metaphors and adapted them to produce something personal and distinctive. For instance, in Plato's Myth of Er the universe is explained as a series of concentric circles, resembling vessels that fit into one another and are shaded in various colors. To those individuals who live a virtuous earthly existence, a wonderful thousand-year voyage through the heavens awaits them.[43] Shelley utilized this cosmology to explain a world that is beautiful in important respects, but not nearly as beautiful as the highest circle. In his elegy on the death of Keats, Shelley wrote,

> The One remains, the many change and pass;
> Heaven's light forever shines, Earth's shadows fly;
> Life like a dome of many coloured glass,
> Stains the white radiance of eternity
> Until Death tramples it to fragments—Die
> If thou wouldst be with that which thou does seek![44]

The British Romantics' main contribution to the debate on Plato was their serious treatment of Plato's artistic imagery and dramatic structure, their general promotion of his thinking at a time when eighteenth-century Anglo-Scottish Enlightenment writers had largely ignored Plato's thought, and their argument that Plato gave poets a unique responsibility to use their imagination for cultivating the individual's and community's ethical sensibilities. Mill was reading Wordsworth and Coleridge closely during the time he was publishing translations of Platonic dialogues with commentaries. But whereas the romantics believe Plato used artistic imagery to give popular and figurative form to moral truth, Mill counters that Plato developed poetic metaphors to cover up or hide reason's limited understanding of morality. Nonetheless, while Mill criticized most of Plato's specific poetic teachings, he acquired from the romantic thinkers an appreciation for Plato's attempts as a poet to cultivate the ethical sensibilities of the individual and the community. This contribution of the romantics to the debate over Plato as well as Mill's own assessment of romantic art would directly contribute to Mill's positions that political philosophers had a *poietic* task of establishing the proper ends of a political society and that England needed an aesthetic culture to cultivate exceptional individuals who would channel their energies to practices that further the public good.

HEGEL'S PLATO

It was Hegel's account of the ancients in general and of Plato in particular that was the most significant of the century, and as such, not surprisingly, the source of critical commentary for generations to come throughout Europe. For Hegel, the Sophists and Socrates initiated the critical break and duality in Western culture from which it was only now beginning to recover, more than two millennia later. Prior to the Sophists, Greece had been characterized by a prereflective culture free of the tensions between the private and public self, the inner and external world: every individual in Athens embraced the laws and customs; each and every one of them experienced in his own person the collective consciousness of the entire polity. In contrast to later ages, the Athenians did not regard their social norms and institutions as alien or oppressive and hence did not attempt to distance themselves from them. The only problem with Athenian culture was that it was experienced without being understood, a problem Socrates drove a decisive wedge into.[45]

This incapacity to ground the religious beliefs and cultural mores of the *polis* in a deeper, more comprehensive understanding was first manifested, ac-

cording to Hegel, when the Sophists submitted them to the scrutiny of reflective reason. The Sophists initiated the shift from the objective to the subjective, from universal to individual standards, and slowly individual resolve
began to assert its rule over the authority of tradition and objective law.
Socrates participated in the Sophistic revolt against unthinking allegiance to
customs and morality. But he also initiated the shift in moral sensibility from
Sittlichkeit to *Moralität.* Before Socrates the Athenians obeyed customs and
derived their ethical life from the ordinances of the *polis.* Now Socrates introduced a reflective moral conscience according to which the individual sought
to determine what is right and good from within. Thought became free, and
the individual asserted his right to evaluate his own conduct. By this process the
Athenians abandoned the religion of the poets and the moral ordinances of the
polis and turned to their own subjective reflection for moral guidance.[46]

Hegel recognizes Socrates' reflective morality as a key step to human freedom, but he also sees that this form of conscience, when isolated from other
considerations, leads to radical subjectivism and ultimately nihilism. Hemmed
in as it is by the self, reflective morality addresses only a part of our psychic
world, and so will not always correspond to what is objectively rational. In the
short run, Socrates' opposition to accepted Athenian norms led to his trial and
death. To Hegel, Socrates' death was not unjust but tragic because "in what is
truly tragic there must be valid moral powers on both sides which come into
collision; this was so with Socrates." In the long run, Socrates initiated the
long-standing split in Western culture between the harmony and unity of the
Greek world and the different quests for subjective freedom through philosophy, Christianity, and, later, commercial activity.[47]

In Hegel's account, Plato's genius was his recognition that the substantive
ethics of his age were being undermined by free thought. On the one hand,
Plato intensified this crisis in a dialogue such as the *Protagoras,* which displays
the use of the negative, critical dialectic in freeing people from what is customary. On the other hand, dialogues such as the *Parmenides* and the *Gorgias* feature Plato's speculative or positive dialectic, which affords insight into how
reason or wisdom can overcome such contradictions. Plato attempted to overcome the ethical crisis by constructing a new republic on a new universalistic
ethos that reestablished shared moral understanding. Plato failed, in Hegel's
view, because he was either unwilling or unable to completely confront the
problem, as he did not integrate the newly founded subjective freedom with his
prescribed universal outlook (an understanding that Hegel would ascribe to
Rousseau). Plato's political plan did little to heal the breach between subjective

notions of right and objective dictates concerning it; on the contrary, his proposals institutionalized the schism. Plato's republic places too many restrictions
on marriage, the family, property, and reason itself. Plato failed to reconcile the
relation between the particular and universal good.

Hegel believed Plato's true contribution to the resolution between subjectivity and objectivity had less to do with his political program and more to do with
his discussion of the nature of "universals." The empiricism of the Sophists and
Socrates sought meaning of abstract terms such as *justice* and *courage* through
an accumulation of instances that exemplified the quality of the item under discussion. Plato argued that one must go the other way: understand a term or
thought in its ideal, absolute reality and then assess the instances of its application to concrete circumstances. In Hegel's account, Plato's doctrine of ideas is
an artistic metaphor designed to help us see that the sensations of external objects and forces that occur in our consciousness do not give us a view of reality.
They are not themselves truly real. The ideal form of a concept is the species or
genus, of which the particular instance is a more or less degraded representative. Hegel concedes that Plato did not focus enough attention on the process
of transition from ideal reality to concrete instance. But Plato's contribution is
nonetheless a signal one. He introduced the intellectual world to ideal concepts
that interact with, without ever being enclosed by, the temporal order. In
Hegelian terms, Plato discovered Spirit.[48]

To Hegel, the conflict that developed at the inception of Western political
philosophy is being resolved in the contemporary period. Indeed, there is a parallel between Hegel's analysis of the evolution of thought from the Sophists,
through Socrates, and culminating in Plato, on the one hand, and the one that
starts with empiricism, proceeds through Kant, and moves to its final stage
with Hegel himself. Like the Sophists, the empiricists of the Enlightenment
undermined the belief in objective truth, which was now represented by the
"innate universals" posited by thinkers such as René Descartes. Like Socrates,
Kant established the sovereignty of the individual moral conscience: a liberating but potentially destructive political morality. But whereas Plato ultimately
failed, Hegel succeeds. Hegel's modern state reconciles the antinomies that
Plato was unable to overcome—reason and freedom: an objective and universalistic ethos, the moral and intellectual achievement of postclassical subjective
freedom.[49]

Throughout Europe for the remainder of the nineteenth century, Hegel's account of Socrates and Plato, both in what it accepted and what it criticized, became pivotal to the analysis of Greek philosophy and politics. As most com-

mentators on Plato maintained the Hegelian conviction that all philosophy is a system in which all parts are pieces of an interconnected whole, they exerted enormous energy explaining how each particular dialogue was like a spoke in a wheel and fit into an overarching Platonic outlook. Many commentators— Eduard Zeller and Benjamin Jowett were the most influential in Germany and England, respectively—set out to deepen Hegel's view that Plato's seemingly contradictory teachings could be explained by his use of two different kinds of dialectic. Other commentators influenced by Hegel discovered unity in the dialogues by placing them in a putatively chronological order of development: a utilitarian dialogue such as the *Protagoras* was situated among Plato's early writings, while the substantive ethics found in the *Gorgias* landed it in a more mature period.[50]

Like Hegel and the Hegelians, Mill will focus on how Plato used different dialogues to reconcile the particular and universal good. But Mill's explanation as to why Plato was unable to accomplish this task will differ dramatically from that of Hegel. Mill rejects the position that Plato failed because he did not integrate the subjective freedom he was stimulating with his newly discovered universals. In Mill's account, it was Plato's failure to discover universal moral ideas to structure human conduct that led him to place restrictions on subjective freedom. Plato's failure served as an additional spur for Mill to reform empiricism's associational psychology and moral theory, which was being assaulted by Kant and other Continental thinkers.[51]

PLATO AS SKEPTIC

Hegel's reading of Plato did not go uncontested. Grote's *Plato, and the Other Companions of Sokrates* was the most comprehensive and innovative response.[52] Grote's claim was provocative: he presented Plato as a protoempiricist. His four-volume work treats the dialogues as distinct pieces published over a period of fifty years, and each dialogue is analyzed in its own right, not as part of a general outlook. Grote's study is one of the first products of Victorian-era classical scholarship to be studied closely by classicists and philosophers on the Continent.[53] His thesis that the Platonic dialogues resist interpretive closure failed to supplant the Hegelian approach, but Grote raised difficult challenges to those commentators who were quick to assume a coherent, unified Platonic outlook.

Grote inverts Hegel's position. He does this by highlighting the image of Plato as the dialectical, skeptical, and critical thinker over the one in which Plato rises to more metaphysical heights.[54] He believes Plato's genius lies in his contributions to a culture that allows critical inquiry to go forward. It lies in Plato's capacity to give life, in literary form, to the first bursts of subjectivity with the ability to challenge the unified and unreflective morality of the social structures we are all born into. Grote's preference for Plato's negative and critical views plainly owes a great deal to empiricist philosophy, which posits that knowledge requires for its supporting ground some specific sensory or perceptible experiences. Grote read Plato as someone who decomposed universal beliefs and values into their constituent parts—humanity's most basic passions and interests. In this way, he compared Plato's dialectic to the modern scientific method, which gains knowledge of physical phenomena by reducing them to a few simple regularities or laws. Such a dialectical outlook, Grote insisted, is crucial to a democratic people, who must learn to judge abstract proposals and values from the perspective of their own interests and needs. Accordingly, Grote rejects Plato's notion that a virtue such as justice is a good in itself. He supports Glaucon's and Adeimantus's view in the *Republic* that many of the obligations of justice are odious and that an individual acts justly when he recognizes a benefit to be gained from the just behavior of other people. In Grote's view, a just morality is the general recognition that the widespread interdependence of interests requires civil association.[55]

Like Hegel, Grote divided the Platonic dialogues according to a negative and positive dialectic. But Grote's distinction was based on the "dialogues of search" and the "dialogues of exposition." The dialogues of inquiry were an extension of the Socratic method, while in the dialogues of exposition Plato proposed political and ethical norms. For Grote, Plato was on the right track in the critical dialogues when he dismantled and challenged the unreflective views of his interlocutors. He was much less impressed with Plato's positive ethical and moral teachings.

Grote's criticism is simple: Plato failed to subject his moral doctrines—the ideal city run by philosophers, the immutable and eternal forms lurking behind a slew of images and opinion, virtue as knowledge—to the same kinds of critical questioning that were employed to confront and undermine the unreflective outlook of Socrates' fellow citizens. Why, asks Grote, does Plato not challenge the position in the *Republic* that justice is an intrinsic good? Plato's just individual attains happiness in book 9 of the *Republic* because he is wholly self-sufficient, but in book 2 Plato explains that men come together to form a simple community by reference to their presocial desires and needs, for example, food and shelter; needs that persist and extend as Plato constructs a more luxurious, elaborate city. Grote writes, "Plato appears so anxious to make out a triumphant case in favour of justice and against injustice, that he forgets not only the reality of things, but the main drift of his previous reasonings."[56] Grote concludes that Plato's ethical teachings ignore human nature, the social environment, and the critical dialectic.[57]

Grote refused to impose any sort of coherence upon Plato's statements and confined himself to detailed examinations of them as they appeared in each dialogue. He judged it "scarcely possible to resolve all the diverse manifestations of the Platonic mind into one higher unity. . . . Plato was skeptic, dogmatist, religious mystic and inquisitor, mathematician, philosopher, poet (erotic as well as satirical), rhetor—all in one: or at least all in succession throughout the fifty years of his philosophical life."[58] Grote's study was a salutary and important antidote to the ceaseless attempts by commentators of his age to overlook or explain away contradictions, ambiguities, and omissions in Plato's thought.

Mill, like Grote, argues that there is an inconsistency in the Platonic dialogues. But unlike Grote, he claims that this inconsistency is explained by Plato's recognition of problems within empiricism, rather than by his abandonment of empiricism. Plato, Mill argues, recognized that dialectical inquiries reveal that the foundation of our moral ideas is *not* discovered by methodological observation and logic. The quest to obtain knowledge of beliefs by resolving them into particular elements often fails. Consequently, Plato developed poetic metaphors and teachings to cover up reason's limited understanding of morality. Still, Mill insists that a *reformed* Platonic dialectic contributes to qualities of character—reason, desires for distinctiveness, the sense of duty to oneself—that will promote human agency and the protection of liberty itself, and he devotes an enormous amount of mental energy to identifying ways to situate this dialectic at the center of society.

Chapter 2 Liberty and the Just Moral Conscience

What excited Mill about reading Plato was what he saw as Plato's attempt to join different ends: creative individuals and the universal good. On the one hand, the Platonic dialogues cultivate reason and aim to create individuals liberated from society's constricting norms. On the other hand, the dialogues are concerned with the development of common ethical bonds. But Mill believed Plato was unable to reconcile these goals and ultimately upset this balance when he allowed the need for stable social forms to overtake the dialectical, liberating side of his thinking, especially in works like the *Laws*.[1] Mill saw Plato as erring too much on the side of social unity at the cost of creative individuality. He aims to harmonize Plato's two ends: Mill wants nothing less than to combine the cultivation of human faculties and the fostering of higher modes of individualism with the pursuit of the common good as understood in an overarching morality of justice and more extended forms of social unity. Empowered by the romantics' critiques of empiricism and cognizant that the backdrop of his own time is much different from Plato's fifth-century Athens, Mill is confident that Plato's roadblock needn't be our own.

That Mill's thought on Plato should focus on the problem of reconciling the egalitarian precept of social unity and the elitist position of developing creative, wise individuals is not surprising. Plato's *political* dialogues regard the reconciliation of these contrasting goals as a most fundamental problem, a problem Mill does not see as insoluble. In the *Statesman,* for instance, the Eleatic Stranger initially discusses the limitations of the rule of law: Rules suffer from a generality that limits their applicability in diverse and new circumstances; laws also fetter those who are wisest, the individuals with the best understanding of how to govern. But eventually the Eleatic Stranger enlarges his perspective and presents the rule of law as the least bad of the realistic political alternatives: the rule of law based on consent is the best we can expect in practice. Why? The immediate cause is that people generally mistrust those who hold power over them and insist on having political matters in their own hands, installing their own opinions as laws and customs. But such a moderate polity does not end the tension between the wisest and the city. The freezing of practices into rules that are sacred, inviolable, and unchangeable is a primary source of the tension between philosophy and politics, especially because the wise must follow rules that are inferior to them in understanding and the law has to punish those who challenge it. Can the philosopher accept such restrictions? Plato's *Statesman* does not provide a definitive answer, although the ultimate fate of Socrates suggests he would not have obeyed a law forbidding him the pursuit of philosophy.[2]

Mill focuses attention on Plato's attempt to reconcile the goals of creative, wise individuals and the universal good because Mill himself mulled over this tension much of his life. In *On Liberty,* for instance, Mill puts at the very center of his argument the objectives of freedom and justice: the goal of cultivating self-commanding individuals, including geniuses; within a society that ensures the liberty and moral development of the general public. Mill also is concerned with freedom and the general good in the Platonic dialogues because nineteenth-century philosophers and commentators on Plato—most notably, Hegel—focused on this theme. These thinkers fiercely debated and divided on the relation between Plato's critical epistemology that cultivated reason and freedom and his proposals of absolute truths and unconditioned moral values. In Mill's account (as I explain in this chapter), these conflicting emphases in the dialogues lay in Plato's fear that reason—or empiricist philosophy—is not discovering the good or foundation of virtue. Further, the liberating dialectic sows confusion over what is right and wrong, good and bad. In Mill's view, consequently, Plato's dialogues coupled dialectical investigations of moral ideas with artistic images that cultivated feelings of sociality and harmony.

The writings examined in this chapter center on moral theory: Mill's assessments of Plato's moral teachings, Adam Smith's theory of moral sentiments, and Kant's conception of the moral conscience. I explain how Mill confronted Plato's moral theory as part of his recognition of the limitations of empiricism's positions on associational psychology and morality. All of this contributes to Mill's developing a conception of justice to challenge Kant's position. This examination and exposition of Mill's theory of justice also establishes a recurrent theme in Mill's thought that bears importantly on *On Liberty;* namely, that the formal liberties of justice can be effective only when there are individuals with qualities that rise above narrow, self-interested activities. For a just society to avoid corruption and generate progress, individuals must develop the capacity for self-mastery and the exertion of human energy. All of these positions are integral parts of Mill's project to harmonize two ends: the cultivation of self-defining, self-commanding individuals and the development of higher modes of social unity.

PLATO'S TWO CONCEPTIONS OF VIRTUE

Like Hegel, Mill emphasizes Plato's inability to develop a moral theory that reconciles the pursuit of particular and universal goods. But Mill rejects Hegel's position that the true significance of Plato is his theory of the forms, where truth is discovered in all its conceptual purity. Mill does not identify the doctrine of the ideas, the pure spirit, or other notions of universal truth as important components of Plato's political philosophy. He also concurs with the romantics that Plato utilized art to cultivate the ethical sensibilities of the individual and the community, yet he rejects the romantics' contention that Plato recognized art to be the foundation of ethics. Mill counters that Plato never comprehended the philosophic foundation of moral behavior and turned to art and poetry to cover up and mitigate philosophy's limitations. This mélange of influences, agreements, and differences contributes to Mill's reformulation of empiricism's moral theory.

Thirty years before the publication of Grote's *Plato, and the Other Companions of Sokrates,* Mill put forth the view that it is not possible to ascribe specific political and moral positions to Plato. The conflict between different dialogues, Plato's failure to appear as his own person in the dialogues, and the consistent use of irony all preclude confidence in any one position.[3] Plato taught a "mode of philosophy"—a method to discover and understand the truth—but he did not create a "philosophy of beliefs" or discover a coherent set of conclusions. With the notable exception of his endorsement of Plato's natural religion in the *Statesman,* Mill considers Plato's moral teachings ill-conceived and notes, "The affirmative Socrates only stands his ground because no negative Socrates is allowed to attack him." Plato, Mill continues, is the great puzzle to posterity that he is because of his refusal to make explicit the internal opposition or dichotomy in his own thinking: the presentation of absolute moral and religious truths in some cases, the liberating method of the dialectic in others.[4]

Of course, Mill's general agreement with Grote that Plato was contradictory is not a surprise. They were personal friends, and Mill considered Grote an heir to Bentham's and his father's utilitarianism. But Mill's affinity with Grote should not be taken to mean he had no position of his own. Mill did not believe that distinguishing Socrates' and Plato's views was pivotal to understanding Plato, and there are other significant differences. Most important, Mill viewed Grote's account of Plato as a reflection of a long-standing problem with empiricism's view of liberty and morality that Plato himself had partly recognized and that Rousseau, Kant, Coleridge, and others had recently criticized.[5]

Mill argues that there is a conflicting idea of virtue in the *Protagoras* and *Gorgias* that crystallizes a general fault line in the Platonic dialogues on the relation between individual happiness and virtue. In the *Protagoras* Socrates' response to his interlocutor's queries invokes a utilitarian doctrine worthy of Epicurus and Bentham: Socrates describes virtue as the knowledge of which actions will produce more pleasure and less pain. There is no discussion of virtue as a general or universal good or as something to be pursued for its own sake. Mill points out that this line of argument can be found in a number of the dialogues. In the *Laws,* for instance, Plato goes further and indicates that all people cannot be persuaded to practice virtue if they do not believe it will produce some kind of reciprocal benefit. Thus, whether true or not, it is necessary to go along with rewards-based arguments on behalf of virtue. In this line of Plato, virtue, whatever its merits, fails to compel the public in and of itself.[6]

Influential commentators often criticize Mill, who in *Utilitarianism* identifies the Socrates of the *Protagoras* as an advocate of utility, for opportunistically enlisting Socrates as a utilitarian.[7] But Mill states in *Utilitarianism* that Socrates advocated utilitarianism in *this* dialogue (*Protagoras*). This noncontroversial assessment about the Socrates of the *Protagoras* is not an explanation of

Socrates' general outlook. Mill argues in other essays that Socrates and Plato present distinct ideas in different dialogues on the character of virtue.

Indeed, Mill does not consider Plato (or Socrates) to be a utilitarian. Rather, "it is doubtful whether [Plato] has adopted on the original foundation of virtue, any fixed creed." This is because in the *Gorgias,* too, Socrates teaches that knowledge is virtue. However, Mill points out that the substance of this knowledge and its relation to individual happiness are explained differently in this dialogue. The Socrates of the *Gorgias* makes a clear distinction between pursuits of knowledge as a universal good that a person chooses for its own sake and actions that result in individual happiness. Whereas in other dialogues, like the *Protagoras,* Socrates collapsed virtue, happiness, and knowledge into the same notion, in the *Gorgias* a chasm opens up between virtue and happiness. In particular, Socrates' claim that somehow the just person who is persecuted, imprisoned, tortured, and universally despised is "better off" than an unjust rich and powerful neighbor who is universally loved strikes Mill as going much too far. Indeed, Mill believes that the chasm created by Socrates, in his description of the just individual who is calumniated and persecuted, between what is good for the body and good for the soul is so wide that no one could be asked to embrace virtue unless he already was predisposed to do so. The *Republic* and the *Philebus,* Mill continues, also sever the relation between our desires for happiness and the quest for knowledge for its own sake, as justice is synonymous with the complete supremacy of reason in the soul irrespective of the condition of the body. Too often in these dialogues, in Mill's view, virtue requires the painful and unworldly overcoming of private good for the sake of reason and the soul.[8]

EMPIRICISM'S LIMITED UNDERSTANDING OF MORALITY

To explain the inconsistencies in Plato's dialogues, Grote had argued that Plato—for reasons Grote could never fully comprehend—periodically abandoned empiricist philosophy that decomposed general ideas into their constituent parts. Mill gets past Grote's stumbling block by adopting and modifying Coleridge's critique of associational psychology to explain that Plato's empiricism was unable to discover knowledge. Here Mill turns to the concept that in his other writings would become central to his critique of empiricism's moral philosophy: morality and virtue as products of "mental chemistry"; the associational process whereby the mind creates complex ideas that are unique and in and of themselves, standing above the psychical particulars from which they originate.

In the moral theory of Hobbes, Locke, and Hume, there are no universal moral ideas: morality is based on experiences that attain pleasure and avoid pain, which allows us to relate ourselves to others so that we may maximize our happiness. In this account of mental association, the guiding principle is that the parts that the analysis yields are the genetic antecedents of the complex idea that is being studied. The many thoughts and goings-on of the mind are deemed to be analyzable into simpler elements of feelings because the inventive process of the mind consisted of reconciling the unit images of the senses. The task of the philosopher is to show how complex moral ideas consist of combinations of original images of perception. When Hobbes, Locke, and Hume provide an account of a moral idea, they identify the various simple ideas that contribute to it and the sensory character of the simple ideas themselves.[9] From this perspective, Grote claimed that Plato's dialectic discovered the specific sensory or perceptible experiences of our moral ideas.

Mill counters that there are processes of learning which, while originating from psychical particulars, create ideas that are qualitatively distinct from their antecedents. The mind often fuses new structured wholes as it forms general ideas from different elements, a process Mill describes as mental chemistry. When associations have been repeatedly experienced simultaneously, then each impression brings forth readily and immediately the idea of the whole group. Those associations often melt and coalesce into one another and appear not as several ideas, but as one. Consequently, many of our moral ideas or complex wholes differ in kind from the sum of the simple ideas that contribute to them. And as the simple parts that contribute to these ideas are now viewed from a new disposition, Mill distinguishes the "genetic antecedents" that originate a complex idea from the "metaphysical parts" that participate in the idea itself. That is, the simple elements that contribute to an idea undergo a qualitative change and are no longer intelligible when they are parts of a new dispositional whole. Just as the elements of oxygen and hydrogen are not recognizable when composing water, the sensations that antecede moral ideas also are beyond recognition. "Mental chemistry," Mill summarizes, is "the view that when a complex feeling is generated out of elements very numerous and various . . . the resulting feeling always seems . . . very unlike any one of the elements composing it, [and] very unlike the sum of those elements." The general idea becomes essentially prior to its parts.[10]

Mill is arguing that the human mind is not aware of many of the simpler parts that cluster into complex ideas. This lack of understanding of our own thoughts is exacerbated by our tendency to unite around our contemporary ideas and practices, which are based on the overcoming or negation of previous experiences. As one mode of thought succeeds another, whatever new view of truth it contains is overemphasized, and whatever truth possessed by the older conception is undervalued. Moral terms such as *virtue, justice,* and *loyalty* are incapable of revealing all of the properties that have contributed to their formation.[11] The hidden characteristics of our complex ideas limit the ability of dialectical inquiries to decompose general beliefs and values into some specific sensory or perceptible experiences.

Mill's thesis of mental chemistry is in part a concession to Coleridge's (and more broadly, Kant's) critique of empiricism's understanding of the Composition of Forces. It is a reaction to how Hobbes and Locke had studied abstract principles by adding the simple effect of one force to the separate product of the other and put down the sum of these separate effects as the joint consequence. Coleridge argued that this mechanical outlook is a limited view of psychology that treats the mind as exclusively passive. The mind, as explained by empiricism, merely accepts sensations and, from these, concepts are formed that leave no room for the active mind. More specifically, Coleridge rejected empiricism's position that all knowledge begins with psychical particulars and then proceeds by way of association to complexity. He argues that this type of associational thinking is a lower or "mechanical" form of understanding. In addition to this "mechanical faculty," Coleridge posits an "imaginative faculty" of the mind in which images of sense are material that the mind assimilates, blends, and transforms based on its ideas. "In all processes of mental evolution," states Coleridge, "the objects of the senses must stimulate the Mind; and the Mind must in turn assimilate and digest the food which it thus receives from without."[12] Coleridge is not going as far as Hegelian idealism and stating that there is no such thing as immediate experience—sensations of isolated particulars "without meaning or relation." But he is arguing that our most important experiences are in "some way intellectual and [infused] with thought." Empirical studies and profound experiences without an animating thought or prior idea are impossible, and discoveries and lessons learned are primarily the product of minds with ideas. Empiricism, says Coleridge, denies the higher plateaus of awareness and understanding and drags human thought to the level of animals.[13]

Mill attributes to a distinct type of *association* what Coleridge attributes to a distinct *faculty.* In the chemical mode of combination, when simple elements are joined, a qualitatively new property or entity comes into being. Merely adding together the simple elements that generate this new property will not produce the entity, as the relational properties of the elements are transformed in composing the whole. Mill's argument is that the chemical mode of combination that occurs in the natural world also occurs regularly in mental associations.[14] The Laws of Obliviscence function in our interactions both with nature and each other: "that when a number of ideas suggest one another by association with such certainty and rapidity as to coalesce together in a group, all those members of the group which remain long without being attended to, have tendencies to drop out of consciousness."[15] Our axioms in mathematics and logic, Mill argues, originate ultimately in the total cumulative effect of experiences, but we go well beyond these original points of sensation when utilizing them. In our understanding that there is an independent external world— most notably, in our ability to judge distances—Mill explains that we are ultimately dependent on a collection of previous sensations, but that the standards that enable us to make practical evaluations do not directly refer back to these specific points of inception. Our notions of "Virtue" and "Duty," Mill continues, are the same as those of "Extension, Solidity, Time, [and] Space," as none are exact copies of the impressions of our senses. All of these ideas "are constructed by the mind itself, the materials alone being supplied to it," and have an independent life beyond the sensations that originated them. In our social life, many psychical particulars "present the character of objectivity"—a common, public world: "The world of possible sensations succeeding one another according to laws, is as much in other beings as it is in me; it has therefore an existence outside me; it is an External World."[16]

Mill's reformed associationism, which moves empiricism's moral psychology in the direction of its romantic critics, was facilitated by the English Romantics, who had a strong preference for concrete, practical, empirical commentaries, which resulted in far fewer theoretical explanations and comprehensive criticisms of associationism than those espoused by their German counterparts.[17] Wordsworth, for instance, both distinguished and collapsed the role of the Imaginative and Mechanical faculties of the mind. The Imaginative is the creative faculty because it introduces new elements into the intellectual universe; nonetheless, he continues, "is it not less true that the [Mechanical] as she is . . . active, is also . . . a creative faculty?" Further, while the Mechanical faculty is creative, the Imagination is associative: both faculties "modify . . . create . . . and associate."[18] While Coleridge drew sharper distinctions between the Imaginative and Mechanical faculties than Wordsworth, he never argued that associationism lacked important explanatory value. Indeed, the proximity of Mill's and Coleridge's positions is revealed by their respective views that each thinker is reconciling or creating a synthesis with the opposing schools of empiricism and romanticism. In consequence, as Mill claimed mental chemistry to be higher-order associations, so Coleridge maintained that mechanistic thinking is a more simple type of understanding.[19]

Ignorance of mental chemistry, Mill concludes, is a fatal blow to the empiricist philosopher who submits existing ideas, laws, and institutions to the test of their own critical rationality. As many of our most important moral ideas have characteristics different from their antecedents, the quest to obtain knowledge of the social world by resolving it into parts and reducing all knowledge to a few lawlike regularities often fails. A psychology based on traditional empiricist assumptions leaves too many general ideas unexplained.

PLATO'S MORAL QUANDARY

Mill argues that the limitations of empiricism's moral psychology explain the difficulties that confront Plato's dialectical searches for the sources and meaning of morality: "The inquiries of Plato into the definitions of some of the most general terms of speculation are . . . indeed, almost perfect examples of the preparatory process of comparison and abstraction; but from being unaware of the law just mentioned [mental chemistry], he often wasted the powers of this great logical instrument on inquiries in which it could realize no result, since the phenomena, whose common properties he so elaborately endeavored to detect, had not really any common properties."[20] Mill discovers in the new laws of association the solution to the problem that he believes bedeviled Plato. How can one be confident that the morality that inclines individuals to be just will not immediately dissolve under the acid of the dialectic? Plato, Mill charges, was unable to discover the basis for justice, so he restricted the cultivation of reason to a small group of philosophers and statesmen while severing the proper relation between cultivating liberated individuals and general moral development. As Mill is much more confident than Plato that a just moral conscience can be generated, he is not fearful that a democratized dialectic and creative individuality will be politically dangerous. His reformed psychology allows him to go down the path that Plato feared:

> Moral associations which are wholly of artificial creation, when the intellectual culture goes on, yield by degrees to the dissolving force of analysis: and . . . the feeling of duty, when associated with utility, would appear equally arbitrary if there were no leading department of our nature, no powerful class of sentiments, with which that

association would harmonize, which would make us feel it congenial, and incline us not only to foster it in others (for which we have abundant interested motives), but also to cherish it in ourselves, if there were not, in short, a natural basis of sentiment for utilitarian morality, it might well happen that this association also, even after it had been implanted by education, might be analysed away.[21]

The conflict in Plato's thinking, according to Mill, is based on a moral quandary that the ancient philosopher confronts. Plato promotes the dialectic as an essential tool for self-knowledge and wisdom. These self-regarding qualities directly contribute to individuals' ability to gain command of their actions and fully realize their natural capacities. Nonetheless, "though the premises of this argument are profoundly true, they only prove that the knowledge in question is one of the conditions of virtue, but that it is not virtue in itself." Plato himself recognizes that justice as well as knowledge is needed to cultivate self-developed individuals; otherwise, some individuals adopt goals that lead to *pleonoxia:* the view that power is the one thing people need to be happy. Or, as Mill would put it in a different context, "It is a very imperfect education which trains the intelligence only, but not the will." Plato, in Mill's view, knows that his portraits of wisdom deepen the understanding of this virtue to those predisposed to embrace it, but that they are unlikely to sway those who are not already motivated to cultivate the mind. "How to live virtuously, is a question the solution of which belongs to the understanding: but the understanding has no inducements which it can bring to the aid of one who has not yet determined whether he will endeavor to live virtuously or not," notes Mill. "It is impossible, by any arguments, to prove that a life of obedience to duty is preferable, so far as respects the agent himself, to a life of circumspect and cautious selfishness."[22]

The *aporia* in Plato's teachings stems from his realization that the dialectic, which fosters qualities such as reason and creativity, does not discover the *nomoi* necessary for justice and order. Rather, the dialectic reveals that many of our cherished and most fundamental views are devoid of rationale. At the end of many of the dialogues, Mill insists, no one ends up with a better understanding of what courage or justice is, as the dialectical inquiries do not discover anything: "The dialogues [never] exhibited a consistent system of opinions, always adhered to and always coming out victorious. . . . [S]o far is this from being the case, that the result of a large proportion of them is merely negative, many opinions in succession being tried and rejected, and the question finally left unresolved. When an opinion does seem to prevail, it almost always happens that in some other dialogue that same opinion is either refuted, or shown to have difficulties which, though frequently passed over, are never re-solved." The dialectic mainly reveals our ignorance and what kinds of criteria a good argument must meet. It shows how our moralities do not derive from rea-son and that reason itself could not constitute the ultimate source of authority. Mill concludes that Plato probably felt that many of our moral understandings are what Locke identified as "mixed modes": our moral values are simple im-pressions and ideas that have been combined more or less arbitrarily from past experiences.[23]

Empiricism's restricted psychology, Mill concludes, contributes to the inabil-ity of both Plato and the contemporary liberal tradition of Hobbes, Locke, and Hume to discover the foundation of morality. What distinguishes Plato from contemporary empiricists is his recognition that his attempts to exclude belief in anything that could not be demonstrated by methodological observation and logic are failing. Plato continues to search for a totality or a spirit to our general ideas as he recognizes the possibility that they are not the simple product of the empirical arrangements that contributed to their formation. Mill explains and criticizes Bentham's attitude toward Socrates and Plato as a symptom of a more general intellectual limitation of contemporary empiricism:

> Socrates and Plato are spoken of in terms distressing to his [Bentham's] greatest ad-mirers; and the incapacity to appreciate such men, is a fact perfectly in unison with the general habits of Bentham's mind. He had a phrase, expressive of the view he took of all the moral speculations to which his method had not been applied, or (which he considered as the same thing) not founded on a recognition of the moral standard; this phrase was 'vague generalities.' Whatever presented itself to him in such a shape, he dismissed as unworthy of notice, or dwelt upon only to denounce as absurd. He did not heed, or rather the nature of his mind prevented it from occur-ring to him, that these generalities contained the whole unanalyzed experience of the human race.[24]

In criticizing empiricism, Mill incorporates and critiques the Hegelian and romantic conceptions of Plato as well. Like Hegel, Mill believes Plato recog-nizes that new moral norms are required to overcome the challenge posed by the reflective intellect. And again, like Hegel, Mill believes Plato failed to rec-oncile the pursuit of particular and universal goods. But Mill does not embrace Hegel's view that Plato developed two dialectics—one to undermine the old ethical order, another to posit that the rational is the spiritual, which is the very essence of the universal—and that Plato failed because he did not integrate the subjective freedom he was stimulating with his newly discovered universals.[25]

In contrast, Mill argues that Plato's dialectic revealed the limited capacity of

reason. It was Plato's failure to discover universal moral norms that led to his restrictions on the subjective will. Plato's dilemma lay in his restricted understanding of moral psychology, which prevented him from identifying how the
passions themselves are part of a complex mix that creates moral sentiments
reconciling particular and general interests. "The feelings of the modern mind
are more various, more complex and manifold, than those of the ancients ever
were," summarizes Mill. "The modern mind is, what the ancient mind was not,
brooding and self-conscious; and its meditative self-consciousness has discovered depths in the human soul which the Greeks and Romans did not dream of,
and which would not have been understood."[26]

In Mill's view, while Plato was right to recognize that reason alone is power-
less to constrain the passions, that does not mean that there are not emotions
and other human qualities that can *aid* reason in doing so. If philosophic reason cannot discover justice, that does not mean that individuals won't be motivated to act justly by a combination of reason and moral sentiments that derive
from promptings such as the desire for self-preservation. If individuals cannot
be induced to seek justice solely through reason, they might still be called to do
so through moral sentiments rooted in fear, especially fear of abuse or death at
the hands of others. By explaining how independent moral sentiments derive
in part from passions, Mill is attempting to offer a solution to the problem of
justice despite a circumscribed view of reason. Hegel overcomes Plato by claiming that a worthy or good life involves some sort of reasoned identification with
modern institutions, most notably the state. Mill will propose to overcome
Plato by identifying how fear, social sympathy, and moral education can be
combined to forge a just moral conscience that enables an individual "to attach
himself to the collective idea of his tribe, his country, or mankind, in such a
manner that any act hurtful to them rouses his instinct of sympathy and urges
him to resistance."[27] Liberty, in short, requires moral development, not wisdom, and justice is built in part upon the moral emotions and is not derived
from philosophic reason.

Mill wishes Plato had managed to articulate an argument on behalf of
morality and ethics; one that made it possible for societies to rely on something
more than the interdependence of interests. Regretfully however, Mill endorses
the romantics' position on Plato: Plato depended exclusively on his imagination and art. Unable to construct a coherent foundation for justice, states Mill,
Plato's dialogues are bifurcated between two conflicting goals: the philosopher's
often "deconstructive," destabilizing search for absolute truth and artistic images that cultivate at best an ethical sensibility of wholeness and harmony. But

whereas the romantics believe Plato used artistic imagery to give popular and figurative form to the truth, Mill counters that Plato developed poetic metaphors to cover up or hide reason's limited understanding of morality. Plato came to the conclusion, Mill summarizes, "that objections insoluble by dialectics could be made against all truths; and, the ethical and political tendencies of his mind becoming predominant . . . he came to think that the doctrines which had the best ethical tendency should be taught, with little or no regard to whether they could be proved true, and even at the risk of their being false."[28]

For instance, Mill argues that Plato's concept of the Ideas contradicts the suppositions of the dialectic. It assumes that ultimate understandings are exogenous creations of nature or the gods, existing by themselves, belonging to another world, and that the conventional opinions we construct are imperfect attempts to conform with these absolute truths. Mill notes that in the *Phaedrus, Phaedo,* and important sections of the *Republic,* the doctrine of the Ideas is posited without serious opposition. It is only in the *Parmenides* that the young Socrates' view on this question is subjected to debate and criticized. But, Mill adds, Parmenides, after rejecting Socrates' formulation, concludes this discussion by teaching that philosophy and dialectics would be impossible unless this doctrine is admitted as the truth! Mill surmises that the concept of the Ideas as well as other important views Plato does not subject to the dialectic is part of the artistic and ethical side of Plato's thinking that stems from his belief that people need myths and views that foster unity, loyalty, and contentment. While the dialectic expresses the side of Plato's thinking that stands opposed to orthodoxy, the doctrine of Ideas reflects his understanding that an imaginative idea of the good must be fostered to generate human sociality and prevent political decay, something impossible to achieve through philosophic reason.[29]

Mill recognizes what motivates Plato's limited and hidden use of the dialectic: philosophers who overemphasize the critical and destructive side of the philosophic task risk provoking popular resentment while promoting the disintegration of social norms. "Whatever encourages young men to think for themselves," Mill writes, "does lead them to criticize the laws of their country—does shake their faith in the infallibility of their fathers and their elders, and make them think their own speculations preferable. It is beyond doubt that the teachings of Sokrates, and of Plato after him, produced these effects in an extraordinary degree." Frustrated by his inability to discover justice, Plato in the dialogues increasingly became concerned with the character and disposition of the philosophers and legislators, while "laws, together with established customs . . . were his real rules of justice for the citizen."[30]

Political philosophy, counters Mill, must be concerned with the qualities of the potentially good citizens from humble backgrounds, such as Aristedes, as well as with the virtues for what Plato considered the highest types. Mill maintains that Plato's self-awareness of the limitations of his own moral theory led him to become distrustful of the dialectic itself. In Plato's last dialogue on politics, the *Laws,* Mill is unable to find it at all. Perhaps, Mill speculates, an older Plato worried that his followers were simply too one-sided in their use of the dialectical method and that philosophy had become a dangerous political tool. Mill criticizes Plato for subordinating the dialectical and liberating features of his thought to the artistic, ethical, and hierarchical currents. Mill concludes that Plato, the founder of the philosophic spirit and method and of many of our "moral and religious props," is honored more for the latter than for the former.[31]

THE GOOD AND THE RIGHT

What is the substantive character of the moral outlook that answers the question Mill believes Plato is unable to overcome: Why would a self-commanding individual be just to others? In *Utilitarianism* Mill provides a succinct answer: "As between his own happiness and that of others, utilitarianism requires him to be as strictly impartial as a disinterested and benevolent spectator."[32] To Mill, the developed individual is both *good* and *right:* the self-commanding individual rises above base impulses by both pursuing self-defined goals and resisting the temptation of unjust acts.[33] Mill's invocation of Adam Smith's "impartial spectator" in defining the *right* requires a brief review of Smith's account of sympathy—one of the most comprehensive statements by an empiricist on the moral conscience. This review will enable us to see how Mill builds a bridge between the moral theories of empiricism and Kant, while overcoming a key weakness he discovers in Plato's political philosophy: the limitation of self-commanding individuals to a select few.

Adam Smith interpreted sympathy as a type of fellow feeling: the imaginative situating of ourselves in the setting of another, representing to ourselves what we would perceive, understand, and do were we in another person's circumstances. To Smith, these natural, subrational capacities for sympathy and imagination enable us to evaluate the passions that move an agent to action, whereupon we determine whether an agent has acted with the virtue of propriety. Sympathy and imagination also enable us to judge whether an agent's actions produce gratitude or resentment in those upon whom the action falls, providing the basis for discerning the merits of an agent's conduct. In short, spectators praise or blame virtuous and vicious behavior on the basis of their sympathy for both the propriety of an agent's passions and the feelings of the recipients of the action.[34]

For Smith, the moral bonds of society are traceable to the natural desire to be admired by others. We abstract from individual cases to principles based on repeated experiences. Just as we judge others, we evaluate ourselves as we feel others interpret us, seeking to understand what pleases or disturbs them, attempting to enter into the minds and feelings of others. The moral conscience is established as we start basing our activities on an imagined "impartial spectator," a "sense within the breast of the individual" of what is considered generally appropriate and meritorious behavior. The moral conscience is our view of what this impartial spectator would sympathize with in this or that situation. The conscience consists primarily of norms and rules attained through experience of what people generally approve or disapprove. For Smith, a moral world stands above or outside the individual, and one's standards of right and wrong are based on an objective order. But this order is not based on a rational order or divine being. It is a moral order immanent to human experience.

In Smith's experiential account of the moral sentiments, he adheres to Lockean principles of association: complex phenomena of the human mind arise out of more simple and elementary impressions and ideas. Moral beings and sentiments "are founded on, and terminated in, these simple ideas we have received from sensation or reflection." Moral ideas, therefore, become norms for attaining pleasure and avoiding pain, and more specifically rules and maxims about how to so relate ourselves to others that we maximize our pleasures and minimize our pain. In short, upon the associationist account of motivation, all apparently nonegoistic motives such as moral sympathy and the moral conscience turn out, given the Lockean mode of analysis, to be after all egoistic.

Smith extends, but does not break from, Locke's associationism by doubling the strains of associations. First, we have desires and actions that are centered on the consciousness of the self; and beyond that there are feelings that derive from the censure and approval of others. "We begin," states Smith, "to examine our own passions and conduct, and to consider how these must appear to them, by considering how they would appear to us if in their situation. We suppose ourselves the spectators of our own behavior, and endeavour to imagine what effect it would, in this light, produce upon us. This is the only looking-glass by which we can, in some measure, with the eyes of other people, scrutinize the propriety of our own conduct. If in this view it pleases us, we are tolerably satisfied."[35] As we become habituated to observing ourselves from others' point of view, our emotions are themselves shaped so as to diminish the motivation to act from a vulgar or narrow sense of self-love. As Smith identifies this matrix of associations, he explains that the moral conscience is established as we mediate between our feelings. The capacity that grants us this moral conscience is sympathy.

SYMPATHY AND MORAL BEHAVIOR

Reasoning such as that of Smith, charges Mill, acts as an acid that dissolves our commitment to moral claims by pointing to their low and pleasure-based *aims* rather than to their pleasure-based *origins*. Utility is the starting point, not the endpoint, of morality. But not only does this argument on morality tend to discredit it; in addition, the thesis assumes that morality is the mere mechanical effects of incentives, a move that at the same time relativizes morality to the pain and pleasure calculations of every single moment, calculations that quite easily shift from situation to situation, person to person, and society to society. Morality and sociability, Mill counters, do not arise naturally in the course of the growth of human associations. While sympathy—the identification of feelings of others with our own—is *a* key source of the moral commitment to respecting the rights and well being of others, it is not identical to it. Sympathy explains everything about the feelings, except the substantive moral character of the feelings themselves: our praise and blame influence conduct, reflecting what we desire to encourage and what we seek to limit, but they do not necessarily reflect a substantive moral outlook, since an agent's conduct could be responding to the sympathetic feelings of others "without any moral feeling in our minds at all." In short, moral sentiments cannot be *solely* the internalization of others' valuations because their values may or may not be based on a moral outlook. Rather, Mill insists, respect for the rights of others must become an end in itself: "[The moral sentiments] must in this manner have become a motive, promoting us to the one sort of acts, and restraining us from the other sort."

Mill believes that the conflation of sympathy and morality continues the empiricist tradition of wrongly ignoring a central element in the constitution of a moral consciousness: the role of the active mind in transforming psychical particulars into independent, general ideas that are in and of themselves. The strictly inductive method of the empiricists, he insists, denies them the ability to formulate an understanding of the development of universal, disinterested norms. There is a greater whole that transcends its parts that the empiricists simply fail to acknowledge at best—fail to even see, at worst. "This portion of the laws of human nature [mental chemistry] is the more important to psychology," Mill concludes, "as they show how it is possible that the moral sentiments, the feeling of duty, and of moral approbation and disapprobation, may be no original element of our nature, and yet may be capable of being not only more intense and more powerful than any of the elements out of which they may have been formed, but may also, in the maturity, be perfectly disinterested."[36]

In Mill's view, empiricism's failure to recognize that the whole idea is not *just* the sum of its parts, and that it can be qualitatively different from those parts, lends credibility to Kant's and other moral idealists' claim that the moral conscience is either innate or somehow not the product of experience. When "phaenomena have been very often experienced in conjunction . . . it is impossible to think the one thing disjoined from the other"; consequently, "the facts . . . answering to those ideas come at least to seem inseparable in existence," and "the belief we have in their coexistence, though really a product of experience, seems intuitive."[37] Mill agrees with Kant that the breed of psychology employed by empiricism has been incapable of explaining genuine universality and so of refuting the charges of egoism and immorality. Indeed, Mill's revisionist psychology is to provide a new defense for empiricism against Kant's claim that moral conduct is disinterested activities that *transcend* experience. In the *Critique of Pure Reason,* for instance, Kant creates a division between a phenomenal or empirical world that is strictly governed by the laws of nature and a noumenal or intelligible world governed by the laws of freedom, which denies that the everyday world of sense, experience, and circumstances generates moral sentiments. Similarly, in the *Groundwork of the Metaphysics of Morals* Kant distinguishes between nonmoral inclinations such as desires and needs and the moral motive of obeying the moral law out of respect for the moral law, severing any links between the passions and ideas of moral worth.[38]

Although Mill embraces Kant's position that the moral conscience provides an ethical outlook for all human conduct, Mill's moral psychology attributes this universal will to a distinct type of association derived from experience, rather than to a distinct faculty of the mind that is independent of experience. They arrive at similar conclusions, but one through experience, the other through a priori reason. The members of "the German school of metaphysical speculation," charges Mill, "prefer dogmatically to assume that the mental differences which they perceive, or think they perceive, among human beings, are ultimate facts, incapable of being explained or altered, rather than take the trouble of fitting themselves, by the requisite process of thought, for referring those mental differences to the outward causes by which they are for the most part produced, and on the removal of which they would cease to exist."[39] To Mill, Kant and his followers confuse the possession of a moral conscience with the capacity to acquire it. The political problem with this aspect of Kant's thinking is not the contemporary critique that it subordinates our various conceptions of the good and unrealistically strips the individual of identity and community.[40] Rather, Mill maintains Kant unrealistically assumes a just moral outlook and community. In short, Kant assumes too much, not too little: "People are mostly so little aware how completely, during the greater part of our species, the law of force was the avowed rule of general conduct . . . and from how recent a date it is that the affairs of society in general have been even pretended to be regulated according to any moral law."[41]

Weaving his way through empiricism and moral idealism, Mill ascribes a more specific, substantive character to the moral conscience than Smith. Whereas Smith spoke of an individual guided by an "impartial spectator," Mill describes an agent who is as "impartial as a disinterested and benevolent spectator."[42] Here Mill's moral conscience comes closer to Kant's categorical imperative: the idea that the individual embraces a moral outlook that is right in itself and not for a particular type of opinion or situation or group of persons. But like Smith and unlike Kant, Mill maintains it is a matter of experience and habituation to learn to view how one's activities affect others: only through association do we learn to feel what is appropriate to feel and, correspondingly, what it is appropriate to praise and blame, what a good and what a harm is.

Mill argues that Enlightenment thinkers underestimated the social conditions required for the cultivation of just moral sentiments. Most eighteenth-century philosophers assumed that such a moral sensibility would generate spontaneously after Christianity's decline. They believed moral feelings "to be more deeply rooted in human nature than they are; to be not so dependent, as in fact they are, upon collateral influences."[43] Mill counters that, while conditions and ideas may be associated, there are variations in just how they are connected, as different orders among sensations are associated with stronger or weaker ideas. Associations between social conditions and ideas that contribute to mental chemistry and become powerful independent entities derive from clear, regular, and habitual connections. "A conjunction," he writes, "however close and apparently indissoluble, between two ideas, is not only an effect which association is able to produce, but one which it is certain to produce, if the necessary conditions are sufficiently often repeated without the intervention of any fact tending to produce a counter-association."[44] Accordingly, there is a far stronger sociological current in Mill's political philosophy than in that of his Anglo-Scottish forebears. Mill places far more emphasis than Locke, Hume, and Smith on reforming and constructing civil society—nongovernmental institutions and practices such as the family, school system, voluntary associations, property relations, religion—to generate the mental chemistry that will form a coherent moral will for modernity. And in so arguing, Mill helps establish within the liberal tradition the long-standing complaint against liberal formalism, initiated by Rousseau and stated succinctly in Karl Marx's "On the Jewish Question," that the informal practices of liberalism create inequalities that cancel out its published principles of equality: the formal equality established by the public sphere creates conditions that allow domination to occur in the private sphere so that the goal of equality is not fulfilled.[45]

THE FAMILY AND MORAL CONSCIENCE

Mill argues that the subjugation of women prevents the formation of a just moral conscience, as it creates two contradictory social conditions. On the one hand, the distinguishing feature of modernity is that individuals are "no longer born to their place in life" and are free to utilize their talents "to achieve the lot which may appear to them most desirable." On the other hand, laws and institutions continue to exclude half of the persons from the "higher social functions" because of the "fatality of birth." Mill points to the incongruity of such a situation. It is "as if a gigantic doleman, or a vast temple of Jupiter Olympus, occupied the site of St. Paul's and received daily worship, while the surrounding Christian churches were only resorted to on Fasts and funerals."[46]

   These contradictory social conditions, Mill charges, prevent the formation of the habits and ideas that cultivate the individual's capacity to be concerned for the rights of others as well as their own. "The education given to the sentiments," he argues, "by laying the foundation of domestic existence upon a relation contradictory to the first principles of social justice, must, from the very nature of man, have a perverting influence of such magnitude, that it is hardly possible with our present experience to raise our imaginations to the conception of so great a change for the better as would be made by its removal."[47] Among men of good character, the conflicting conditions sow moral confusion, while among the worst of men the condition of force and obedience regarding the treatment of women cultivates a class of tyrants. Concomitantly, among the most active and energetic women the absence of liberty leads to a willful pursuit of power through the control of others in the family: "To allow to any human beings no existence of their own but what depends on others, is giving far too high a premium on bending others to their own purposes."[48] Among weaker women, by contrast, the tyranny fosters a passive, submissive character.

Mill claims that because the private sphere predominates over the public sphere in modern life, civil institutions such as the family play a crucial role in establishing a spirit of justice in society. "Citizenship in free countries," he states, "is partly a school of society in equality; but citizenship fills only a small place in modern life, and does not come near the daily habits of inmost sentiments."[49] Because the modern family, the most fundamental unit of sociality and the venue where children learn social norms, is based on inequality, English society is unable to cultivate fully a just morality. To place women on a more equal setting in the family, Mill makes his well-known proposal that husbands and wives develop a division of labor based on their respective strengths and weaknesses. This doctrine of reciprocity and equal rights is not solely concerned with every individual expanding his or her respective capacities and happiness.[50] It also is pivotal to the cultivation of a morality of justice that will, in turn, infuse society as a whole. Equal rights and reciprocal relations between marital partners are "the only means of rendering the daily life of mankind, in any high sense, a school of moral cultivation." Such a justly constituted marital relationship forges a highly cultivated sense of self-control in which an individual learns to show consideration for other human beings. The parents show children by both example and precept that reciprocity contributes to one being both respectable and able to respect; and that the way one develops views and proper concern for one's self is inseparable from the process by which one takes into account the views and well-being of others:

> What is needed is, that it [the family] should be a school of sympathy in equality, of living together in love, without power on one side and obedience on the other. This it ought to be between the parents. It would then be an exercise of those virtues which each requires to fit them for all other associations and a model to the children of the feelings and conduct which their temporary training by means of obedience is designed to render habitual, and therefore natural to them. The moral training of mankind will never be adapted to the conditions of the life for which all other human progress is a preparation, until they practice in the family the same moral rule which is adapted to the moral constitution of human society.

The family becomes the "school of virtues for freedom," training individuals in the moral qualities that enable them to act justly in their associations throughout society.[51]

JUSTICE AND OTHER OBLIGATIONS

In developing his argument for the modern moral conscience, Mill distinguishes justice from other obligations in a variety of ways. Justice is the preeminent moral obligation—it is necessary to the very existence of society. Unlike other obligations, justice is based on precise rules and enforced through violence. Justice is also primarily, although not exclusively, a negative virtue as it centers on not harming others. Finally, Mill argues that an individual can be just without embracing other qualities of character that contribute to self-developed or higher forms of individuality, but that self-developed individuals must be just. Mill's theory of justice anchors his views on the proper relation between a culture that cultivates character and a rule-abiding morality.[52]

Mill derives a pivotal feature of his conception of justice from premises at least in part borrowed from the natural law jurists. Central to Mill's argument on the distinctive character of justice is the idea of the perfect obligation, while other duties are identified as imperfect obligations. The distinction between perfect and imperfect obligations had been initiated by Hugo Grotius and elaborated by Samuel von Pufendorf. Grotius's distinction is based on the reciprocity of rights: perfect or complete rights involve property ownership, contracts, and other rules of agreement which are enforced through violence because their violation directly threatens the security of individuals. Imperfect or incomplete rights, such as the poor's claim for charity from the wealthy, are not enforceable, as they are not based on reciprocal responsibility. They are not essential to society's survival. Pufendorf focuses on responsibilities, not rights. He argues that perfect duties are those on which the very existence of both the individual and society is dependent. The performance of perfect duties could be enforced by either violence in presocial existence or through the courts in society; a perfect duty in society is always precise, explaining exactly how much money or service each obligation requires. In contrast, imperfect duties improve the quality of a society but are not necessary for its self-preservation. Imperfect duties are not specifiable.[53] Locke, Hume, Smith, and other members of the Anglo-Scottish tradition remain within this general framework. All agree that positive virtues such as beneficence are an extra: they make society flourish and happy; but respect for the life and property of others is essential for a society to sustain itself. As Smith puts it, "Beneficence . . . is less essential to the existence of society than justice. Society may subsist, though not in the most comfortable state, without beneficence: but the prevalence of injustice must utterly destroy it."[54]

In Mill's account of justice, the individual has the perfect or absolute duty to live in accordance with a largely commutative idea of justice that specifies the sorts of harm that can be done to another individual's person, property, and reputation as well as the specifications of punishment and redress of those injuries. Broadly speaking, just individuals respect the rights they themselves enjoy, making civil peace possible. They are angered by violations of rights even if those violations do no harm to themselves and conversely do not resent a harm to themselves unless it is of a "kind which society has a common interest with them in the repression of." Their sense of justice is irretrievably linked with their idea of a social good. In contrast, as the virtues of charity and benevolence are not linked to either the security of society or our own rights, they are products of compassion and nonenforceable. "Justice implies something which it is not only right to do, and wrong not to do, but which some individual can claim from us as his moral right," Mill summarizes. "No one has a moral right to our generosity and beneficence, because we are not morally bound to practise those virtues towards any given individual. . . . Wherever there is a right, the case is one of justice, and not of the virtue of beneficence."[55]

A pivotal point of departure between Mill's view of justice and that of natural law jurists and Anglo-Scottish thinkers is Mill's bid to explain justice as an ethical outlook. The natural law jurists conceived of justice as the following of a set of rules that protected the rights that one enjoyed. "Justice," according to Grotius, consists entirely in "abstaining from that which is another's" regardless of whether one has good or bad motives. Locke recognizes the value of morality but held that "whatever standard soever we frame in our minds the idea of virtues or vices, . . . their rectitude, or obliquity, consists in the agreement with those patterns prescribed by law." Smith divorces the idea of justice from ethics, as one could not assume an individual would be impartial on issues that directly affect his self-interest. To Smith, virtues require individual evaluation of ends or rules rather than simply following the rules themselves, and in matters of justice "the man who refines the least and adheres with the most obstinate steadfastness to the general rules themselves, is the most commendable and the most to be depended upon."[56] In contrast, the just person for Mill is not simply the one who follows rules that protect the rights of others. The Millian idea of justice is intended to apply to the moral maxims of sincere and conscientious individuals in everyday life.

Indeed, Mill is suspicious of the attempt to divorce acting justly from being just. He argues that the just person is not simply the one who follows rules that protect the rights of others. Human nature left to take care of itself inevitably decays, and Mill questions the value of an administration of justice that focuses exclusively on perfecting the machinery, the rules, and contrivances of its operation, while ignoring the task of moral education. Justice, a normative good, cannot be so mechanized. We mustn't forget the lessons of the ancients, "that there is an incessant and ever-flowing current of human affairs toward the worse, consisting of all the follies, all the vices, all the negligences, indolences, and suppinenesses of mankind." "Any society . . . which is not improving, is deteriorating."[57] The value of the State, Mill argues, in the long run

> is the worth of the individuals composing it; and a State which postpones the interests of *their* mental expansion and elevation to a little more of administrative skill, or that of semblance of it which practice gives in the details of business; a State which dwarfs its men, in order that they be more docile instruments in its hands even for beneficial purposes—will find that with small men no great thing can really be accomplished; and that the perfection of the machinery to which it has sacrificed everything will in the end avail it nothing, for want of the vital power which in order that the machine might work more smoothly, it has preferred to banish.[58]

Mill recognizes that individuals without a just disposition should not be considered unjust if they do not break the rules of justice; rather, these individuals are "not *consciously* just" (emphasis added). They slide by without initiating trouble more by passivity than any greater concern with justice or the social good. He argues that a moral outlook that closes the gap between just actions and the just being must be cultivated and sustained continuously. While law and public opinion are external sanctions that enforce justice, the ultimate source of this quality is the moral conscience: "a feeling in our own mind; a pain, more or less intense, attendant on violation of duty, which in properly cultivated moral natures rises, in the more serious cases, into shrinking from it as an impossibility."[59]

This moral conscience motivates the just individual to adhere to the rules of justice because of the self-respect that it generates, states Mill. It operates on a higher plane, one not so lofty as the ancients' perfected individual but not as low as the Anglo-Scottish thinkers' rule-following person. The just individual exemplifies self-control. He is neither driven by unbridled passions nor cowers in fear of the law. His refusal to harm others is part of his perseverance in a self-commanding life. "The word 'do' must be understood as including forebearances as well as acts."[60] This self-command is a characteristic of developed individuality. As Mill puts it, "If the desire of right and aversion to wrong has yielded to a small temptation, we judge them to be weak, and our disapprobation is strong. If the temptation to which they have yielded is so great that even strong feelings of virtue might have succumbed to it, our moral reprobation is less intense. If again, the moral desires and aversions have prevailed, but not over a very strong force, we hold that the action was good, but that there was little merit in it; and our estimate of the merit rises, in exact proportion to the greatness of the obstacle which the moral feeling proved strong enough to overcome."[61]

In describing this inner court of conscience, Mill's thought is moving closer to that of Kant, who defines the moral conscience as a "state of consciousness which in itself is duty," meaning it is the "moral faculty of judgment passing judgment on itself." The moral conscience does not evaluate actions in relation to external laws and criteria but acts as reason itself evaluating our conduct. This "inner judge" of the moral law by which everyone "find themselves observed, threatened, and in general kept in awe" issues warnings before an action is undertaken and prosecutes after the deed is done. These internal disputes between our desires and conscience are not settled amicably, according to Kant, as "the judge of conscience has to pass sentences, acquitting or condemning. An acquittal does not bring reward or happiness but only a relief of anxiety." Moral conduct consists of acts that overcome what the individual really wants. As we do not have a rational will that is perfect and automatic, we often feel the moral law operating within us as a constraint because it reacts against the pull of our desires.[62]

Mill and Kant part company at Kant's claim that the moral conscience is based on contracausality: choosing one course of action while preferring another. In Mill's account, the just moral conscience creates the *desire* to do right: just acts are forms of self-fulfillment, not self-renunciation. This moral conscience is derived from human nature, human equality, and reason. The moral conscience is rooted in a feeling of resentment common to all animals: a desire to harm those who have hurt, or those who it thinks are about to hurt, itself or its young. Mill also refers to the key role of sympathy in reformed civil societies that promote equality. Free individuals, feeling themselves equal to their fellow citizens, can, through their imaginations, enter into sympathy with the lives of their compatriots. Here the individual *learns* to be compassionate and respect the rights of others, literally feeling what another human being is feeling. Finally, these feelings of resentment and compassion must be mobilized by moral education so that an individual, "by virtue of his superior intelligence, even apart from his superior range of sympathy," shrinks from activities that would conflict with the basic rights of others and resents actions that harm society as a whole.[63] "The object of moral education," Mill summarizes, "is to educate the will: but the will can only be educated through desires and aversions; by eradicating or weakening such of them as are likeliest to lead to evil; exalting to the highest pitch the desire of right conduct and the aversion to wrong; cultivating all other desires and aversions of which the ordinary operation is auxiliary to right, while discountenancing so immoderate an indulgence of them, as might render them too powerful to be overcome by the moral sentiment, when they chance to be in opposition to it."[64]

Mill and Kant agree that many individuals are conflicted by morally responsible and irresponsible motivations. But they disagree when Mill insists that this is not a conflict between an individual and some outside or transcendent power. Mill never refers to morally just behavior as "other-regarding conduct" (despite this term's being the subject of countless books and essays on Mill), as it indicates moral conduct requires transcendence of the self and its desires.[65] The two motives that compete with one another here come from the appetites, from the desires the individual has. Reason will point us in the direction of higher and lower aims; it also will help us determine what will happen as a consequence of a choice we make—but the choice of ends is always going to be a choice of desires, and never between reason and desire. The just individual does not cheat, steal, or partake in other actions that harm others, because his moral conscience informs his desires and prevents him from taking actions that—in his view—reflect a debased character.

> "I" am both parties in the contest; the conflict is between me and myself; between (for instance) me desiring a pleasure, and me dreading self-reproach. What causes me, or if you please, my Will, to be identified with one side rather than with the other, is that one of the Me's represents a more permanent state of my feelings than the other does. After the temptation has been yielded to, the desiring "I" will come to an end, but the conscience stricken "I" may endure to the end of life. I therefore dispute altogether that we are conscious of being able to act in opposition to the strongest present desire or aversion. The difference between a bad and a good man is not that the latter acts in opposition to his strongest desires; it is that his desire to do right, and his aversion to doing wrong, are strong enough to overcome, and in the

case of perfect virtue, to silence, any other desire or aversion that may conflict with
them. It is because this state of mind is possible to human nature, that human beings
are capable of moral government: and moral education consists in subjecting them
to the discipline which has most tendency to bring them into this state.[66]

Mill's moral conscience is a bid to provide us what Kant's moral reason is supposed to provide, but without the problematic distinction between an empirical world driven by the laws of nature and a noumenal world animated by the
laws of freedom, which diminishes the moral worth of different types of desires,
experiences, and circumstances.

NATURE AND MORALITY

Mill's reform of empiricism's conception of justice—especially his position
that human nature left to itself will inevitably decay—seems to suggest that he
sides with Rousseau and Kant's position that humanity is capable of lifting itself above the "slavery" imposed by nature. In opposing the natural law jurists,
Rousseau had argued that if the moral law did not exist in the state of nature,
then it must owe such reality as it now possesses to the political community and
positive law—in which case, it cannot constitute an independent, natural standard above them. On the contrary, the moral law is then an artificial human
creation, wholly subordinated to the needs of politics and positive law, which
are different from one society to another. To Rousseau, "the historical debate
over the character of the state of nature" delves into "the relative causal and on-
tological priority of morality on the one hand, and (politics) on the other." And
in refuting the natural law view of a self-subsisting morality, Rousseau argues
that the full development of humankind's reason and consciousness is dependent on politics. Rousseau, in short, founded a new and radical separation between the moral-cultural world and nature.[67]

Kant substitutes reason for Rousseau's politics. In the Preface to the second
edition of the *Critique of Pure Reason,* Kant writes that "reason has insight only
into that which it produces a plan of its own" and that "it [reason] must not allow itself to be kept, as it were, in nature's leading strings, but must itself show
the way with principles of judgment based on fixed laws, constraining nature to
give answers to questions of reason's own determining." It is due to this ordi-
nance, Kant continues, that the scientific study of nature now makes huge advances, "after having for so many centuries been nothing but a process of
merely random groping."[68] The *Critique of Practical Reason* continues this line
of reasoning: freedom of the will is consistently opposed to the necessity of na-

ture, and the fundamental problem of practical philosophy is posed as one of reconciling natural and free causality. This Kantian distinction of nature and freedom contributes to the concept of the nature-nurture dichotomy that animates contemporary popular discourse and literature.[69]

Once again, however, Mill weaves together a position that straddles empiricism and romanticism. While opposing traditional empiricism's restricted conception of nature as matter in motion, Mill also rejects Rousseau's and Kant's positions that a political or moral outlook permits the transcendence of our animal selves. "If, as is my own belief," he writes, "the moral feelings . . . are acquired, they are not for that reason less natural. It is natural to man to speak, reason, to build cities, to cultivate the ground, though these are acquired faculties. . . . Like [these] acquired capacities, the moral faculty, if not a part of our nature, is a natural outgrowth from it . . . and susceptible of being brought by cultivation to a high degree of development."[70] In a sense, Mill returns to classical political philosophy or, more specifically, to Aristotle's conception of a second or higher nature to reform empiricism's conception of nature *and* to address Rousseau's and Kant's concerns regarding moral autonomy. In the *Nicomachean Ethics* Aristotle explains that humans, solely by virtue of being human, effect and carry out natural capacities in a distinct way from other species of animals: that is, through the raising of the young in a regime, our natural capabilities for speech, deliberation, and ethics are cultivated and harnessed. When properly cultivated, these potentialities develop as a "second nature" that maintains an ongoing relationship with our primary nature. Individuals who are habituated and trained poorly do not attain this second or higher nature. For Aristotle, these individuals are "unnatural," as they are unable to reflect the higher capacities of the human species. As Aristotle puts it, "The virtues arise in us neither by nature nor against nature. Rather, we are by nature able to acquire them, and reach our complete perfection through them."[71]

In "Nature," Mill argues that nature itself is incapable of establishing an ethical standard of the good. Yet, while nature is a source of far more evil than beneficence, it is to be studied, not ignored: "If the useless precept to follow nature were changed into a precept to study nature; to know and take heed of the properties of the things we have to deal with, . . . we should arrive at the first principle of intelligent action." Like Aristotle, Mill views human nature as not wholly determinate of human actions, but not irrelevant to it either. Human nature is a source of difficulties to be addressed and capacities to be structured. "The duty of man," Mill summarizes, "is the same in respect to his own nature as in respect to the nature of all things, namely not to follow but amend."[72]

Mill knits together the position that ethics are based on fostering habits that overcome our natural instincts, but that virtues reflect an assessment of the ways humanity can possess either base or noble ends and are not mere conventions. "That there must be the germs . . . of virtues in human nature . . . I am ready to admit," states Mill. "But the weeds that dispute the grounds of these beneficent germs . . . are luxuriant growths" that will not be overcome unless there is well-conceived habituation and education. For example, the human tendencies toward selfishness and cruelty necessitate the cultivation of social ethics, while the human capacity for such virtues as cleanliness, courage, honesty, self-control, and justice presupposes habits that "in some happily circumscribed specimens of the human race, the most elevated sentiments of which humanity is capable become a second nature, stronger than the first, and not so much subduing the original nature as merging it into itself." Mill stresses the particular importance of moral training among those individuals with the "finest nervous organizations," as they realize their impulses in manners that have the greatest effect on the well-being of others.[73]

Influential commentators on political thought such as Stephen Holmes and Julia Annas confuse Mill's position that nature is neither wholly determinative of good and bad human conduct nor irrelevant to it. Holmes calls Mill's "Nature" a brilliant essay and rightfully points out that Mill rejects nature as a standard for right and wrong. But Holmes ignores Mill's assessment that nature is a set of capacities and Mill's injunction that the task of humanity is to amend, not follow, nature. Consequently, Holmes mistakenly states that Mill contradicts "Nature" in On Liberty when Mill asserts that the free individual chooses a way of life that reflects one's higher natural capacities. Annas also misunderstands Mill's view that the nature of a thing means its entire set of capacities for exhibiting phenomena and that distinct circumstances contribute to different realizations. Annas is confused by Mill's position that women display different characteristics in distinct environments. She complains that Mill is inconsistent when he states that women both lack an intrinsic nature and develop passive qualities due to repression, ignoring Mill's argument that one's lower natural capacities are cultivated in specific environments.[74]

To be sure, Mill is only in partial agreement with Aristotle. He rejects Aristotle's metaphysical conception of nature and virtue that extracts norms from a conception of the specie's highest point of developmental possibilities. True, Mill's distinction between just and unjust individuals does assume, like Aristotle, a difference between living through the power of self-mastery versus being the passive tool of a ruler's needs, public opinion, customs, or one's imme-diate physical desires. To Mill, maintaining a commitment to justice is an in-trinsic good for a human being. But Mill rejects Aristotle's position that what is most desired is a life in accordance with nature, with the highest "accordance" understood as the realization of the universal, natural human potential for a life of *logos*. Mill's just individual places self-command above instrumentality, but that in itself does not define the life that the just individual should lead. Mill combines the Aristotelian premise of cultivating higher human attributes with the modern conception of justice to revise traditional empiricism's mechanical conception of nature as matter in motion, while also breaking down Rousseau and Kant's separation of morality from nature.[75]

LIBERAL VIRTUES

Mill's treatment of justice—as an ethical outlook and not mere adherence to rules—can be interpreted as a straddling between the ancients' virtue-centered ethics and the moderns' rule-governed moralities. The central point about the virtue-centered view, which is generally associated with the ancients, is that key ethical decisions are judgments that reflect the character of agents: the virtuous person's proper conduct emanates from a fixed disposition that is a composite of our rational capacities, emotions, bodily constitution, and sociality. In the classical understanding, the virtues are excellences of character that are objec-tive goods; they have worth to others as well as to the bearer of virtue. Virtue-centered ethics may incorporate rules as maps or aids to social interaction, but these rules should not replace the concern for how the regime and its social and cultural institutions shape the character of the individual. Rules, in short, serve the virtues. Finally, virtue-centered ethics maintain that while virtue is learned and is not easy to acquire, it addresses our social and political nature. Living alone, and living without virtue, is not good for us.[76]

In contrast, rule-governing moralities, which are generally associated with the moderns, identify how we can know what to do by appealing to laws, rules, or principles which spell out or give us a method for finding out what is right, permitted, or obligatory. The rules or principles can be known and applied by individuals irrespective of their character or disposition. The accepted agenda of these act-centered ethics is to formulate a supreme and universally applicable moral principle—for example, Kant's categorical imperative, Bentham's great-est happiness for the greatest number, and John Rawls's two principles of justice—together with criteria for recognizing relatively different kinds of moral situations. Then moral conduct is the activity that best accords with the applicable rules in given situations.[77]

In Mill's commemorative essay on Bentham in 1838 that marked his final break with the utilitarian school, he questioned whether a moral philosophy could focus exclusively on rules. "Morality consists of two parts," Mill reasons. "One of these is self-education; the training by the human being of his affections and will. That department is blank in Bentham's system. The other and co-equal part, the regulation of his outward actions, must be altogether halting and imperfect without the first." Bentham's principles, Mill continues, will restrict individuals from killing, burning, and stealing; but how will they cultivate higher aspects "of human behavior, or for laying down even the greater moralities as to those facts which tend to influence the depth of character." From the writing of "Bentham" until his death in 1871, Mill attempted to construct a political and moral philosophy that combined ethics centered on developing self-commanding individuals within the framework of a rule governing morality.[78]

In Mill's account, justice is both a quality of character and a rule-governing morality. In addition to addressing one's desire for self-protection, it is the self-command and self-respect of the individual that drives one to refrain from base desires and uphold a general obligation to the well-being of others. As George Kateb puts it, "Individuals [in Mill's view] are as they should be only if they do not trample on others: and only if they feel their refusal to trample as part of that individuality. A true individual will not impair the individuality of any of his fellows or harm their interests."[79] This conception of the just individual can be viewed as higher or lower, more or less noble, than the virtue-centered ethics of the ancients. On the one hand, the ethical decisions of the subject are lower, as they are *not* rooted in complex, unique, and challenging circumstances— true tests of character—but rather acts of conformity to uniform rules. From this perspective, the quality of justice is adherence to a social rule, and there is nothing particularly noble or distinct about it. To be just is a limited version of self-command, as one need only obey the same rules that every citizen obeys. On the other hand, one can take the position that our actions ought not be confined exclusively to our own well-being and character development. From this perspective, Mill's just individual can be viewed as higher than the traditional virtue-centered individual, as the just moral conscience directly contributes to the general good: it provides an important cross-current to the narrowness and egoism of self-interest that pervade much of modern life.

THE LIMITATIONS OF JUSTICE

Mill's idea of justice emphasizes the capacity for individual self-command and not only the adherence to rules. But, Mill continues, while a just outlook is a part of self-developed individuality, the two are not the same. Self-development also requires other qualities of character: reason, strong will and desires, a sense of dignity, to name a few. By establishing equal rights and free human conduct, the rules of justice provide *a* condition for every individual to elevate himself and develop all of these qualities of character. But these same rules of justice, Mill continues, can lead to moral atrophy and social decay. English society, Mill warns, will stagnate if compliance with just rules becomes the sole criterion of the good human being.[80]

Here Mill recognizes, once again, that individuals who lack a just outlook should not be considered unjust as long as they do not break the rules of justice. Modern liberty, in short, requires *not* doing unjust acts, not a just disposition. Distinguishing perfect and imperfect obligations, Mill also reasons that individuals who refrain from committing unjust acts are not required to be self-developed. As justice is the only enforceable practice, individuals can be criticized, but not legally coerced, for being imprudent, wasteful, or exercising what Mill calls "miserable individuality." Finally, Mill concedes that some unjust actions will have "proceeded from qualities entitled to praise." While this recognition of higher qualities will modify the estimation of the agents themselves, in almost all cases it will not free them from punishment for committing unjust actions. In a conflict between qualities such as creativity or desire for distinctiveness and the requirements of justice, one's obligation is to obey the rules of justice. Liberal societies presuppose toleration as the highest virtue, and rules of justice are the foundation of civil peace and the one absolute requisite of civil society: "Justice . . . is . . . to be the chief part, and incomparably the most sacred and binding part, of all morality." Justice establishes "moral requirements" that "stand higher . . . and are therefore of more paramount obligation, than any others."[81] In short, Mill posits that the good liberal society will recognize the distinction between the excellent individual and the rule-abiding citizen: the egalitarian principle of the authority of the self is raised above the task of cultivating higher types of individuals.[82]

Herein—the "liberal virtues"—lies a vital tension in Mill's thought. Mill argues that self-commanding, energetic individuals allow liberal societies to prosper as individuals raise themselves above narrow, self-interested activities. They develop desires for excellence, break traditions, and create new practices. But

Mill also is arguing that the cultivation of these qualities of character must be subordinated to the self-interested activities of individuals who comply with the rules of justice. As compliance with the rules of justice stands above self-development, there will be a general tendency for free societies to devalue the qualities of character that allow it to prosper. The advantage of equal justice is its ability "to repress wrong through all departments of life, by a fit exertion of the superior strength which civilization has given it," and thus to offer protection through law for the weak and vulnerable members of society, who are no longer dependent on the "chivalrous character" of stronger types. The disadvantage of equal justice is that, while the contributions of the heroic and creative individual "are still what they were . . . the rights of the weak and the general comfort of human life, now rest on a far surer and steadier support."[83] To Mill, the self-developed life is one possible mode of existence in liberal societies—one among many others. And the adherents of self-amended lives must recognize the need for coexisting with individuals who do not place self-development at the center of their existence.[84]

Further, as the rules of justice regiment and demand uniformity, there is a tendency for modern people to follow rules, customs, and public opinion and nothing else. In England, where, Mill believes, the laws of justice are most advanced, he consistently complains that the individual spends all of his time following rules and customs. Mill appreciates that this English rule-governing morality has cultivated a degree of civility and "tenderness of conscience" in mutual interactions: "In this we have had on the whole a real superiority, though one principally negative; for conscience is with most men a power chiefly in the way of restraint—a power which acts rather in staying our hands from any great wickedness." But "in England, rule to a great degree has substituted itself for nature. The greater part of life is carried on not by following inclination under the control of a rule, but by having no inclination but that of following a rule."[85]

The English aristocracy is particularly wanting in the qualities of character that lead to higher forms of individuality and exertions of human energy. This class, bemoans Mill, which sets a spiritual tone in society, "every year shows more & more their *pitoyable* absence of even that very moderate degree of intellect, & that very moderate amount of will and character" which characterize an independent existence, "owing to the total absence of habit of exerting their minds for any purpose whatever." The rising middles classes are little better: their attention is "almost confined to money-getting." While the passive outlook of the English restrains individuals from committing acts of great wickedness, it fosters a type of character that has little love of nation, of human improvement, of human agency, of virtue. Unlike the French, the English are unwilling to inflict pointless suffering, but they also are unwilling to exert human energy unless it leads to their material improvement.[86]

Mill's fear is that "the inevitable growth of social equality . . . should impose on mankind an oppressive yoke of uniformity in opinion and practice." Exacerbating this problem, liberal philosophers—Smith, the utilitarians, classical political economists, among others—established the view that the narrowly self-interested existence is the best life. "I am not charmed," confesses Mill, "with the ideal of life held out by those who think that the normal state of human beings is that of struggling to get on; that the trampling, crushing, elbowing, and treading on each other's heels, which form the existing type of social life, are the most desirable lot of human kind, or anything but the disagreeable symptoms of one of the phases of industrial progress."[87]

To Mill, England is confronting the dark side of liberty, because people are free to be barely human, not think, not create, just follow. The consequence is that, compared with former times, in England there is "much more of the amiable and humane, and much less of the heroic. . . . [The English] shrink from all effort, from everything which is troublesome and disagreeable. The same causes, which render them sluggish and unenterprising, make them, for the most part, stoical even under inevitable evils. But heroism is an active, not a passive quality; and when it is not necessary to bear pain but to seek it, little needs to be expected from the men of the present day." Mill complains that "English opinion is sure to be against the side . . . that seems to be attempting to alter an existing order of things." The English mind, he summarizes, "is distinguished only for a kind of sober good sense . . . and for doing all those things which are best done where man most resembles a machine, with the precision of a machine."[88]

Mill concludes that equal justice—"a necessary stage in the progress of civilization"[89]—is a one-sided morality that must be complemented by civil practices and values that cultivate reason, strong desires, fortitude, and other qualities that engender strong exertions of human agency. While the rules of modern justice promote self-interested activities that yield commercial benefits, those who defend justice and equality only to protect property will fail to maintain justice itself. "The ascendancy of the commercial class in modern society and politics is inevitable, and, under due limitations, ought not to be regarded as an evil," cautions Mill. "Any counterbalancing power can henceforth exist only by the sufferance of the commercial class; but that it should tolerate some such limitation, we deem as important as that it should not itself be a vassalage."[90]

To be sure, Mill continually argued for further developing civil association, whereby equal rights would be gradually extended to all those hitherto neglected or excluded, whether they were the English working class or Negro slaves or women. But the rules of justice can be effective only when there are individuals with qualities and characteristics that will lead them to use liberty well. "Torpidity and cowardice, as a general characteristic, is new in the world. . . . [I]t is a natural consequence of the progress of civilization, and will continue until met by a system of cultivation meant to counteract it." Mill's aim is not to replace the rules of equal justice with hierarchy but to discover the qualities of developed individuality that protect civil association and promote (ultimately) social unity. "We must beware, too, of mistaking its [equal rights] virtues for faults, merely because, as is inevitable, its faults mingles with its virtues and colour them."[91]

The modern English emphasis on civil intercourse creates important social advances: "the multiplication of physical comforts . . . the softening of manners; the decline of . . . personal conflict; the progressive limitation of the tyranny of the strong over the weak; the great works accomplished . . . by the cooperation of multitudes." At the same time, these advances exact a high price: "the relaxation of individual energy and courage; the loss of proud and self-relying independence; the slavery of so large a portion of mankind to artificial wants; their effeminate shrinking from even the shadow of pain; the dull unexciting monotony of their lives, and the passionless insipidity, and the absence of any marked individuality, in their characters." Where there is a common set of positions and ways of life, concludes Mill in discussing equality's tendency to override individuality, there also will be common partialities, desires, prejudices, "and absolute power." "[This] is the way to render the corrections of these imperfections hopeless; to make one narrow, mean type of human nature universal and perpetual, and to crush every influence which tends to the further improvement of man's intellectual and moral nature." "Only when, in addition to just institutions, the increase of mankind shall be under the deliberate guidance of judicious foresight," concludes Mill, will modern societies have a comprehensive morality that promotes both excellent individuals and "the means of improving and elevating the universal lot."[92]

In Mill's vision of the good liberal society, the quest for human excellence and developed individuality will exist for a long time among many other ways of life, most of which are more rooted in the institutions and principles of equal justice than self-commanding individuality is. This increases the need to consciously cultivate excellent individuals. "The beautifying of existence," he writes, "is as worthy and useful an object as the sustaining of it; but only a vitiated taste can see any such result in the fopperies of so-called civilization, which myriads of hands are now occupied and lives wasted in providing."[93] To Mill, developing civil practices and values that cultivate self-commanding individuals is as important as establishing the rules and mores of justice.

Chapter 3 The Cultivation of the Individual and Society: J. S. Mill's Use of Ancient and Romantic Dialectics

Mill is reputed to be the unequivocal defender of all human conduct not deemed harmful to others. It is a legacy that paints an incomplete picture of Mill's political philosophy. In Mill's view, liberal societies can neither self-preserve nor prosper without values and civil practices that raise some individuals above narrow, self-interested activity. It simply isn't enough for an entire society to subsist via the harm principle. Mill believes that the morality and rules of justice will limit potential instabilities or troubles that energetic, willful individuals may engender. However, even if creative individuals periodically cause conflicts and tensions, the problems they create for liberal societies are minimal in contrast to the stagnation spawned by a society that no longer generates such individuals. The "great difficulty" of "democratic society," explains Mill, is that it has been unable to do what all other flourishing societies have done—create "a social support, *a point d'appui,* for individual resistance to the tendencies of the ruling power; a protection, a rallying point, for opinions and interests which the ascendant public opinion views with disfavour."[1]

As this chapter explains, Mill looked to the teachings of Plato,

Coleridge, Kant, and others, both ancient and romantic, to discover resources for a type of liberalism that, in addition to defending individual rights, would emphasize the capacity for individual self-mastery and the exertion of willfulness. To Mill, the dignity and happiness of human beings rest on the power to command, to be the determinant of one's own aims, rather than the instrument of customs, rules, public opinion, or one's base desires. Mill believes both ancients and romantics explored this human capacity much more thoroughly than the philosophers of the Anglo-Scottish Enlightenment, whose goals rarely extended beyond the engendering of civil peace and commerce. English liberalism, Mill charges, fails to take responsibility for developing self-commanding modes of existence and is driving English society into the muck of social homogeneity.

EMPIRICISM AND ROMANTICISM ON LIBERTY

Political philosophy has always been deeply concerned with the role the passions play in both the individual and society. While not politically homogeneous, seminal philosophers of empiricism generally posited reason as an instrumental tool of the passions, whether in the realm of the purest theorizing or, more important, in the foundation of a civil life—a life they saw as based chiefly on the pursuit of private satisfactions. "Reason," Hobbes states, "is nothing but Reckoning," that is, discovering which means are most appropriate to attain desired ends. To Hobbes, desires and impulses do not respond to a perceived idea of the good. Rather the desires themselves are the sources of good and evil in the world. The objects that compel us toward them we identify as good, and those that repulse us we call evil. In this way, the passions are the source of all human action. Reason is merely another tool we have to respond to our passions. As Hobbes felt that self-aggrandizing ends generally animate our passions, he saw no way for us to bring them under self-control. Only an outside rule-making power could be a sufficiently credible threat to our lives to cause us to restrain them, a power that we accepted because of our overriding fear of death.[2]

Locke generally follows Hobbes's view of the relation between human desires and the idea of the good. "What moves desire?" Locke asks, and answers, "Happiness and that alone." It is pleasure and pain that determine good and evil. Thus, "that which is properly good or bad, is nothing but barely pleasure and pain," and "things also that draw after them pleasure and pain, are considered good and evil."[3] For Locke, "it is present unease, not the prospect of a future good, which determines our" actions. We feel discomfort in relation to the "amount of pain of an evil, and so we always desire to avoid it. But we do not feel restless about an absent good that is proportionate to the amount of good" we would enjoy if we actually came to possess it. The most common error is that we remain satisfied with the goods of this life, which, it might appear, we can secure through our own execution.[4] If we feel more pain from hunger than from a desire for heaven, we will act to relieve the greater uneasiness. Locke believes our desires to be more idiosyncratic than did Hobbes, as the strength of different passions is shown in the varying degrees of uneasiness everyone feels at the thought of absent goods. Locke does maintain, like Hobbes, that since we primarily attempt to avoid pain, we can be controlled by the rule of law and the norms of morality. Thankfully, our reason is adequate to establish the laws and concepts that give us what we want: the security to pursue actions and possessions as we please.[5]

Claude-Adrien Helvétius, the philosophe who deeply influenced Bentham and James Mill (as well as the young John Stuart Mill), embraces the Hobbesian framework of the relation between the passions and the good. Man, says Helvétius, flees from bodily pains and seeks bodily pleasures, and it is to this persistent quest that is given the name of self-love. Social circumstances are unable to change these fundamental drives—they only determine the way that we pursue these ends. The good is the means we use to seek power, avoid pain, and gain pleasure: "Riches, honor, glory, reputation, justice and virtue, in a word, all the factitious passions, are really but the love of power, disguised under different names." To Helvétius, a monarch in power already has the requisite for personal pleasure, and one cannot assume that he or she will have a reason to promote reform that serves the public good. Frederick the Great and Catherine of Russia may introduce a few reforms to heighten their power and gain a reputation for enlightenment, but the principles of human nature will prevent them from introducing comprehensive reforms that will contribute to the general welfare. At the same time, individuals tend to be loyal to small groups, which generally are opposed to the general interests. Only representatives in a democracy have the self-interest to ingratiate themselves with the general public and establish laws that will promote the general happiness and, in the long run, educate individuals to understand the relation between their own desires and those of the nation.[6]

Hobbes and other empiricists rejected arguments that, since human conduct is a product of causation and antecedents, the individual is not free. Compatibilism, as most fully articulated by Hobbes and Hume, asserts that freedom and determinism are not antithetical, since the causal factors of agents' desires have no bearing on their right to choose. When causal factors lead to human action, the two are simply conjunctions of events, not a relation of necessity. Only coercion from external sources impedes action, and an agent is free when he does what he desires, even if his desires and decisions are themselves the influences of more remote causes, outside the agent. From this perspective, one is free to act, even if not free to will, as the antecedent causes determining the will always exist. The architects of a naturalistic epistemology, Hobbes and Hume argue that we are a part of nature and are not alien to it or capable of rising above it.[7]

For Hobbes, the mind consists of tiny particles of matter which function like visible bodies. External objects make different impressions on our bodies, leading to distinct passions. Conflicting desires and pains lead to "deliberation," and its outcome—the last appetite—leads to action, which is an act of the will. These deliberations and actions are themselves motions that can be explained by laws of physics. What determines every action "is the sum of all things, which now being existent, conduce and concur to the production of that action hereafter, whereof, if nay one thing were now wanting, the effect could not be produced." But Hobbes maintains that this determinism does not reduce freedom: an individual is free when he is not impeded from his actions, even if he is not really in control of his actions. Liberty consists merely in the absence of interference with the exercise of our choices, not the absence of causal determination in their formation. "I acknowledge this *liberty*," Hobbes states succinctly, "that I *can* do if I *will*; but to say I can *will* if I *will*, I take to be an absurd speech."[8]

The will does not play an independent role in Hume's theory of human conduct either: "By the *will*, I mean nothing but *the internal impression we feel and are conscious of, when we knowingly give rise to any new motion of our body, or new perception of our mind.*" But while Hobbes speaks of "nature and the intrinsic quality of the agent," Hume's empiricism takes him a step further.[9] The picture of human conduct that Hume strives to reject is the one provided by Hobbes, in which self-interested bundles of desires and aversions interact with each other solely on what promotes their needs, and indeed perhaps momentary needs at that. Morality, Hume counters, structures our actions by shaping the motivations that drive our desires and passions. Moral approval further stimulates, and moral disapproval tames, our desires. A mind "is nothing but a heap of collection of different perceptions, united together by different relations." There is no such thing as a self, or an agent, beyond the impressions it has and the bodily acts to which these lead. This regular determination of the will by other factors is one important aspect of the causal uniformity on which a science of human conduct is to be founded. It is beside the point that an agent may feel a "liberty of indifference" or freedom from antecedents in his conduct. The necessity of actions consists in the fact that the philosopher or scientist of human nature may infer our actions from our motives, character, and circumstances. The explanation of human behavior is of the same sort as the explanation of physical events because "there is but one kind of *necessity*, as there is but one kind of cause, and that the common distinction betwixt *moral* and *physical* necessity is without any foundation in nature." To Hume, this assessment that almost all of our actions are predictable does not mean that we are not free: to predict an act is not to compel an individual to act. Liberty is "*a power of acting or not acting, according to the determinations of the will;* that is, if we choose to remain at rest we may; if we choose to move, we also may."[10]

Rousseau, Kant, and other romantics criticized this negative conception of liberty. To these thinkers, self-determination could not "mean simply the unfettered pursuit of one's empirical desires." It meant something higher—"being determined by views that reflect one's most authentic or spiritual nature." If we are to be consistently free, we must be autonomous, directing our lives in a way wholly self-imposed and self-regulated. Rousseau and Kant begin the trend of seeing humans in terms of authentic and inauthentic modes of being. Freedom for them must presuppose a distinction between the self and its environment.[11]

Rousseau initiated this outlook, insisting on the importance of free agency and arguing that while physics might explain the "mechanism of the senses," it could never make intelligible "the power of willing or rather of choosing," a power in which, he says, nothing is to be found but acts which are purely spiritual and wholly inexplicable by the laws of mechanism.[12] Rousseau distinguished the "physical" and "metaphysical and moral" aspects of humanity. Viewed as a physical entity, humanity is simply an ingenious machine driven by appetites and desires that can be analyzed through the laws of physics. Viewed from the moral and metaphysical perspective, however, the human species is inherently distinct from all others. In this view, we are agents who have the capacity to will, choose, and transcend our natural appetites, making progress and perfectibility for the species possible and rendering us able to speak of freedom in a way the empiricists wouldn't dare.

In Rousseau's view, classic liberalism, with its cherished private sphere protected from the limited state, fosters only the physical and selfish aspect of humanity, as dealings among individuals are at best contractual, always with an eye to gain. He proposed two alternative roads—moral idealism and romantic/expressive individualism—for the individual seeking spiritual or authentic freedom. On the one hand, in the good regime based on the social contract, the individual learns to reconcile and even displace his desires with the general will of the citizenry. What occurs in this act of virtuous self-conquest is not the overcoming of one natural desire by another but the triumph of that unique human faculty—the will—to resist or rise above all natural impulses: "the voice of duty replaces physical impulse and right replaces appetite."[13] Here the citizen overcomes those desires that run counter to the good of the community. On the other hand, for the person who lives in a hopelessly corrupt society, Rousseau puts forth the value of self-expressive individuals—the solitary artist or romantic dreamer. This individual withdraws from corrupt political and social engagements and communes with his soul. He becomes absorbed with his unconscious sentiments and emotions, develops as a self-defining, self-grounding subject, with the aim of discovering his distinct nature or "what am I."[14] Having found his way free of the false needs created by a corrupt civil society, this self-developed individual is capable of developing his unique ethical sensibilities.

Kant builds on Rousseau's critique and develops the idea of a free will to contrast empiricism's idea of freedom of action. One's will in this sense is one's decision, choice, or dominating aim. Kant asks: Even if one is free to follow one's strongest desires and hence has freedom of action in the compatibilist sense, does one have any control over those choices and desires themselves? Can one influence the strength of one's desires? Or are they determined by external influences? Just how much of the real world did the mind receive through sensory apparatus, and how reliably? Kant argues that one might be a compatibilist with respect to free action and determinism, but an incompatibilist with respect to free will and determinism. Whereas Hobbes, Hume, and empiricism understand freedom in opposition to restrictions on movement, Kant identifies freedom in opposition to a will determined by the necessity that governs the natural and sensible world. For Kant, living under laws that allow free movement or action is, at best, an external freedom secured by public law in accordance with right. Here one's actions are still being controlled by external causes such as the appetites and the passions. Inner or true freedom is attained when one's actions move beyond that of natural necessity and are based on a will that acts from a universal law that one recognizes and respects as prescribed by reason. To frame Kant's conception of liberty positively, freedom is the power of complete self-determination, enabling us to judge and act solely because of our own reasoning, regardless of tangible circumstances. To put it more negatively, freedom is the complete independence of any prior causes other than our own will or practical reason, our "power to restrain and overcome inclinations by reason."[15]

MILL'S TWO CONCEPTIONS OF LIBERTY

Mill's deepest philosophic treatments of empiricism's and romanticism's contending ideas of liberty are found in the *Logic* and *Hamilton*. In both works, Mill confronts the romantics' challenge to empiricism's conception of liberty.[16] Here Mill concedes that, while empiricism holds a deeper understanding of the role law and other circumstances play in limiting the coercive actions of others, the romantics' "free will doctrine has . . . fostered in its followers a much stronger spirit of self-culture." The earlier liberalism is better at freeing the individual from many external restraints but has not thought through the psychological basis of human liberty. As a result, it fails to distinguish higher and lower forms of individuality. The romantics' conception of liberty was developed "because the supposed alternative of admitting human actions to be *necessary* was inconsistent with every one's instinctive consciousness, as well as humiliating to the pride, and even degrading to the moral nature, of man."[17] In sum, Mill saw the value of empiricism's focus on shaping circumstances that protect individual rights, but he also agrees with the romantics' view that too often a more substantive view of freedom—one that educated and cultivated the individual to use freedom well—was ignored.

Mill confesses in the *Autobiography* that as a young man he too embraced the traditional empiricist position on the compatibility between liberty and necessity. Looking back, he complains that this outlook left him without hope that he could "begin the formation of my character anew, and create in a mind now irretrievably analytic, fresh associations of pleasure with any of the objects of human desire." In his youth, Mill saw himself as "a made or manufactured man, having had a certain impress of opinion stamped on me which I could only reproduce." Mill found there was no place for an irrepressibly self-conscious state of mind in empiricism's associational psychology, where being "conscious of the feeling" was not distinguished from "merely having the feeling. . . . I felt as if I was scientifically proved to be the helpless slave of antecedent circumstances; as if my character and that of all others had been formed for us by agencies beyond our control, and was wholly out of our own power."[18]

Nonetheless, in both the *Logic* and *Hamilton* Mill rejects the contrast by Kant between the free will and causation. According to Kant, the individual is free if and only if his or her action is the result of a will that has no empirical cause. "The philosopher of Königsberg saves inconvenient facts at the expense of the consistency of his theory," states Mill. Kant cannot hold one explanation for one kind of actions, and another explanation for other kinds of actions: "When we voluntarily exert ourselves, as it is our duty to do, for the improvement of our character, or when we act in a manner which (either consciously on our part or unconsciously) deteriorates it, these, like all other voluntary acts, presuppose that there was already something in our character, or in that combined with our circumstances, which led us to do so, and accounts for our doing so."[19]

In response, Mill maintains that the romantics' goal of elaborating a more self-defining conception of freedom is compatible with universal causality: it requires that part of that causality must be the consciousness of our ability to determine our volitions and reshape our character. "Though our character is formed by circumstances," Mill writes, "our own desires can do much to shape those circumstances; and what is really inspiriting and ennobling in the doctrine of free will, is the conviction that we have real power over the formation of our own character; and that our will, by influencing some of our circumstances, can modify our habits or capabilities of willing." In Mill's account, now that we are cognizant that our dispositions and desires are shaped by chains of causation, we have the capacity to shape those chains to cultivate the desire for a life of dignity and self-commanding individuality. The free society creates circumstances in which the individual learns he can command himself. The character of an agent's mind becomes one of the constitutive forces of circumstances, the significance and role of mind becomes more of a question and philosophical problem for empiricism.[20]

Mill finds himself at the interface of what Bernard Williams calls "Internal and External Reasons:" "those political philosophers influenced by Hobbes, Hume, and empiricism, for whom any rationale to act could be a reason only if it offered some sort of means to the satisfaction of the passions, or, more broadly, a prior disposition, and those influenced by Rousseauist and Kantian concerns about the origins of such desires and motivations and so the problem of autonomy."[21] Mill works to fill this lacuna in empiricism's notion of freedom in the *Logic* and *Hamilton*. He defines "moral freedom" as the *opportunity* for the self-development of character based on the cultivation of mental faculties. To be self-conscious is not only to be aware of a world of things; it is also to be aware of one's awareness of things. Self-development is thus characterized by an ability to stand back from one's self and reflect upon one's state of mind. True freedom is not just being able to effectively calculate how to move toward already determined ends, but to possess the ability to express and defend one's own goals. Mill defines freedom of *action* as the freedom to do what a person enjoys, while higher freedom means the individual wills the desires one desires. To Mill, the opportunity to gain self-command of one's aims requires the traditional empiricist goal of limiting the determination of our actions and allowing the freedom to make choices. However, moral freedom also requires that individuals have the *option* of self-amendment of character. "[The] feeling of our being able to modify our own character *if we wish,* is itself the feeling of moral freedom which we are conscious of," summarizes Mill in the *Logic*.[22]

While a self-amended life requires a measure of qualities that not all of us can or do muster—or even desire to have—it is crucial that individuals should have the opportunity to claim a sphere or way of life for which they are fitted, whatever that might be. Mill recognizes that some individuals' objectives are not the development of a new way of life, but rather its maintenance. These individuals also are morally free as long as they know that if they were desirous of changing, they could do so. In *On Liberty,* Mill argues that the actualization of different ways of life will induce people to make choices about their own character, thus promoting self-determined modes of existence. "Freedom, instead of being the capacity to satisfy any desire that might occur, becomes the capacity to satisfy a particular desire—that of modifying or choosing one's character."[23]

Mill's position in both the *Logic* and *Hamilton* that all individuals must have the *opportunity* to self-amend helps clarify his view in relation to polarized positions in contemporary political theory on Mill's vision of liberty. John Gray, for instance, argues that Mill articulated two ideas of liberty—the universal right to free action, the "moral right to autonomy, [which] is possessed, not by all men, but only by those possessing in some minimal degree the capacities of an autonomous agent." In opposition, Wendy Donner and Nadia Urbinati charge that Gray's interpretation unfairly associates Mill with elitism and that he did not have higher and lower conceptions of liberty. They counter that Mill identified free human conduct and the self-amendment of character as a single egalitarian principle. In the *Logic* and *Hamilton,* Mill—consistent with Gray's account—maintains that only some individuals self-amend. But Mill also maintains the egalitarian current identified by Donner and Urbinati in positing that all individuals must have the option of self-amendment of character.[24]

Furthermore, Mill's insistence that all individuals have an opportunity—but not an obligation—to self-amend answers the misguided charge of John Rawls, Charles Larmore, William Galston, and others, who claim that Mill's vision is too "comprehensive" and ultimately illiberal because it would lead the state to end outlooks and ways of life that do not center on autonomy.[25]

Mill's distinction between different kinds of liberty is an explicit response to Kant's charge that empiricism fails to distinguish between free action and the free will.[26] Mill's vision of a self-developed life is a challenge to Kant's conception as well. Kant's pronounced tendency is to restrict autonomy or free will to the achievement of only one sort of excellence: moral excellence. Prudence is mere *Klugheit,* or cleverness, while the autonomous dictates of reason are the laws of morality. To be free, therefore, is to embrace moral duty. "A free will," states Kant, "and a will under moral laws are one and the same."[27] To have moral value, our actions must conform to what duty requires and must be done for the sake of the duty itself. The moral character of an action is completely determined by the motive or the intention that informs it—respect for the moral law—and is entirely independent of whatever consequences may result from it. Morality does not derive from a practical reason that is heteronomous and inextricably linked to our desires. Any moral outlook that attempts to base an ethical outlook on desired changes that we produce will fail, for all such natural goods are also caused by contingency and unknown reasons.

To Kant, our rationality is not unique unless our reason transcends our desires. If we are only able to accomplish what nonrational and thus nonmoral events also can bring about, then humanity is little more than an animal that walks upright. As Kant puts it, the human being is "not so completely an animal as to be indifferent to all that reason says on its own and to use reason merely as a tool for the satisfaction of his needs as a sensible being. For, that he has reason does not at all raise him in worth above mere animality if reason is to serve him only for the sake of what instinct accomplishes for animals; reason would in that case be only a particular mode nature had used to equip the human being for the same end to which it has destined animals, without destining him to a higher end."[28]

Like Kant, Mill argues against traditional empiricism in claiming that liberty is fully realized only if there is more to life and human conduct than a response to the stimuli of rules, public opinion, and customs. Being human and truly free entails more than the empiricists were willing to admit. Differing with Kant, Mill argues that concerns for higher goods are not solely motivated by selflessness.[29] To Mill, the desire for dignity, the courageous resistance to public opinion, the quest for self-respect and self-fulfillment—all maintained in the context of a just moral outlook—are powerful and ennobling springs of action serving as preconditions for progress and human liberty. In short, Mill is challenging a dichotomy, present to this day in contemporary political theory, between Hobbes, Locke, and empiricism's "interests" and Kant and moral idealism's "autonomy." To the former, freedom is self-interested activities and has neither a higher or lower content nor a direct relation to the public good, but to the latter, autonomy is a higher form of freedom and it centers on what we do for the universal good and not for ourselves. In contrast, Mill is arguing that some forms of self-interested conduct are both higher forms of freedom and contributors to the general good.[30]

THE GOOD AND DESIRES

At first glance Mill's view is reminiscent of the classical view, somewhat Platonic or neo-Epicurean, whereby the mental faculties represent something as a good that an agent might attain, thereby calling into action a type of desire. As the passions are essentially representations of good and ills, improvement in the idea of the good, or mental and moral cultivation, fosters a higher view of what is pleasure. "What it is the man's interest to do or refrain from," Mill writes, "depends less on any outward circumstances, than what sort of man he is. If you wish to know what is practically a man's interest, you must know the cast of his habitual feelings and thoughts." Because internal channeling of the passions is possible, the passions do not have to be feared. Those who attack pleasure "represent human nature in a degrading light; since the accusations suppose human beings to be capable of no pleasures except those of which *swine* are capable."

What is needed is education and public policies as aids in facilitating the cultivation of higher mental and moral faculties: "I regard any considerable increase of human happiness, through mere changes in outward circumstances, unaccompanied by changes in the states of the desires, as hopeless; not to mention that while the desires are circumscribed in the self, there can be no adequate motive for exertions tending to modify to good ends those external circumstances." Thus, while Mill places enormous value on free human conduct, he also has other criteria for evaluating the quality of laws and civil practices: "The rights of individuals, which other individuals ought to respect, over external things, are in general sufficiently pointed out by a few plain rules, and by the laws of one's country. But it often happens that an essential part of the morality or immorality of an action or a rule of action consists on its influence upon the agent's own mind; upon his susceptibilities of pleasure or pain; upon the general direction of his thoughts, feelings, and imagination; or upon some particular association." A great danger, Mill insists, is that contemporary "man as well as the 'woman who deliberates' is in imminent danger of being lost."[31] As Jeremy Waldron puts it, "[Mill] *evaluates* the processes by which preferences are generated. Large parts of his ethics—for example, the distinction between higher and lower pleasures—are unintelligible apart from the assumption that the generation of preferences is a proper subject for ethical scrutiny."[32]

Mill's views on universal education are strongly affected by this vision of higher forms of individuality. Mill opposed the state's being the sole provider of general education: he was concerned about the polarization that would develop over the substance of a uniform curriculum. In the event of a consensus, he feared a uniform curriculum would further society's general tendency to cultivate mass conformity. Nonetheless, Mill consistently proposes that the state enforce a universal standard of education for all children through the mechanism of public examinations.[33] He recognizes that education must combat the natural tendency toward rest and complacency and that it is extremely difficult to change narrow, restricted outlooks of what is good once they become fixed and settled. To ask a selfish individual to be concerned for other people or for his or her country "is like preaching to the worm who crawls on the ground, how much better it would be for him if he were an eagle."[34]

Universal education is an absolute requirement for ethical development, Mill insists, because the educated individual is generally associated with "prudence, temperance, and justice, and generally by the virtues which are of importance in our intercourse with others." Such education must not be limited to teachings on how "to get on in life"; rather, "knowledge and culture, which have no obvious tendency to better the fortunes of the possessor, but solely to enlarge and exalt his moral and intellectual nature, shall be . . . obtruded on the public." Mill argues that, as education for the world of business, trade, and many professions is self-generating, the state is not required to ensure the teaching of anyone but the most destitute in how to make a living. What must be ensured is that "all instruction which is given, [teaches] not that we may live, but that we may live well; all which aims at making us wise and good . . . as the majority have neither the desire, nor any sufficient notion of the means, of becoming much wiser or better than they are." The aim of universal education is neither the dissemination of specific beliefs nor the identification of a distinct specially gifted elite. What is sought here is the development of the habit of reflecting about one's desires and aims, of wanting to be able to infuse our desires with thought. Next to unbridled selfishness, Mill concludes, "the principal cause which makes life unsatisfactory, is the want of mental cultivation."[35]

Indeed, Mill thought mental cultivation such a laudable goal that he was willing to restrict some individual liberties for the goal of universal education. "It still remains unrecognized that to bring a child into existence without a fair prospect of being able . . . to provide . . . instruction and training for its mind is a moral crime, both against the offspring and against society; and that if the parent does not fulfill the obligation, the State ought to see it fulfilled at the charge, as far as possible of the parent." Mill did not oppose laws in those countries on the Continent that forbade marriage to couples who were unable to prove they were capable of raising their offspring well. Similarly, universal suffrage depends on universal education: "if society has neglected to discharge solemn obligations, the more important and fundamental of the two must be fulfilled first: universal teaching must precede universal enfranchisement." To Mill, creating conditions for the cultivation of higher forms of individuality is as important as establishing equal rights for all.[36]

"CLASSICAL" REASON IN SERVICE OF EXPRESSIVE SELF-DEVELOPMENT

But while reminiscent of classical themes, Mill's cultivation of the good is not to be confused with ancient teleological views that extract norms from some conception of a specie's highest point of developmental possibilities. All living creatures love themselves, noted Cicero, because nature bestows an instinct for self-preservation through the maintenance of themselves in the best condition possible. "Every living creature therefore finds its object of appetition in the thing suited to its nature. Thus arises the Ends of Goods, namely to live in accordance with nature and in that condition which is the best and most suited to nature that is possible."[37] The ancients viewed the human species as a distinct being structured by its parts in their interplay. They evaluated humans exclusively by standards intrinsic to its own entity: body and soul, reason and emotion. These common and unique features that separate man from animal should find their place in a complete and harmonious development of one's nature. Reason was accorded the highest place in determining the character of the good life.

In the *Nicomachean Ethics,* for instance, Aristotle posits that the good existence is the life according to the natural order of the human soul, with reason steering the passions toward virtue. When he reviews the various characteristics of human conduct, Aristotle focuses on "the activity of the soul in conformity with a rational principle" as the distinctly human function and outlines the distinct ways in which the soul may be said to conform to reason. Persons can exercise reason in either practical or purely philosophical matters. The first suggests that the good existence consists in the practical life of moral virtue, the second that it consists in the life of philosophy. Most of the *Ethics* is devoted to the moral virtues, but the final book favors philosophy as the highest and most choice-worthy good. It is humanity's closest approach to perfection or divine activity.[38]

In contrast, Mill maintains empiricism's view that humanity is an appetitive species that seeks to satisfy desires with the aid of reason, and he does not prescribe the content and sum of goods that an individual should seek to realize. The specific end or good that individuals strive for is less important than conceiving a goal and displaying reason in striving to re-form their lives in its name. Like the ancients, Mill distinguishes better and worse ways of life: freedom through the power of self-mastery is higher than a life of subservience to customs or one's most immediate physical needs. But unlike the ancients, Mill does not identify the life that the self-commanding individual should lead. "Great and strong and varied faculties are more wanted than faculties well proportioned to one another; a Hercules or a Briareus more than an Apollo," writes Mill.[39] The goal of reason is the romantic-expressive aim of self-development rather than the good, or a life that is good because self-developed. As Antony Thorlby puts it, "What is peculiar in Mill's picture of the soul, or 'higher parts of our nature,' as he calls it . . . is that he cares so little *what* 'fresh and living conviction' gets into it, so long as something does."[40]

Mill straddles ancient and modern thought as he explains that there are two poles to happiness: tranquility and excitement. Like the ancients, Mill maintains that self-mastery is a good that leads to the greatest pleasure. Unlike the ancients, Mill argues that such self-mastery requires engagement in the world, as the realization of actions and aims contributes to our sense of self-development. One becomes involved in practice as a means to self-develop rather than withdrawing into one's mind. "It is only those in whom indolence amounts to a vice, that do not desire excitement after an interval of repose." Happiness is not an end state, a completion or fulfillment; rather, the happy life is characterized by active pleasures predominating over the passive. "Those only are happy . . . who have their minds fixed on some object other than their own happiness . . . on some art or pursuit, followed not as means, but as itself an ideal end. Aiming thus at something else, they find happiness by the way."[41]

But unlike his forebears of empiricism, Mill seeks to restore some of the classical dignity of reason. Mill feels that empiricism's naturalistic understanding of man, which he himself did not completely abandon, needed to be supplemented by the self-knowledge that the knowing subject had of itself, as only by understanding the causes and aims of our desires do we gain power over them. Mill insists that the individual who develops the capacity to deliberate and make particular choices with a good life in view leads a happier and better existence. Invoking von Humboldt, he announces "the end of man, or that which is prescribed by the eternal or immutable dictates of reason, and not suggested by vague and transient desires, is the highest and most harmonious development of his powers to a complete and consistent whole."[42]

Once again, however, Mill does not identify the specific end or good the agent should pursue. "Different persons . . . require different conditions for their spiritual development: and can no more exist healthily in the same moral, than all the variety of plants can in the same physical, atmosphere and climate. The same things which are helps to one person towards the cultivation of higher nature are hindrances to another."[43] What is being argued here is that the highest good is not the pursuit of some specific good. Self-development that accompanies activities that pursue any good, as long as those activities do not undermine the capacity of other individuals to self-develop and self-govern their lives, becomes the highest good. This account of higher or developed individuality is based on a teleology of striving; namely, actions are good if structured by purposiveness. But it is not based on an intrinsic teleology: the purposive development of a specific entity or type.[44] In Mill's view, the mind and will are not focused on *the* good but on oneself in the purposeful pursuit of *a* good—this good or another. He locates the pinnacle of freedom in a person's ability to "desire for its own sake, the conformity of his own character to his standard of excellence, without hope of good or fear of evil from other sources than his own inward consciousness." To Mill, only the highest type of individuals attain "complete freedom," which is the successful remolding of our character in light of our own image of what is good, "and hence it is said with truth, that none but a person of confirmed virtue is completely free."[45]

In sum, Mill is a romantic-expressive liberal. The focus of Mill's attention is upon the relation of reason to self-realization, and the idea, underlined by such terms as "self-development" and "inner consciousness," is that the best life is distinctive and authentic, something every individual can discover for himself. But Mill is not a complete romantic-expressive liberal. He defends empiricism's liberty of action as a good in itself and as a condition for self-development. He insists that not all individuals are obligated to self-amend and that many individuals will choose to maintain their way of life. He argues that the discovery and realization of one's unique self are consistent with empiricism's universal causality, rather than the transcendence of circumstances. He posits that self-development of one's own character does *not* involve core features of romantic thought: exploring the unconscious; extolling the imagination; establishing an intimate relationship with nature.[46] There also remains a classical current in Mill's thought, as self-development requires feelings and desires being supervened upon a mind cultivated on the pursuit of *a* good. To discover one's good and then to pursue it is virtue, for it releases the vital energies of life—most notably, reason and the will—so long held down and constrained by customs and conventional practices. Finally, Mill consistently points out that both the romantics and the ancients advocate the cultivation of qualities that foster human agency, and he persistently develops arguments from both schools, in the process of reforming English liberalism, which he charges has neglected the task of cultivating self-commanding individuality.[47]

PLATO AND MILL ON HAPPINESS

Mill's debt to Plato in establishing a conception of liberty connected to "the development of higher faculties"[48] is exemplified by his discussions of higher and lower pleasures in *The Subjection of Women* and *Utilitarianism*. In each essay, Mill appropriates parts of Socrates' discussion in book 9 of the *Republic* on why the philosopher is happier than the tyrant to explain why a self-developed existence is superior to a life centered on the pursuit of unbridled passions. At the same time, Mill democratizes Socrates to incorporate his views into a more romantic-expressivist conception of liberty.[49]

In the *Republic* Socrates aims to convince Glaucon that the tyrant is the unhappiest individual. First, Socrates argues that tyrants are unable to fulfill their desires. The tyrant allows his passions to increasingly dominate him: he becomes hated and isolated as he seeks to dominate more things. To Socrates, the tyrant is the least self-sufficient individual, utterly dependent on external things and thus full of anxiety. Second, Socrates distinguishes three kinds of individuals corresponding to three parts of the soul: wisdom-loving, victory-loving, and gain-loving. Socrates states that the individual who knows all three pleasures would be the best judge of which is the greatest pleasure. Only the philosopher knows all three, however, and he chooses the pleasure of philosophy. Socrates does not base the philosopher's preference for wisdom on either the instrumental advantage it brings to himself or the benefits philosophy provides for others. The philosopher's sole criterion is the kind of pleasure that is produced by the respective modes of existence. "Of the three pleasures," Socrates concludes, "the most pleasant would belong to that part of the soul with which we learn; and the man among us in whom this part rules has the most pleasant life."[50]

In *Subjection of Women,* Mill explains that without equal civil and political rights for women, there is no effective check on the power of individual males over females. Further, Mill's modern tyrannical man, who is cultivated by the laws that subjugate women, is unable to check himself. He grows unhappy for the same reasons as Plato's lawless individual in book 9 of the *Republic.* Like Plato's tyrant, Mill's modern male is a bully in his domestic setting. Both tyrants also move from one material object to another as their domestic power unleashes an insatiable appetite for base or low desires. Rather than self-developing character, their energies and passions are channeled outward at others. As Mill puts it, this "power seeks out and evokes the latent germs of selfishness in the remotest corners of his nature—fans its faintest sparks and smoldering embers—offers to him a license for the indulgence of those points of his original character which in all other relations he would have found it to repress and conceal, and the repression of which in time would have become a second nature."[51]

Mill, like Plato, paints a portrait of tyrants as anxious individuals desperately seeking external objects, lacking independence, and terrorized by insecurity. They are unhappy beings who are unable to satisfy and control their lower appetites, and as a result suffer an isolated existence, mistrusting and misunderstanding even those who are closest to them. Plato's and Mill's tyrants also refuse to abdicate power owing to their fear that they will be unable to interact with others unless they maintain a superior status. "They [men] are afraid," Mill charges, "lest they should insist that marriage should be on equal conditions: lest all women of spirit and capacity should prefer doing almost anything else, not in their own eyes degrading, rather than marry, when marrying is giving themselves a master, and a master too of all their earthly possessions." What appears as a masterful position is revealed by Plato and Mill as being a slave to the lowest in oneself.[52]

Mill's democratization of Plato's conceptions of mental cultivation and human happiness also contributes to important distinctions between Plato's and Mill's tyrants. In the *Republic,* the tyrant moves beyond the domestic setting, attaining power at the pinnacle of the political order. Plato also juxtaposes the unhappiness of the tyrant and the happiness of the philosopher, who seeks to understand everything. In *Subjection of Women,* the actions of the tyrant remain centered on the domestic setting: tyranny sits at the base, not the pinnacle of society. Mill also finds the potential for happiness at the foundation of society. He contrasts the unhappiness of the domestic tyrant with the happiness of free individuals who develop their mental and moral faculties through the exercise of thoughtful choice over this or that practice or way of life.[53]

In chapter 2 of *Utilitarianism,* Mill evokes themes from the second argument in Plato's contrast of the philosopher and tyrant's happiness in book 9 of the *Republic.* Here he adopts Socrates' discussion that emphasizes the philosopher's happiness, rather than the tyrant's unhappiness, while addressing why self-government by reason and moral principles is more pleasurable than a life driven by lower, selfish principles. In formulating his answer, "If one of the two [pleasures] is, by those who are competently acquainted with both, placed so far above the other that they prefer it . . . and would not resign it for any quantity of the other pleasure which their nature is capable of, we are justified in ascribing to the preferred enjoyment a superior in quality, so far outweighing quantity as to render it, in comparison, of small account." It is an unquestionable point, Mill continues, that those individuals equally acquainted with and equally capable of enjoying both kinds of pleasures do give a clear preference to the modes of existence which develop their higher faculties.[54]

A developed mind, Mill argues, forms a type of human character that becomes a good in itself. We may attribute this preference to "pride . . . to love of liberty and independence," and, most important, to a "sense of dignity . . . which is so essential a part of the happiness of those in whom it is strong, that nothing which conflicts with it could be otherwise than momentarily, an object of desire to them." Instead of being the instrument of one's base passions, the mentally and morally developed person realizes the capacity for self-determination. His dignity preserves a prideful disdain of certain actions. His unwillingness to yield to animal impulses proves to the individual that he is capable of conscious, self-generated conduct—his freedom and happiness. Consequently, "no intelligent human being would consent to be a fool, no instructed person would be an ignoramus, no person of feeling and conscience would be selfish and base, even though they should be persuaded that the fool, the dunce, or the rascal is better satisfied with his lot than they are with theirs."[55]

As in *Subjection of Women,* Mill modifies Plato's conception of the mentally cultivated individual. Plato's philosopher of book 9 seeks to understand the truth, while Mill's mentally developed individual chooses ways of life and implements practical projects that exercise one's higher capacities. While Mill's mentally cultivated individual deliberates and judges, he does not require a degree of knowledge that extends too far beyond one's local situation. Millian wisdom, in short, is an attainable type of virtue that a liberal democratic society should be able to cultivate generally. Plato also maintains that only a few individuals are capable of becoming mentally cultivated, while Mill argues that the "present wretched education, and wretched social arrangements, are the only real hindrance to its [mental and moral development] being attained by almost all." Plato does not discuss whether the philosopher's life is socially useful or circumstantially helpful to the philosopher himself, while Mill maintains that the mentally cultivated individual contributes to both the general happiness of society and his own situational good. Nonetheless, Mill's congruity with book 9 of the *Republic* is striking as he concludes, "It is better to be a human being than a pig satisfied, better to be Socrates dissatisfied than a fool satisfied. And if the fool, or the pig, is of a different opinion, it is because they only know their side of the question. The other party to the comparison knows both sides."[56]

REFORMING PLATO'S DIALECTIC

Mill most appreciates, adopts, and revises the current of Plato's dialectic where accepted views of justice, beauty, virtue, and other standards of good and bad are challenged through questioning and cross-examination. Unlike Grote, Mill did not assume that Plato's dialectic was primarily critical: that it taught students only to expose fallacies and protest against thoughtless affirmations. Mill found a more positive, constructive lesson of the dialectic. It fostered the discipline and focus that allowed the mind to begin classifying common elements and developing principles beyond the most primitive and metaphysical views. More important, according to Mill, the dialectic primarily contributed to the ethical cultivation of the individual. Plato recognized the problem generated by characters such as Alcibiades: that many of the qualities we recognize as virtues—courage, creativity, and the rest—may be so used to do harm as to do good. Individuals require wisdom to determine when certain virtues may be employed and to what end.[57] Finally, and most important, Mill believed that, by adopting and revising Plato's dialectic and integrating it with the dialectics of Coleridge and the German Romantics, English liberalism would begin to cultivate self-commanding individuals who will contribute to the development of higher modes of existence and social unity.

Mill's account of the Platonic dialectic argues that it is a crucial step on the staircase to cultivating the mental faculties and self-commanding individuality. Plato's dialectic derives from the recognition that we assume knowledge when there is really ignorance: "The close searching *elunchus* by which the man of vague generalities is constrained either to express his meaning to himself in definite terms, or to confess that he does not know what he is talking about; the perpetual testing of our general statements by particular instances; the siege in form which is laid to the meaning of abstract terms. . . . [A]ll this, as an education for precise thinking is inestimable."[58] Mill argues that the dialectic has made enormous contributions to the development of great thinkers and human excellence. "Human invention." he writes, "has never produced anything so valuable, in the way of both stimulation and of discipline to the inquiring intellect, as the dialectic of the ancients, of which the many works of . . . Plato exhibit the practice.[59]

Mill puts forth that Plato's dialectic is as relevant today as it was in antiquity because contemporary views on most "mental and moral subjects" are not based on knowledge: "they are, just, as much, the wild fruits of the undisciplined understanding—of the '*intellectus sibi permissus*,' as Bacon phrases it; rough generalizations of first impressions, or consecrations of accidental feelings, without due analysis of mental circumspection." Plato's dialectics were primarily negative discussions of the great questions of philosophy and life that helped convince people that many of their ideas of the good are not based on a full understanding. Even when Plato was unable to discover the ideas that lie at the bottom of our opinions, it was no small benefit to expel the false views of knowledge; to make individuals aware of their ignorance regarding things most required to be known; to fill them with embarrassment at their own being, "and rouse a pungent internal stimulus, summoning up all of their mental energies to attack these greatest of all problems, and never rest until, as far as possible, the true solutions are reached."[60]

But that is not the end of the matter, as Mill also reforms Plato to accord with his romantic-expressive conception of liberty. First, Mill democratizes the dialectic. Mill's account of Plato argues that the ancient thinker concluded that philosophy can be maintained only by placing the dialectic on the margins of society. "In the *Republic*," Mill complains, "we find him [Plato] dwelling on the mischiefs of a purely negative state of mind, and complaining that Dialectics are placed too early in the course of education and are taken up by immature youths, who abuse the license of interrogation, find all of their home-grown opinions uncertain, and end by losing all positive convictions." The teachings of the dialectic in the Platonic dialogues, Mill notes, are primarily private education for elites in private settings.[61]

This option to hide dialectic debate around the most important moral and political questions is no longer necessary or possible, states Mill. It is not necessary because Mill believes that the modern moral conscience limits the ability of the dialectic to create mischief. It is not possible in Protestant countries, since Protestants believe, "at least in theory," that the responsibility for analyzing and making moral and religious choices must be borne by each for himself and cannot be relegated to an elite. Finally, as contemporary intellectuals now debate and exchange ideas in writing, it is almost impossible to hide dialectical exchanges from the uninstructed.[62] Thus, while the Platonic dialectic must be reintroduced to the highest type of thinkers, it "is now as much and even more indispensable to enable average human beings to attain the mental stature which they are capable of." Mill envisions extending the dialectic into the center of society. For example, Mill claims that people are not insincere when they say that they uphold central tenets of the New Testament. They believe these truths, as they believe all truths that they have always heard praised and never debated. But the lack of public discussion and exchange on Christianity or on any set of beliefs precludes the tenets of Christianity or any value system from being a living moral outlook which influences and structures human conduct. Moral ideas become received truth rather than spiritedly upheld values, and when this happens understanding leaks out and they grow crusty from lack of use.[63]

Next, Mill reforms the dialectic into a source of positive political and moral beliefs and actions. In his commentaries on Plato, Mill broke from the traditional view, as notably expressed by the romantics and Hegelians of his century, which places specific beliefs such as the pure spirit or doctrine of ideas at the center of Plato's thought. Mill held that Plato cannot be associated with a specific idea of the good or cosmology. Plato never specifically wrote on the subject of nature.[64] More important, the Platonic dialogues examine the assumptions underlying different opinions and reveal how all beliefs presuppose faulty understandings of the whole and metaphysics. The dialogues do not establish a specific idea of the good. They debunk others' false and ungrounded ideas of the good. Philosophers and commentators who present an exposition of the comprehensive or total Platonic worldview are easily refuted and confounded by passages in the dialogues which contradict the exposition: "Many definitions are tried, and shown to be untenable, and the dialogue[s] often conclude without any result but the confession of ignorance. Even when one of the definitions examined seems to be accepted in one dialogue, it is often contested, and apparently refuted, in another: so that the result, on the whole, is rather one of method than of doctrine; though striking fragments of truth come to the surface, in the general turning up of the subject which the process involves. The confutations, too, though of marvelous ingenuity, are, frequently, to us, obvious fallacies."[65] In short, Mill argues that Plato loves and pursues but does not claim to possess *the* good or knowledge of nature's first and highest principles. What distinguishes Plato's understanding of the philosopher from the outlook of all others is nothing but the knowledge of one's ignorance. Socrates' wisdom consists in knowing what he does not know, in realizing that he does not possess anything like the knowledge claimed by the politicians, poets, and artisans: "He, Sokrates, did not pretend to know anything, except his own ignorance; but inasmuch as other people did not know even that, Sokrates, who did, deserved the palm of wisdom assigned to him by the Delphian Oracle."[66]

In contrast, Mill argues that democratic dialectical inquiries serve as the prerequisite to positive political and moral beliefs and human agency. Only individuals who can rebut an opposing opinion and successfully defend their own against an opponent have the right to think they have sufficient knowledge for right actions and right beliefs. "No one's opinions deserve the name of knowledge," Mill states, "except so far as he has either had forced upon him by others or gone through himself" negative criticism. While such criticisms are worthless as an ultimate result, they are a "critical means to attaining any positive knowledge or conviction worthy the name . . . and until people are . . . trained to it [the Platonic dialectic], there will be . . . a low general average of intellect."[67] "This is the principal lesson of Plato's writings . . . [and] . . . dialectics, thus *understood,* is one branch of an art which is the main portion of the Art of Living [prudential, moral, and aesthetic activities]—that of not believing on sufficient evidence; its function being that of compelling a man to put his beliefs into precise terms, and take a defensible position against all objections that can be made to it." In Mill's reformed dialectic, the examined life does not pursue philosophic truth or *the* good: it is not an ascent from thoughtless assumptions to fleshed out universals and knowledge. Neither does the dialectic establish questions as an end in itself: the relentless critique of all accepted categories of our moral culture.[68] Rather, the transformed Platonic dialectic contributes to the individual's discovering and embracing *a* good on his own: "If the cultivation of the understanding consists in one thing more than another, it is surely in learning the grounds of one's opinions. Whatever people believe . . . they ought to be able to defend against at least the common objections." Mill's reformed dialectic contributes to the free or self-developed individual, one who has thought out and can defend his actions and way of life. Through the challenges of the dialectic the individual gains courage, defense of principle, independence, and self-mastery.[69]

Mill finds the Platonic dialectic valuable because it enables our actions to be based not only on consent, but on a more romantic-expressive conception of freedom; it allows us to discover our distinct feelings and thoughts. He argues that existing and striving are not good and desirable if characterized by ceaseless and futile quests for ever-elusive satisfactions. The individual must aim somewhere and get there. In addition, almost all of us accept traditional opinions and common sentiments as ultimate facts. Whoever cannot answer dialectical inquiries about his main goals, Mill warns, is wandering in a cave, has no standard by which his judgments are regulated and kept consistent with one another. Such individuals have no principle or rule that they know and can stand by for the guidance of their lives: "Any one who does not think the description applicable, with slight modifications, to the majority even of educated minds in our own times and all times known to us, has not brought either the teachers or the practical men of any time to the Platonic test."[70] Reason, in Mill's view, serves us by granting thought-out beliefs about the most important questions in one's life. "There is no such thing as absolute certainty," Mill writes, "but there is assurance sufficient for the purposes of human life. We may, and must, assume our opinion to be true for the guidance of our own conduct. . . . Complete liberty of contradicting and disproving our opinion is the very condition which justifies us in assuming its truth for purposes of action; and on no other terms can a being with human faculties have any rational assurance of being right." Reason is vital to human agency; and without dialectical inquiries, one's conduct isn't so far from what traditional empiricists thought: mere responses to impulses or external forces such as public opinion, customs, or rules.[71]

Mill also broadens the category of the type of individual who challenges prevailing customs and conventions well beyond Plato's philosopher. As Mill put it, Plato "exalt[ed] the philosopher to a region above nature and the earth, making him akin to the gods, who . . . live in perpetual contemplation of these glorious and superterrene experiences." Conversely, Mill's desire to generate both lively ideas and relative certainty in our own beliefs leads him to champion heretics, eccentrics, atheists, religious dissenters, and all men whose minds are strong enough to challenge prevailing views and conventions. Without these oppositionists, Mill argues, the public will not be awakened from its political and moral slumber and will remain unsure of itself. Conflict of a spirited and rhetorical kind within the parameters of liberal justice will spur all individuals, elite and mass alike, to become more self-defining. In short, free. "If there are any persons who contest a received opinion," Mill asserts, "or who will do so if law or opinion will let them, let us thank them for it, open our minds to listen to them, and rejoice that there is someone to do for us what we otherwise ought, if we have any regard for either the certainty or the vitality of our convictions."[72]

Among all of Mill's revisions of the Platonic dialectic, the most surprising is his explanation of the dialectic as a source of fortified beliefs and right actions. After all, Mill distinguishes himself from almost all commentators on Plato of his age with his position that Plato primarily teaches a "mode of philosophy"— a method to understand and discover the truth—and not a "philosophy of beliefs." Rather than holding Hegel's position that Plato failed to integrate subjective freedom with his newly discovered universals, Mill charges Plato with failing to discover the universal. Rather than embracing the romantics' position that Plato used artistic imagery to give popular and figurative form to truth, Mill argues that Plato's art covers up or hides reason's limited understanding of the truth. In Mill's commentaries on the Platonic dialogues, he repeatedly insists that *all* of Plato's dialectical inquiries on political and moral matters fail to discover knowledge. The dialectic shows that Socrates' interlocutors were caught in self-contradictions or often unable to give account of themselves, and Socrates couldn't "rescue" them—his own positive notions would have failed the test of his own dialectical inquiries. Socrates' investigations encouraged agents who were certain about what was right to reflect on the adequacy of their ways of posing problems and their sense of range of options: "If there is one thing more than another which Plato represents Socrates as maintaining, it is that knowledge, on the subjects to man, did not yet exist, though everybody was living under the false persuasion of possessing it."[73]

REGENERATING HUMAN AGENCY

Why did Mill reformulate the Platonic dialectic into a source of lively ideas and positive political and moral beliefs? The answer in part can be found in Mill's view that higher freedom resides in the self-legislation of all pursuits, contributing to Millian reason having a constructive current. To Plato, liberation resides in complete understanding—Platonic reason has more passively contemplative or acquisitive qualities.[74] The answer also can be explained in part by Mill's account of the different relations between thought and action in ancient Athens and Victorian England. In Mill's view, the Athenians were an unusually energetic people, and Athens was a place where thought and action, word and deed, were not estranged and illusionary ideas and principles had enormous political consequences. By inducing debate and self-examination over what the good and bad, just and unjust, were, Plato aimed to add thoughtfulness to Athenian political practice.[75]

To be sure, Mill believed the English also suffered illusions. He repeatedly attacks the general tendency of the English to conflate arbitrary practices and values with timeless truths. The people of England mistake the conventional way of organizing existence for the condition of reality and the universal forms of thought, and Mill always insists that it lies within the individual to discover what parts of England's customs and practices are appropriate to his own circumstances and character.[76] But rather than illusionary ideas misdirecting human energy, Mill believes he lives in a Victorian world in which one feels an acute sense of weakness, whether engendered by enervating remnants of Christian beliefs that are not being challenged, the loss of strong minds and character in the face of the rule of public opinion, or simply the vague idea that customs operate with a disturbingly blind indifference.[77] As Mill complained, "Scarcely anyone, in the educated classes, seems to have any opinions, or to place any real faith in those which they profess to have."[78] Thus Mill had what his friend John Morley called "double viewing," combining criticisms of prevailing customs and conventions with the recognition that new beliefs are needed to renew human agency. Mill's project was to be positive and constructive in addition to negative. His goal was to rebuild, not just to limit or tear down.[79]

In an earlier stage of his thinking, Mill's proposed reforms emphasized changing policies and institutions rather than human character. But by the midpoint of his life, he recognized that many of these reforms had either already been realized or were about to be, and he expressed disappointment with the results: "They have produced very little improvement in that on which depends all real amelioration in the lot mankind, their intellectual and moral state." "Nine-tenths of all the true opinions which are held by mankind are held for wrong reasons," states Mill. "And this is one cause why the removal, now so constantly going on, of particular errors and prejudices does not much improve the general understanding. The newly admitted tenth commonly rests on as mistaken principles as the old error. What is the remedy? There can be none short of the reconstruction of the human intellect *ab imo.*"[80]

Looking around the world, Mill saw moral ideas as the key source of human agency and long-term fundamental change. "One person with a belief is a social power equal to ninety-nine with interests. . . . It was not by any change in the distribution of material interests, but by the spread of moral convictions, that negro slavery has been put to an end in the British Empire and elsewhere," argues Mill. "The serfs in Russia owe their emancipation, if not to a sentiment of duty, at least to the growth of a more enlightened opinion respecting the true interests of the State. It is what men think, that determines how they act." Looking at England, Mill saw little thinking and moral atrophy. This stagnation harms everyone and every facet of life: "At present I expect very little from any plans which aim at improving even the economical state of the people by purely economical or political means. We have come, I think, to a period, when progress, even of a political kind, is coming to a halt, by reason of the low intellectual and moral state of all classes; of the rich as much as of the poorer classes." The positive political and moral teachings of the reformed dialectic reflect Mill's belief that the nearly century-long attempt to change the human condition through institutional reform had run its course, and that a focus on "moral progress and intellectual culture for the public" is needed to generate human energy and the highest form of freedom.[81]

COLERIDGE'S DIALECTIC

But the complete explanation for Mill's revision of the Platonic dialectic lies in his positing a second important feature to the dialectical process: identifying it as the source of new synthetic truths. Here Mill puts forth the complementariness of opposites and argues that there is generally an element of truth in the views that individuals oppose, as well as partiality or falsehood inhering in the perspectives one embraces. As agents rebut opposing views and defend their own against critics, a dialectical process emerges that, by convincing people of their limited views and pointing out the value of alternative positions, discovers new, positive positions.[82] Mill's reformed Platonic dialectic, whereby self-developed and creative individuals challenge opponents and defend themselves against opposition, contributes to a broader *social dialectic* of competing views of right and wrong that provide raw material for new synthetic truths.

Of course, by the time Mill came to it, a good deal of reflection had already been devoted to the role of polarities. Plato, for instance, had treated polarity in the *Timaeus,* in which sameness and difference are the constituent elements of the World Soul. In the *Sophist,* the concept of Being houses the opposition of these two poles.[83] Mill recognized that the theme of opposition or polarities as a creative and dynamic principle had an ancient history. The *logos* of the pre-Socratic Anaximander, Mill notes, is the principle of becoming through conflict. Mill argues that Plato also recognized polarity as creative and understood that the discovery of truth required working one's way through apparent contradictions: "Truth, in everything but mathematics, is not a single but a double question; not what can be said of an opinion, but whether more can be said for it than against it. . . . [T]his . . . lesson of Plato's writings, the world and many of its admired teachers have very imperfectly learned."[84]

But Mill goes beyond Plato as he joins ranks with Coleridge and the German Romantics in his understanding of dialectics. It is evident that Mill was strongly impressed with the necessity Coleridge felt of always mentioning the positive, rather than the negative, features of antinomies. Coleridge comments, "Always to bear in mind that profound sentence of Leibniz that men's intellectual errors consists chiefly in *denying.* What they *affirm* with *feeling* is, for the most part, right—if it be a real affirmation and not affirmative in form, and negative in reality." "Great good," continues Coleridge, "therefore of such revolution as alters, not by exclusion, but by an enlargement that includes the former, though it places it in a new point of view."[85] In order to constantly realign one's perspective to fit with new truths, one did not just discard old truths but continued to reorganize them into a more comprehensive outlook. Mill follows in kind. "It might be plausibly maintained," he argues, "that in almost every one of the leading controversies, past or present, in social philosophy, both sides were in the right in what they affirmed, though wrong in what they denied; and that if either could have been made to take the other's view in addition to its own, little more would have been needed to make its doctrine correct." What is true in the philosophic realm is true in the popular realm as well. Popular opinions are generally true, but never or rarely completely true, and thus "they are part of the truth, sometimes a greater, sometimes a smaller part, but exaggerated, distorted, and disjoined from truths by which they ought to be accompanied and limited."[86]

From this positive perspective, the synthesis which comes after any division constitutes a third stage which is higher than the original unity because it maintains the antinomies it has reconciled. As Coleridge put it, "The two component counter-powers actually interpenetrate each other and generate a higher third, including both the former."[87] It is a process in which polarities clash with one another, link up, and create a new phenomenon in which both currents exist, but at a higher level of organization. Accordingly, Mill identifies the antinomies that animate modern political and social development: democracy-aristocracy; property-equality; cooperation-competition; luxury-abstinence; sociality-individuality; liberty-discipline; and looks forward to the time when all of these conflicts will be incorporated within the parameters of one political party: "In politics, again, it is almost commonplace that a party of order or stability and a party of progress or reform are both necessary elements of a healthy political state, until the one or the other shall have so enlarged its mental grasp as to be a party equally of order and progress, knowing and distinguishing what is fit to be preserved from what ought to be swept away." Going further, Mill identifies the greatest two antinomies that must be reconciled and recombined in future England: the Enlightenment's reason and the romantics' ethical sensibilities; ancient creativity and Christianity/modernity's obligation to obey universal authority.[88]

There is another aspect of Mill's view of dialectics which he learned from Coleridge and the German romantics: the role higher-type thinkers perform as reconcilers and synthesizers in a world of contradictory political and social agencies. If the polarities are to be related and integrated there must be some individuals who can create the third terms in which they meet and interpenetrate. In Coleridge's view, the highest human types do not merely establish a new pattern or relationship between contending agencies; they synthesize the animating tension between opposing forces and create a new entity, or what he called "a multieity in unity." To Coleridge, the highest type of thinker was the Artist, whose power "reveals itself in the balance of reconcilement of opposite or discordant qualities; of sameness, with difference; of the general with the concrete; the idea with the image; the individual with the representative; the sense of novelty and freshness with old and familiar objects; a more than usual state of emotion with more than usual order; judgment ever awake and steady self-possession with enthusiasm and feeling profound or vehement." Coleridge envisioned himself as one of the "Philosophers and the Bards" who uses "plastic might" to reshape the "chaos of a disintegrating culture" to reconstitute forms, which derive from their "brightest visions of the day." His proposed constitution revolves around reconciling the spirit of "permanence," as provided for by a representation of landed proprietors; and that of "progression," by a representation of personal property and of intellectual achievement. He identified a specific class of men, the clerisy, as the mediators of the contributions of the two classes and the creators of a national culture that morally developed the citizenry.[89]

Mill's idea of reconcilers and synthesizers is ultimately connected with Coleridge's view. Nevertheless, he adds some nuances of his own. One difference is that the synthesizing role Coleridge assigned to the "Philosopher and Bard," Mill commissions solely to the philosopher in the realm "of the highest order of moral and intellectual greatness."[90] Mill's highest elite in the day-to-day civil and political realm is not a castelike elite or clerisy. It is not as well structured or as set off from the mass as Coleridge's elite. Mill assigns this task to the more vaguely defined "impartial judges of human affairs," "the opulent and lettered classes," and "the instructed minds."[91]

For instance, in philosophy the truths established by Bentham and Coleridge separately were equally necessary to comprehending the advantages and disadvantages of the Enlightenment's assault on the medieval world. "To Bentham," Mill wrote, "it was given to discern more particularly those truths with which existing truths and institutions were at variance; to Coleridge, the neglected truths which lay *in* them." In every respect the two thinkers were contrasting counterparts: "The strong points of each correspond to the weak points of the other." It would be easier to identify the best political road forward, he continues, if either half of their respective positive teachings were all of their teachings. As to whether their respective views are reconciled "depends on whether these half-thinkers are or are not followed in the same track by complete thinkers." No doubt thinking of himself, Mill comments that whoever masters and combines the outlooks of both "would posses the entire English philosophy of their age." Similarly, the *Logic* itself is designed to improve philosophy, which "can only consist in performing, more systematically and accurately, operations with which, at least in their elementary form, the human intellect in some one or other of its employments are already familiar." Mill even stated that the goal of the *Political Economy* was to "rescue from the hands of such people the truths they misapply, and by combining these with other truths to which they are strangers, to deduce conclusions capable of being of some use to the progress of mankind."[92]

Mill saw himself more as a "conceptive" philosopher than a "creative" thinker; that is, a philosopher who, without originating any completely new truths, discovers new truths by reconciling and recombining philosophies created by others. Philosophy has a tendency to go too far to one side and then to the other—like a seesaw—and Mill sees himself standing in the middle evening it out, making sure philosophy does not tip too far in one direction and lose the insights of the other direction. The recent appreciation of this type of thinking is due to insights of Continental philosophers, states Mill. Instead of making the mistake that discovering the truth and avoiding falsehood is the great danger confronting philosophy, these thinkers recognized that "in the present imperfect state of mental and social science," antagonistic modes of thought are of great value. Continental thinkers recognized that all previous great thinkers had developed one-sided outlooks and that if any one of them could have been made to adapt the opponent's view in addition to their own, little more would have been needed to make their fundamental teachings correct.[93] Mill elaborates that the most difficult task for the philosopher is detecting both the errors of his predecessors "and . . . the inaccuracies of current modes of thought." Or, to put this more positively, the philosopher must "fortify the weak side of his own intellect, by study of the opinions of mankind in all ages and nations, and most of all the speculation of philosophers of the modes of thought most opposite to his own." As one of the few individuals of his age who found himself in sympathy with both ancients and moderns, both transcendentalists and empiricists, Mill decided he was "much superior to most of his British contemporaries in willingness and ability to learn from everybody" and was therefore obligated "to serve as a mediator among fiercely opposed schools of thought."[94]

The whole truth in the realms of politics and morality also involves a synthesis of contrasting half-truths. For instance, in this era of moral unanimity, Mill advocates diversity. The different modes of existence expand "moral freedom"—providing examples of self-amended lives—and engender discussion and debate over which way of life is better or worse. Concomitantly, there is no one political power in society, including popular power, "of which the influences do not become mischievous as soon as it reigns uncontrolled— . . . by being able to make its mere will prevail, without the condition of a previous struggle. To render its ascendancy safe, it must be fitted with correctives and counteractives, possessing the qualities opposite to its characteristic defects."[95] Important social and political outlooks, Mill argues, are generally characterized by being good for parts, but not the whole, of society. The dialectical interaction between the conflicting ideas of the good places restraints on the other, induces toleration, and forces advocates and partisans to sharpen and clarify their viewpoints.[96] Liberal toleration is a good in itself, but it is also a means, because the conflicting ideas create higher modes of existence and greater truth for everyone.

MILL'S *BILDUNG*

Here Mill develops his conception of *Bildung,* or the relation between opposition and unity, self-development and unified moral and political beliefs. *Bildung* was derived from the romantics in late eighteenth-century Germany, establishing an ideal of self-development that refers to the cultivation of an individual's unique capabilities as well as what he learns about the world outside of himself. The self and world, individual and society, synthesize between what an individual uniquely contributes and what a reformed culture makes of him. This back and forth process leads to higher forms of individuality and more social and political unity. To Herder, a lower type of individual develops through learning a craft, a higher type cultivates his faculties through an art, and the highest type, in doing one thing well does it all, uniting the society in harmonious cooperation.[97] Further, persistent movement and change, rather than an end state, characterizes *Bildung.* The culture is constantly forming and reforming as society synthesizes the contributions of individuals into higher modes of human existence. The central focus in this romantic-expressivist thinking is, on the one hand, the desire of the individual to be himself and to realize his distinct nature to the full, while, on the other hand, to change in the culture that makes the individual through the development of unifying values and practices. As Steven Smith puts it, "The emphasis here [*Bildung*] . . . is on the cultivation of given talents and the imposing of form on inchoate matter."[98]

In Mill's account, the collision of opinions around better and worse ways of life and opposed political outlooks creates a social arena of effort, struggle, self-development, and grand purposes for creative individuals and political partisans, while also stimulating the mental energies of the general public.[99] Individual freedom of thought, discussion, and lifestyle creates *"ethical confrontation*—the open clash between earnestly held ideals and opinions about the nature and basis of the good life."[100] At the same time, the collisions of opinions have a salutary effect upon the "highest minds"—the "calmer and more disinterested bystander"—who gain insights into the advantages and disadvantages of the contending political outlooks and different ways of life. These bystanders—the careful defenders of competing currents of truth—learn to combine a more complex pattern out of the materials presented to them by the contrasting currents, creating Coleridge's synthetic truths.[101] While Mill does not envision this intellectual elite authoritatively establishing its views with the public, he is confident they will elevate the general political and moral qualities of England as they identify the higher and lower civil practices and political beliefs being generated by society. In Mill's view, the standards established by the intellectuals should constantly spread and deepen over the course of time so that the principles of liberty and higher modes of existence come to be understood and applicable to a wider array of individuals. There are limits that the views of the intellectuals in a liberal state must not breach. But within those bounds the educative role of intellectuals is legitimate and necessary and must be robust.

In today's era of unity around superficial beliefs, Mill argues, the most innovative thinkers have the particularly difficult task of promoting outlooks and practices that dissolve conventional beliefs while thoughtfully recombining new truths from the competing elements that attempt to fill the vacuum. These intellectuals will function at two levels of efficiency: those who fashion compromises from the differences that are generated; those who derive new synthetic truths from the conflicting outlooks and practices that are stimulated. "In the present age," Mill reasons, "the writers of reputation and influence are those who take something from both sides of the great controversies, and make out that neither extreme is right, nor wholly wrong. By some persons, and on some questions, this is done in the way of mere compromise; in some cases, again, by a deeper doctrine underlying the contrary opinions; but done it is, in one or the other way, by all who gain access to the mind of the present age: and none but those who do it, or seem to do it, are now listened to." By combining a reformed Platonic dialectic, whereby individuals challenge conventions and defend their way of life, with a Coleridgean dialectic that synthesizes contrasting views, Mill brings a new conception of *Bildung* to England. In *On Liberty* Mill predicts that many and varied experiments in living will provide the opportunity for the "teachers of mankind" to discover improved social practices and modes of life through a process of comparison, debate, and synthesis.[102]

ATHENS AND SPARTA

Mill's turn to the ancients to endow empiricism with an idea of liberty that was not limited to the natural desires of self-preservation and property protection extended beyond his study of Plato. When Mill looks back to the ancient foundation of the West, he holds the position that the modern way of life is superior. Modernity builds better institutions and promotes more freedom for more people. It is more humane, practices milder manners, and is moving toward the abolition of slavery. But in contrast to Hobbes, Locke, and Hume, Mill asserts that Athens and Sparta provide valuable lessons for the moderns. Notwith-standing all the hope that modernity had to offer, these ancient regimes hold fundamental lessons grounded in contrasting experiences. Mill extols the will of Athens that led to creativity and greatness and praises the role education and public opinion played in fostering political stability in Sparta. At the same time, Mill maintains that Athens was too dependent on the qualities of its most outspoken and forceful citizens, while also criticizing Sparta for being too ac-quiescent to custom. Each represents another case of contrasting or partial truths that must be reconciled and recombined. Mill will address these respec-tive strengths and weaknesses of Athens and Sparta as a backdrop to his formu-lation of how society can pursue moral ends while encouraging strong exertions of human agency within it.[103]

In Mill's account, the distinct character of Athens and Sparta is well articu-lated by an enemy of Athens, the Corinthian speaker who urges the Spartans to go to war in Thucydides' *Peloponnesian War.* The Athenians and Spartans em-body two very different human types or drives. Self-assertion and creativity on one side are at odds with the claims of stability and public good on the other side. The Athenians are wedded to innovation, and their plans are characterized by swiftness both in conception and execution. The Spartans favor self-preser-vation, and their plans generally are cautious. The Athenians enjoy the dangers that accompany their self-imposed tests, which often push them beyond the limits of their own power and understanding. The Spartans mistrust their judg-ments and remain focused on political security.[104]

Mill believes that the respective "national characters" of Athens and Sparta create a duality or dialectic that all political societies must generate and recon-cile if they are to prosper: human creativity and the public good. Unfortu-nately, neither "one of the ancient forms of society contained in itself that sys-tematic antagonism, which we believe to be the only condition under which stability and progressiveness can be permanently reconciled with one an-other."[105] Athens and Sparta, Mill maintains, provide the clearest examples of the advantages and disadvantages of these different human characters as their respective regimes centered on the cultivation of each. Both are extremes, and conveniently (for the modern philosopher at least), clashed with one another in war.

To Mill, the root of Athens's ethos of creativity was the innovative war-fight-ing strategy required to defeat the Persian invasion. The result was an empire that rivaled Sparta. In following their natural desires and inclinations to avoid defeat and pursue gain, Athenian creativity was consistent with empiricism's position that the will is determined by something outside the agent. But over time, Mill continues, Athens's persistent, indeed habitual, emphasis on creativity transformed this instrumental practice into the standard for evaluating all human conduct. This strong creative will is the core of the unique Athenian character, which pushed its citizens to pursue the goal of innovation—ultimately to its detriment. The Athenian will reveals the powerful capacity for human agency, the ability to remold and amend one's circumstances: "We ought . . . to look up with reverent admiration to a people, who, without any of our adventitious helps, and without the stimulus of preceding example, moved forward by their native strength at so gigantic a pace."[106]

The Athenian democracy, Mill insists, was characterized by a quality noticeably absent in modern societies, an "idea of human excellence" or "an accepted standard of virtuous conduct." The Athenians embodied the virtues of social tolerance, cultivated taste, and a "lively interest and energetic participation in public affairs." This emphasis on experimentation and freedom in society was a part of the general ethos or will that emphasized human creativity to serve the public good, "while in the ethical practice of the moderns, this is exactly reversed, and no one is required by opinion to pay any regard to the public, except by conducting his own private concerns in conformity to its expectations."[107] The Athenians, Mill explains, came to recognize that founding-type individuals—persons willing to overcome prevailing standards of right and wrong in order to create new practices—are necessary to attain political and social progress. To put Mill's views in Arendt's terms, the Athenians were characterized by "action:" imposing one's will for "natality," or founding practices, against the regularized process of nature and society.[108] As Mill put it, the Athenians understood that "originality is not always genius, but genius is always originality; and a society which looks jealously and distrustfully on original people—which imposes its common level of opinion, feeling, and conduct, on all its individual members—may have the satisfaction of thinking itself very moral and respectable, but it must do without genius."[109] This love of human excellence points to the human capacity to conceive higher goals and re-form our lives in its name.

What Mill most wants to emphasize with his analysis of the Athenian national character is that the marriage of thought and action, intellect and deed, creates an explosive level of human agency. In Athens, the good life was understood to be contingent upon one's resolution to live up to a set of goals or purposes. The Athenians were "bred to action, and passing their lives in the midst of it." Their speculations "were for the sake of action, [and] all their conceptions of excellence had a direct reference to it." "This was the education," Mill writes, "to form great statesmen, great orators, great warriors, great architects, great sculptors, great philosophers; because, once for all, it formed *men,* and not mere knowledge-boxes; and the men, being men, had minds, and could apply them to the work, whatever it might be, which circumstances had given them to perform." The Athenians' greatest marks of honor were its fortitude and resolve in leading their city-state through the fiery trials of war to the founding of the West's most significant practices and beliefs: "They were the beginners of nearly everything, Christianity excepted, of which the modern world makes a boast."[110]

But to Mill's regret, the Athenians did not avoid dependence on chance or forceful leaders, as the direction of innovation that a Pericles or an Alcibiades provided was to a large extent based on their qualities as individuals. While the Athenian will engendered fortitude and self-assertion, this drive to overcome prevailing conditions did not necessarily promote the public good. The combination of reason and action is not virtue in itself because creative practices need the anchoring of just rules and, most important, the just moral conscience. Intellect and deed are virtuous when they serve just principles, but this combination is potentially very dangerous and often morally wrong. Athenian excellence required tremendous and rare individuals. The history of Athens, Mill insists, "is one series of examples how often events on which the whole destiny of subsequent civilization turned, were dependent on the personal character for good or evil of some one individual."[111]

While some leaders, most notably Pericles, ingeniously led the Athenian citizenry to find new ways to pursue the public good, others, such as Alcibiades and Nicias, employed debased versions of the charismatic charm and common sense that enabled Pericles to be a great leader. Athenian political decisions often were products of demagoguery as they were made in the popular assembly based on speeches delivered by self-selected participants: "The Athenian Many, of whose democratic irritability and suspicion we hear so much, are rather to be accused of too easy and good-natured confidence" in those who asserted new practices and leadership. "Ever variable," Mill continues, "according to the character of the leading minister of the time; alike prudent and enterprising under the guidance of a Pericles; carelessly inert or rashly ambitious when their most influential politicians were a Nicias or an Alcibiades."[112]

Mill goes on to point out that the Athenian public opinion was so unstructured that, after Pericles died, it was only the antagonisms generated by the demagogues Cleon and Hyperbolus that prevented Athens's immediate downfall. By the time another leader with the qualities of Pericles emerged, Demosthenes, the Athenians lacked the moral energy to stand up to Philip of Macedonia. In short, Athens teaches that reason and will are hallmarks of human agency. But Athens also teaches that these qualities are not always positive because they may engender unjust deeds. Without justice, intellect and deed may undermine the public good. Whoever knows what Athenian "society was (or indeed any society consisting of an active and spirited people, in an imperfect state of the social union)," Mill concludes, "is well aware that lawlessness, in such a society, is the prevailing mischief, the great moral and political danger to be combated against."[113] A key question that Mill will address in *On Liberty* is how to limit the dangers that arise from powerful exertions of human energy without also ending the energy itself, which would be fatal to liberty.[114]

Urbinati ignores this lesson Mill learns from Athens in her analysis of the influence of the ancients on Mill's thought. Urbinati's determination to interpret Mill as a deliberative democrat leads her to exaggerate Mill's praise for Athenian democracy, ignore his criticisms of the Athenian decision-making process, and fail to discuss Mill's view of the Athenian idea of human excellence. In her account, Mill's praise for ancient Athens centers on its being the archetype *modern* polity, with a regulated process of deliberation that both involved the largest possible number of individuals and exalted the learning function of discussions in public. "Mill . . . located Athens' vitality and modernity in its political order," states Urbinati. "[His] intellectual journey through the institutions and culture of the Athenian polis allowed him to anticipate the vision of politics as communicative power, the idea the public process of opinion formation and exchange legitimizes democratic government and frames and supervises the administrative power of the state." However, Mill's praise for Athens centers on its popular standard of human excellence or *summun bonum:* the combination of reason and fortitude. Moreover, as illustrated by his discussion of Pericles, Nicias, and Alcibiades, Mill argues that individuals were the decisive factor in determining whether the Athenian public made better or worse political decisions. There is nothing, Mill posits, that the Athenian *demos* did "not seem capable of understanding, of feeling, and of executing; nothing generous or heroic to which they might not be roused; and scarcely any folly, injustice or ferocity into which they could not be hurried, when no honest and able adviser was at hand to recall them to their better nature." Athens "furnishes the most extreme example of" the reliance on extraordinary individuals "to be found in history." Mill summarizes that, while the Athenians teach important lessons in regard to cultivating dynamic, great individuals, "in political and social organization, the moderns . . . have a more unqualified superiority over [Athens]."[115]

Mill argues that Alcibiades and Nicias represent two great political dangers. Alcibiades, who flattered the public into policies that encouraged his own good irrespective of public expense, the "crowning act" of which was the proposal for the ill-starred expedition to Syracuse, teaches the need for a morality of justice to channel the creative will and provide protection against political zealotry. In Athens, innovation and the pursuit of immortal deeds were permitted too wide an influence in activities that should have been guided by additional norms. At the other extreme, Nicias, who promoted himself through representing ordinary sentiments and opinions, ultimately leading to his submission to the unfavorable circumstances of the campaign in Syracuse and Athenian defeat, represents the danger posed by the socially acquiescent individual.[116]

Mill's view of the advantages and disadvantages of these different human types—Alcibiades and Nicias—plays a crucial role in Mill's vision of the good liberal society. In *On Liberty,* Mill's criticism of individuals with the disposition of Nicias is well known. It is a central part of Mill's charge of the newest threat to liberty and the *summum malum,* the highest evil: the society-manufactured individual. If one's compliance with rules, public opinion, and customs is too complete, then one's conduct is no different from that of a machine—the individual is not free. In Mill's discussion of human excellence in *On Liberty* we also find him explicitly addressing the problem of Alcibiades as part of the need for liberal societies to cultivate the *summum bonum,* the single best way of life. On the one hand, liberal societies must learn to control such individuals, as their uncontrolled energies can easily spin out of control and do more harm than good. On the other hand, too much social control—including the kind of obedience warned against in *On Liberty*—will excessively tame the creativity of society's best leaders and innovators. The potential danger of these willful types can be avoided by establishing rules and mores of justice that prohibit actions that harm others. At the same time, one must remember that the prosperity of a society based on the rules and mores of justice will not be realized unless the innovative will is cultivated among citizens.

SPARTAN MORAL EDUCATION

Mill recognizes that influential political philosophers' understanding of Athens's weaknesses contributes to an appreciation of some features of the Spartan polity. To individuals who feel "called upon to stand up for Law against Will, and for traditional wisdom against the subtleties of sophists and the arts of rhetoricians, Sparta was the standing model of reverence for law, and attachment to ancient maxims." Mill primarily had a critical view of the Spartans: they were the Tories of Greece as law, custom, and conservation were raised above self-assertion, liberty, and creativity. Nor was Sparta the reformist regime of political participation and egalitarian property relations that writers such as Rousseau believed it to be. Rather, Mill counters, collective self-determination and equality were reforms initiated by King Agis and Cleomenes in the second-century BC to regenerate public support for a regime that had decayed. These features of a late, declining Sparta were mythologized by Plutarch, eventually becoming objects of admiration to those moralists and philosophers who were in despair at contemporary tendencies to overemphasize individualism.[117]

By unveiling the myth of a reformed Sparta, Mill emphasizes that its accomplishment of unparalleled political stability was a testimony to the powerful influence of comprehensive education in creating a will that shapes public behavior. While this Spartan will originated from a quest to preserve its position as the most powerful city-state in Greece, Spartan education, which included general military education, public tables and meals, and a common culture, is the finest example of the powerful role that moral education can play in society. It cultivated a will for the common good, citizenship, and stability despite the existence of hierarchy. Once again, Mill charges that Sparta's emphasis on preserving custom, security, and the state held back creativity and contributed to its ultimate decline. Nevertheless, Mill learns from Sparta that the will can be cultivated in many different directions through early education and the sanctioning force of public opinion. He invokes Sparta in his argument that belief in gods is no longer necessary for the cultivation of a moral will for modernity.[118] Sparta teaches "the wonderful pliability, and amenability to artificial discipline, of the human mind." If Spartan-type moral education centered on establishing a sense of public good and citizenship had been combined with the Athenian ethos of creativity, the ancient societies would have harmonized the two ends vital to the good society: the cultivation of self-defining, self-commanding individuals and the development of higher modes of social unity.[119]

GENERAL CONSCIOUSNESS AND THE WILL

While Mill recasts reason for empiricism to overcome its mere role as the scout of the passions, his analysis of the distinct "national characters" of Athens and

Sparta serves to account for another part of human conduct for which empiricist philosophy had no position—the will. Practices, Mill believes, arise as means to pursue pleasure and avoid pain, but through habituation these instrumental means become ends or goods in themselves.[120] To develop this account of the will, Mill refers to the concept that is central to his project to revitalize empiricism's associational psychology: general ideas as products of mental chemistry. Here what is crucial to Mill is the distinction between "complex ideas *consisting* of simpler ideas and complex ideas being generated by simpler ideas of which, however, it does not *consist*."[121] There are, he argues, "cases of mental chemistry, in which it is proper to say that the simple ideas generate, rather than they compose, the complex ones." This difference is vital to Mill, as he can now posit that the mind itself is an autonomous center of human conduct: certain simple states of mind generate further states of mind that are qualitatively different from those simpler ones. The sensory character of our simple ideas does not explain all human conduct: "On this theory [of traditional empiricism] the uniformities of succession among states of mind would be mere derivative uniformities, resulting from the laws of succession of the bodily states which cause them. There would be no original mental laws, no Laws of the Mind . . . and mental science would be a mere branch, though the highest and most recondite, of the science of physiology."[122] Under the previous empiricist approach, the self could not be separated from its environment and therefore be authentically free. As Michael Mandelbaum puts it, "What is important to note is that this psychological doctrine allows for the self-transformation of man: what was originally dominant in the individual's nature becomes transformed by association, and may in fact altogether cease to be dominant as an operative force in that individual's life."[123]

Mill explains that empiricism had not been able to explain the individual capable of desiring a good for its own sake, who sought to fit his character to his standard of excellence, which derived from no other source than his own consciousness. Bentham, for instance, failed to recognize that a sense of honor, personal dignity, love of beauty, love of order, love of power, love of action, are all powerful springs of action. This is the starting point to higher freedom for Mill, yet the empiricists are convinced that human motivation is entirely intelligible in terms of the desire for pleasure and the aversion to pain. It is not, Mill observed, that pleasure and pain do not have considerable jurisdiction in the determination of human affairs, but rather that they are considerably more complex and heterogeneous than empiricists imagined.[124]

Mill says that the time comes when, through the formation of habits and a general consciousness, we continue to will an act or a course of conduct to which we are accustomed, without any reference to its being pleasurable. The will, as "the active phenomenon, is a different thing from desire, the state of passive sensibility, and though originally an offshoot from it, may in time take root and detach itself from the parent stock; so much so, that in the case of a habitual purpose instead of willing the thing because we desire it, we often desire it only because we will it." To be human and to avoid the nonentity of mechanical existence, Mill insists, individuals and groups must have forceful and distinctive characters, "and the will, once so fashioned, may be steady and constant, when the passive susceptibilities of pleasure and pain are greatly weakened or materially changed." Individuals have "confirmed characters" when they fashion a will around a conceived purpose. National character, the feelings and will that people in a nation hold in common, is "what makes such a thing as society possible and which, to a large extent, determines the difference between one nation and another."[125]

Mill's revised conception of the will is a response to Kant's critique of empiricism and has important points of agreement with Kant's position: both agree that the body is geared toward the pursuit of happiness and both maintain that the will does not merely respond to the stimuli of pleasure and pain. Of course, Kant identifies distinct faculties of the mind—the will and passions—and he equates this separate will with a practical reason that imposes a universal form on the givens we feel as desires by acting in accordance with what is right or Duty. Duty, "the necessity to act out of respect for the [moral] law," must be formal because it cannot refer to contingent ends.[126]

Like Kant, Mill argues that the will structures a way of life and initiates practices that are not reducible to the calculation of pleasure and pain. Unlike Kant, Mill argues that the will is not necessarily universalizable and generates different types of human drives. "In this manner it is." he argues, "that habits of hurtful excess continue to be practiced although they cease to be pleasurable; and in this manner also it is that the habit of willing to persevere in the course which he has chosen, does not desert the moral hero, even when the reward, however real, which he doubtless receives from the consciousness of well doing, is anything but an equivalent for the suffering he undergoes, or the wishes he may have to renounce."[127]

In sum, Mill's analysis of the Athenian and Spartan wills illustrates two important differences with Kant's position. Desires do not have to be overcome by the will, states Mill. In fact, it is through the habitual pursuit of desires that means become ends and the will is formed: Athens and Sparta exemplify that powerful desires are the raw material for a strong will. Mill also argues that the will is not necessarily a moral faculty. The Athenian and Spartan wills, for example, were capable of both noble and base conduct.[128] The strong will is a source of both excellence and danger, and it is Mill's self-imposed task in *On Liberty* to identify the conditions that will cultivate the former and prevent the latter.

REASON AND HABITS OF LIBERTY

Every thoughtful reader of Mill is confronted with the problem of reconciling Mill's views on reason and the will and yet identifying how each quality contributes to the free individual. On the one hand, Mill argues that higher forms of individuality require thoughtfulness. Only by understanding the causes of our practices do passions and customs no longer unconsciously determine our conduct. From this Mill's ideal becomes the free or autonomous person who employs reason to redefine his character in the pursuit of *a* good—self-understanding is critical to self-development. On the other hand, Mill posits that it is from the habitual pursuit of desires that the will and person of character forms, whereby we continue to pursue an act or course of conduct without any reference to the motives that are behind them. How can both the conscious and the habitual be key characteristics of the free individual? How can Mill's ideal of self-development be resolved with his view of an enduring self with a persistent identity and will? Important commentators on Mill argue that his attribution of reason and settled practices as primary qualities of the free individual is incoherent.[129]

In answering these questions, it is important to recall that Mill's free individual values self-mastery and the qualities necessary to achieve it. This self-mastery is in part justified by our possession of faculties such as reason, but just as importantly by the use that we make of them. Part of using our faculties well lies in resolutely pursuing those desires we desire. In short, reason and fortitude are essential Millian qualities of the free individual. Actions ought to be dependent on thoughts, but actions will further develop those thoughts, and both thoughts and action are necessary for self-development. The free individual, who possesses a cultivated reason and will, is characterized by a conscious volition, but this volition is resolutely pursued and put into operation by continual practices. This "habitual act of will in the individual instance is not in contradiction to the general intention prevailing at other times, but in fulfillment of it; as in the case of the person of confirmed virtue, and of those who pursue deliberately and consistently any determined end."[130]

In short, Mill's self-developed individual is characterized by conscious desires and fortitude. The *vita activa,* or active engagement in the world, as well as the cultivated mind, contributes to our freedom and self-mastery. A life dominated by custom is one of servitude and weakness because of our inability to control our actions, whereas the free life is one in which the more we *reflect* on and *realize* the coherence and power of our ideas, the greater becomes our awareness of self-mastery and free agency. Individuals make their desires their own as they take a hand in the making of their character and amending it in light of a *reflective commitment* to substantive aims.[131]

Mill's *On Liberty* appropriates and revises the Platonic dialectic and the Athenian will to build a bridge between the empiricists' and romantics' conceptions of liberty. He argues that the state and society must create a protective sphere around the individual. He also recognizes that an individual can be estranged from or foreign to one's wants, and that many desires do not reflect one's true self. To Mill, all modes of existence that are not subject to external restraints are not equally free. The best reason for an agent to choose a way of life is that such *practices* best allow the individual to become a developed, self-determined individual: "He who chooses the plan for himself, employs all of his faculties. He must use observation to see, reasoning and judgment to foresee, activity to gather materials for decision, discrimination to decide, and *when he has decided firmness and self-control to hold to his deliberate decision.* . . . Among the works of man, which human life is rightly employed in perfecting and beautifying, the first in importance is surely man himself" (emphasis added).[132]

Higher freedom as it emerges in Mill's corpus is tied to self-development, the ability to overcome social and personal barriers such as public opinion, customs, and one's own unbridled desires. Mill is convinced that England's increasingly egalitarian society can remain free only by cultivating the qualities of self-developed individuality. In England people are becoming increasingly similar to one another and can no longer be distinguished by individualistic characteristics. Reason, will, strong desires, the sense of duty to oneself, dignity, and the desire for distinctiveness prove to be crucial supports for genuine individualism and springs to practices that allow social and political progress.

In *On Liberty,* Mill will show the shortcomings of English liberalism, which fails to cultivate these qualities of character; but he also shows that, if English liberalism engages in a rapprochement with ancient and romantic ideas, there are areas in English society in which support for self-development of character will emerge. More to the point, Mill's *On Liberty* argues against a one-sided morality in England that emphasizes obedience to universal rules and fiercely resists outlooks—romantic or classical—that focus on the development of the human faculties. This is a potential disaster, as Mill's indictment of English liberalism makes the case that the qualities tied to the self-development of character are at least as important to individual liberty as equal rights.

Chapter 4 *On Liberty:*
Overcoming the West's
One-Sided Moral Development

At the very center of *On Liberty* Mill places the objectives of both the good and the right: the goal of cultivating higher forms of individuality, including the exceptional individual, or genius; and the aim of ensuring justice and moral development among the general public. Mill presents each respective objective as an expression of opposed conceptions of liberty and posits that each of these perspectives is dangerously one-sided and in need of balance by the other. By setting up the contrasts between these conflicting ideas of liberty in chapter 2, Mill prepares the way for an idea of human excellence in chapter 3 that combines and synthesizes each: reason, will, strong desires, the sense of duty to oneself, the desire for distinctiveness, *and* justice—the moral obligation not to harm other individuals—are the hallmarks of developed individuality.

Mill argues that society must combine these two perspectives on liberty if political thinkers are to overcome the constant oscillations in Western morality between opposing outlooks. Each one-sided moral development has different characteristics, expressed on either side of the channel. On the Continent—most notably, in France—justice is required to restrict and channel the creative will of forceful individuals who, in the pursuit of great deeds or of any other objects they strongly desire, permit themselves to do harmful acts that the just English individual could not bring himself to consent to. In England, the task is to counter modern equality's tendency to undercut the conditions that foster reason, strong desires, high ambitions, fortitude, and individual agency.[1] As the next two chapters explain, the process of discrimination and fusion in England requires broaching a sensitive issue that the Anglo-Scottish Enlightenment did not fully comprehend: namely, that Enlightenment thought is too great a compromise with Christianity, which ignored the positive contributions of the ancients and failed to cultivate positive qualities that lead to the exertion of human energy. After the ancients exhausted us, Christianity enervated us, and modern England has not developed values and practices to regenerate human energy. The fundamental point of Mill's discussion of freedom of thought in *On Liberty* is English liberalism's failure to break with the Christian tradition of obedience and its fear of the creative will.

Contemporary commentators claim that chapter 2 of *On Liberty* is primarily directed at Christianity's mystical hold on the Victorian mind,[2] or in a more general sense the hold of a monolithic opinion of any kind.[3] In this chapter and chapters 5 and 6 below I explain that Mill's concern about these limitations on freedom is an integral *part* of his fundamental goal to reform English liberalism and hopefully balance the one-sided or distorted moral development of the West. It explains Mill's position that, if English society is to generate higher forms of liberty and human excellence, the Anglo-Scottish Enlightenment's universal rules of justice and reformed Christianity, or natural religion, must be augmented by civil practices and values that cultivate the qualities of character that engender strong exertions of human agency. Mill aims to harmonize and synthesize the constituent elements of a morality that cultivates the complete human character: creative individuality and right conduct.

THE PHASES OF LIBERALISM

Mill opens *On Liberty* by situating his concerns regarding freedom within the history of modern liberal thought. While noting the common views shared by all liberal philosophers, his goal is to identify "the different and more fundamental treatment" that liberty requires for those people "who are in the stage of progress into which the more civilized portion of the species has now entered."

Mill is concerned both with ridding the individual of unnecessary restraints on external activities and, more important, the denuding of individual character.[4]

In Mill's account, each phase of liberal thought responds to a problem created by a prior phase. Modern liberalism itself arose in response to the Hobbesian type of sovereigns, who themselves had developed to answer the question of how to reduce the state of perpetual war and conflict. Those sovereigns held absolute power for the sake of establishing and maintaining peace and used this authority to determine the laws of property, to declare war, and to decide which doctrines are fit to be taught. "Their power was regarded as necessary," Mill writes, "but also as highly dangerous; as a weapon which they would attempt to use against their subjects, no less than against external enemies. To prevent the weaker members of the community from being preyed on by innumerable vultures, it was needful that there should be an animal of prey stronger than the rest, commissioned to keep them down." The modern liberal outlook, which begins with philosophers such as Locke, emphasizes inalienable rights and constitutional forms while defining the state as an instrument—a limited one at that, for the sake of such private goods as security and property. This phase of liberalism answered and addressed what was regarded as an unresolved problem in the Hobbesian form of sovereignty: arbitrary rule stemming from the establishment of absolute power in the government.[5]

The progress of Lockean-type liberalism, Mill continues, led to a new question: why should the government be a power independent from society? This problem is most fully addressed by concepts like Rousseau's general will, whereby people treat the government as the collective power of a united people. This "mode of thought or . . . feeling" gained predominance in Continental, but not British, liberalism. In this new understanding of liberalism, everyone is willing to give over all rights to the sovereign so that the accumulated power of the citizens' will encounter no restrictions. Because the government is the representative of everyone, no one need fear putting himself under the arbitrary control of another, including the government: "What was now wanted was that the rulers should be identified with the people, that their interest and will was the interest and will of the nation. There was no fear of its tyrannizing over itself." This liberalism, in turn, gave rise to Tocquevillian liberalism, which emphasized how such democratic rule was inimical to the freedom of the individual and the rights of minorities. As Mill argues, "The limitation, therefore, of the power of government over individuals loses none of its importance when the holders of power are regularly accountable to the community, that is, to the strongest party therein."[6]

Mill distinguishes himself from the liberal tradition of which he is a part by his recognition that a new form of despotism is arising from society, one that prevents people from realizing their capacity to claim control and responsibility for their own desires and actions. "Reflecting persons" recognize that liberty is more than the absence of impediments to action: liberty is also the pursuit of self-defined goals. The new despotism is not characterized by "civil penalties" that limit the actions of individuals. Rather, it is a tyranny of opinion, feelings, and circumstances that penetrates "much more deeply in to the details of life . . . enslaving the soul itself." The new threat to liberty is the socially manu-factured individual who has no control over his passions, habits, and concerns —the furthest idea from a self-made, reflecting character essential to true free-dom. Consequently, an effective defense of liberty cannot stop at legal protec-tions for individuals; rather, "there needs protection also against the tyranny of the prevailing opinion and feeling, against the tendency of society to impose, by other means than civil penalties, its own ideas and practices as rules of con-duct on those who dissent from them; to fetter the development and, if possi-ble, prevent the form of any individuality not in harmony with its ways, and compel all characters to fashion themselves upon the model of its own."[7] The solution to the problem of liberty is no longer as concrete, not legal, more indi-vidual, and deeply concerned with civil practices and the social ethos.

INCORPORATING ROMANTICISM AND REFORMING EMPIRICISM

Why doesn't Mill turn to Rousseau's general will or Kant's categorical impera-tive for this critique of English liberalism? Surely they offered solutions to the problem of the mass individual who is incapable of claiming autonomous re-sponsibility for his desires and actions. Certainly Mill recognizes that when he writes that people who "are generally without either opinions or feelings of home growth, or properly their own" are unfree, he is indebted to Rousseau's charge that the modern individual found it "necessary for his advantage, to show himself to be something other than what he in fact was. Being something and appearing to be something became two completely different things."[8] Mill himself notes in *On Liberty* that "the enervating and demoralizing effects of the trammels and hypocrisies of artificial society" is an idea that has never been ab-sent from thoughtful individuals "since Rousseau wrote."[9]

But Rousseau's insights regarding the mass individual are followed by an er-ror in the *Social Contract* that exacerbates the problem rather than fixing it. For him, the free man alienates himself entirely to the "general will" or "common self." Rather than opposing the excessive socialization of humans, Rousseau argues the solution is to radicalize it. We must come to understand ourselves and our individual egos, in a wholly new way, as intimately bound up with the will of all other citizens. Acting for ourselves in the usual way requires acting in the service of what others have taught us to desire. Only by freely subjecting and identifying ourselves with the universal, wholly objective good in the form of the general will can we be self-determining.[10] In other words, in the face of the social conformity he so brilliantly described, Rousseau opted for a cure that threatened to enforce even more obedience and social conformity.

While Mill embraces key parts of Rousseau's critique of modern life, he rejects Rousseau's position that only as a social participant can the individual be a free subject able to see himself in his deeds and practices. Mill argues that the size of modern political communities and, more important, the modern right of freedom of religion create poor conditions for a regime that intrudes so deeply into private life. He also rejects an idea of freedom that is based exclusively on obedience to a general moral law. Indeed, to Mill, this singular emphasis on obedience to a general law, which has "been wielded more strenuously against divergence from the reigning opinion in self-regarding than even in social matters," reflects modernity's continuation of the Christian emphasis on obedience and submission. Rousseau is one of "those modern reformers who have placed themselves in strongest opposition to the religions of the past [and] have been no way behind either churches or sects in their assertion of the right of spiritual domination." Rousseau's thought "destroys the past" but is "impotent" for directing future innovation and creativity.[11]

Kant also fails to offer Mill a viable solution to the problem of individual freedom. A central goal of Mill's *On Liberty* is to *reconcile,* not sever, universal determinism and human freedom. The traditional compatibilist position of Hobbes and Hume is that there is no contradiction in holding that human actions are both caused and free, as the history of an individual's desires is strictly irrelevant to an individual's power to act. Hobbes and Hume argue that just because human conduct is caused does not imply it is coerced, for the causal relation is merely a constant conjunction of events, not a relation of necessity. Freedom consists merely in the absence of interference with the exercises of our choices, not the absence of causal determination in their formation.

To be sure, having been influenced by Coleridge, Kant, and the romantics' critique of empiricism, Mill had come to understand that what most individuals establish as marks of independence in society—property, prestige, family—

and the self we wind up caring so much about, everywhere involve a slavish dependence on the opinion of others. Rationality is not and ought not to be a means to the realization of desires and inclinations that derive from outside the individual. Reason is, rather, essential for and internally related to the full development of individual liberty. Thus, while Mill affirms empiricism's traditional concern regarding external coercion of the individual, he also shares romantic thinkers' concern that almost no members of society have the opportunity to determine their own character.

Mill, however, did not go as far as those moral idealists like Kant and Fichte, who posited the view that reason could somehow transcend desires. To Mill, it is possible for us to determine our own characters and thus make our desires genuinely our own because the *desire* to self-amend or self-develop one's character can be fostered as a causal antecedent: "His character is formed by his circumstances (including among these his particular organization); but his own desire to mould it in a particular way, is one of those circumstances, and by no means one of the least influential."[12] Mill accepts the view so prominent in Rousseau and Kant that true self-determination requires self-legislation, but he cannot accept the notion that such self-determination involves an identification with the general will or a subjection to the categorical imperative. The first is a false unity of particular and general happiness; the second, a permanent dualism between reason and desires. Everything in Mill's position must then revolve around his view on self-legislation. Mill posits that the reconciliation of the opposing forces in Western morality—the cultivation of qualities that lead to self-mastery and the obligation to obey universal laws and norms—is the key to developing this new conception of liberty.

Why did Mill give only limited credit to Tocqueville in *On Liberty* for his position on the newest threat to liberty? Mill praises Tocqueville for identifying how democracy engenders tyrannous legislation, but he does not elaborate on Tocqueville's warnings about social despotism. Mill and Tocqueville certainly agreed that social atrophy is the greatest danger confronting democratizing and liberalizing societies. But as Mill had put forth this thesis as early as 1831 in "The Spirit of the Age"—five years before the publication of the first volume of *Democracy in America*—he may not have felt obliged to credit Tocqueville for founding this position. Mill also had been exposed to Coleridge's and Wordsworth's writings on the tyranny of custom in the late 1820s and early 1830s. Furthermore, scholars tend to emphasize only the concord that existed between Tocqueville and Mill. Yes, these two great thinkers of their day concurred that social equality was the wave of the future, that political and social quietude

would challenge the viability of future democratic regimes, that political cen-
tralization would also pose a problem in the future, and that inductive analysis
of social phenomena was vitally important. But Mill and Tocqueville also
sharply disagreed about the role that women, Christianity, intellectuals, and
nationalism would play in overcoming problems generated by social equality.
This discord no doubt fettered their respective desires to point to the other as
the great thinker of their age.[13]

While Mill believes his comprehensive morality of the future is relevant to
the entire West, *On Liberty* is devoted to the weaknesses of British empiricism
and English liberalism.[14] In England, where a spirit of Lockean liberalism predominates, empiricism's view of liberty and morality contributes to a new
despotism over the soul. Here the prevailing political outlook is largely consistent with the negative view of liberty. Negative liberty is the freedom to act or
forbear from acting where the laws are silent: law and liberty are regarded as
mutually antagonistic.[15] "In England," Mill writes, ". . . [the] yoke of . . . law
is lighter than in most other countries of Europe; and there is considerable jeal-
ousy of direct interference by the legislative or executive power with private
conduct, not so much from any just regard for the independence of the individual as from the still subsisting habit of looking on the government as representing an opposite interest to the public."[16] Consistent with his critique of
empiricism's position on the compatibility of liberty and necessity, Mill argues
that this exclusive focus on restraining the government's ability to limit liberty
of action ignores the question of whether the desires and motives of an agent
are his own. The English are socially manufactured individuals cultivated to
like and dislike what they as a collective prefer and pursue: "Both their feelings
and their intellectual faculties [remain] undeveloped, or develop themselves
only in some single or limited direction; reducing them, considered as spiritual
beings, to a kind of negative existence."[17] The individual has the capacity to
satisfy many desires that arise, but he is unaware of his capacity to realize one
particular desire: the desire to cultivate his character.

Empiricism's moral theory of sympathy, Mill continues, which insists that
human conduct should be based on realizing our self-interest through public
approval, also contributes to the new social despotism:

> People are accustomed to believe, and have been encouraged in the belief by some
> who aspire to the character of philosophers, that their feelings on subjects of this na-
> ture [right and wrong conduct] are better than reasons and render reasons unneces-
> sary. The practical principle which guides them to their opinions on the regulation
> of human conduct is the feelings in each person's mind that everybody should be re-

quired to act as he, and those with whom he sympathizes, would like them to act. No one, indeed, acknowledges to himself that his standard of judgment is his own liking; but an opinion on a point of conduct, not supported by reasons, can only count as one person's preference; and if the reasons, when given, are a mere appeal to similar preferences felt by other people, it is still only many people's liking instead of one. To an ordinary man, however, his own preference, thus supported, is not only a perfectly satisfactory reason but the only one he generally has for any of his notions of morality, taste, or propriety, which are not expressly written in his religious code, and his chief guide in the interpretation even of that.[18]

The most advanced liberal thinkers in England, Mill argues, do not aspire to create a new kind of liberal polity that embraces a new kind of liberal individual. They focus more attention on developing specific ideas of the good, rather than the qualities that enable individuals to strive after their own notions of it: "They have occupied themselves rather in inquiring what things society ought to like or dislike than in questioning whether its likings or dislikings should be a law to individuals." Mill recognizes that some great thinkers during the Protestant Reformation and seventeenth-century religious wars in the United Kingdom helped turn authority to the individual as the sole judge of Scripture and religious beliefs. This rejection of hierarchy coupled with the development of inner freedom is a pivotal moment in Mill's understanding of liberty. For the first time in this battle for religious liberty what counted most was the broad principle of freedom "and the claim of society over dissentients openly controverted": "We cannot be blind to the sharpening and strengthening exercise which such topics give to the understanding—the discipline in abstraction and reasoning which such mental occupation brought to the humblest layman."[19]

But Mill finds fault even in this one successful foray into the realm of freedom, as most seventeenth-century English liberals were intolerant of religious views they opposed. Their endorsement of toleration fell far short of recognition of the value of diversity. Toleration was extended for the most part only to the most powerful dissenting Protestant sects. These architects of religious freedom primarily responded to the devastating religious wars, establishing a theoretical justification for people to stop killing one another over religious differences. The new political principles—human equality under the law, toleration, and reduction of ecclesiastical power—were directed to the goal of civil peace, not human liberty. The point was not to affirm the creative control of every individual over his life, but only to provide enough freedom to avoid the dangers of civil conflict. The free religious mind, Mill concludes, is primarily a product of a compromise brokered because no party, church, and sect gained predominance over others.[20] Mill will target this compromise as the principal source of the cultural and intellectual passivity plaguing England.

The English, in Mill's view, are habitually conscious of the need to conform to the basic standards of right and wrong, and nothing higher. Their social feelings and intellectual faculties remain undeveloped. In Mill's account, these types of human beings—"low, abject, servile"—are far beneath the self-interested individuals described by Locke. While Locke did not think an individual was capable of transferring certain rights to the civil authorities, Mill fears that the modern Englishman will alienate liberty to public opinion—or already has. "The modern regime of public opinion is," Mill warns, "in an unorganized form, what the Chinese educational and political systems are in an organized; and unless individuality shall be successful to assert itself against the yoke, Europe, notwithstanding its noble antecedents and its professed Christianity, will tend to become another China."[21]

FREEDOM OF THOUGHT AND DISCUSSION

As currently understood then, the "moral sense" of British empiricism—with its focus on rights and its blindness regarding individual self-creation—necessarily fails to generate higher forms of liberty. Mill knows that the legal right to free speech is not endangered. Thus he opens chapter 2 of *On Liberty* by saying that there is little need to focus attention on removing legal or external restrictions on the general freedoms associated with the liberty to publish alternative or controversial views: "The time, it is to be hoped, is gone by, when any defense would be necessary of the 'liberty of the press' as one of the securities against corrupt or tyrannical government." Mill does not discount the possibility of future instabilities and periods when freedom of political discussion might be interfered with, but he expresses confidence that "the era of pains and penalties for political discussion has, in our country, passed away."[22]

Mill's sanguine attitude toward legal persecution of published works is not based on Baruch Spinoza's and Locke's pragmatic or political arguments that such policies generally backfire on the ruling authorities.[23] Indeed, Mill believes history teaches that attempts to legally control the content of thought, far from breeding conflict and ultimately revolution, often breed harmony and stability. There is, to begin with, the tendency for people to assume that the general prevailing views are naturally right. Society often impairs the capacity for reasoned judgment, and one cannot assume a diversity of views that will be too difficult for the governing authorities to control. "On any matter not self-evident," states Mill, "there are ninety nine persons totally incapable of judging of it, for one who is capable; and the capacity of the hundredth person is only comparative." People also are often disinclined to hear out all voices. In the name of what is moral and pious, society is more likely to strike down the newest, "best and noblest doctrines." As the fate of Socrates shows, society does not like to review or evaluate their most cherished views and as a result often resents challengers.[24] History teaches that there have been many periods of successful censorship because of the fear imposed by ruling authorities, notes Mill: "The dictum that truth always triumphs over persecution is one of those pleasant falsehoods which men repeat after one another till they pass into commonplaces, but which all experiences refutes. History teems with instances of truth put down by persecution." The success and failure of persecution of the truth, Mill summarizes, is a political question based on the balance of forces in a regime.[25]

Legal persecution is now less warranted, Mill argues, because by prescribing a single notion of good character through the powerful instrument of public opinion, modern society manages, as effectively as any government policies, to limit human thought. The distinguishing feature of the modern world, he claims, is that societies are themselves shaped by public opinion. Once we in turn are socialized, our sense of our own existence, in which we take so much pride, is not in fact ours but depends on others. As most of us act thoughtlessly, unreflectively, or in mere conformity to prevailing conditions, we allow the direction of our life to be charted by others and in this way circumscribe the mind and limit human agency.[26]

SEVERING WISDOM AND LIBERTY, THOUGHT AND DEED

Mill contends that the primary casualties of today's persecution are wisdom and liberty. Freedom of thought and opinion would be of no value were it not for a particular "quality of the human mind" which he calls "corrigibility," the human capacity to correct one's errors through the exercise of developed judgment. This capacity, he says, is "the source of everything respectable in man either as an intellectual or as a moral being." Mill situates his position between what Rousseau called perfectibility and Kant called pure reason—that is, the capacity to overcome our desires and experiences—and the reason of Hobbes and Hume, which is limited to acting as a guide for the satisfaction of desires and inclinations. Mill's corrigibility denotes the capacity human beings have to exercise improved judgments concerning the activities they engage in. This type of reason is acquired, and its acquisition requires thoughtful minds that debate the advantages and disadvantages of different experiences. A human being "is capable of rectifying his mistakes by discussions and experience. Not by experience alone," states Mill. "There must be discussion to show how experience is to be interpreted. Wrong opinions and practices yield to fact and argument; but facts and arguments, to produce any effect on the mind, must be brought before it. Very few facts are able to tell their own story, without comments to bring out their meaning."[27] Here Mill's reformed Platonic dialectic, whereby people submit their beliefs and practices to opposition and criticism, contributes to fortified beliefs and developed actions. Mill argues, "In the case of any person whose judgment is really deserving of confidence, how has it become so? Because he has kept his mind open to criticism of his opinions and conduct. Because it has been his practice to listen to all that could be said against him: to profit by as much of it as was just, and expound to himself, and upon occasion to others, the fallacy of what was fallacious."[28]

The executions of Socrates and Jesus are the outstanding instances of the grave mistakes the persecutors of new ideas commit. Mill chooses his examples with a view to linking the condemnation of restricted speech and thought with his conception of the two heretofore contradictory outlooks required for the comprehensive morality of the future. For Socrates is the founder of reason, which, in Mill's view, is a key source of human agency, and Jesus' way of life was so extraordinary that it founded a moral outlook, which obligates individuals to take into account the well-being of others.[29]

Mill explains that contemporary religious persecution also does not center on legal penalties. Official restrictions on atheism are but the "rags and remnants" of old-style despotism. Rather, it is the values that people hold and the feelings they believe to be most important which make "this country not a place of mental freedom." In Mill's account, the consequences of this new type of religious despotism are clear. Pivotal qualities that embody Mill's free and developed individual—reason and resolute engagement with the world—are lost: "Who can compute what the world loses in the multitude of promising intellects combined with timid characters, who dare not follow out any bold, vigorous, independent train of thought, lest it should land them in something which would admit of being irreligious or immoral?" Liberty of thought and discussion is essential because it fosters the development of reason and individual faculties. The speculative thinker is victimized as the constriction on public discussion has a narrowing effect—"mental development is cramped, and . . .

reason cowed by the fear of heresy." The result is that the higher mind's attention is turned to the prosaic and the mundane. Many intellectuals narrow their thoughts and interests "to things which can be spoken of without venturing within the region of principles, that is, to small practical matters which would come right of themselves . . . [while] free and daring speculation on the highest subjects—is abandoned." Thought and action, intellect and deed are estranged, and the human mind is diminished.[30]

Important new moral and political theories exist, Mill claims, but they remain within narrow circles of thinking, smoldering among the highly educated where they originate, "without ever lighting up the general affairs of mankind with either a true or deceptive light." There are too few "public moralists"[31] because "our merely social intolerance kills no one, roots out no opinions, but induces men to disguise them or to abstain from any active effort at their diffusion." No doubt thinking of himself, Mill states that a few of the highest type of thinkers are able to present some of their most important political and moral teachings in this environment, by "spending a life in sophisticating an intellect which he cannot silence, and exhaust[ing] the resources of ingenuity in attempting to reconcile the promptings of his conscience and reason with orthodoxy." But these "great thinkers" have shown throughout history that they have the capacity to survive in all kinds of environments of "mental slavery." It is society as a whole that suffers the greatest loss, as the relation between wisdom and the public, knowledge and action, is completely severed, and the mass individual loses the opportunity to develop his mind. "It is much and even more indispensable," Mill writes, "to enable average human beings to attain the mental stature which they are capable of. . . . Where there is a tacit convention that principles are not to be disputed; where the discussions of the greatest questions which can occupy humanity is considered to be closed, we cannot hope to find that generally high scale of mental activity which has made some periods of history so remarkable."[32]

Thoughtful commentators on Mill—most notably, Joseph Hamburger, Shirley Letwin, and Maurice Cowling—argue that Mill's primary concern in this discussion of religious despotism is the public's continued support for *revealed* Christianity. In Hamburger's account, for instance, Mill placed great hope on freedoms accorded to atheists and freethinkers. He thinks that Mill believed open debate would lead to a withering of support for such mystical teachings of the New Testament as the divinity of Jesus, miracles, the immortal soul, original sin, and the idea of an omniscient and omnipotent Deity. This erosion of mystical beliefs, Hamburger continues, was a necessary condition of

Mill's plan of moral reform: "Religious notions would be 'put on the logical rack' and subjected to 'the discipline which purges the intellect itself.' This would follow from the Socratic *elunchus* which, through full freedom of thought and discussion, would be applied to religious belief in his own time."[33]

To be sure, there is an important parallel between Mill's discussion of the diminished modern individual and seminal arguments in political philosophy that the revealed teachings of Christianity are inimical to the spirit of liberty. For instance, both Niccolò Machiavelli and Rousseau charged that Christianity promoted disengagement from political activity, leaving people unfit for political life. In the *Discourses on Livy,* Machiavelli explains how the sense of quiescence that accompanied the rise of Christianity, erodes the desire for political liberty. Christianity taught the individual to devalue this world relative to the afterlife.[34] Rousseau's writings often charge that Christianity's exclusive otherworldly orientation teaches "nothing but servitude and dependence." The doctrine of original sin, in Rousseau's view, withers man's sense of freedom and moral responsibility. It teaches that everyone enters the world as a sinner and thus that the individual has no free will and cannot escape evil. This doctrine, continues Rousseau, renders people passive, disengaged, and resigned to their limitations while they await God's salvation. "The history of the species outlined in the "Discourse on Inequality" and the instruction of the child in *Émile* are" both written to oppose the biblical account of humanity's inherently bad character, supplying an opposing argument of the origin of man's fall that frees him of his shackling guilt "by shifting the blame to society."[35]

But the same criticism that Machiavelli and Rousseau directed at the teachings of a revealed Christianity, Mill brings against "a convenient plan for having peace in the intellectual world," a "tacit convention that principles are not to be disputed," and the position that "discussions of the greatest questions which can occupy humanity [are] closed." It is a philosophic compromise, not the New Testament or mystical views, that produces

a state of things very satisfactory to some minds, because, without the unpleasant process of fining or imprisoning anybody, it maintains all prevailing opinions outwardly undisturbed, while it does not absolutely interdict the exercise of reason by dissentients afflicted with the malady of thought. A convenient plan for having peace in the intellectual world, and keeping all things going on therein very much as they do already. But the price paid for this sort of intellectual pacification is the sacrifice of the entire moral courage of the human mind. A state of things in which a large portion of the most active and inquiring intellects find it advisable to keep the general principles and general convictions within their own breasts, and attempt, in what they address to the public, to fit as much as they can of their conclusions to premises which they have internally renounced.[36]

Unlike Machiavelli and Rousseau, Mill charges that the problem of the timid, circumscribed existence derives from a philosophic outlook which compromises principles for the sake of intellectual peace and security. "Intellectual pacification" keeps people in a stage of tutelage and immaturity. Mill's *On Liberty* does not focus on why revealed religion is inimical to liberty. Rather, Mill devotes the second half of chapter 2 to explaining how the failure to debate Christianity's traditional principles has led to the New Testament *no longer* being an effective moral doctrine. It is not only the foundation of Christian beliefs that has been forgotten in the absence of discussion, but too often the meaning of the belief itself: "By Christianity, I here mean what is accounted by all churches and sects—the maxims and precepts contained in the New Testament. These are considered sacred, and accepted as laws, by all professing Christians. Yet it is scarcely too much to say that not one Christian in a thousand guides or tests his conduct by reference to those laws." The public has a "habitual respect for the sound of them [revealed Christian beliefs], but no feeling which spreads from the words to the things signified and forces the mind to take *them* in and make them conform to the formula. Whenever conduct is concerned, they look around for Mr. A and Mr. B to direct them how far to go in obeying Christ."[37]

CHRISTIANITY'S AND MODERNITY'S NEGATIVE MORALITY

The problem of a culture of self-abasement and passivity identified in *On Liberty* emerges after, not during, the heyday of Christianity. Enlightenment philosophers in the United Kingdom compromising with Christianity far more than they recognized turns out to be the source of the problem. "What is called Christian, but should be termed theological [revealed] morality," Mill argues, ". . . was . . . built up by the Catholic Church of the first five centuries, and though not implicitly adopted by moderns and Protestants, has been much less modified by them than might have been expected."[38] Mill applauds the contributions that this Christian/modern morality has made to the formation of a culture characterized by equality and restraint; "but I do not scruple to say of it that it is, in many important points, incomplete and one-sided, and that unless ideas and feelings not sanctioned by it had contributed to the formation of European life and character, human affairs would have been in a worse condition than they are now. . . . It is essentially a doctrine of passive obedience."[39]

Mill's most fundamental critique of English liberalism's reconciliation with Christianity in chapter 2 of *On Liberty* centers on a moral explanation: both Christianity and modern justice are negative moralities that have overlooked the half of the truth they have superseded. For instance, the ancients and Christians made different contributions to human development but seemed to be, as well as believing themselves to be, enemies of one another. In truth, however, the ancients and Christians made equally important contributions to a fully rounded conception of humanity. They are not at loggerheads with one another, as they appear to be. But the putative schism created a legacy that helps prevent English liberalism from introducing a conception of liberty that combines qualities of character that promote human agency with the universal obligation to act justly with one another.[40]

The good political society, Mill asserts in chapter 2 of *On Liberty*, is characterized by two kinds of beliefs and practices. The first consists of those values and practices that establish obedience, equality, and moral development among the general public. Many of these practices were initiated in the Christian "reaction" or "protest" against the surfeit of uncontrolled and wildly creative types of the pagan world. The central issue that Christianity and English justice have been designed to solve is the imposition of universal obedience. Christianity compelled obedience to a universal faith, while modern justice compels obedience to universal law. It cannot be denied that real differences exist between traditional Christianity and modern England, and the modern Englishman in fact benefited from this new environment because modern justice makes few epistemic demands on its adherents. It allows more space for free human conduct than Christianity.[41] But the continuity is significant, and the English liberal tends to underrate its consequence: the main object of modern justice is to compel general obedience to the law. This Christian-derived morality is "negative rather than positive; passive rather than active; innocence rather than nobleness; abstinence from evil rather than energetic pursuit of the good. . . . In its horror of sensuality, it made an idol of asceticism *which has been gradually compromised away into legality*" (emphasis added).[42]

Once again, Mill insists that while "mankind owes a great debt to this morality," when devoid of its antagonists, it promotes passivity, acceptance, failure to actively pursue virtue, and a prosaic selfishness: "And while, in the morality of the best pagan nations, duty to the State holds even a disproportionate place, infringing on the just liberty of the individual, in purely Christian ethics that grand department of duty is scarcely noticed or acknowledged." Mill concludes, "It is a great error to persist in attempting to find in the Christian doctrine that complete rule for our guidance which its Author intended it to sanction and enforce, but only partially to provide. . . . I believe that other ethics than any which can be evolved from exclusively Christian sources must exist side by side with Christian ethics to produce the moral regeneration of mankind."[43]

The second kind of beliefs and practices that a good political society requires are those whose purpose is to promote the health of the individual's character, chiefly our mental and moral development. These types of practices are, properly speaking, reflections of positive, self-regarding qualities. As it was the aim of the classical civilizations to bring human beings to excellence, the ancients are *one* important resource for these qualities. A society of citizens constantly buttressing their character leads to human flourishing in both the public and the private spheres. "What little recognition the idea of obligation to the public obtains in modern morality is derived from Greek and Roman sources, not from Christian," states Mill. "As, even in the morality of private life, whatever exists of magnanimity, high-mindedness, personal dignity, even the sense of honor, is derived from the purely human, not the religious part of our education, and never could have grown out of the standard of ethics in which the only worth, professedly recognized, is that of obedience."[44] Mill recognizes that some conditions of modern England—most notably, the predominance of the private sphere over the public sphere—make cultivating these qualities and practices more difficult than it ever was for the ancients. But English liberalism has "greatly overrat[ed] the amount of unlikeness between the men of modern and those of ancient times, [and] indulged the belief that the whole of the difference was in their own favor." He concludes that in England the Christian/modern persistence in cultivating a restricted morality is "becoming a grave practical evil, detracting greatly from the value of the moral training and instruction which so many well-meaning persons are now at length exerting themselves to promote." The discarding of values and practices that foster human agency, "which heretofore coexisted with and supplemented Christian ethics, receiving some of its spirit, and infusing into it some of theirs" will produce "a low, abject, servile type of character," who is incapable of higher forms of individuality or human excellence.[45]

Mill's account of the schism between the ancients and moderns charges that the ancients were as guilty of one-sidedness as the moderns, albeit in the opposite direction. Mill understood the "love of freedom" found among the ancients to be "an intense feeling of the dignity and importance of his own personality; making him disdain a yoke for himself, of which he has no abhorrence in the abstract, but which he was abundantly ready to impose on others for his own interest."[46] Mill believes that Plato recognized this danger and sought to address it by having the Socrates of his dialogues argue with noble youth about the true meaning of such terms as happiness, courage, and justice. Socrates sought to convince his interlocutors that the individual's capacity to reason is the key determinant in what an agent views as happiness, and that improvement of the idea of the good—or mental cultivation—fosters a higher view of what is happiness. While Mill believes that this Platonic dialectic further developed the ancient conception of cultivating dignity and the importance of one's own desires, he regrets that Plato did not ultimately manage to articulate a persuasive case for the moral solidarity of society's members. Still, Mill learns from Plato the need for a value system with two equally valid ends: the promotion of individuals who attain self-command of character and the development of a civilization characterized by just sympathetic bonds among its members.

Mill's *On Liberty* blames both the ancients and moderns for abusing their respective position over their opponents and preventing the formation of a comprehensive morality. Not only did they know only half the truth, but also they refused to even recognize another half, let alone foster it! He unfolds this criticism around his analysis of Marcus Aurelius's persecution of Christianity. Mill, who privately expressed "extreme admiration" for Marcus and posited him as a standard of human excellence for the "Religion of Humanity,"[47] fittingly portrays him sympathetically in *On Liberty*. He was an individual of the "tenderest heart," one whose ethical teachings "differ scarcely perceptibly, if they differ at all, from the most characteristic teachings of Christ." Mill sympathizes with the difficult conditions he encountered: Marcus was responsible for the entire civilized world of his day, "the summit of all previous attainments of humanity," which was now being engulfed by fissures, strife, and injustice. Marcus appreciated the need for unity, while confronting an emergent Christian religion that threatened to end the prevailing pagan orthodoxy. Unfortunately, Mill continues, Marcus did not recognize how, if the old religion dissolved, a new religion "could be formed to knit it [the civilized world] together." Christianity's superstitions and rituals disgusted him and made him incapable of distinguishing its advantages and disadvantages. He chose not to adopt or integrate the new religion, and so "it seemed to be his duty to put it down." Marcus Aurelius, "the gentlest and most amiable of philosophers and rulers, under a solemn sense of duty," chose not to incorporate the religion that might have saved his empire and "authorized the persecution of Christianity."

The conclusion Mill draws is emphatic: "To my mind this is one of the most tragical facts in all history. It is a bitter thought how different a thing the Christianity of the world might have been if the Christian faith had been adopted as the religion of the empire under the auspices of Marcus Aurelius instead of those of Constantine."[48] Mill's primary criticism of Marcus's policy of persecution centers on his failure to integrate Christianity into a larger comprehensive morality. Despite his wisdom and deft political abilities, Marcus missed this golden historical opportunity. To Mill, Marcus Aurelius represented the West's primary lost chance to integrate the dynamic activity of antiquity into a universal morality that would have tamed the excesses of the age. The violation of Christianity's civil liberties prevented the union of the ancient ethos of self-development and creativity with the moral norms of universality and equality.

Mill concludes chapter 2 of *On Liberty* by evoking Coleridge's concept of synthetic truths, asserting that the highest type of philosophic outlook does not play favorites but must recognize that for every thesis there is generally a valid antithesis. Instead of wedding itself to what has long appeared to be a true position, the philosopher is flexible enough to look for value in opposite positions. Mill regrets that neither Christianity nor modern England has learned from Marcus's mistake, and the one-sided development of the United Kingdom's morality continues. "If Christians would teach infidels to be just to Christianity," Mill reasoned, "they should themselves be just to infidelity. It can do truth no service to blink the fact, known to all who have the most ordinary acquaintance with literary history, that a large portion of the noblest and most valuable moral teaching has been the work, not only of men who did not know, but of men who knew and rejected, the Christian faith."[49]

INSURGENT PHILOSOPHERS AND RELIGION

Who developed this compromise or reconciliation between Christianity and the Anglo-Scottish Enlightenment? Why is Mill referring to England as being Christian, while also arguing that traditional Christian beliefs are no longer significant? And why is Mill being so cautious and discreet in explaining the philosophic foundation of this compromise between English liberalism and Christianity? Answers to these questions can be found in Mill's writings on why philosophers and the deepest thinkers are prone to compromising political and moral principles.

Mill argues that when religions are unable to explain the meaning of human existence a vacuum develops, which allows new philosophical and scientific explanations to come forward: "With the decline of polytheism came Greek philosophy; with the decline of Catholicism, the modern."[50] A period of conflict then ensues between the prevailing religious faith and the new philosophic and scientific understandings. Mill charges that when the highest thinkers confront this conflict between faith and reason, they tend to either compromise or disengage completely from political discourse, so as to be able to continue contemplation and the pursuit of the newly discovered truths. Those few intellectuals who challenge the gods are persecuted. The schism between wisdom and the public, knowledge and action, is established, and society as well as the intellectuals suffer because of it.

Mill argues that, while religions are products of the Imagination, they are not arbitrary constructs. Religions emerge from the human desire to understand the meaning and highest form of human existence and develop in relation to prevailing philosophic and scientific understandings. For instance, ancient Greek religions addressed the needs of a people struggling to move beyond the presocial stage of existence: the legends offered a sense of continuity with the past; and the heroic founders of family, tribe, or race (whether mythical or not) provided deities that cultivated a courageous attitude toward the future. These polytheistic religions also conformed to the prescientific understanding that the phenomena of nature seem to be the result of forces altogether variant, each taking its force without relation to the other.[51]

This is not Mill's final say on ancient religions, however. Mill explains that after centuries of "travel, communication, and more than all, the commencement of physical, scientific, and the intelligent observation of nature . . . a mode of interpreting phenomena . . . [engaged in] . . . continuing conflict with the simplicity of ancient faith." More specifically, Mill explains that as Anaxagoras, Plato, Aristotle, and the philosophers and natural scientists of ancient Athens systematically studied natural phenomena, they discovered that every natural event depends for its existence on some antecedent and that each of these relations is influenced by other types of regularities or laws. From this complex understanding the belief followed that a Being controls all of nature. Equally important, when the philosophers and scientists attempted to explain physical phenomena by physical causes, they were regarded as sacrilegious:

"Anaxagoras was banished for it (according to some authorities, even sentenced to death), Aristotle had to fly for his life; and the mere unfounded suspicion of it contributed greatly to the condemnation of Socrates."[52] Faced with the challenge of overcoming both persecution and the weight of an entire tradition of thought, the highest minds of the ancient world were either unwilling or unable to challenge polytheism. Almost all reconciled the new reason with the old faith:

> Mankind do [*sic*] not pass abruptly from one connected system of thought to another: they first exhaust every contrivance for reconciling the two. To break entirely with the religion of their forefathers, would have been a disruption of old feelings, too painful and difficult for the average strength of even superior minds; and could not have been done openly, without incurring a certainty of the fate which, with all the precautions they adopted, overtook Anaxagoras and Socrates. But even of the philosophers, there were at first very few who carried the spirit of freethinking so far. In general, they were unable to emancipate themselves from the old religious traditions, but were just as incapable of believing them literally. . . . The legends, in their obvious sense were no longer credible: but it was necessary to find for them a meaning in which they could be believed. . . . Rejected in their obvious interpretation, the narratives were admitted in some other sense. . . . They were represented as ordinary histories, colored by poetic ornament, in which moral instruction, physical knowledge, or esoteric religious doctrines, were designedly wrapt up.[53]

Many centuries would pass before polytheism was finally laid to rest, and to Mill's deep regret, philosophy did not contribute to its replacement.[54]

Mill frames the conflict between reason and faith for the contemporary English intellectual in the same way he did for the ancient thinker: "We are too well acquainted with this form of religious sentiment [persecution in Athens] even now, to have any difficulty in comprehending what must have been its violence then."[55] While a few contemporary thinkers wage ill-tempered polemics against Christianity, the most important thinkers respond to this conflict by compromising or disengaging from direct debate on moral and religious doctrines. These individuals mask their views in mystery, afraid to speak out their genuine beliefs. "A strong premium is placed on dishonesty on their part," Mill notes in a letter, "and those that have a natural energy of character are drawn into violence of language which hurts the feelings of other people and arouses in themselves something of that very intolerance from which they are sufferers."[56] In a passage that parallels Mill's assessment of intellectual and cultural life in England in *On Liberty,* Mill explains in "The Utility of Religion" how the contemporary English intellectual approaches religious questions:

Many who could render giant's service both to truth and to mankind if they believed that they could serve one without loss to the other, are either totally paralysed, or led to confine their exertions to matters of minor detail, by the apprehension that any real freedom of speculation, or any considerable strengthening or enlargement of the thinking faculties of mankind at large, might, by making them unbelievers, be the surest way to render them vicious and miserable. Many, again, having observed in others or experienced in themselves elevated feelings which they imagine incapable of emanating from any other source than religion, have an honest aversion to anything tending, as they think, to dry up the fountain of such feelings.[57]

Like the ancient intellectuals of late polytheism, English intellectuals have great difficulty either disengaging from or directly confronting their religious tradition, and both the society and its intellectuals suffer.

THE ENLIGHTENMENT'S COMPROMISE

Even more important, Mill explains that, just as the ancient thinkers compromised with polytheism, the circumscribed intellectual outlook of contemporary England is the result of a too similar compromise—that between the Anglo-Scottish Enlightenment and Christianity. Rather than directly challenge Christian beliefs, states Mill, the Enlightenment of the United Kingdom reformed Christianity to show it contained nothing offensive to society. In fact, Christianity's highest teachings were reworked to support the requirements of a new liberal state. The reformers claimed natural religion—establishing an understanding of God through the exercise of our cognitive powers—had "as much right to the religious argument as their opponents, and that if the course they recommended seemed to conflict with some parts of the ways of Providence, there was some part with which it agreed better than was contended for on the other side."[58] Mill summarizes the overall outcome of this compromise between the Anglo-Scottish Enlightenment and Christianity:

Thus, on the whole, England had neither the benefits . . . of the new ideas or the old. . . . We had a Church, which had ceased to fulfill the honest purposes of a church, but which we made a great point of keeping up as the pretence or *simulacrum* of one. We had a highly spiritual religion (which we were instructed to obey from selfish motives), and the most mechanical and worldly notions on every other subject; and we were so much afraid of being wanting in reverence to each particular syllable of the book which contained our religion, that we let its most important meaning slip through our fingers, and entertained the most groveling conceptions of its spirit and general purpose.[59]

It is now clear why Mill continually refers to England as being Christian, even though he believes that few English embrace traditional Christian beliefs. The gravity of Mill's charges in *On Liberty* of a "convenient plan for peace in the intellectual world" and a "tacit convention that principles are not to be disputed" is now becoming apparent.[60] Mill is arguing that the Enlightenment advocates of natural religion set themselves the task of domesticating Christianity's religious authorities and their zeal for persecution. They preferred to turn Christianity against itself, rather than directly attacking it, "being often themselves not free from the feeling (of Christian belief), and in any case afraid of incurring the charge of impiety by saying anything which might be held to disparage the Creator's power."[61] Mill charges that this compromise freed the intellectual and the general public from ecclesiastical supervision and persecution, but that it also failed to challenge the Christian tradition of obedience and fear of the creative will.

Mill argues that the new religious teachings flowed from Enlightenment philosophers' first recognizing, then taking advantage of, a contradiction in the traditional Christian outlook that an all-good, all-wise, and all-powerful God created nature. The Enlightenment knew that during Christianity's period of dominance, Christian theology largely embraced the ancient philosophers' view that humans are wild, but crafty, animals and that instilling ethical obligations into recalcitrant human material was a highly valued task. The modern philosophers also understood that during this Christian era, the paradoxical idea that an omniscient, omnipotent, and benevolent Deity created a wicked, evil human nature which needed to be tamed was a source of moral confusion. Rather than directly challenge Christian beliefs, the Enlightenment took advantage of this contradiction to develop an alternative view of the Deity's relationship to morality and human nature. What resulted is the argument for a new liberal civil theology centered on self-preservation and human happiness, an approach more consistent with the Christian belief in an all-powerful, all-wise, and all-good Deity. The Enlightenment, Mill continues, was confident it would "win" this compromise in the long run: "In this mode of dealing with the great *a priori* fallacies, the progress of improvement clears away particular errors while the causes of errors are still left standing, and very little weakened by each conflict: yet by a long series of such partial victories precedents are accumulated, to which an appeal may be made against these powerful pre-possessions, and which afford a growing hope that the misplaced feeling, after having so often learnt to recede, may some day be compelled to an unconditional surrender."[62]

Indeed, Mill recognizes that through a long series of partial victories, the British reformers weakened most features of the revealed Christian morality, including ecclesiastical supervision of philosophy and religion. Christianity has accommodated itself to the prevailing philosophy of the day and now borrows "a considerable part of its color and flavor from sentimental deism." The Church of England's primary goal is civil peace, serving as a "sedative to the religious spirit, to preventing it from disturbing the harmony of society and the tranquility of states." After the Revolution of 1688, Christianity's moral doctrine had dropped spiritually minded goals and embraced the prevailing self-interested ethos. As Mill states, "One of the crotchets of the philosophy of the age was, that all virtue is self-interest; and accordingly, in the textbook adopted by the Church . . . for instruction in moral philosophy, the reason for doing good is declared to be, that God is stronger than we are, and is able to damn us if we do not."[63]

Mill praises the religious compromise for contributing to liberating the individual from bondage to superstition and ecclesiastical authority.[64] But Mill argues that the Enlightenment's resolution of the religious question also created costs—at best underestimated, at worst completely unforeseen. First, Mill charges that, as the new religion does not teach anything other than rational obedience to liberal rules of justice, it is incapable of establishing the higher modes of individuality that either the ancients or romantics foster and that the new liberal society requires. Mill argues that religion, like art, should establish something more than the devotion to practical aims. Religion creates a strong imaginative picture of what human perfection is and how to realize it. The Enlightenment's reformed Christianity is now a "hereditary creed" that no longer examines the meaning and highest forms of human existence. Christianity remains "as it were outside the mind, incrusting and petrifying it against all other influences addressed to the higher parts of our nature; manifesting its power by not suffering any fresh and living connection to get in, but doing nothing for the mind or heart except standing sentinel over them to keep them vacant." "The evil is," Mill summarizes, "that such a belief [natural religion] keeps the ideal wretchedly low; and opposes the most obstinate resistance to all thought which has a tendency to raise it higher. Believers shrink from every train of ideas which would lead the mind to a clear conception and an elevated standard of excellence, because they feel (even when they do not distinctly see) that such a standard would conflict with many of the dispensations of nature, and much of what they are accustomed to consider as the Christian creed."[65]

Second, Mill charges that the Anglo-Scottish Enlightenment compromise with Christianity contributes to a modern England that is a secularization of biblical themes in key ways, and none more so than the Christian tradition of obedience and fear of the creative will. Like Christianity, the founders of British liberalism (such as Locke and Hume) saw the virtues of the ancients—most notably, honor and courage—as contributors to instability and strife. Rather than ennobling human conduct, these virtues promoted human misery.[66] This continued emphasis on restraint of the will is, for Mill, ultimately at odds with his conviction that attention needs to be paid to developing a more creative will in the face of modern civilization's normalizing tyranny: "There has crept over the refined classes, over the whole class of gentlemen in England, a moral effeminacy, an inaptitude for every kind of struggle. . . . They cannot undergo labour, they cannot brook ridicule, they cannot brave evil tongues: they have not hardihood to say an unpleasant thing to any one whom they are in the habit of seeing, or to face."[67]

Third, Mill argues that the Anglo-Scottish Enlightenment compromise with Christianity had limited English liberalism's capacity to develop institutions that cultivate the positive qualities that lead to human agency and moral development. For instance, unlike many of his liberal forebears, Mill did not object that England's established church violated the liberal doctrine of separation of church and state. Civil and ethical, state and church, Mill argued, are not as opposed to one another as many liberal thinkers suggest. Each provides different means to the same end: the mental expansion and moral development of the individual. The civil laws protect the liberty and security of the individual; the church helps shape individual and national character.

Mill argues that for Enlightenment thinkers a "case for the feudal and ecclesiastical institutions of modern Europe was by no means impossible: they had a meaning, had existed for honest ends, and an honest theory of them might [have been] made."[68] Mill was particularly attracted to Coleridge's position on the need for a national institution focused on the advancement of knowledge, ultimately encouraging the civilization and cultivation of the national community. Such a "church" could require that all citizens be instructed in "all the evidences of Christianity," although it would not require adherence to specific Christian teachings. Under this system, young people "would be brought up either churchmen or dissenters as they now are, the State merely taking care that they be instructed churchmen, or instructed dissenters."[69]

However, despite his attraction to Coleridge's view of a national institution focused on moral development, Mill rejects Coleridge's position that the Church of England could eventually perform this task. Mill claims Coleridge's standard represents the "severest satire" on what the Church of England is. He charges that the Church of England is a victim of the compromise brokered between the Anglo-Scottish Enlightenment outlook and the prevailing Christian authorities: "What neither party cared about, the *ends* of existing institutions, the work that was done by teachers and governors was flung overboard." In this compromise, the Church retained its form, rituals, and establishment, but the Church no longer embodied an independent moral outlook. It stopped being "the champion of arts against arms, of the serf against the seigneur, peace against war, or spiritual principles and powers against the domination of animal forces." The Church was envisioned "by philosophers" as a bulwark for civil peace and tranquility. The clergy of the establishment thought they had a good compromise on these terms "and kept its conditions very faithfully."[70]

Mill argues that an entirely new institutional framework will have to be established in the future as an organized body, set apart and subsidized and having the task of cultivating and diffusing higher forms of knowledge. From this perspective, Mill defends the principle of state educational endowments for *higher* education against the attacks that had been made upon them by such liberal thinkers as Bentham and Smith. A people might be free and secure and yet in an abject state of mental degradation. As early as 1833, Mill insists that maintaining higher education is not "one of those marketable commodities which the interest of rival dealers can be depended on for providing, in the quantity and the quality required," and he reiterates this position in the *Autobiography.*[71]

Finally, the most important impact of the Enlightenment-Christianity compromise in England is on the "freed" intellectuals themselves, who are now restricted and weakened by adhering to beliefs they either do not believe or do not fully comprehend: "Their minds were once active—they are now passive; they once generated impressions—they now merely take them." Just like the confused ancients, who could not figure out how to engage the weight of an entire religious tradition they in part rejected, the compromised modern intellectual lives in a mental fog: "This simple and innocent faith can only, as I have said, co-exist with a torpid and inactive state of the speculative faculties. For a person of exercised intellect, there is no way of attaining anything equivalent to it, save by sophistication and perversion, either of the understanding or of the conscience."[72] In Mill's account, late Christianity, like late polytheism, is characterized by a condition of progressive intellectual disengagement:

When the philosophic minds of the world can no longer believe its religion, or can believe it with modifications amounting to an essential change to its character, a transitional period commences, of weak convictions, paralysed intellects, and growing laxity of principle, which cannot terminate until a renovation has been effected in the basis of their belief leading to the elevation of some faith, whether religious or merely human, which they can really believe; and when things are in this state, all thinking or writing which does not tend to promote such a renovation, is of very little beyond the moment.[73]

Mill concludes, "It is time to consider . . . whether all this straining to prop up beliefs which require so great an expense of intellectual toil and ingenuity to keep them standing, yields a sufficient return in human well-being." It is preferable, he continues, to apply our mental energies to the sustenance and maintenance of those other sources of human character—most notably, the ancients and the romantics—that are not linked to a reformed Christianity. To produce a comprehensive morality that will promote "the moral regeneration of mankind," Mill advocates a reconciliation of those outlooks that promote human agency with those that establish universal obligations, as opposed to the already existent reconciliation of Christianity with English liberalism.[74]

NATURAL RELIGION

The Enlightenment of the seventeenth and eighteenth centuries provides us with the grounds for understanding, if not accepting, Mill's position that natural religion fails to cultivate human agency and higher modes of human existence. Those who founded the Enlightenment saw themselves as engaged in a bitter, long-drawn-out battle with the adherents of religion or orthodoxy, who continued to have faith in such supernatural phenomena as miracles, creation, and heaven. Biblical dogma, what Hobbes called the "kingdom of darkness," had to be pushed into the background to allow for civil peace and the rational pursuit of truth. The problem ran deeper than the hierarchy and superstition promoted by the ecclesiastics. "By asserting that the will of God is a standard above the positive laws of the state and by making themselves the sole interpreters of that will," religious dissenters and zealots "had carved out a lawless kingdom of their own within" society.[75]

Most of Mill's great predecessors in modern political philosophy, when they discussed the political consequences of Christianity, drew a line of demarcation between a false Christianity, which had bad consequences, and a true Christianity, which they held to be perfectly compatible with their understanding of the requirements of a free political society. Seminal Enlightenment thinkers developed a rational Christianity as an alternative to the scriptural theology of the

New Testament. Pufendorf, Hobbes, Spinoza, and Locke, among many others, devoted enormous energy to biblical commentaries and interpretations that replaced the rule of Scripture with natural religion, which established an understanding of God's will based on our cognitive capacity to recognize his laws of nature. Most of the standard-bearers of this new Christianity saw the attainment of civil peace and avoidance of strife as the most important ends of a political society. The precepts of the new theology tended to be simple, few in number, and stated with precision. They posited such things as a belief in the existence of an omnipotent and omniscient God, punishment of the wicked, and the sanctity of the rules of justice. As Spinoza put it, "Scriptural doctrine contains not abstruse speculation or philosophic reasoning, but very simple matters able to be understood by the most sluggish mind. . . . God . . . asks no other knowledge of himself than the knowledge of his divine justice and charity, that is, such attributes of God as men find it possible to imitate by a definite rule of conduct."[76] The simple doctrinal core of the Enlightenment's new natural religion accomplished the goal of civil peace by limiting the possible challenges to God's will by ambitious religious ideologues and moralists who escaped and subverted positive law through appeals to a higher law. Even Rousseau, who opposed the Enlightenment's position regarding laws of nature, put forth the need for a civil religion characterized by general and simple truths that each citizen has a right to interpret in his own way as long as these interpretations contain nothing contrary to the duties of citizenship.[77]

Modern natural law theorists stated that by "reasoning from observable facts we discover how to confront the moral and political problems that afflict our lives. Experience yields the evidence we need in order to infer that God exists and cares for us. Part of what we learn from experience is that God has made the proper structure of our common life independent of any larger cosmic scheme. Even if there is a divine harmony in the universe, we are unable to appeal to it to determine how we ought to live. Once we understand that God governs us, the observable facts about ourselves in this world provide the rational basis for working out the proper moral direction." We can determine what it is God wills for humankind not by consulting Scripture, but by considering what must be done if a man, made as God has made him, is to be preserved from his fellow man. "It means partly," states Pufendorf, "that law can be explored by the light of reason, and partly that at least the common and important precepts of natural law are so plain and clear that they meet with immediate assent, and become so ingrained in our minds that they can never thereafter be wiped from them, however the impious man may strive wholly to extinguish his sense of them, to lay to rest the stirrings of his conscience. On this ground, too, it is said in the Holy Scriptures to be 'written in the hearts of men.'"

The laws of nature, Grotius argues, are rooted in God's wisdom that "we should be weak, and should lack many things needed in order to live properly, to the end that we might be the more constrained to cultivate the social life." The laws of nature, Grotius continues, are "abstaining from that which is another's, the restoration to another of anything of his which we may have, together with any gain which we may have received from it; the obligation to fulfill promises, the making good of a loss incurred through our fault, and the inflicting of penalties upon men according to their deserts." On the one hand, this modern natural law outlook conforms to the Christian idea that nature is a product of a wise, powerful, and benevolent Creator. On the other hand, the focus of this outlook takes morality and law out of the disputed territory over which religious wars were being fought. Instead, reason is emphasized as key to understanding the morally good and bad. As Locke put it, human reason is to be established as our "only Star and compass."[78]

Indeed, Pufendorf argued that by diverting Christianity from other worldly goals and redirecting it toward more sociable and peaceful ends, Christianity itself was addressing the basic characteristics of human nature created by God: an instinct for self-preservation and sound judgment as to what makes life with others possible. God's command to man, as discovered by human reason (as opposed to revelation) was to live in conformity with these natural laws, that is, to live in accordance with natural justice—giving each his due, refraining from doing harm to others. Based on these natural laws, we can have society and thereby the fundamental elements of moral life, whereas if we neglect them and act on the basis of that neglect, we can have neither society nor humanity. "It follows," Pufendorf writes, "that God wills that a man should use for the preservation of his nature the powers within him in which he is conscious of surpassing the beasts; and that he also wills that human life be different from their lawless life. Since he cannot achieve except by observance of natural law, it is also understood that he is obligated by God to observe it as the means which God Himself has established expressly to achieve this end, and which is not a product of man's will and changeable at his pleasure."[79]

Later Continental thinkers—most notably, the German Romantics—eventually replaced natural religion with culture as the source of moral integration and self-direction.[80] But natural religion—as exemplified by the writings of Locke, Smith, and William Paley, for instance—was rarely challenged by Anglo-Scottish thinkers.[81] Britain continued to center Christianity on a handful of basic beliefs to limit challenges to the law by ambitious ideologues and moralists. Indeed, Anglo-Scottish thinkers had extended the characteristics of human nature created by God to be even more compatible with the new liberal state. Locke, Smith, and Paley propounded that compliance with the laws of justice established by the "Author of nature" created the basis for human happiness as well as self-preservation. "The happiness of mankind, as well as of all other rational creatures, seems to have been the original purpose intended by the Author of nature, when he brought them into existence," states Smith. "By acting according to the dictates of our moral faculties, we necessarily pursue the most effectual means for promoting the happiness of mankind, and may therefore be said, in some sense to co-operate with the Deity, and to advance as far as in our power the plan of Providence."[82]

To be sure, the advocates of natural religion did not believe that a political society should end Christian beliefs altogether. There remained a need for some type of inner disposition to inform human conduct and make distinctions between right and wrong, just and unjust. The reformed Christianity would diminish the threat of lawlessness by reminding individuals of the seriousness of life outside the immediate questions that afflicted them. Belief in the soul and its afterlife would moderate materialism; and the sure answers Christianity offers to the most fundamental questions can strengthen individual judgment in both private and public life. "For in natural liberty," states Pufendorf, "if you do away with fear of the Deity, as soon as anyone has confidence in his own strength, he will inflict whatever he wishes on those weaker than himself, and treat goodness, shame and good faith as empty words; and he will have no other motive to do right than the sense of his own weakness."[83]

In Locke's account, the newly formulated Christianity, serving as an extension of the social requisites for human happiness, makes virtue more available to the public. As opposed to the previous requirements for virtue, which were obscure, the new basic requisites—respect for the life, liberty, and property of others—can be simply viewed as a profitable investment. "The view of heaven and hell," Locke argues, "will cast a slight upon the short pleasures and pains of this present state, and give attractions and encouragements to virtue, which reason, and interest, and the care for ourselves, cannot but allow and prefer. Upon this foundation, and upon this only, morality stands firm, and may defy all competition. This makes it more than a name, a substantial good, worth all our aims and endeavours; and thus the gospel of Jesus Christ has delivered it to us."[84]

Advocates of natural religion differed over what institutional arrangements flowed best from their reformed Christianity. Locke, Smith, and others proposed a more decentralized framework—the encouragement of multiple religious communities within a general framework of toleration. From this perspective, there was always potential for conflict among individuals and groups around religious questions, and the means for preventing this potential volatility from spilling over into civil war was through maintaining a balance of power among multiple, competing sects. "The teachers of each little sect," stated Smith, "finding themselves almost alone, would be obliged to respect those of almost every other sect, and the concessions which they would mutually find it convenient and agreeable to make to one another, might in time probably reduce the doctrine of the greater part of them to that pure and rational religion, free from every mixture of absurdity, imposture, or fanaticism." The inability of one sect to dominate other sects would cultivate Christian virtues of moral restraint and toleration. Local Christian communities would further encourage the Protestant sense of inwardness and self-cultivation that newly freed societies required. The church and state must be separate, Locke insisted, because, while religion is responsible for men's souls, "all the power of civil government relates only to men's civil interests. . . . [It] is confined to the things of this world, and hath nothing to do with the world to come." As only what is mindfully embraced can please God, policies of religious coercion are impious. The state can legitimately use coercive power for the goal of protecting the "civil goods" of security and property, but the state must eschew compulsion in regard to religious beliefs.[85]

Other Enlightenment thinkers, chiefly Hobbes and Spinoza, argued that the political sovereign's control of religion derives from the natural law or right of self-preservation. Indeed, political control over religion is necessary for the sake of civil peace and for the sake of religious liberty itself: the chief obstacle to the realization of each is the ambitions of religious ideologues and moralists who escape and subvert the law through the appeal to some higher law. "How many rebellions hath this opinion been the cause of," Hobbes wrote in the midst of the English civil war, "which teacheth that the knowledge whether the commands of kings be just and unjust, belongs to private men; and that before they yield obedience, they not only may, but ought to dispute them!" If any man shall, Hobbes continued, "by most firm reasons demonstrate that there are no authentical doctrines concerning right and wrong, good and evil, besides the constituted laws in each realm and government . . . surely he will not only show us the highway to peace, but will also teach us how to avoid the close, dark, and dangerous by-paths of faction and sedition; than which I know not what can be thought more profitable." From this perspective, either the sovereign controls scriptural rights or religious advocates will control temporal rights. "For what decisions can be taken by sovereigns if this right is denied them?" asked Spinoza. "They can decide nothing whatsoever, whether concerning war or peace or any other matter, if they are to wait on the utterance of another who will tell them whether that which they judge to be beneficial is pious or impious. On the contrary, everything will be done according to the decree of him who has the right to judge and decide what is pious or impious, right or wrong."[86]

In order to maintain civil peace, declare Hobbes and Spinoza, the political sovereign has the right to determine civil and religious laws. The undivided political sovereign is posited as a vehicle for freeing the individual from the authority and conflicts of competing religious groups. The centralized state is envisioned as the only possible neutral power in regard to civil and religious conflict. By refuting all rival sources of morality, ending misplaced obedience, and removing all loyalties and associations that stand between the solitary individual and the sovereign, the interests of both individual and state are reconciled.[87] Hume reinforced this "political control" position in his argument that the state limit religion's role in shaping human motivations through bribery of the established church. Hume charged that religion promoted two harmful tendencies. On the one hand, the independent (Catholic) church promoted itself by fostering human passivity and superstition. On the other hand, when competing (Protestant) religious sects are free from the state, efforts are continuously launched to foster religious enthusiasm, producing fanaticism. It is preferable, he continues, to bribe the priests' indolence. Putting clerics on the dole eliminates their incentive for activism and their emphasis on preventing their patrons from straying outside the boundaries of the church. As Hume put it, the civil magistrate makes it "superfluous for them to be further active than merely to prevent their flock from straying in the quest for new pastures."[88]

England adopted the "political control" model of church-state relations. The Church of England formed after breaking with the universal Catholic Church. In a series of statutes, the Reformation Parliament of 1529 recognized that England was and always had been an empire, independent of all external jurisdictions. They claimed the monarch supreme over all of his subjects, whether clerical or lay. Over the next 160 years, state and Church struggled over this relationship. The monarch and parliament established an Erastian solution, as they were concerned to gain unchallenged political sovereignty. A Christian state, in their view, had the right to settle and interpret Scripture and thus authoritatively determine the Law of God and Nature. Without this authority, they believed, it would be impossible to govern.[89]

TOWARD A NEW SYNTHESIS

So the Enlightenment devoted an enormous amount of energy to the goal of supplanting the Scripture of the New Testament, the traditional authoritative guide and teacher of morality, with a new kind of religion based more on reason than ever before. This new Christianity promised a "new world" of civil peace: toleration, security, happiness, private property, and equality under the law. But Mill raises a daunting question: Is the Enlightenment's new religion a sufficient break from the Christianity it has compromised with? He recognizes that no philosopher can now be "found who like the institutional writers of former times, adopts the so-called Law of Nature as the foundation of ethics, and endeavors consistently to reason from it." Nonetheless, the outlook established by this theory "must still be counted among those which carry great weight in moral argumentation." We live in an era, Mill states, "in which the real belief in any religious doctrine is feeble and precarious, but the opinion of its necessity for moral and social purposes is universal; . . . [T]hose who reject revelation, very generally take refuge in an optimistic Deism, a worship of the order of Nature and the supposed course of Providence, at least as full of contradictions, and perverting to the moral sentiments, as any of the forms of Christianity. . . . Yet, very little, with any claim to philosophical character, has been written by skeptics against this form of belief."[90]

In Mill's view, resolving the conflict between cultivating practices required for exerting human agency and creating conditions that ensure general moral development is the primary task for generating humanity's progress and happiness. England's past has been animated by a great, insoluble conflict between these two contrasting outlooks and practices. Unlike Hegel and many romantics, Mill does not maintain that a negation or division between contrasting counterparts necessarily leads to reconciliation and unity at a higher level: yet such a synthesis is what Mill desires.[91] In modern England, however, this long-term, seesaw battle is waning, and Mill worries that an age of lifeless quiescence is at hand. "The new synthesis is barely begun, nor is the preparatory analysis completely finished," he writes, but it is necessary to proceed with the project, for "the old edifice will remain standing until there is another that is ready to replace it."[92]

English liberal society is an improvement on Christianity in ensuring human equality and general moral improvement. But English society has not broken from those features of Christianity that limit human agency: "For mankind are always growing better than their religion, and leave behind one after another of the more vicious parts of it, dwelling more and more exclusively on those which are better, or admit at least of a better sense. But this holding fast in theory to a standard ever more and more left behind in practice is one great cause why the human intellect has not improved in anything like the same ratio as the senti-ments." Mill argues in the posthumously published *Autobiography* that the era of remaining silent on religious questions must end. "On religion in particu-lar," he writes, "the time appears to have come, when it is the duty of all who be-ing qualified in point of knowledge, have on mature consideration satisfied themselves that the current opinions are not only false but hurtful, to make their dissent known; at least if they are among those whose station, or reputa-tion, gives their opinion a chance of being attended to."[93] Accordingly, Mill devotes an enormous amount of mental energy to understanding the advan-tages and disadvantages of religion and its role in developing human energy and a conception of the best life for modernity.

Chapter 5 Reforming Reformed Religion: J. S. Mill's Critique of the Natural Religion of the Enlightenment

Before identifying how Mill developed his critique of natural religion and proposed Religion of Humanity in his political philosophy, I want to address two important questions. Why are Mill's most comprehensive statements on revealed Christianity, natural religion, and the Religion of Humanity found in his *Diary*, private correspondence, and posthumous publications the *Autobiography* and the *Three Essays on Religion?* And why are Mill's criticisms of Christianity an understated or subordinate theme in the essays—most notably, *On Liberty* —published during his lifetime? It cannot be said that Mill failed to publicly criticize Christianity during his lifetime, but neither did he make his criticisms as polemical or as comprehensive as he did in those writings he knew would be read after his death. One must turn to Mill's private correspondence and posthumous publications to find him forthrightly raising the question, "How can morality be anything but the chaos it now is, when the ideas of right and wrong, just and unjust, must be wrenched into accordance with the notion of a tribe of barbarians in a corner of Syria three thousand years ago, or with what is called the Order of Providence?"[1]

The most obvious explanation is that Mill practiced a literary strategy of indirection in his commentaries on religious questions for prudential considerations, such as self-protection from persecution or fear of social dissolution.[2] After all, Mill admits being taught as a child by his father that, as his opinions regarding religion were contrary to those of the world, he should prudently avoid publicly avowing them.[3] Fears of legal persecution and moral ostracism and concerns that the loss of Christian beliefs would undermine obligation and result in social chaos affected almost all British writers who spanned the Victorian age—Thomas Carlyle, Charles Darwin, George Grote, George Henry Lewes, Henry Buckle, Alfred Tennyson, Thomas Hardy, Herbert Spencer, Henry Sidgwick, T. H. Huxley, among many others—either concealing or hedging their true feelings on Christianity and religion.[4] Concern for their own security or concern for the security of England as a whole discouraged the Victorian intellectuals from raising explicitly challenging and tenacious inquiries regarding the most fundamental religious beliefs of the English. Darwin, for instance, records in his diary the concern that he will suffer the same fate as Galileo. He held back publishing his teachings on evolution for decades and even then did not explicitly reject Creation, which led him to admit later that he had compromised his position out of a fear of persecution and denigration.[5] The late Victorian Sidgwick summarized why he failed to speak out against Christianity, despite his inability to discover a coherent rational argument for the Christian hope of happy immortality: "It seems to me that the general loss of such a hope, from the minds of average human beings as now constituted, would be an evil of which I cannot pretend to measure the extent. I am not prepared to say that the dissolution of the existing social order would follow, but I think the danger of such dissolution would be seriously increased, and that the evil would certainly be great."[6]

No doubt Mill's moderate public rhetoric on the religious question was motivated in part by prudence. As a candidate for the House of Commons, he hardly could have been elected, or as a parliamentarian been effective as a spokesman for unpopular causes, had he been immoderate in expressing his religious views. But there are evident difficulties in the position that caution *exclusively* motivated Mill to avoid, in the essays published during his lifetime, explicit discussion of the advantages and disadvantages of either natural religion or the Religion of Humanity. First, Mill maintained religion was no longer necessary in Western civilization for the maintenance of political stability and the cultivation of the just moral conscience.[7] Next, courage was not a problem for Mill. He admired this quality, and he exemplified it in his literary, political, and personal life; and he was known to even his severest opponents as the model figure of his age for stirring controversy.[8] Mill often displayed the courage of his convictions by taking principled stands against prevailing public or elite opinion and by resolutely defending his views in the face of withering criticisms. Mill's parliamentary proposals for women's suffrage, his role in the Hyde Park affair, his defending of the Union military action in the American Civil War, his public critique of Bentham and the utilitarian school, and his relationship with Mrs. Taylor are an indicative showing of Mill's willingness to accept risk and isolation.[9]

Third, Mill's contemporary friends and foes maintained that Mill employed rhetorical strategies in *all* of his writings to gain maximum advantage in attaining his political goals. Mill worked very hard at reconciling his large-scale theories in identifying far-reaching aims with political considerations so that "the choice of principles for present application is guided by a systematic appreciation of the state and exigencies of society."[10] Rather than being motivated by a concern for personal security or political stability, these contemporaries believed Mill cultivated a writing style that garnered the largest alliances to have maximum political effect. As the Mill critic James Fitzjames Stephen's wrote, Mill believed that a "zig-zag mode of approach [in writing] is good in controversy as well as sieges," that if Mill had tried "to storm the town now," he would "simply be knocked on the head."[11] Another Mill critic, James Martineau, warned,

> No writer it is possible was ever more read between the lines; his authoritative force of the intellect, his perfect mastery of his material, his singular neatness of exposition, marked him as a great power in the speculative world. But, as usual, the real interest was less scientific than moral—as to the direction in which that power would work. A certain air of suppression occasionally assumed by Mill himself, with hints for a revision of the existing narrow-minded morals, has increased this tendency. This suppressive air is the greatest fault we find in him; it is his only illegitimate instrument of power; for it weighs chiefly on the weak: and the shadow which it passes across his face is sometimes so strong as almost to darken the philosopher into the mystagogue.[12]

Similar comments were voiced by his supporters—as points of praise, rather than criticism. John Morley, for example, writes that Mill "was unrivalled in the difficult art of conciliating as much support as was possible for novel and extremely unpopular opinions." To Morley, "Mill husbanded the strength of truth and avoided wasteful friction."[13]

Finally, and most important, Mill's private correspondence with Auguste Comte reveals that he presented his views on religion to have maximum political impact. They disclose Mill embracing the same strategy toward Christianity as the Enlightenment thinkers he criticizes: namely, establishing a compromise with Christianity that will slowly swing the balance of forces toward the creation of a more progressive liberal order. In these letters to Comte, Mill makes it clear he could not publish all of his thoughts about religion, and he indicates that in what he wrote he would make the kind of presentations which he regarded the most politically effective. In one letter Mill agrees with Comte that a social philosophy or religion directed toward humanity is needed to replace the present outlook that remains associated with God. But, Mill adds, he has had a "rare fate" compared to most members of his country—he has never believed in God. And even with his background, he states that it is impossible to appreciate this new secular outlook "without some kind of emergency in the life of any man whose moral nature is incapable of meeting the obligations it imposes." Consequently, while Comte will find Mill's work too metaphysical, "it still seems to me very appropriate for easing the conversion from the metaphysical to the positive spirit."[14]

In another letter, Mill explains that he is unwilling to translate Comte's *Discourse on the Positive Spirit* because "the time has not yet come when we in England shall be able to direct open attacks on theology, including Christian theology, without compromising our cause." Mill notes that, as almost all of those in England who have a degree of religious emancipation and scientific knowledge read French, no loss in effect will occur if only the French version of Comte's work circulates. Mill reiterates the same theme in a letter rejecting a request from Comte to cosponsor a journal. While Mill looks forward to the day when he can "refuse all compromises, even tacit, to theories of the supernatural," he must make such concessions now for the times still demand it. Finally, Mill implores Comte to distinguish his private and public views of religion. He notes that a private letter of Comte's to a mutual acquaintance has further shaken that individual's faith in God. But Mill insists that this person was already "half-detached" and that Comte should not assume that she represents the norm in England. "Today," Mill insists, "one ought to keep total silence on the question of religion when writing for an English audience, though indirectly one may strike any blow one wishes at religious beliefs."[15]

Mill's artful presentation of his views on English liberalism's limited disengagement from Christianity was motivated, then, by more than simply the goal of self-preservation and security. He was also driven by a political strategy that aimed to move English liberalism beyond the stage created by the compromise that the Anglo-Scottish Enlightenment had brokered with Christianity. Of course, a few of Mill's contemporaries believed that Christianity was such an extreme problem that it called for a radical response, that moderation or a political approach was unprincipled.[16] Mill's rejoinder is that the best political stand may not be the most moral stand, but the political stand is right because it makes the victory of the moral stand possible. As Alexander Bain, Mill's friend and biographer, reports, Mill never published his complete views on Christianity while alive: "He had long determined to throw off the mask entirely, when the time should be ripe for it. He was prevented from an earlier avowal of these [unpopular religious views], solely by the circumstance that the silent course of opinion was serving the interests of progress better than any violent shock, on his part would have done."[17] Bain knew of Mill's strategy of compromising with Christianity while undermining or further reforming it because Mill wrote to him about this approach. "I have not written it [*Utilitarianism*] in any hostile spirit towards Xtianity," notes Mill in a letter to Bain, "though undoubtedly good ethics and good metaphysics will sap Xtianity if it persists in allying itself with bad. The best thing to do in the present state of the human mind is to go on establishing positive truths . . . & leave Xtianity to reconcile itself with them the best way that it can." On religion, Mill states in another letter to Bain that explains *On Liberty*, "Certainly I am not anxious to bring over any but really superior intellects & characters to the whole of my opinions—in the case of all others I would much rather, as things now are, try to improve their religion than destroy it."[18]

THREE ESSAYS ON RELIGION

Mill's *Three Essays on Religion,* published posthumously, articulate a new idea of human excellence for modern England. While examining the weaknesses of the Enlightenment's natural religion, the articles explain a "new religion" that has a feature that characterizes all religions: an imaginative picture of human perfection. As Mill writes in his *Diary,* "Religion, of one sort or another, has been at once the spring and regulator of energetic action, chiefly because religion has hitherto supplied the Philosophy of Life, or the only one which differed from a mere theory of self-indulgence." At the same time, Mill maintains the general orientation already noted in his assessments of Athens, Plato, and, most important, modern justice, namely, that human agency augments, not supplants, general moral development. An understanding of Mill's views on Christianity and religion is critical to a deeper understanding of *On Liberty* and his overall political philosophy.[19]

Mill opens "The Utility of Religion" by noting moral and ethical concerns that are characteristic of all religions: an object of the good by reference to which our everyday actions are to be judged and an imaginative picture of human perfection. "The first question," he asserts, "is interesting to everybody; the latter only to the best." In discussing the value of religion, Mill identifies his dilemma as being similar to the predicament he ascribes to Plato. Mill is being pulled apart by the "two noblest of all objects of pursuit, truth, and the general good."[20] Mill fears social disintegration as society becomes driven solely by negative, critical knowledge and suggests that religion is intellectually unsustainable but politically justifiable. However, he immediately questions whether religion itself is an extension of the requirements of moral and political order. Putting forth the model of Sparta, Mill argues that it is comprehensive education around a unified, authoritative framework, not religion, which provides the moral foundation for good and bad behavior. It is our opinions alone, not the heavens, which create the primary external incentives and sanctions that deter the weak from failing to live up to their social obligations, while also establishing the means for the ambitious to realize their aims. He continues,

> The love of glory; the love of praise; the love of admiration; the love of respect and deference; even the love of sympathy, are portions of its [public opinion's] attractive power. . . . The fear of shame, the dread of ill repute, or of being disliked or hated, are the direct and simple forms of its deterring power. . . . And again the attractive, or impelling influence of public opinion, includes the whole range of what is commonly meant by ambition; for except in times of lawless military violence, the objects of social ambition can only be attained by means of the good opinion and favorable disposition of our fellow creatures; nor, in nine cases out of ten, would those objects even be desired, were it not for the power they confer over the sentiments of mankind. . . . And we ought to note that this motive is naturally strongest in the most sensitive natures, which are the most promising material for the formation of great virtues.[21]

Mill concedes that using supernatural gods to establish moral norms is appropriate to the rudest and most primitive times, human beings stuck in ignorance and superstition. But what in earlier times could be conveyed only by means of god and faith can now be apprehended by moral education. Indeed, once its historical function of introducing social morality is complete, the continued use of the supernatural maintains people in a condition of political tutelage and immaturity. "Belief, then, in the supernatural, great as the services which it rendered in the early stages of human development, cannot be considered to be any longer required," summarizes Mill, "either for enabling us to know what is right or wrong in social morality, or for supplying us with motives to do right and to abstain from what is wrong."[22]

Turning to the question as to whether supernatural beliefs are necessary for the perfection of human character, Mill argues that religion, like poetry, primarily addresses the human desire to live a meaningful and beautiful existence. Our existence is but a secluded moment in a world of infinite time and space, as "the past and future are alike shrouded from us: we neither know the origin of anything what is, nor its final destination." With reason unable to comprehend the whole, we are able to address the human desire to understand the purpose of human existence with the imagination only: "The imagination is free to fill up the vacancy with the imagery most congenial to itself: sublime and elevating if it be a lofty imagination, low and mean if it be a groveling one." And Mill argues that religion and art are the main instruments the imagination uses to put forth the meaning and highest forms of human existence.[23]

In Mill's account, religion differs from art in that it demands to know if our conceptions of the meaning and highest forms of human existence "have realities answering to them in some other world than ours." He asks whether pursuing this good requires traveling beyond the horizons in which we live, "or whether the idealization of our earthly life, the cultivation of a high conception of what it may be made, is not capable of supplying a poetry, and, in the best sense of the word, a religion, equally fitted to exalt the feelings, and (with the same aid from education) still better calculated to ennoble the conduct, than any belief respecting the unseen powers."[24]

Mill is aware that a complete rejection of the idea of a transcendent Being could contribute to the further promotion of short-term, self-interested behavior. Therefore a new religion, a Religion of Humanity, must look to the seemingly endless character of the species, as well as to humanity's inexorable drive for improvement, "offering to the imagination and sympathies a large enough object to satisfy any reasonable demand for grandeur of aspiration." Mill projects a religiously informed idea of creative deeds for the public good, associating this outlook with ancient pursuits of permanent greatness and immortal deeds. Turning to Cicero, Mill notes that ancient quests for immortality provided an uplifting, creative will both for the heroic individual and the *polis,* or regime. Cicero extolled the Athenians and Romans for being committed to their own glory, but Mill's Religion of Humanity will combine ancient and modern aims: establishing heroic contributions to the general good of humanity as the basis for distinguishing the highest types of individuals.[25]

The key figures of Mill's Religion of Humanity, in whose light one would scrutinize his or her own activities, are primarily founders of beliefs and practices that serve the public good: Socrates, the founder of rationality; George Washington, the founder of the American Republic; Marcus Aurelius, the philosopher-ruler of the Roman Empire, who recognized the need to combine innovation with moral obligations; Jesus Christ, the founder of a moral way of life; and John Howard, the founder of the prison reform movement in England.[26] Mill explains how such an idea of perfection would help influence individual behavior. Among the "individuals of superior natures," these standards for emulation would attach sympathy and benevolence to their quests to excel. "The highest minds, even now," he writes, "live in thought with the great dead, far more than with the living; and next to the dead, with those ideal human beings yet to come, whom they are destined never to see." Among the general mass, this idea of perfection would promote a reference point that would contribute to the public's ability to distinguish the "excellent and shameful."[27]

Mill rejects the position that the absence of God in the Religion of Humanity means that he is proposing a type of moral outlook and not a religion. To Mill, his proposed religion contains the defining feature of all religions: "the strong and earnest desires toward an ideal object, recognized as of the highest excellence, and as rightfully paramount over all selfish objects of desire." Religion, like art, establishes something more than devotion to practical aims. It creates a strong imaginative picture of what human perfection is, a picture that is regularly appealed to by the most creative individuals in making conscientious decisions on the most difficult, fundamental questions.[28]

A potential weakness of the Religion of Humanity, Mill concedes, lies in the failure of its idea of immortality to address the widespread desire for an afterlife. It establishes meaning for the highest type of life on earth, but nothing for afterwards. Mill's hope, however, is that as this new religion is cultivated and takes hold, its central ethic—creative deeds for the public good—will contribute to the eradication of conditions that lead people to long for another world. After all, Mill continues, the ancient Greek conception of afterlife held little attraction for their feelings and imagination, but this did not lead them to enjoy life less or fear mortality more than other people.[29]

JESUS AND PLATO AS TEACHERS
OF THE HEROIC

Indeed, Mill compares this new religion favorably to Christianity. Rather than basing its appeal for human excellence on the self-interested goal of eternal happiness, the Religion of Humanity will establish innovation for the public good as a good in itself: "It carries the thoughts and feelings out of self, and fixes them on an unselfish object, loved and pursued as an end for its own sake." This religion will not worship the maker of an unrighteous world, but rather will recognize worldly plights and inequities as challenges to be conquered.[30] In "The Utility of Religion" and "Theism," Mill distinguishes Jesus from Christianity and advocates that Jesus be put forward as a morally excellent being, creating a standard of greatness and imitation for the Religion of Humanity. Despite the moral confusion fostered by Christianity—attributing a wicked world to an omnipotent, perfect Creator—it has established the life of Jesus as the embodiment of the idea that selfless devotion to the welfare of all is the good. While the philosopher is enabled "to form a far truer and more consistent conception of Ideal Goodness"—*creative deeds* that serve the public good—the life of Jesus is an excellent example of human perfection. This standard, though not in itself "amounting to what can be called a religion, seems to me excellently fitted to aid and fortify that real, though purely religion, which sometimes calls itself the Religion of Humanity, and sometimes that of Duty."[31]

Accordingly, Mill argues that a feature of Plato's art contributes to the Religion of Humanity. Here Mill's assessment of the ethical character of Plato's poetry differs from that of romantics such as Coleridge and Shelley. In Mill's reading, Plato's artistry does not create an "aesthetic state"—a society that overcomes materialism and disunity—as understood by Coleridge. Neither does Mill point to specific moral teachings like Shelley—the doctrine of recollection, the Myth of Er, among others—that paint a pervasive beauty that lies beyond the civilized world.[32] Finally, Mill rejects the romantics' position that Plato's art gives figurative form to moral truths. In Mill's account, Plato's dialogues generate feelings that lead to a few great individuals' gaining the consciousness that creative deeds that serve the public good is the best life. The beauty of the Platonic dialogues cultivates feelings that lead to a love for noble virtue or what Mill often refers to as human excellence.[33] The Socrates of the *Gorgias,* Mill explains, makes all other evils more tolerable than injustice of the soul, not by logically proving it, but by the sympathy he calls forth with his intense feeling of it: "He inspires heroism, because he shows himself a hero. And his failures in logic do not prevent the step marked by the *Gorgias* from being one of the greatest ever made in moral culture—the cultivation of a preference of duty for its own sake, as a higher state than that of sacrificing selfish preferences for a more distant self-interest." The love of noble virtue, Mill concludes, is a feeling that is inspired by loved ones, heroes, and artists—not philosophy—and no writer has promoted more admiration for excellent individuals than Plato. "It is this element which completes in him the character of a Great Teacher," he writes. "Others can instruct, but Plato is one of those who form great men, by the combination of moral enthusiasm and logical discipline."[34]

Mill is rejecting early British romanticism's position that Plato's art expresses moral truth in figurative form. But Mill is not completely ignoring romanticism. He is incorporating Plato's dialogues into what *mid-Victorian* romantics such as Matthew Arnold and Alfred Tennyson were calling the "grand style" of writing. "Grand Style" writings are characterized by "men in a state of enthusiasm"—that is, individuals who feel strongly and nobly, who focus on delineating "human character and form in their utmost, or heroic, strength and beauty."[35] This mid-Victorian desire by romantic writers to reinstall the heroic tradition in England was a response in part to the new democratic theory which limited political leaders to being instruments of the people. It also was a backlash to the mechanistic views of history as an interrelated play of class and cultural forces under the imperious control of social laws. Most important, the mid-Victorian romantics believed that, as society was abandoning belief in God, poetry is the form that must take its place in putting forth what is the best life. Writers such as Arnold and Tennyson believed that, given the great confusion of the present transitional period from a religiously informed moral life to a secular-based ethics, the potentially noble individual needed a map and source of inspiration to lead him through the complexity, a guide to identify for him the goals and practices he should keep in mind. The grand style would encourage the individual to engage in activities that will allow him to realize heroic aims.[36]

Mill's position that Plato's and Jesus' respective moral teachings reside primarily in Plato's portrayals of heroism and Jesus' inspiring moral existence is a radical break from the long tradition in the study of the history of political philosophy that has maintained that in works like the *Republic* and *Gorgias* Plato laid the basis for the Christian view of the world as a fallen and unredeemable place—a dark cave indeed. Against this world, Plato, and then Jesus and the Apostle Paul, promoted a transcendent notion of the Good, located in the Forms and in Heaven, respectively. In Hegel's account, for instance, Plato's noble but flawed attempt to establish a new substantive ethics[37] foreshadows Jesus' and Christianity's imperfect bid to establish a new universalistic outlook. On the one hand, Jesus taught a new communal outlook based on universal love and friendship. On the other hand, Jesus recognized that reforming the corrupt Jewish community would compromise his new substantive ethics. Like Plato, who did not take into account the subjective freedom initiated by the Sophists and Socrates, Jesus chose to ignore the larger society and focused exclusively on his friends and disciples. He ultimately decided that his message of universal love was not of this world. Paul's division between the earthly and heavenly realms was to be the fate of Christianity and Western culture. "The Christian religion," states Hegel, "has certainly adopted the lofty principle that man's inner and spiritual nature is his true nature, and takes it as its universal principle, though interpreting it in its own way as man's inclination toward holiness; but Plato and his philosophy had the greatest share in obtaining for Christianity its rational organization and bringing it into the kingdom of the supernatural, for it was Plato who made the first advance in this direction."[38]

Mill does recognize the value of a specific moral teaching of Plato, but it has nothing to do with transcendent notions of the Good. In "The Utility of Religion," Mill explains that the only view of supernatural origin and government of the universe that is consistent with the Religion of Humanity is the natural religion of Plato's *Statesman*. This is "the only form of belief in the supernatural—one only theory respecting the origin and government of the universe—[that] stands wholly clear both of intellectual contradiction and moral ubiquity."[39] In the *Statesman*, the Stranger explains that an intelligent, but not omnipotent, god shaped the world from already existent and not fully changeable matter and force. This god was unable to create a very good world, leaving it to humanity to push this task forward. The world, in short, is a product of a conflict between god's contrived goodness and an intractable matter that is unable to be fully reshaped and reformed.[40] Mill believes that this view of a deity is more consistent with what reason infers from the workings of nature and is a far firmer basis for a morally beneficent god than the natural religion of the Enlightenment. In the *Autobiography*, Mill explains that his father taught him the value of this teaching, and "I . . . heard him express surprise that no one revived it in our time." Accordingly, in the "Inaugural Address," Mill speaks of the existence of a ceaseless conflict between good and evil, warning the students that they can neither avoid being a part of this battle nor abstain from a responsibility to side with the good. From this perspective, the Religion of Humanity cultivates individuals to become a "fellow labourer with the Highest, a fellow combatant in the great strife." Mill admits that the evidence of Plato's god in the *Statesman* is too "shadowy and insubstantial" to be a substitute for the Religion of Humanity, but the two outlooks "may be held in conjunction," and there is no harm created by Plato's god providing some with the hope of a bright future.[41]

In the "Inaugural Address" Mill discusses the importance of training the highly educated mind to appreciate the art of Plato and, more generally, an aesthetic culture that establishes creative deeds that serve the public good as the highest type of life. This form of art focuses on perfection of the individual, not the community. Anticipating some of the themes found in Nietzsche's monumental history,[42] Mill explains that the ethical aim of aesthetic culture is the presentation of scenes and characters that play upon the feelings in such a way as to establish love for the noblest conduct. If fully communicated, the standard of excellence becomes a model of inspiration and imitation to the few individuals who seek to transcend the safe but ordinary qualities of the many and realize great deeds. "Thus feeling," Mill notes, "we learn to respect ourselves only so far as we feel capable of nobler objects . . . and . . . to sustain ourselves by the ideal sympathy of the great characters of history: shall, I add, of ideal perfection embodied in a Divine Being?"[43]

The value of aesthetic culture for social life throughout history has been that from the heroic characters "not only the noblest minds in modern Europe derived much of what made them noble, but even the commoner spirits what made them understand and respond to nobleness." The goal of aesthetic culture, then, was the cultivation of the potentially heroic to be heroic and to make the general public appreciative of such risk-taking conduct. Mill called this study of aesthetic culture a part of general education as well and stated that "it would be well if the more narrow-minded portion, both of the religious and scientific education-mongers, would consider whether the books which they are banishing from the hands of youth, were not instruments of national education to the full as powerful as the catalogue of physical facts and religious dogmas which they have substituted."[44]

Whereas Mill's account of Plato and Jesus breaks radically with much of the Western philosophic tradition, it is instructive to note that Mill's account of aesthetic culture and human perfection still maintains important parallels with Kant's and other romantics' thinking. Kant, for instance, like Mill, argues that moral education and a high culture are necessary for moral perfection: "The fact that virtue must be acquired (and is not innate) is contained already in the concept of virtue. . . . That virtue can and must be taught follows from the fact that it is not innate." Here Kant places particular emphasis on philosophers contributing to a high culture for the citizenry. "That kings should philosophize or philosophers become kings is not to be expected. . . . But that kings or royal peoples (ruling themselves by laws of equality) should not let the class of philosophers disappear or be silent but should let it speak publicly is indispensable . . . so that light may be thrown on their business; and, because this class is by its nature incapable of forming seditious factions or clubs, it cannot be suspected of spreading *propaganda*." In certain respects, Mill's emphasis on the shift from the basic desires of self-interest to the principled desire to be original, to found new practices and beliefs, and break customary practices parallels Kant's hierarchical order of the morally good over the interest-driven individual, but it is not the same. Mill's highest type of individual is subrational, in Kantian terms, because he remains concerned with himself, his uniqueness, his practices, and his contributions. A founder must be unique by definition.[45]

The ethical significance of Mill's aesthetic culture and Religion of Humanity, then, resides in their ability to inspire and raise some individuals beyond the level of civil association. This art transcends attachment to things or objects by directing exceptional individuals to channel their energies to higher ideals, while also cultivating a public standard of human excellence. An ennobling pleasure, Mill insists, comes from learning about individuals who have accomplished great deeds, and this aspiration of looking up to excellence is needed by the English people more than any other as they are increasingly attending to the mundane. "The more prosaic our ordinary duties," Mill writes, "the more necessary it is to keep up the tone of our minds by frequent visits to that higher region of thought and feeling, in which every work seems dignified in proportion to the ends for which, and the spirit in which, it is done." The existence and cultivation of exceptional individuals in the general culture is crucial if English society and state are to progress and avoid becoming mere instruments for the satisfaction of substantive wants.[46]

Thoughtful commentators of Mill—Joseph Hamburger, Maurice Cowling, Shirley Letwin, among others—argue Mill envisioned the Religion of Humanity or aesthetic culture ultimately becoming the general ethos of society, creating a level of social obligation inimical to human liberty. But Mill's view of religion and culture exemplifies his use of religious, ancient, romantic, *and* liberal themes: Mill uses the romantic conception of the aesthetic to combine the religious idea of human perfection with the ancient ethos of founding practices of lasting importance and the modern idea of contributing to the universal good. Mill's aim is not to replace the rules of equal justice with an aesthetic culture but to discover the values and practices that cultivate human excellence compatible with civil association. He seeks to win the public to a standard of human excellence by establishing it as a desirable object rather than as an imposed obligation.[47] In sum, Mill's Religion of Humanity and aesthetic culture perform their function in two ways: by emphasizing the value of individuals who found new practices, this poetry embraces religious and ancient teachings regarding human perfection and immortal deeds; by emphasizing the importance of lives that further the general good and extend the sympathetic bonds among members of society, this poetry acts universally and fosters liberty and equality. Finally, Mill reconciles all of these themes through the romantic use of the imagination: the ability to frame and shape values that brings meaning to human existence.

Mill uses this combination of human excellence and liberty to distinguish his position of the Religion of Humanity from that of Comte. Mill praises Comte for showing that a religion does not require a god to direct the energies of people to noble goals, but he criticizes Comte for increasingly placing individualism in conflict with his creed. Mill argues that Comte—"a morality-intoxicated man"—should learn from Catholicism's distinction between a morality obligatory on all believers and the standards required for attaining perfection. But "like the extreme Calvinists, [Comte] requires that all believers shall be saints, and damns them (after his own fashion) if they are not." In both *On Liberty* and the *Autobiography,* Mill charges that the elderly Comte's idea of religion as the singular aim of society is tyrannous.[48]

RATIONAL AND MORAL CRITIQUES

Mill's proposal for a Religion of Humanity stems from humans' inherent need for explanations to the most fundamental questions. It provides a vision as to what is the meaning and best forms of human existence. Mill's "Nature" and "Theism" tackle the same question from the opposite direction: the natural religion of the Enlightenment provides a low or vulgar picture as to what is the meaning and best forms of life.

Mill is keenly aware that his assessment that the Enlightenment's natural religion is irrational, immoral, and a detriment to self-development stands or falls in part on the validity of the method he proposes to assess it. He initially attempts to explain the existence of God by means of strictly natural causes. On nature, Mill adopts a Baconian outlook: a vast and interlocking network of efficient causes.[49] In order to explain God one must ultimately know if he is the cause whereby all things are determined. Mill's "famous methods of experimental enquiry are designed specifically to locate, by means of eliminative reasoning, a salient condition preceding or accompanying a phenomenon 'with which it is really connected by an invariable law.'" From the precepts of his inductive method, Mill analyzes arguments for Theism, focusing primarily on whether nature reflects Design.[50]

Mill's inductive *method of agreement* suggests that some parts of nature may have been designed by an intelligent will. The thought behind Mill's method of agreement is that no feature *not* common to the circumstances in which the phenomenon occurs can be its cause, since the phenomenon is capable of occurring in its absence. In short, if there is a sole feature common to all the different cases, this is the only remaining candidate to play the causal role.[51] While Mill considers this method the weakest of his four inductive approaches, he asserts that this particular argument is a strong one for this type. For instance, Mill cannot disprove the hypothesis that the eye has been designed. The disparate components of the eye resemble one another in that they all enable the eye to see. The conjunction of parts that form the eye had a foundation in time, suggesting another antecedent. The eye exists in a diverse set of animals, reducing the possibility of chance and suggesting a common antecedent. The distinct components of the different animals' eyes contribute to one end— sight—suggesting the possibility of Design.[52] Mill declares that the idea of a Creator cannot be denied, although it must be placed on the lower level of possibilities: "Though [this] ground is unsafe we may, with due caution, journey to a new destination on it." Skepticism is the right theoretical attitude toward God.[53]

However, the principles of scientific investigation are a necessary but insufficient condition for developing valid views of God, states Mill. It is not enough that God's existence be evaluated naturalistically. It is also necessary to distinguish the *moral meaning* of God from his *existence*.[54] This distinction can be understood better when seen in light of Hume's criticism of natural religion. For Hume, what is critical as we attempt to understand God is the way he works in nature. Accordingly, Hume's Philo in the *Dialogues on Natural History of Religion* explains how the physical world compromises or disproves all beliefs in God's existence. Hume's larger aim in doing this is to free our understanding of morality from any need of appeal to supernatural origins and maintenance. Human nature is adequate to evolve its own directives, and morality need not be imposed on us from above. "No action can be virtuous or morally good," states

Hume, "unless there be in human nature some motive to produce it, distinct from the sense of its morality."[55] Like Hume, Mill studies nature to determine God's existence. Unlike Hume, Mill also examines the moral implications of the view that a good and just Being created and governs the world. For Mill, our understanding of the immoral character of nature provides clues to the possible wisdom, power, and goodness of God. And Mill argues that "God still can be worshiped even if his power is limited, perhaps even if his intelligence is limited, but not if his moral character is questionable." Unlike Hume's, Mill's analysis of natural religion centers on the ethical and moral character of God and nature.[56]

Mill's "moral" approach to God and religious questions more generally differentiated his analysis of Darwinian and Theistic views on the origin of the species from that of his contemporaries. For instance, T. H. Huxley, W. H. Lecky, and Herbert Spencer viewed Darwinian and Theistic positions as the latest battle in the permanent conflict between reason and faith. In contrast, Benjamin Jowett and the Essayists who led the Broad Church party felt that Darwinism or any other result from scientific inquiry could not harm the teachings of Christian faith: all truth is God's truth. To Mill, Theism and Darwin offer different explanations of nature, and the philosopher reasons to evaluate the rational quality *and* moral implications of each theory.[57]

In "Nature" and "Theism," Mill primarily examines the modern natural law theorists' position that the existence and cohesion of civil society are the result of the natural power of morality. From this perspective, an objective, naturally recognized and followed standard of justice that predated society, enabled it to emerge, and now sustains it, is a real force in the world. Mill counters that there is no objective, rational standard of order derived from nature that constitutes a binding code of morality or natural law. He demonstrates this through his account of nature, which explains that, without the artificial aid of human activity, nature does not provide ends or purposes; it is chaotic, meaningless, and unjust:[58]

> Nature impales men, breaks them as if on the wheels, casts them to be devoured by wild beasts, burns them to be devoured, crushes them with stones like the first Christian martyr, starves them with hunger, freezes them with cold, poisons them by the quick or slow venom of her exaltations, and has hundreds of other hideous deaths in reserve, such as the ingenious cruelty of a Nabis or a Domitian never surpassed. All this, Nature does with the most supercilious disregard both of mercy and of justice, emptying her shafts upon the best and noblest indifferently with the meanest and the worst; upon those who are engaged in the highest and worthiest enterprises, and of-

ten as the consequence of the noblest acts; and it might almost be imagined as a punishment for them.[59]

How can a reckless nature, Mill asks, which ushers in anarchy, chaos, and injustice, be attributed to a God at once good and omnipotent? The problem remains that, for those with an "exercised intellect" to reconcile these conflicting views, there is no way to sustain belief, "save by sophistication and perversion, either of the understanding or of the conscience." It is only in the context of the artificial construct of civilization, Mill continues, "that the notion . . . ever could have grown up, that goodness was natural: because only after a long course of artificial education did good sentiments become so habitual, and so predominant over bad, as to arise unprompted when occasion called for them."[60]

Mill repudiates two key precepts of natural religion—that the machinery of nature creates a reciprocity of rights that is the foundation of justice and all social existence, and that the design of nature indicates a Deity who wills happiness for his creatures. Mill complains that these principles transform the conception of a developed existence into an essentially selfish existence. It debases the meaning of religion and insulates a prosaic, self-interested morality from scrutiny and reform: "This falling below the best of the ancients, and doing what lies in it to give human morality an essentially selfish character . . . disconnects each man's feelings of duty from the interests of his fellow creatures, except so far as a self-interested inducement is offered to him for consulting them."[61] Mill recognizes that human happiness exists, and that one cannot rule out that an Author of nature included this capacity in his design. But to infer from this capacity that the single or highest aim of the Creator is human happiness "is not only not justified by the evidence but is a conclusion in opposition to such evidence as we have."[62] Unfortunately, "the same slovenliness of thought, and subjection of the reason to fears, wishes, and affections, which enable them [the public] to accept such a theory involving a contradiction in terms, prevents them from seeing the logical consequences of the theory."[63]

Mill goes further and qualifies Pufendorf's position that God wills humanity's self-preservation. Observation of the species, responds Mill, reveals that little more can be said than that the Creator "does not wish His works to perish as soon as they are created." Mill concludes that "that much applauded class of authors, the writers on natural theology, have, I venture to think, entirely lost their way. . . . If the maker of the world *can* will all that he will, he wills misery, and there is no escape from the conclusion."[64] Mill summarizes a morally and intellectually consistent position for natural religion on the attributes of God:

"A Being of great but limited power, how or by what limited we cannot even conjecture; of great, and perhaps unlimited intelligence, but perhaps, also, more narrowly limited than His power: who desires, and pays some regard to, the happiness of his creatures, but who seems to have other motives which he cares more for, and who can hardly be supposed to have created the universe for that purpose alone. Such is the Deity that Natural Religion points to."[65]

Going on the offensive, Mill argues that the continued association of an omnipotent and omniscient God with an "immoral" nature contributes to the love of God being based on the worship of power. Such a view diminishes the distinction between noble and maleficent force and lowers the idea of a good human being: "The tendency of the human mind to the worship of power, is well understood." Now, God is worshiped by an immense majority as "the Almighty, not as the All-good, as he who can destroy, not as he who has blessed."[66] Equally important, the stance that nature reflects God's will contributes to a political and moral outlook that is not interventionist toward nature, including human nature. Natural religion, in Mill's account, reinforces traditional empiricism's restricted view that justice and the good existence are mere mechanical effects of incentives. This view that human conduct is automated obedience to causal natural laws turns its back on an integral dimension of the human condition: mental and moral development. "When the mind is no longer compelled . . . ," Mill writes, "to exercise its vital powers on the questions which its beliefs present to it, there is a progressive tendency to forget all of the belief except the formularies, or to give a dull and torpid assent, as if accepting it on trust dispensed with the necessity of realizing it in consciousness, or testing it by personal evidence, until it almost ceases to connect itself at all with the inner life of the human being."[67]

Mill charges that natural religion contributes to a vague notion "that though it is very proper to control this or that natural phenomenon, the general scheme of nature is a model to imitate: that with more or less liberty in details, we should on the whole be guided by the spirit and general conception of nature's ways." He counters that "to bid people conform to the laws of nature when they have no power but what the laws of nature give them is an absurdity." Although nature may at times fill us with awe and wonder, no one who has studied it seriously would establish nature as a normative standard or ought: "Nature cannot be a proper model for us to imitate. Either it is right that we should kill because nature kills; torture because nature tortures; ruin and devastate because nature does the like; or we ought not to consider at all what nature does, but what it is good to do." If confronted by a choice between nature and artifice,

Mill clearly opts that the side of freedom and progress is certainly with the latter. "There is hardly anything valuable in the natural man except capacities," declares Mill, "a whole world of possibilities, all of them dependent upon eminently artificial discipline for being realized." The Enlightenment's natural religion, Mill concludes, limits the role of artificial discipline and fetters development of higher modes of human life.[68]

REASON AND POETRY

Mill concludes the last essay of the *Three Essays on Religion,* "Theism," by staking out a position on natural religion that will further his goal of cultivating human agency and self-development. Mill posits that, at most, we are left with the hope that there is a creator and an afterlife. He now asks, What is the proper attitude the philosopher should take to this god whose very existence is considered to be only marginally possible, whose power over matter is not absolute, whose love for his creatures is not his single actuating aim? Should the philosopher include this god in the ethics and morality of the future? Mill is asking himself the same question that he believes Plato unsuccessfully confronted: What is the proper relation between reason and poetry, reason and faith?[69] That is, what is the relation between philosophy's quest to discover the truth and the social need for ennobling poetical and religious teachings?

In answering these questions, Mill once again weaves his way through empiricism and romanticism—expanding beyond the bounded, reproductive view of the imagination posited by the Anglo-Scottish tradition, while also rejecting the boundlessly creative imagination of the German Romantics. To an early Anglo-Scottish thinker such as Hobbes, the poet was a mere recorder, whose imagination was only a "sort of decaying memory." Moreover, Hobbes emphasized that the human imagination's response to fear of the unknown led to "the greatest part of the religion of the gentiles in times past, that worshiped satyrs, fawns, nymphs, and the like; and now-a days the opinion that rude people have of fairies, ghosts, and goblins, and the power of witches." For later Anglo-Scottish thinkers such as Hume and Smith, the imagination had a slightly wider significance: a type of aggregative power that may, by a process of association, rearrange ready-made elements so as to establish a new pattern. The imagination has the potential to provide extra, adding beauty or color to the impressions of truth known through sensory experience. But because the imagination has the potential to create both deception and harmony, these thinkers never overcame their ambivalent attitude toward it. On the one hand, states

Hume, "nothing is more dangerous to reason than the flights of the imagination, and nothing has been the occasion of more mistakes among philosophers." On the other hand, Hume continues, we save ourselves from the total skepticism of the world created by philosophy "by means of that singular and seemingly trivial property of the fancy, by which we enter with difficulty into remote views of things."[70]

For the German Romantics, the objects that impressions throw off are always of far less consequence than the imagination, by means of which the individual—most notably, the artist—seeks to control and reshape the outside world. To these thinkers, the mind does not reflect external objects; it is a radiant projector that shapes and reshapes the world we see. Many German Romantics rejected the idea that objective laws solely govern an external world, arguing that the artist's imagination is the tool with which to transform and create the world. Here the most creative individuals combine nature and art, both the knowledge of understood rules and a spontaneous creativity that transcended conventions and prevailing practices. The former can be taught and learned, but the latter is a gift of nature.[71]

Mill argues that the German Romantics have gone too far. He is unwilling to endorse such a radical subjectivism. Mill insists that the imagination is not a blind or spontaneous agent: it must respect the laws of nature and society that have been discovered by science and philosophy. "The Germans . . . have perverted both thought and phraseology," he writes, "when they made Artist the term for expressing the highest order of moral and intellectual greatness. The older idea is true—that Art, in relation to Truth, is but a language. Philosophy is the proper name for that exercise of the intellect which enucleates the truth to be expressed. The Artist is not the Seer; not he who can detect truth, but he who can clothe a given truth in the most expressive and impressive symbols."[72]

Mill also denies the view prevalent among nineteenth-century Anglo-Scottish thinkers that scientific investigations can provide normative guidance to philosophers on the proper goals and ends of a political society.[73] To Mill, science primarily enables philosophers who aim to create or legislate such goals to avoid foolish and futile proposals. He explains that the philosophic legislator's Art or Poetry shapes chaotic nature into a harmonious whole and structures human conduct at different levels and ends. To Mill, the artistic side of political philosophy—the *poietic* feature of political philosophy—defines and proposes ends to be attained by different sections of society and hands them over to science for investigation. The scientific side of the political philosopher studies the aims and sends them back to Art with a theorem of the combination of circumstances by which they could be produced. At this point, Mill concludes, "Art then examines these combinations of circumstances, and according as any of them are not in human power, pronounces the end attainable or not." The philosopher's vision of the good society "is thus a joint result of laws of nature disclosed by science, and of the general principles of what has been called . . . the Doctrine of Ends."[74]

In Mill's account, the political and moral philosopher combines in himself the elements of art and reason, the ability to create meanings for human existence within the context of knowable laws of nature and society: "Now, the imperative mood is the characteristic of art, as distinguished from science[,] . . . and ethics or morality is properly a portion of the art corresponding to the sciences of human nature and society. . . . The complete art of any matter includes a selection of such a portion from the science as is necessary to show on what conditions the effects which the art aims at producing depend."[75] Mill posits that the imaginative mind that does not conflict too sharply with philosophic and scientific understandings of the truth is a powerful constructive influence in society. Art is good as long as it hovers around the understanding of reason, as opposed to conflicting with reason, as religion often does.

CHRISTIANITY OF THE FUTURE

Mill retains this framework on the relation between Art and Science in his assessment of the role Christianity or any type of theism will play in the morality of the future. Anticipating the prosaic character of modernity, Mill cautions future philosophy to leave as much room as possible to "even small probabilities on this subject [God] which furnish the imagination with any footing to support itself upon." To Mill, it is legitimate to establish hope for the Christian idea of God provided that it is a God of limited powers. Consistent with his support of Plato's natural religion in the *Statesman* and his view that Christianity is moral as long as it continues to reform itself, Mill states that if people need a God let them conceive in their imagination a Being unlimited in goodness but limited in power, thereby freeing themselves of the moral confusion created by the idea of the all-powerful and benevolent God: "If the maker of the world *can* all that he will, he wills misery, and there is no escape from the conclusion." The recognition of such a God of limited powers could possibly help check ideas that life is insignificant. More important, it provides a moral imperative to the tasks of encouraging human energy and cultivating human character. Rather than regarding life and nature as reflections of the moral character of the Deity, Christianity should see the world as the product of a conflict between God's contrived goodness and an intractable matter.[76]

Mill believes that this type of Christianity is not inconsistent with his proposed Religion of Humanity, which puts forth creative deeds that serve the public good as the highest type of life. He also believes that this position on natural religion avoids the problem he identifies with most of Plato's art, as this poetic idea of God does not conflict too sharply with reason. "Truth is the province of reason," states Mill, "and it is by the cultivation of the rational faculty that provision is made for its being known always, and thought of as often as is required by duty and circumstance of human life. But when the reason is strongly cultivated, the imagination may safely follow its own end, and do its best to make life pleasant and lovely inside the castle, in reliance on the fortifications raised and maintained by Reason round the outward bounds."[77]

How seriously Mill took to the possibility of a restoration of deep beliefs in a Christian God can only be a matter of speculation. We do know for certain that Mill felt such beliefs should not center on the idea of an omnipotent creator. Still, he is willing to maintain God's goodness, however facetious or serious Mill may be. Christianity must take another step, however. Only by reforming the natural religion that had reformed revealed Christianity, concludes Mill, could Christian beliefs contribute to ending intellectual and moral confusion and help establish practices and values that generate human creativity that contributes to the public good.

CHRISTIANITY AND MODERNITY

Mill's position that modern England is a secularization of Christian beliefs in key dimensions has important continuities and differences with positions developed by seminal Continental philosophers. By situating Mill's position in relation to some of these thinkers, Mill's (and the other philosophers') self-imposed task for formulating a morality of the future grows clearer. Kant, for instance, maintained that Christianity inaugurated "the moral law" that created "a thoroughgoing revolution in doctrines of faith." The Christian religion, Kant writes, taught what no prior ethical philosophy—whether Cynic, Epicurean, or Stoic—had recognized: The moral law in all its purity provided both an opportunity and a necessity for our own moral development. Among all historical faiths, Christianity best embodied the essence of pure, rational ethical religion, discoverable behind the symbolism of its various dogmas and rituals. What enabled Christianity to develop this universal character, Kant continued, is its founding as a moral, rather than a statutory, religion: "and as thus entering into the closest relation with reason so that, through reason, it was able of itself, without historical learning, to be spread at all times and among all peoples with the greatest trustworthiness." Jesus' essential message was the public promulgation of a "pure rational faith," a "moral religion" consisting of the same moral law that all persons already find in their hearts. Kant's self-imposed task was to complete the revolution initiated by Christianity. This required the negative task of clearing up the inconsistencies and mystical notions of the old historical religions, including those of Christianity, which had to be done before the constructive goal of establishing a new moral religion of reason could be fully accomplished.[78]

In his accounts of Plato, and then of Jesus and the Apostle Paul, Hegel argued that all were unable to integrate subjective freedom with a new universalistic outlook; a failure that continued to plague Western culture.[79] However, to Hegel, the secularization and diffusion of the Protestant moral conscience had begun to overcome this schism and become the great engine of history from the Reformation to the French Revolution, "as everything in the moral and spiritual world began to be submitted to subjective thought." Human beings "are unwilling to acknowledge in their attempts anything which has not been justified by thought," states Hegel. This subjective freedom "is the characteristic property of the modern age, as well as being the distinctive principle of Protestantism." Hegel maintains that this subjective point of view, "one that ties moral evaluation to the purity of intentions and admits as good only intentions to obey" subjective freedom, "is itself a historical practice." It does not simply discover at a certain time what "pure reason determines as obligatory." Indeed, in Hegel's assessment of Socrates, this moral conscience, when isolated from other moral considerations, necessarily leads to radical subjectivism and nihilism.[80]

Indeed, Hegel's self-imposed task is to allow the present historical epoch to understand itself, as the subjective will derived from Protestantism realizes the objective determinations of right and duty: "In this way the ethical substantial order has attained its right, and its right to validity. That is to say, the self-will of the individual has vanished together with the private conscience that had claimed independence and had opposed itself to the ethical substance."[81] Modern institutions such as family, civil law, commerce, association in corporations, some form of representative political life, and a world order of states all embody modern social roles within which the subjective freedom of agents derived from Protestantism is realized. These institutions are the true objects of the subjective will and the embodiment of human freedom. The philosopher's task is to comprehend and identify this realization.[82]

Mill also embraces the idea that modern England is a secular realization of Christian principles in important dimensions. But Mill emphasizes the negative consequences that stem from this continuity. In his account, both outlooks continue the historical tendency of new modes of thought, discarding the half-truths of that mode of thought it supersedes. English liberalism continues Christianity's opposition to the active and energetic human qualities that lead to high ambitions, dignity, self-respect, self-command, and exertions of human energy. While the modern Englishman is more just than the ancient Greek, he has far less faith in himself as an agent of his own desires, has less energy, and, in important respects, is less free:

> Comparing the best Grecian with the best modern community, is the superiority solely on the side of the moderns? Has there not been deterioration as well as improvement, and the former perhaps almost as marked as the latter? There is more humanity, more mildness of manners, though this only from a comparatively recent date; the sense of moral obligation is more cosmopolitan, and depends less for its acknowledgement on the existence of some special tie. But we greatly doubt if most of the positive virtues were not better conceived, and more highly prized, by the public opinion of Greece than by that of Great Britain; while negative and passive qualities have now engrossed the chief part of the honour paid to virtue; and it may be questioned if even private duties are, on the whole, better understood, while duties to the public, unless in cases of special trust, have almost dropped out of the catalogue: that idea, so powerful in the free States of Greece, has faded into a mere rhetorical ornament.[83]

Mill also is far less hopeful about an imminent realization of principles of freedom than either Kant or Hegel. The antagonistic relations between opposing ideas demonstrate that one-sidedness is the rule and synthesis is the exception. And there does not seem to be any alternative to this constant action and reaction of historically significant modes of thought. Public opinion rallies around the dominant idea of truth, while oppositionists, rather than aiming to add to the "suppressed and neglected truths" that form the necessary balance to the received ones, establish an alternative one-sided idea as the whole truth. "One-sidedness has always been the rule . . . ," Mill asserts. "Even progress, which ought to superadd, for the most part only substitutes one partial and incomplete truth for another; improvement consisting chiefly in this, that the new fragment of truth is more wanted, more adapted to the needs of the time, than that which it displaces."[84] Mill's position that a synthesis of contrasting ideas of liberty is not imminent will lead to a dramatic—and arguably self-defeating—innovation in his political philosophy.

Thus, in Mill's account, contrasting ideas of Western morality have issued conflicting lessons. On the one hand, the classical and romantic-expressive outlooks (in different ways) teach that the will, powerful desires, developed rationality, pride, and the desire for distinctiveness and excellence are powerful springs for human agency. On the other hand, Christianity's moral universalism and English liberalism's justice instruct the importance of equality, obedience, and general moral development. Mill summarizes that neither of these outlooks is the law of human development, as their admirers are prone to make them. He believes that the political philosopher in general and himself in particular must desire and work for the reconciliation of these giant adversaries. The resolution of their respective thesis and antithesis into the synthesis of a comprehensive morality of the future is the philosopher's highest goal. Is Mill capable of mediating this fault line in Western morality?

Chapter 6 *On Liberty:* The *Summmum Bonum* of Modern Liberalism

Modern liberal thought does not center on human perfection or the best life. "Liberalism's deepest conviction is in place" from its very inception, in the belief of the earliest defenders of toleration, born in horror at the religious wars, "that cruelty is an absolute evil, an offense against God or humanity." It is because of that tradition that liberal political philosophy has generally resisted views that there is a *summum bonum,* or best way of life.[1] Liberal thinkers have generally feared that a standard of what is best could easily grant political authorities the unconditional right to impose beliefs and practices on the citizenry to that end. Enlightenment views and shifts in theoretical outlooks reinforced this view—in particular, scientific skepticism about a moral order external and independent of human beings— which revealed that the idea of the best life was a human invention and often a product of a society's particular needs and values. Hence liberals generally insist that the quest for perfection be relegated to the private sphere of religious beliefs or aesthetic self-expression. Liberalism generally focuses on the characteristics of a political order that will avoid the *summum malum,* the highest evil, making the aim of politics the more limited goal of avoiding the worst rather than realizing the best. Mill sets out to fill this putative vacuum in liberal thought in *On Liberty*.

Mill's goal in chapter 3 of *On Liberty* is to establish a quality which characterized Athenian democracy but is noticeably absent in modern societies: an idea of human excellence or "an acceptable standard of virtuous conduct."[2] Mill's *initial* portrait of human excellence is clearly consistent with his admiration for both the Platonic dialectic and the Athenian creative will, as both Socrates and Pericles are projected as the highest type of human beings throughout the chapter. Indeed, Pericles is presented as the standard of human excellence or *summum bonum* for humanity, representing as he does the creative individual who transcends ordinary practices and views to realize the public good. At the same time, however, Mill also invokes themes in this discussion consistent with his appreciation for Sparta, the goal of Plato's moral teachings, and, most important, the modern moral conscience. The celebration of willful, creative individuals, warns Mill, must not be allowed to degenerate into support for types like Alcibiades, individuals who transcend the ordinary to pursue private gain at public expense. To this end, he fuses or synthesizes the Christian/modern conception of universal justice, which is represented by the Calvinist reformer John Knox, with the ancient creativity of Pericles.

This initial discussion of the best life, however, does not end Mill's examination of human excellence in *On Liberty*. Upon analyzing the type of environment that must be fostered to cultivate human flourishing, Mill reformulates his own proposal on human excellence and adopts a more expressive conception of the highest life. Here the developed individual distinguishes himself through his uniqueness and opposition to public opinion, encouraging alternative modes of existence that will contribute to new synthetic truths and higher modes of existence. In England, Mill warns, the long term, back and forth battle between contrasting conceptions of liberty has faded, and an era of listless quiescence is arriving. To replenish our capacity for human agency, which is a precondition for human progress and human liberty, we need to encourage and support alternative modes of existence, with individuals experiencing conflict between themselves and society.

The movement of Mill's thought in chapter 3 of *On Liberty* is through the two major discussions that constitute its basic structure: the essential need for a conception of human excellence that synthesizes ancient and modern conceptions of liberty, and an expressive idea of the best life that is characterized by spontaneity, struggle, and self-development. I examine both visions of developed individuality—showing what they invoke, what qualities they exemplify, how they are similar, how they are different, why each conflicted with English liberalism, and why, in Mill's view, the expressive conception of human excellence is ultimately preferable. Mill's hierarchical politics, as I show, are linked to his expressive conception of the best life, and Mill envisions intellectuals reconciling and synthesizing diverse ways of life into new synthetic political and moral truths for society.

THE FREE INDIVIDUAL

In chapter 3 of *On Liberty,* Mill's various analyses of the developed individual revolve around the various themes examined in this book: the cultivation of reason (Plato); the necessity for strong desires and will (Athens); the continuity between Christianity and modernity (fidelity to a universal authority); a picture of human perfection that combines creativity and concern for the public good (Religion of Humanity and aesthetic culture); the overcoming of the oscillations in Western morality between competing conceptions of liberty (ancient versus moderns, empiricism versus romanticism); the integration of the reformed Platonic dialectic with the synthetic dialectic of Coleridge and the German Romantics; and the necessity to reform compatibilism—that is, the need to formulate a conception of liberty that combines empiricism's causality and the romantic conception of free will. Mill introduces his discussion of a modern idea of human excellence while praising von Humboldt's view that freedom and variety of situations are the requisites to human individuality. Mill grants the value of previous experiences but argues that what distinguishes humanity from other species is the capacity of individual members to choose which parts of the past are appropriate for his or her needs. "No one's idea of excellence in conduct," states Mill, "is that people should do absolutely nothing but copy one another." Trends and customs may be too restrictive and, more important, may fetter the creative individual, to the great loss of society as a whole.[3]

Mill posits that a free approach to customs is desirable because it fosters a certain type of human being. In understanding the causes of our actions and desires, we no longer acquiesce to them but proactively and consciously submit them to the control of our rational faculties. Choice in regard to different modes of existence performs the same task as Plato's dialectic, allowing for the development of individual judgment, which is the highest quality of human life: "The human faculties of perception, judgment, discriminative feeling, mental activity, and even moral preference are exercised only in making a choice." Rather than being subjected to the pursuit of one's empirically given desires, this individual knows himself to be a creature of social practices that he neither blindly submits to nor vainly rejects but takes an active interest in identifying their value. This liberated self is a master of his passions and his goals. He thinks about life and the roads he is required to take in developing it. He is truly free.[4]

More important, Mill argues that freedom of action is necessary if individuals are to realize the qualities essential to self-mastery. Strength of character is forged through making decisions and realizing aims. If the individual does not actively engage the world, "he gains no practice in discerning or desiring what is best." If an individual fails to consciously choose and resolutely pursue a way of life, his distinct human qualities of reason and will atrophy, for "the mental and moral, like the muscular powers, are improved only by being used." By contrast, "he who lets the world, or his own portion of it, choose his plan of life for him, has no need of any other faculty than the ape-like one of imitation." The value of human life, Mill continues, depends not only on what an individual does but also upon what he becomes. An individual who leads a decent and productive life but allows his life to be completely structured by others is no more than a machine. "It is possible that he might be guided in some good path, and kept out of harm's way, without any of these [reason and will] things. But what will be his comparative worth as a human being?" Mill asks. "Human nature is not a machine to be built after a model, and set to do exactly the work prescribed for it, but a tree, which requires to grow and develop itself on all sides, according to the tendency of the inward forces that make it a living thing."[5] Whereas the key figures of romanticism, Rousseau and Kant, had consistently juxtaposed the human species with machines and other animals to identify a supposed supranatural or transcendent character of the human species, Mill uses the same contrast to make his argument more morally compelling, while eschewing Rousseau's and Kant's assumption that human beings have the capacity to overcome nature.[6]

Human excellence, however, demands not only the cultivation of reason and energy, but also the elevation of the will. Mill puts forth the positive role of impulse in enabling the individual to gain self-command. Consistent with his analysis of Athens, Mill posits that powerful desires contribute to strong wills, and that the stronger the will, the more raw materials exist for an autonomous existence that originates new practices. Mill concedes that such drive is a double-edged sword. It may be the source of either good or evil energy: "but more good may always be made of an energetic nature than that of an indolent and impassive one . . . as . . . one whose desires and impulses are not his own has no character, no more than a steam engine has character." Unable to comprehend the proper relation between strong desires and the general good, English liberalism has instead focused on circumscribing the passions, cutting willfulness off at the source rather than trying to trim the bad and keep the good. Mill counters with the same lesson he drew from his engagements with Plato and the Athenian creative will: the key to the moral character of human agency and energy is the cultivation of the just moral conscience; the drives and desires that inspire action are moderated, channeled, and uplifted by a morality of justice. "It is not because men's desires are strong that they act ill: it is because their consciences are weak. There is no natural connection between strong impulses and a weak conscience," argues Mill. "Desires and impulses are as much a part of a perfect human being as beliefs and restraints; and strong impulses are only perilous when not properly balanced, when one set of aims and inclinations is developed into strength, while others, which ought to coexist with them, remain weak and inactive." Internal direction of the desires by equally important forces of reason, will, and justice, Mill concludes, contributes to human perfection, and a society that denies the role of strong desires does not progress.

Mill anticipates objections to his position that a will forged around strong desires contributes to developed individuality. Not only does the denial of such a will stabilize a stagnant status quo, but, worse yet, this self-denying conformity is lauded as human excellence. Here is where Mill reintroduces his thesis that English liberalism is a secular extension of Christianity in an important domain. The modern conception of fidelity to law, Mill argues, continues the Calvinist tradition of cultivating the passive, obedient individual as the highest type. While many liberals in England do not recognize this affinity with Calvinism, these moderns, in fact, merely substitute obedience to one external authority for another, the first in heaven, the current in rules and public opinion. The Christian and English modern obey external authority:

> It is so, on the Calvinistic theory. According to that, the one great offense of man is self-will . . . and it is held, in a mitigated form, by many who do not consider themselves Calvinists; the mitigation consisting in giving a less ascetic interpretation to the alleged will of God, asserting it to be his will that man should gratify some of their inclinations, of course not in the manner that they prefer, but in the way of obedience, that is, in a way prescribed to them by authority, and, therefore, by the necessary condition of the case, the same for all. . . . Many persons, no doubt, sin-

cerely think that human beings thus cramped and dwarfed are as their Maker designed them to be, just as many have thought that trees are a much finer thing when clipped into pollards, or cut out into figures of animals, than as nature made them.[7]

Once again, Mill laments the one-sided development of Western morality. He recognizes the contribution of the moral universalism of Christianity, which gave rise to a Church that assumed responsibility for heaping its precepts on all sectors of society, including the warlike kings and other barbarous types: "There was a time when the element of spontaneity and individuality was in excess, and the social principle had a hard struggle with it. The difficulty then was to induce men of strong bodies or minds to pay obedience to any rules which required them to control their impulses." But history swung too much to the other side. The exclusive emphasis on taming individuality has existed for too long and now threatens to eradicate completely humanity's capacity to will and create. Mill suggests that those inculcated in this sort of regime, who "become incapable of any strong wishes or native pleasures," have their human nature "maim[ed] by compression, like a Chinese lady's foot."[8] To put this in terms of Mill's understanding of some of the topics already discussed: Sparta's stability is being raised above Athenian creativity; Nicias, not Pericles, represents human excellence; Plato's poetry and moral statements stand above the liberating dialectic; Kant's idea of human excellence prevails over Mill's idea of the best life.

Consistent with his view of both the Religion of Humanity and natural religion, Mill argues that a religion more consistent with the idea of a "good Being" would establish human excellence as a life in which the "human faculties . . . [are] . . . cultivated and unfolded, not rooted out and consumed."[9] Here Mill puts forth the historical figures of Pericles, Alcibiades, and Knox to illustrate human perfection: the fusion of ancient and modern qualities leading to the highest possible good. Pericles, of course, is the Athenian statesman who creatively led the Athenian citizenry to serve the public good, and Mill consistently puts him forward as the model of human excellence: "It is impossible to estimate how great a share this one man had in making the Athenians what they were. A great man had, in the unbounded publicity of Athenian political life, extraordinary facilities for molding his country after his own image; and seldom has any people, during a whole generation, enjoyed such a course of education, as forty years of listening to the lofty spirit and practical wisdom of Pericles must have been to the Athenian Demos." Mill emphasized Pericles' ability to combine reason and action, intellect and deed, quoting that part of Pericles' "Funeral Oration" which posits that intellectual speculation does not lead to enervation. Pericles said, "Far from accounting discussion an impediment to action, we think it an evil not to have been instructed by deliberation before the time of execution arrives. For, in truth, we combine in a remarkable manner boldness in action with full debate beforehand on that which we are going about: whereas with others ignorance alone imparts daring, debate induces hesitation." As Alexander Bain summarizes, "Pericles . . . was [Mill's] greatest hero of antiquity."[10]

But Mill recognized that Pericles was not the typical Athenian leader. He regretted Athens's unstructured public opinion, which contributed to its political fortunes being dependent on the whims of forceful leaders, as the direction of leadership that innovative types provided was to a large extent based on their qualities as individuals. And to Mill, Alcibiades, the general who flattered the Athenian public into adopting policies that encouraged his own good irrespective of public expense—as most notably expressed by his proposal for the Sicilian invasion while Athens was in a militarily vulnerable position—teaches the dangers of the innovative will when severed from the morality of justice. While Pericles was good and right, the creative will that combines reason and fortitude is not virtue in itself and not always politically constructive because it may engender unjust deeds. Pericles and Alcibiades were both tremendously willful, but their wills served different ends, one leading to Athens's greatest glory, the other to its demise.[11]

Finally, Mill, who studied Thomas M'Crie's laudatory biography, *Life of John Knox,* as a child, considered Knox to be a "heroic figure by the side of Martin Luther." Mill's attraction to Knox is not a surprise.[12] Knox had led the Protestant Reformation's opposition to superstition and ecclesiastical authority in Scotland and, more important, significantly contributed to Christianity's development as a universal morality. Knox, for instance, had held that to participate in the Catholic mass was irrevocably to violate "the league and covenant of God," which "requires that we declare ourselves enemies to all sorts of idolatry."[13] Knox's biblical commentaries and interpretations centered on establishing the precepts of Christianity as a universal moral law. In the *First Blast of the Trumpet,* he declared that the fundamental authority was "the law moral . . . the constant and unchangeable will of God to which the Gentile is no less bound than the Jew." Knox combed through the Old and New Testaments to create a biblical "case law," establishing precedents that were universally binding because they revealed to humankind the immutable laws of God.[14] In Mill's account, Knox represents Christianity and English liberalism's emphasis on obedience to a universal authority, a contribution which has directly led to the English being far more just to their fellow citizens than the Continental people are to the members of their respective societies.

For a new idea of human excellence, Mill argues, one must reach back beyond Christianity to the ancient age, when "pagan self-assertion" (Pericles and Alcibiades) was encouraged. But he also realizes that society's cultivation of a creative will can produce individuals who put forward their will at the expense of others (Alcibiades) as well as individuals who assert themselves in order to pursue the public good (Pericles). He concludes that there is a need to develop an idea of human excellence that synthesizes the reason and fortitude of Pericles with the ideas of self-control represented by Plato and, most important, John Knox: "There is a different type of excellence[,] . . . a Greek ideal of self-development, which the Platonic and Christian ideal of self-government blends with, but does not supersede. It may be better to be a John Knox than an Alcibiades, but it is better to be Pericles than either; nor would a Pericles, if we had one in these days, be without anything good which belonged to John Knox."[15]

Mill is well known for the assertion in *On Liberty* that only by establishing the overcoming of uniformity as human excellence "will human beings become a noble and beautiful object of contemplation," and that *these* individuals are the source of creativity, the geniuses that generate new knowledge about what is true. But it is generally overlooked that Mill also argues that such individuals are not merely the product of willfulness or self-creation; they also are the products of "compression," "restraint," and "rigid rules of justice."[16] Alan Ryan, for instance, misses this point and makes the same one-sided, half-truth mistake that Mill spends all of his time railing against. Whereas Mill posits a dialectical relation or Coleridgean synthesis between an ancient ethos of creativity and the Christian/modern quality of obedience to universal authority, Ryan sees only the praise of self-assertion and paganism and the rejection of self-restraint and Christianity. "The target of Mill's assault was self-abnegation," states Ryan. "He contrasted Christian with pagan self-assertion. . . . One can forgive Mill for following Machiavelli in praising pagan self-assertion to the detriment of the Christian ideal of self-abnegation. In gross at any rate that contrast holds up perfectly well."[17]

But Mill advocates the *blending*, not the severance, of the contrasting aims of self-development and self-government. A person who has reason, strong will, and justice (Pericles) would be a great individual, one who combines the good and the right and as a result is a higher type than one who had only justice. But the just individual (Knox) would also be right, while those with only creative wills are not necessarily right (Alcibiades). In fact, they can be downright horrible for society. After identifying the goal of combining the qualities of Pericles and Knox, Mill explains,

> As much compression as is necessary to prevent the stronger specimens of human nature from encroaching on the rights of others cannot be dispensed with; but for this there is ample compensation even in the point of view of human development. The means of development which the individual loses by being prevented from gratifying his inclinations to the injury of others are chiefly obtained at the expense of the development of other people. And even to himself there is a full equivalent in the better development of the social part of his nature, rendered possible by the restraint placed on the selfish part. To be held to rigid rules of justice for the sake of others develops the feelings and capacities which have the good of others for their object. But to be restrained in things not affecting their good, by their mere displeasure, develops nothing valuable except such force of character as may unfold itself in resisting the restraint. If acquiesced in, it dulls and blunts the whole nature. To give any fair play to the nature of each, it is essential that the different persons should be allowed to live different lives. In proportion as this latitude has been exercised in any age has that age been noteworthy to posterity.[18]

In this densely worded paragraph Mill is focusing on the proper relation between founding-type individuals and the moral outlook and rules of justice, and he argues that the forceful desire for human excellence is channeled and raised by adherence to principles of justice that uphold the universal good. Mill asserts that to prevent the innovative from encroaching on the rights of others (Alcibiades), authoritative rules are required. But the creative are amply compensated for the limitations they must endure. Social imperatives and injunctions prevent the creative themselves from being harmed and, more important, cultivate human sociality and concern for the well-being of others among those who are capable of creating new norms and conventions (Pericles). Moral universalism (Knox), in Mill's account, is not inimical to human perfection: the rules and mores of justice contribute to self-preservation and, by channeling creative practices in a more public direction, contribute to a more comprehensive outlook and the fuller development of character. Authoritative rules and norms are only harmful, Mill continues, when they are established irrespective of the public good—inducing either uncontrolled willfulness or acquiescence. An age is noteworthy, Mill concludes, the more it is able to establish obligatory assumptions that induce strong-willed individuals to be creative in ways that address the needs of those that live within the common framework, allowing both types of natures—the creative (Pericles) and the obeying (Knox)—to co-exist and attain their true character.[19]

ANCIENT AND MODERN JUSTICE

On the basis of Mill's teachings on Pericles and Knox and his call for "fair play" with divergent types of natures, a new vision of justice begins to appear, one that reconciles crucial features of the ancient and modern conceptions. For the ancients, justice exhibits a fit between an individual's distinct nature, understood as one's capacities and aptitude and one's social and political position. Aristotle, for instance, argues in *The Politics* that it would be unjust to treat the better sort of individual like everyone else: "Justice is held to be equality, and it is, but for equals and not for all; and inequality is held to be just and is indeed, but for unequals and not for all."[20] Plato, of course, is a prototypical ancient thinker on this theme, maintaining that the philosopher must discern the various kinds of soul, whether to identify the focus of discourse appropriate to each[21] or to discover the appropriate roles in a political regime. Not that Plato envisioned the construction of a just regime to be an easy political task. In attempting to describe a perfectly just city in the *Republic,* Socrates initially depicts a simple city centered on addressing only the basic needs of its members. Although simple, this city exhibits a division of labor because by focusing on a specific task people do a better job than they would as generalists. Beyond the specialization, what characterizes this city is that each person in it displays a fitness for some particular task important to the city. Every individual chooses an occupation according to his natural capacities so that everything corresponds to his desires or talents. Each contributes according to his ability and receives according to his needs, and this is justice. Each of us, summarizes Socrates, "is naturally not quite like anyone else, but rather differs in his nature; different men are apt for the accomplishments of different jobs." In such a just city, there is a complete correspondence between private interests and the public good.[22]

Unfortunately, however, not all of the tasks of the city are equal. Socrates' interlocutor, Adeimantus, notes that for a farmer or a craftsman to idly sit by in the marketplace waiting for buyers would be tedious. To this difficult problem of filling jobs of distinct desirability, Socrates reaffirms that individuals' natures should decide what positions they occupy. In the healthy or just city, he continues, those whose bodies are weak would occupy the market; those whose bodies are strong would be wage laborers. "There are," states Socrates, "some . . .

servants who, in terms of their mind, wouldn't be quite up to the level of part-nership, but whose bodies are strong enough for labor. They sell the use of their strength and, because they call their price a wage, they are, I suppose, called wage earners." From this perspective, each person being suited by nature to his task characterizes the just city, and each task is necessary to the city. All of the necessary positions are filled, no positions are unnecessary, and every individual contributes to the city to the best of his talents. The just city enables each per-son to realize his natural capacities and serve the general good.[23]

However, except in this most basic city, which Glaucon refers to as the "City of Sows," Socrates indicates that the fit between an individual's nature and so-cial and political position will be very difficult to accomplish. Warriors, for in-stance, are required to defend feverish and luxurious cities. These warriors must be suited by nature to their task, but their natures must also be carefully culti-vated. And even after such careful attention is paid to individual natures and their education, Socrates broaches issues that suggest the just regime is not pos-sible. After all, the city needs a lie to legitimize the distinct social and political positions: this noble lie falsely claims that the distinct classes of the city are dis-tinguished at birth. The souls of rulers are mixed at birth with gold, guardians with silver, while more plebeian types are distinguished in their constitution by iron and bronze. Plato's politics of the noble lie suggest that there is an arbitrary character to the ancients' "natural" hierarchy, that not all individuals' natures fit the position that they perform, and that the reconciliation of the particular and general good is a problematic task.[24]

Closer to modern thought, Machiavelli's political outlook also centers on the task of discovering the proper fit for different human kinds—ruler and ruled, or the commanding and the obeying. There are, Machiavelli said, "two diverse humors to be found in every city," "two diverse appetites," and they are ex-pressed in turn in "the people" and "the great," the ruled and the ruler.[25] In-deed, up until Machiavelli, there is a consistent discussion of founders or legis-lators such as Lycurgus, Solon, Moses, Theseus, Romulus, Numa, and Cyrus in analyses of political regimes. It was taken for granted that tasks such as the for-mation and maintenance of a political union or the attainment of deeds of last-ing importance required individuals of surpassing talents to achieve them, and that these individuals often had to utilize ruthless practices.

In contrast, the seminal thinkers of British empiricism shift the emphasis to-ward identifying the contract or agreement that is the foundation of civil order, where all that is required of individuals is that they be clear about their personal interests and where they intersect with those of others. The formation of the civil state is posited to be almost automatic. Hobbes, Locke, and Hume saw that the aspirations of so-called heroic types contributed to humanity's problems, on the grounds that the heroic encouraged fanaticism and warlike qualities. Hobbes, for instance, claims that although everyone is self-interested only a small section of people are strongly ambitious or contentious from a love of glory or salvation. While the majority of people are compliant, a minority of the populace is intemperate. "For one man, according to that natural equality which is among us, permits as much to others as he assumes to himself," Hobbes writes; "which is an argument of a temperate man, and one that rightly values his power. Another, supposing himself above others, will have a license to do what he lists, and challenges respect and honour, as due to him before others; which is an argument of a fiery spirit. This man's will to hurt ariseth from vain glory, and the false esteem he hath of his own strength." The fiery types cause civil wars: they are prepared to risk death and organize the compliant for the sake of realizing their ambitions. They forms clans, factions, sects, and other associations and use these assemblages to divide sovereignty and undermine political authority. To eliminate the destructive violence of civil war, it is necessary to restrict those beliefs and practices that lead individuals to defy death. In a good society, people will, for the most part, rationally pursue self-preservation, oblivious to the temptations of aristocratic glory and religious redemption.[26]

The leading figures of the Anglo-Scottish Enlightenment—Locke, Hume, Smith, among others—posited justice as a political principle that cut against conceptions of higher and lower, better and worse. Rather, justice sustains a minimal level of civility—or "rules of convenience"[27]—in a society consisting of naturally equal, self-interested beings. The mind, according to Locke, is capable of identifying justice, "that most unshaken Rule of Morality, and Foundation of all social Virtue": that one should act toward others as he would be acted unto. "Justice and Truth are the common ties of Society; and therefore, even Outlaws and Robbers, who break with all the World besides, must keep Faith and Rules of Equity amongst themselves, or else they cannot hold together." In contrast to the ancient views that justice requires "Precedency" for those human types characterized by *Virtue . . . Excellency of Parts and Merit,"* the fundamental premise of Locke's view of justice—the natural freedom and equality of all—means that no man is by nature subject or subordinate to the will of any other man.[28]

Hume and Smith articulate themes regarding justice similar to those of Locke. To Hume, justice derives from individuals becoming aware that stability of possessions is in their specific interests and everyone realizing that they must not disturb one another's property. The foundation of justice rests on obeying the laws or customs concerning property which are current in our society, but this morality is strengthened by our ability to extend our sense of self so that self-interest comes to include respecting the interest of others with whom we form a cooperating society. According to Smith, justice was the "main pillar" of society. In his account, every individual should be free to follow his own interest in his own way, but only as long as he does not inflict injury or harm to others. Justice is a "negative virtue, and only hinders us from hurting our neighbor. The man, who barely abstains from violating either the person, or the estate, or the reputation of his neighbors, has surely very little positive merit. He fulfills, however, all the rules of what is peculiarly called justice. . . . We may often fulfill all the rules of justice by sitting still and doing nothing."[29]

If there is an analogue among modern thinkers to the ancient conception of higher human types or drives, it can be found in Continental thinkers such as Descartes and Rousseau, who put forth the positive role to be played by individuals who wish to accomplish great deeds. Far more than the philosophers of British empiricism, these thinkers extol the value of great individuals who are legislators for new regimes or modes of thought. Descartes' higher types are characterized by rationality, self-control of the passions, and a drive to find new and more useful ways to serve the public good. The goal to attain rationality and "detach oneself from all beliefs one has once accepted as true is not an example that everyone should follow," states Descartes. "The world consists almost completely of two kinds of people and for these two kinds it is not at all suitable: namely those who, believing themselves more capable than they really are, cannot help making premature judgments and do not have enough patience to conduct their thoughts in an orderly manner; thus if they take the liberty to doubt the principles they have accepted and to keep away from the common path, they could never keep to the path one must take to go in a more forward direction—they would remain lost all of their lives." Among the benefits to the public these higher types of rational individuals can offer are "an infinity of arts and crafts," which are the fruits of modern science. In discussing the need for a new mode of thought, Descartes posits the importance of a human being he can only imagine: an individual trained solely in rationality. This individual would be most fit to be a legislator, for he establishes a new people on rational laws that would supplant our own heritage, which is rooted in religion and ancient Greek myths.[30]

Rousseau feels compelled to introduce the great legislator as the founder of the social contract, the individual who is capable of establishing the laws and institutions that transform the self-interested individual into a citizen. The virtuous citizen is the effect, not the source, of such a system of laws: "How will a blind multitude, which often does not know what it wants (since it rarely knows what is good for it), carry out on its own an enterprise as great and difficult as a system of legislation? . . . The good path it seeks must be pointed out to it." This legislator's great ability "is, so to speak . . . to change human nature, to transform each individual. . . . In a word, he must deny man his own forces in order to give him forces that are alien to him and that he cannot make use of without the help of others." The founder needs to be great himself but also needs historical opportunity. Accidents will be required to bring together an extraordinary individual such as this and a people open or receptive to laws that will fundamentally transform their character.[31]

Nonetheless, both Descartes and Rousseau—and Continental thinkers more generally—play down the distinct role of these higher types far more than the ancients or Machiavelli and accommodate the modern concern for natural equality. Descartes' most fundamental political advice to the new scientists is to embrace a "provisional morality" that "obey[s] the laws and customs of one's country,"[32] so that they will avoid persecution and quietly introduce new modes of thinking and ways of life. Rousseau also limits the role of his highest type of individuals in the regime based on the social contract.[33] After the founding, the legislators must conduct ongoing activities behind the scenes and in secret: "I am speaking of mores, customs, and especially of opinion, a part of the law unknown to our political theorists but one on which depends the success of all the others [laws]; a part with which the great legislator secretly occupies himself, though he seems to confine himself to the particular regulations that are merely the arching of the vault, whereas mores, slower to arise, form in the end its immovable keystone." Aside from the founding or refounding of the social contract, Rousseau's individuals of superior wisdom and talent are to function at an informal and unofficial level.[34] In sum, Descartes, Rousseau, and other Continental thinkers advocate a greater role for founding-type individuals than the philosophers of British empiricism. But they do not advocate a return to the ancient conception of justice—a fit between one's capacity and one's social and political position—and generally emphasize the modern idea of the natural equality of all human beings.

LIBERALISM AND FOUNDERS

Like the ancients, Mill explicitly acknowledges the role of founding-type individuals in originating practices of lasting importance. All "good customs" presuppose that "there must have been individuals better than the rest," who set these practices going. Rather than referring to an original contract or agreement, Mill recognizes that founders of people gain heroic status by introducing a combination of astonishing and useful practices. Partly through admiration and partly through the fear they generate, they "obtain the power of legislators, and . . . establish whatever customs they pleased." The need for such founders does not end with the formation of a people: "There is always need of persons not only to discover new truths and point out when what were once truths are no longer, but also to commence new practices. . . . The initiation of all wise or noble things comes and must come from some one individual. The honor and glory of the average man is that he is capable of following that initiative; that he can respond internally to wise and noble things, and be led to them with his eyes open."[35]

Mill insists that the "greatest thoughts are the greatest events," that the character of speculative thought is the most decisive factor in creating and establishing social practices. For human beings to conform their actions to any set of opinions, ideas must exist. The necessary elements for the mental and moral development of Western civilization required founders. "Philosophy and religion are abundantly amenable to general causes," states Mill. "Yet few will doubt, that had there been no Socrates, no Plato, and no Aristotle, there would have been no philosophy for the next two thousand years, nor in all probability then; and that if there had been no Christ, and no St. Paul, there would have been no Christianity."[36] In short, Mill consistently advances an ancient conception that there are human beings who can "become a noble and beautiful object of contemplation," that these individuals reflect a perfection of our nature, that they are the source of creativity, including the new knowledge about what is true. Such excellent individuals may never be very numerous, yet they justify and preserve civilization itself: "Unless there were a succession of persons [of genius], whose ever-recurring originality prevents the grounds of beliefs and practices from becoming merely traditional[,] . . . there would be no reason why civilisation should not die out."[37]

We saw in chapter 2 that Mill's conception of justice straddles the ancient emphasis on virtue-centered ethics and the modern ideal of a rule-governing morality. On the one hand, Mill identifies justice in a variety of modern ways:

justice is primarily, although not exclusively, a negative virtue that centers on not harming others; justice is the preeminent moral obligation, as it centers on the very existence of society; justice is based on precise rules and enforced with violence. On the other hand, Mill also defines justice as an ethical disposition that reflects the character of agents. It is the self-control of the just individual that is his defining characteristic. The punitive power of the law is not required to prevent him from harming others and society.

Justice, however, is not exclusively concerned with our common need for self-preservation and protection of rights, continues Mill. The modern conception of justice is also conducive to the perfection of human nature. This perfection is not diminished but enhanced by natural equality. In Mill's conception of human excellence, the ancient distinction between higher and lower natures is fully justified only if there is equal opportunity for every individual to discover what social and political role fits with his or her nature. The ancient view that identifies specific groups of people as higher or lower types is no longer tenable. The advantage of the modern conception of justice that ensures the natural equality of all is the ability to generate the greatest variety in ways of life, which allows individuals to realize their distinct natural capacities:

> It is not that all processes are supposed to be equally good, or all persons to be equally qualified for everything; but that freedom of individual choice is now known to be the only thing which procures the adoption of the best processes, and throws each operation into the hands of those who are best qualified for it. Nobody thinks it is necessary to make a law that only a strong-armed man shall be a blacksmith. Freedom and competition suffice to make blacksmiths strong-armed men, because the weak-armed can earn more by engaging in occupations for which they are more fit. In consonance with this doctrine, it is felt to be an overstepping of the proper bounds of authority to fix beforehand, on some general presumption, that certain persons are not fit to do certain things. It is now thoroughly known and admitted that if some such presumptions exist, no such presumption is infallible.[38]

Mill denies that anyone can discover or realize his or her complete natural capabilities as long as people live in unequal relations to one another. The premodern practices of philosophers and rulers of interfering in behalf of natural right, for fear that nature should not succeed in effecting its purpose, is an altogether unnecessary endeavor. Under the modern rules of justice, higher types of individuals are not a result of contrived barriers, but a product of self-development. What people by nature cannot do, it is quite superfluous to forbid them from doing. What they can do, but not so well as others who are their competitors, competition suffices to exclude them from.[39] Mill synthesizes the ancient conception of human perfection with the modern goals of self-preservation and equality for all.[40]

This is not the end of the matter, however. Mill insists that the rules and mores of modern justice and equality are a necessary, but not sufficient, condition for developing higher forms of individuality and human perfection. The natural capacity for human excellence is more or less randomly distributed among the human race, but the laws and practices of different nations meet with better or worse results in cultivating this capacity. The problem with the English is that they, more than any other people, are exclusively a product of a rule-governing morality. English liberalism has not established the practices and values that develop the individual's higher capacities and attitudes.[41] England is the country in which obedience to general rules has most succeeded in suppressing whatever is liable to conflict with them. The Englishman has been trained to recognize what is wrong and to eschew unjust actions to realize his goals, but he is too narrow-sighted and incapable of thinking of anything but the enrichment of himself and his family. English obedience causes human nature to remain undeveloped or to develop only in a limited direction: "As is usually the case with ideals which exclude one-half of what is desirable, the present standard of approbation produces only an inferior imitation of the other half. Instead of great energies guided by vigorous reason and strong feelings strongly controlled by a conscientious will, its result is weak feelings and weak energies, which therefore can be kept in outward conformity to rule without any strength of either will or of reason."[42]

Mill elaborates in *On Liberty* how the relations between the perfected individual and the general public in a free society can be deeply problematic. Excellent individuals have a sense of personal distinction. "Persons of genius," he declares, "are, *ex vi termini* [by definition], more individual than other people." They ask themselves, "What do I prefer? Or what would suit my character and disposition? . . . Or what would allow the best and highest in me to have fair play and allow it to grow?" This sense of one's individual worth runs counter to the prosaic ordinary desires of the mass individual, who by definition does not see himself as special or unique, who sees himself the way everyone else sees themselves: "Thus the mind itself is bowed to the yoke: . . . [T]hey become incapable of strong wishes or native pleasures, and are generally without either opinions or feelings of home growth, or properly their own."[43]

Once again, Mill challenges a long-standing dichotomy in Western political theory between empiricism's interests and moral idealism's autonomy: interests motivate narrow, selfish behavior, and autonomy is what we do for the general good. Mill argues that what the highest type of individual does for himself is not motivated by mere selfishness, yet his concern for higher goals is not motivated purely by selflessness. Mill explains that the goals of the perfected individual and those of the masses differ. The highest good for the perfected individual is neither self-preservation, nor the life of democratic freedom, nor the attainment of wealth, but creativity for the public good. Their endeavors are extraordinary and go beyond ordinary expectations and processes. They discover new truths, point out when old truth are suffering from limitations, commence new practices, and set an example of more enlightened conduct. In contrast, the public, by definition, is unable to recognize that the average is not necessarily the good and that small minorities and individuals originate new truths and progress. "Originality is the one thing which unoriginal minds cannot feel the use of," Mill states. "They cannot see what it is to do for them: how should they? If they could see what it is to do for them, it would not be originality."[44]

Mill openly worries that the potentially creative individual will respond in one of two ways to this tension between himself and the public. Innovators may respond timidly and consent to be formed into one of the molds established by the public, restricting their own practices, limiting the role of wisdom, curtailing genius. Conversely, creative types may attempt to compel the public to recognize their teachings. Here innovative individuals will not only be restricting the development and freedom of all of society, but also corrupting their own character.[45] This stepping on others' toes, as advocated by Carlyle (late in his career) is not for the best because it violates liberty and cultivates a class of tyrants.

It is not surprising, then, that so many readers of *On Liberty* have often found it difficult to reconcile Mill's defense of liberty with his passionate commitment to human excellence.[46] The distinction between the goals and needs of the perfected individual and the general public runs like a thread through the first half of chapter 3. It is precisely his recognition of this distinction that makes him resist striving to overcome it. Mill does not advocate the rule of the perfected individuals who might enforce new ideas of the good. No society, however organized, can compel its members to self-develop and become creative. At the same time, Mill recognizes that, in addition to the laws and mores of justice, specific conditions are required to cultivate the types of desires that are springs to human agency and developed individuality. Mill concludes that the goals of human excellence *and* modern justice are neither mutually exclusive nor the same. His vision of a liberal society is made up of two parts, and his political philosophy cannot be understood if one of the two poles is ignored or taken for the whole.

HUMAN CREATIVITY AND MORAL RESTRAINT

Mill's writings on the rise and fall of particular peoples and values place his ethical and moral philosophy in the larger context of his historical outlook. We have seen that Mill identifies the ancients and moderns—Pericles and Knox—as representatives of the complementary goods of the best political regime. His insistence that creative individuality must function within the context of an overarching morality of justice also parallels his analysis of the proper role of moralities in ancient monarchies and medieval regimes. In *Considerations on Representative Government,* Mill notes that monarchy and hierarchy were needed to tame and civilize the ancient Jews, Egyptians, and Chinese. The Egyptian and Chinese rulers taught their people to be obedient in a way that was not different from slaves' obedience, but "the Jews, instead of being stationary like other Asiatics, were next to the Greeks, the most progressive people of antiquity, and jointly with them, have been the starting-point and main propelling agency of moral cultivation." The uppermost idea of the Greeks is thoughtful action; the uppermost idea of the Jews is right or moral conduct. What is unique about the Jews, in Mill's account, is that the kings were not the exclusive molders of character. Might did not automatically translate into right because Judaism granted room for an Order of Prophets, allowing people of genius and high religious tone to comment on the activities of the hierarchy and on Judaism in general. The prophets were far more than an equivalent to the modern idea of a free press. Their ability to criticize the rulers and interpret Judaism placed rules and moral parameters on the rulers' activities, while also offering a legal and moral framework among the public that was under constant renewal. As Mill summarizes in *Utilitarianism,* the ancient Hebrews founded the primitive element of the idea that fidelity to universal law is justice.[47]

Mill argues that the Catholic Church also played a positive, albeit one-sided role, in the moral development of Europe during the early Middle Ages. On the one hand, the Catholic clergy taught restraint to the lower classes, "that howsoever defective the morality which they taught, they had at least a mission for curbing the unruly passions of mankind, and teaching them to set value on a distant end, paramount to immediate temptations, and to prize gratifications consisting of mental feelings above bodily sensations." In important ways, Mill argues, the Catholic Church created conditions that led to the formation of the moral conscience. The Church's separation of temporal and spiritual power is based on the idea that material force has no right or hold over the mind, beliefs, or truth: "Enormous as have been the sins of the Catholic Church[,] . . . her assertion of this principle has done more for human freedom, than all the fires she ever kindled have done to destroy it." At the same time, the Catholic Church of the early Middle Ages was the only institution capable of placing moral parameters on the willful and warlike activities of the competing sections of the ruling aristocracies and monarchs, "menacing the great with the only terrors to which they were accessible, and speaking to their consciences in the name of the only superior whom they acknowledged on behalf of the low." It required a pope to speak with authority to the kings and emperors, insists Mill. Nothing but an authority recognized by all people and nations—and not necessarily dependent on any specific group—could in that era have been adequate to the task. "That the Pope, when he pretended to depose Kings, or made war upon them with temporal arms, went beyond his province, needs hardly, in the present day, be insisted on," Mill writes. "But when he claimed the right of censuring and denouncing them, with whatever degree of solemnity, in the name of the moral law which all recognized, he assumed a function necessary at all times, and which, in those days, no one except the Church could assume, or was in any degree qualified to exercise."[48]

In Mill's vision of modern liberty, the masses, not the monarchs and aristocrats, will have the opportunity to be more innovative and willful. But like the progressive monarchies of Judaism and the aristocracies of medieval times, modern individuals must assert themselves within the framework of a comprehensive moral underpinning. Furthermore, Mill aims to negate the oscillations between the one-sided Hellenism and Hebraism, of humanity's creative and moral impulses, which have characterized Western morality by combining and synthesizing the goals of human creativity and moral restraint.[49] Mill's ideal of a complete, harmonious human nature requires nothing less than the negation of the historical process, which continually sends Western civilization into a back and forth process between two incomplete views of human nature.[50]

NIETZSCHE'S CHALLENGE

Despite Mill's reputation as a merely reformed utilitarian, it is quite striking how close Mill's argument gets to a thinker whose name is not usually paired with his: Friedrich Nietzsche—especially Nietzsche's discussion of master and slave moralities, or "Rome vs. Judea," found in the first essay of *Genealogy of Morals*. Rome represents those—Athenians, Romans, the Florentine's Renaissance, Napoleon—who create values and cultivate human excellence in terms of status and personal qualities. Judea stands for the Judeo-Christian tradition, which attains power through *ressentiment,* the angry demand to punish and restrict those who are preeminent or more creative. In contrast to the justice of the masters, which creates a pathos of difference between distinct human types, the justice of slaves is nothing more than the unyielding demand of the weak seeking revenge. In Nietzsche's view, the modern quest for social justice is akin to the Christian passion for redemption, as both have the same psychological origins and serve the same inner needs. Modern justice creates rights, promulgates laws, and establishes principles of equality that protect the weak and resentful, at the cost of the strong and willful.[51]

To Nietzsche, the slave morality is primarily derivative and negative but extremely successful—its victory has forced the higher types to accept its rules. Nietzsche knew that the most important product of this outlook, the moral conscience, had for the first time made humanity into what he called an "interesting animal," by giving depth to the human soul and making it capable of both good and evil. Still, the one-sided victory of the slave morality diminished the role of contradiction in modernity, which contributes to a general aimlessness and loss of creativity.[52]

However, the parallels that link Nietzsche's and Mill's views on Western morality—the conflict between diverse human drives, modern justice as a secular extension of Christianity, the one-sided victory of modern justice—should not obscure fundamental differences in their views. To Nietzsche, the relation between the ancient and modern conceptions of justice always was, and always will be, a polarizing conflict. Following the classical view, Nietzsche charges that "one has duties only to one's equals, toward the other one acts as one thinks best: justice can be hoped for (unfortunately not counted on) only *inter pares* [among equals]." Higher types may have an obligation to their peers, but they owe nothing to the general public. Injustice, charges Nietzsche, "lies in the claim to 'equal rights,'" in a political order that has the nerve to make claims on "the higher, greater, richer." Today, Nietzsche insists, no individuals have "the courage any longer for privileges, for masters' rights, for a sense of respect for oneself and one's peers—for a *pathos of distance*. Our politics is sick from this lack of courage."[53]

In "In the Tarantulas" of *Thus Spoke Zarathustra,* for instance, Zarathustra and his enemies clash over the ancient and modern conceptions of justice. The chapter outlines a battle between the partisans of universal equality and Zarathustra, who explains the justness of inequality. Zarathustra charges that justice as universal equality is an outlook that the many embrace in response to the disproportionate talents distributed by nature: nature gives superior talents to the few and inferior abilities to the many—this division engenders resentment and vengeance among the latter. Zarathustra explains that the teachers of equality are motivated by envy and the desire for power, and they demand that all members of society, high and low, live under the same rules. How does Zarathustra answer this challenge? "I do not wish to be mixed up and confused with these preachers of equality," he responds. "For to *me,* justice speaks thus: 'Men are not equal.' Nor shall they become equal." Zarathustra advocates a return to the ancients' *agonistic* politics: only a politics centered on freedom and competitive challenges for higher types will revivify creativity and natural inequalities: "And behold, my friends: . . . the ruins of an ancient temple rise; . . . that struggle and inequality are present even in beauty, and also war for power and more power: that is what he teaches us here in the plainest parable." Rather than a Millian blending of ancient and modern conceptions of justice, Nietzsche's Zarathustra advocates conflict between the ancients and moderns. He sees a synthetic reconciliation as being impossible.[54]

Nietzsche's thought, however, does not center on such political themes as the best political regime, the organization of agonistic politics, and political or moral obligations. Set against his comprehensive critiques of modern religious, social, and cultural values and practices and coupled with his genealogical explanations of how they developed qualities inimical to human flourishing, Nietzsche's political proposals are a marginal concern. Nietzsche's fundamental challenge to Mill centers on how the death of God—with its consequent loss of moral standards rooted in nature, reason, and revelation—threatens modern culture. To Nietzsche, the death of God signifies the beginning of an era of widespread recognition that the human will is the ultimate ground of values. But God was once alive: the endeavor to mobilize the will to create new values has been subverted by the centuries-long taming of the will characteristic of both Christianity and the Enlightenment, along with their valuations of the weak over the strong. Nietzsche argues that, unlike the ancient Greeks and Romans, moderns confront the lack of transhistorical spiritual values with a weak will and a heavy conscience. This condition raises the possibility that the species will "no longer launch the arrow of [its] longings beyond man," leading to the degeneration and diminution of humanity into the perfect herd animal. Nietzsche rejects a Millian-type position that ancient-style creativity can be simply integrated into modern culture.[55]

Nietzsche predicts that this modern moral crisis will produce an intellectual culture with residues of Christianity and the Enlightenment, a combination of weak-willed skepticism with egalitarian moralism. The modern intellectual will be characterized by either the curious observation (social science) or tepid celebration (historicism) of the human will's creation of prosaic values.[56] While Mill anticipates many of Nietzsche's characterizations of modern culture, Nietzsche believes that this problem is more intractable. In Nietzsche's account, attempts to blend ancient thought and practices—or values from other civilizations—with modern culture would further weaken the modern intellectual, who would now be dwelling upon difference and celebrating ambiguity. This intellectual, states Nietzsche, "simply needs a costume. . . . To be sure, he soon notices that not one fits him very well; so he keeps changing." These moderns are characterized by an eye for "quick preferences and changes of style of the masquerade: also for the moments of despair over the fact 'nothing is becoming.'"[57] Does Mill know what to do about modernity's loss of confidence in the creative will? Mill addresses this question in the second half of chapter 3 of *On Liberty,* and his answer leads to an important shift in his political philosophy.[58]

MILL'S SLIDE TO EXPRESSIVISM

After completing his conception of developed individuality midway through chapter 3 of *On Liberty,* Mill's focus of attention takes a sharp turn. Mill recognizes that times change. English liberalism today no longer has easy access to the beliefs, practices, and institutions from which it could once confidently draw to sustain the qualities of human excellence: "In ancient history, in the Middle Ages, and in a diminishing degree through the long transition from feudality to the present time, the individual was a power in himself; and if he had either great talents or a high social position, he was a considerable power." The actualization of the principle of equality, Mill acknowledges, bears no small responsibility for the stiff challenge English liberalism now faces. For the liberal principle of equality has worked to weaken the sources of the qualities of human excellence in a liberal order. "The only power deserving the name is that of the masses . . . ," Mill writes. "This is as true in the moral and social relations of private life as in public transactions. . . . They [opinions] are always a mass, that is collective mediocrity." Mill is not complaining about *all* of this, as he recognizes that the age of equality produces many valuable political and social effects. But as much as the excellent individual needs a society of justice and equal opportunity to flourish, these conditions may undermine him. Mill feels compelled to warn that "no government by a democracy or a numerous aristocracy, either in its political acts or in the opinions, qualities, and tone of mind which it fosters, ever did or could rise above mediocrity except in so far as the sovereign Many have let themselves be guided by the counsels and influence of a more highly gifted and instructed *one* or *few*."[59]

Because English liberalism's principles have withered the roots and eroded the soil on which human excellence relies for its nourishment, Mill is unable to do what he would like to do: end the discussion on human development: "For what more or better can be said of any condition of human affairs than that it brings human beings themselves nearer to the best that they can be?" The weakening or exhaustion of these resources does not bring about a weakening of England's need for developed individuality; it only weakens England's capacity to satisfy this need. What Mill must do is somehow show that "these developed human beings are of some use to the undeveloped." This task necessitates overcoming "the indifference of persons in general to the end [human excellence] itself." To meet this challenge, Mill modifies his conception of human excellence and slides toward an expressive conception of liberty.[60]

Throughout *On Liberty* Mill has noted that a self-developed existence, the achievement of real command concerning both philosophic issues and "the great practical concerns of life," requires for its development a peculiar discipline. This outlook, which Mill finds notably lacking in modern democracy, is best cultivated by the dialectic found in the Platonic dialogues. Such dialectical exercises "test the certainty and vitality of our convictions" and cultivate the quality of "many sidedness," a virtue Mill associates with Socrates and Goethe, who both had "the capacity to recognize what is true in diverse and rival perspectives and practices."[61] But few people can receive a proper education in the Platonic dialectic, in part because such private teachers are rare, in part because many individuals are either unwilling or unable to be schooled in the rigors of the dialectic. But, most challenging, the social dialectic that is most favorable to self-examination—clashing outlooks regarding "both what is it [life] and how to conduct oneself in it"—no longer exists. "Until people are systematically trained to it [the dialectic]," Mill argues, "there will be few great thinkers and a low general average of intellect in any but the mathematical and physical departments of speculation."[62]

Mill laments key features of modern life. In the wake of centuries-long taming of the will and the growth of equality, "mediocrity" and "public opinion" are the "ascendant powers of mankind," and there is little discussion of what the higher and lower social practices and ways of life are. In the past, Western civilization was characterized by a remarkable diversity of character and culture, inducing many kinds of human development and ultimately leading the Western group of nations to become both tolerant and improving. "Individuals, classes, nations have been extremely unlike one another," Mill says; "they have struck out a great variety of paths, each leading to something valuable; and although at every period those who traveled in different paths have been intolerant of one another, and each would have thought it an excellent thing if all the rest could have been compelled to travel his road; their attempts to thwart each other's development have rarely had any permanent success, and each has in time endured to receive the good which the others have offered." The strength of the West had always been its ability to generate social dialectics, which challenge its own truths by presenting alternative possibilities: "Europe is, in my judgment, wholly indebted to this plurality of paths for its progressive and many-sided development." These contrasting paths forced advocates to justify their own ideas and practices, and the conflicts generated brought forward excellent individuals with developed minds and fortitude. In short, competing sites of power were good for human excellence as they were good for liberty.[63]

But unlike these previous European societies, in liberal England everyone now reads, listens to, and sees the same thing. Thus, although Mill says the struggle for liberty is "far from being new," he recognizes it now "presents itself under new conditions, and requires a different and more fundamental treatment." "Comparatively speaking," all persons now have the same hopes and fears and aspire for the same freedoms and liberties: "And the assimilation is still proceeding. All the political changes promote it, since they all tend to raise the low and to lower the high." If opposition "waits till life is reduced *nearly* to one human type, all deviations from this type will come to be considered impious, immoral, even monstrous and contrary to nature."[64]

In the circumstances of this uniformity of opinion and diminishment of human character, Mill argues, spontaneity and creative modes of life, irrespective of whether they are directed toward the public good, as well as freedom of discussion and opinion are the best contrivances for the cultivation of the mind and the best available substitutes for the education provided for by either the Platonic dialectic or clashing ideas of the good:

> In other times there was no advantage in their doing so, unless they acted not only differently but better. In this age, the mere example of nonconformity, the mere refusal to bend the knee to custom, is itself a service. Precisely because the tyranny of opinion is such as to make eccentricity a reproach, it is desirable, in order to break through that tyranny, that people should be eccentric. Eccentricity has always abounded when and where strength of character has abounded; and the amount of eccentricity in a society has generally been proportional to the amount of genius, mental vigor and moral courage which it contained. That so few now dare to be eccentric marks the chief danger of our time.[65]

Mill, in short, proposes that a wide variety of spontaneous practices and opinions emanating from civil society will create experiences and discussions that allow individuals to discover the best life and have the opportunity to gain more control over their desires and mental and moral faculties.

Mill's excellent individuals are now characterized by spontaneous inclinations. They "act upon their opinions—to carry these out in their lives without hindrance, either physical or moral, from their fellow-men." They conduct "experiments in living," are unrehearsed, and are not fettered by fear of being called eccentric.[66] In a certain sense, this shift in *On Liberty* from a conception of human excellence that combines the ancient and modern conceptions of justice to the idea of the best life as expressivist is a demotion in Mill's account of human excellence and "developed individuality." In Mill's prior discussion, he had identified the qualities required for the complete, harmonious development of one's nature, in which reason, will, and justice should find their integral places in a fully formed human character. Reminiscent of classical conceptions of human perfection, human excellence here consists in the degree to which the individual succeeds in developing a set of qualities or virtues which are specifically appropriate to a human being considered as an object of its own kind and as an end in itself. Mill established this ideal life by singling out the leading qualities of human conduct and making them the regulative principle of all human activities—for humanity is developed not merely by changing, but by realizing its highest peaks.

With the new emphasis on self-creation and self-expression, Mill's goal is not humanity at its highest, but our distinctiveness and individuality. Eccentricity is valuable because our self is unique and unrepeatable. Mill's new excellent individual is not to rest and conform to an established standard but to move, on ceaseless journeys courageous and innovative, celebrating the value of new experiences, with a desire for deeper self-discovery. Here the immediate purpose is to produce an individual, a unique or authentic personality, rather than a perfectly developed human nature. Coleridge makes this distinction nicely in his comparison of Sophocles and Shakespeare as respective representatives of the ancients and moderns: "Upon the same scale we may compare Sophocles and Shakespeare: in the one there is a completeness, a satisfying, an excellence on which the mind can rest; in the other we see a blended multitude of materials, great and little, magnificent and mean, mingled, if we may say so, with a dissatisfying, or falling short of perfection, yet so promising of our progression, that we would not exchange it for that repose of mind which dwells on the forms of symmetry in acquiescent admiration of grace."[67]

Moreover, unlike the prior catalogue of virtues, Mill's expressivist outlook does not define certain motivations as virtuous in terms of public actions they move us to. What is now required is not the strong desires and will toward some goal that serves the public good, but rather a unique way of expressing our lives, our distinct desires and fulfillments, our special good. In Mill's reformulated vision of the best life, the highest types of human experiences break from the unthinking practices of the community. Removed from conformity, the creative individual now longs for self-realization, which consists of new practices on a higher level of self-awareness. The excellent individual is to be understood, then, as an agent who questions established social practices, developing choices "properly their own" as they call society's standards into question.[68]

To be sure, consistent with Mill's view that both classical and romantic-expressivist outlooks are united in their concern for the development of human faculties, Mill's new excellent individual remains characterized by a strong will and developed mind. Dignity, courageous resistance to public opinion, desire for self-respect and self-fulfillment, creativity, and refusal to be hemmed in by custom all capture crucial characteristics of both of Mill's formulations of the developed individual. Mill's spontaneous individual, for instance, is driven by "great energies guided by rigorous reason and strong feelings controlled by a conscientious will."[69] But it is now the experience of conflict between the individual and society that gives meaning to one's decisions and spurs mental development and fortitude. Of course, Mill's prior discussion on human excellence also identified individual differences. But the new emphasis on difference is no longer just variations or distinct types within the same basic natural capacities. Rather, the new expressivist current posits that each one of us also has an original path on which we ought to tread: "There is no reason that all human existence should be constructed on some one or some small number of patterns. If a person possesses any tolerable amount of common sense and experience, his own mode of laying out his existence is the best, not because it is the best in itself, but because it is his own mode." Our obligation now is to live up to our originality: "The same mode of life is a healthy excitement to one, keeping all of his faculties of action and enjoyment in their best order, while to another it is a distracting burden which suspends or crushes all internal life."[70]

PRELUDE TO NEW SYNTHESIS

Mill's shift to a more expressive conception of excellence and developed individuality in *On Liberty*, as dramatically illustrated by his invocation of "Socrates and Goethe," is the great gamble in his political philosophy. Mill's explicitly stated goals in *On Liberty* in advocating many and varied experiments in living are *liberty* and *wisdom*, or perfection of the individual *and* society: that is, the promotion of self-determined modes of existence and the discovery of the best ways of life and practices "in order that it may in time appear which of these fit to be converted to customs." Mill counsels that individuality, rightly understood, refers to the developed capacity to undertake experiments in living and form one's character in accordance with one's particular powers. At the same time, we must remember "that the unlikeness of one person to another is generally the first thing which draws the attention of either to the imperfection of his own type and the superiority of another, or the possibility of combining the advantages of both, of producing something better than either."[71]

As noted, Mill's ultimate purpose in equating human excellence with eccentricity is not to champion a process that promotes the infinite malleability of the human personality; neither does he intend to glorify arbitrary or aimless defiance of conventional opinion. "Human beings," Mill insists immediately after making his call for eccentricity, "should be for ever stimulating each other to increased exercise of their higher faculties, and increased direction of their feelings and aims towards wise instead of foolish, elevating instead of degrading, objects and contemplations."[72] Mill consistently recognizes that a standard of perfection is preferable to differences in imperfection and that discovering the former is a vital social and political goal. But he believes that the limited conflict between competing conceptions of liberty has existed for so long that the future practices that develop human faculties—most notably, reason and will—need to be based on evaluations of what is better and worse from an infinite variety of experiments in living. "The period of decomposition . . . is not yet terminated, . . . and . . . the new synthesis is barely begun, nor is the preparatory analysis completely finished," writes Mill in his evaluation of Auguste Comte's proposal for an immediate imposition of new standards of human excellence. In "Bentham," Mill warns that "the field of man's nature and life cannot be too much worked, or in too many directions; until every clod is turned up the work is imperfect; no whole truth is possible but by combining the points of view of all the fractional truths, nor, therefore, until it has been fully understood what each fractional truth can do by itself." He made the same warning against a premature synthesis in his assessment of Goethe. Goethe's idol was symmetry, but he rarely succeeded in developing it in any of his own work,

> showing the utter impossibility for a modern, with all the good in the world, to tight-lace himself into the dimensions of an ancient. . . . Every modern thinker has so much a wider horizon, & there is so much deeper a soil accumulated on the surface of human nature by the ploughing it has undergone & the growths it has produced. . . . It is too soon by a century or two to attempt either symmetrical productions in art or symmetrical characters. We all need to be blacksmiths or ballet dancers with good stout arms and legs, useful to do what we have got to do, and useful to fight with at times—we cannot be Apollos and Venuses just yet.[73]

In *On Liberty,* Mill makes the same point. While "mankind are imperfect," it is useful that there should be varied views, "so is it that there should be different experiments of living; that free scope should be given to varieties of character, short of injury to others; and that the worth of different modes of life be proved practically."[74] Mill is recognizing the challenge that Nietzsche will identify a few decades later: that the centuries-long taming of the will characteristic of Christianity and modern justice has subverted the endeavors to mobilize the will to create new values and practices. Mill is responding to this challenge with a call for eccentricity and difference. The diverse modes of existence are at the present time an opening step to higher civil practices and beliefs that are to be attained in the future.

INTELLECTUALS AS SYNTHESIZERS

Mill believed that English liberalism's commitment to the principle of diversity would eventually shift public opinion and make the reconciliation of differences and the development of new moral truths a practical outcome both for the difference makers and, more important, for the general public. How is

Mill's conception of *Bildung*—a back and forth process that effects a synthesis between what individuals uniquely contribute to the society and what the culture of the society makes him—to be realized? Is there an invisible civic hand that mediates and reconciles competing interests and ideas of the good? Or must interconnections and synthesis be consciously produced?

On one level, Mill thinks that by stimulating the energies and vibrancy of individuals and sectors of society, these individuals and groups will be forced to defend one set of beliefs and practices against those who hold opposite views—promoting the liberal virtue of toleration and a balanced set of views. "There is always hope when people are forced to listen to both sides," states Mill. "Each of these modes of thinking derives its utility from the deficiencies of the other: but it is in great measure the opposition of the other that keeps each within the limits of reason and sanity."[75] By calling into question the way of life of all people who follow public opinion and customs, even without saying so directly, those who live differently act as Socratic gadflies and awaken the majority to the possibility that their way of life may not be the right one. The differences that set them apart are an indication of the possible qualities of character that the majority may or may not wish to embrace. Mill argues that, on the one hand, when an individual develops an "eminent" set of qualities, "he is so much nearer to the ideal perfection of human nature" that he becomes a proper object of public admiration. On the other hand, if an individual's behavior is characterized by "lowness or depravation of taste," while it "cannot justify doing harm to the person who manifests it," it renders that individual "necessarily and properly a subject of distaste, or, in extreme cases, even of contempt."[76]

But while Mill poses the *possibility* that social dialectics—or public conflicts over varying outlooks and ways of life—will promote toleration, balance, and excellent individuals, he also warns that the public by itself is unable to generate a sufficient amount of toleration and wisdom from these collisions. Mill is not Habermas. He does not, that is, assume that whenever advocates put forward a claim as one for whose truths they believe they have good reasons, they anticipate an ideally rational conversation, because to believe they have rationales for their assertions implies an understanding that in a good conversation they will win others over to their views.[77] Rather, Mill recognizes the potentially injurious effects of the ideological conflicts he insists on: "I acknowledge that the tendency of all opinions to become sectarian is not cured by the freest discussion, but is often heightened and exacerbated thereby; the truth which ought to have been, but was not, seen, being rejected all the more violently because proclaimed by persons regarded as opponents." There also is the tendency for people to assume that the general prevailing views are naturally right. Most are disinclined to hear out alternative positions. People are rarely concerned about anything in regard to public behavior other than actions and feelings different from their own. This standard of evaluation, while not presenting itself as such, is held up to humanity as the core of religion and philosophy by almost all moral and philosophic teachers. "These teach that things are right because they are right: because we feel them to be so," charges Mill. "They tell us to search in our own minds and hearts for laws of conduct binding on ourselves and on all others. What can the poor public do but apply these instructions and make their own personal feelings of good and evil, if they are tolerably unanimous in them, obligatory on the world."[78]

The problem Mill here addresses is *not* how to make intolerant advocates and antagonisms in society less sectarian or polarized. Mill does not believe that the most unlimited use of the freedom of discussion of all possible opinions and ways of life "would put an end to the religious or philosophical sectarianism. Every truth which men of narrow capacity are in earnest about is sure to be asserted, inculcated, and in many ways acted on, as if no other truth existed in the world." To hesitate, to balance advantages and disadvantages, to advocate a policy or way of life with due recognition of its one-sidedness or limitations is almost impossible psychologically to partisans and advocates of contending political outlooks and alternative modes of existence. Further, those with distinct and original characters tend to be more contentious than consensual.[79] And indeed, Mill advocates persistent strife in society: "Wherever some such quarrel has not been going on"—wherever conflict has been ended by the complete victory of one of the contending outlooks or ways of life, and no new contention has taken the place of the old—"society has either hardened into Chinese stationariness, or fallen into dissolution. A center of resistance, round which all the moral and social elements which the ruling power views with disfavour may cluster themselves, and behind whose bulwarks they may find shelter from the attempts of that power to hunt them out of existence, is as necessary where the opinion of the majority is sovereign, as where the ruling power is a hierarchy or aristocracy."[80] As Jeremy Waldron puts it, "The good effects of ethical confrontation, in Mill's account, will not accrue unless views are put forward passionately, forcefully, and directly, in a manner that opponents of these views cannot practicably ignore."[81]

Mill's solution to the problems of intolerance and strife pivots on the role of the intellectuals—"the sober," "honest," and "impartial judges of human affairs"—so that they will encourage and defend a wide variety of outlooks and ways of life, while also reconciling and synthesizing the discordant civil practices and beliefs.[82] By encouraging individuals and groups to challenge conventions and defend their ways of life, "the opulent and lettered classes" would create more choices for the individual and pave the road to a new, unified, impartial outlook among the intellectuals themselves, an outlook which "might partially rival the mere power of the masses, and might exercise the naturally salutary influence over them for their own good." The collisions of ideas and modes of existence, while stimulating developed individuality, also allow the intellectuals to develop new understandings of what is good and bad, and "though the persuasions and convictions of average men are in a much greater degree determined by their personal position than by reason," Mill argues, "no little power is exercised over them by persuasions and convictions of . . . the united authority of the instructed. When therefore the instructed in general can be brought to recognize one social arrangement, or political or other institution as good, and another as bad, one as desirable, another as condemnable, very much has been done toward giving to the one, or withdrawing from the other, that preponderance of social force which enables it to subsist."[83] To envision the values of the future, Mill summarizes in *The Subjection of Women*, has always been the "privilege of the intellectual elite, or of those who have learnt from them; to have the feeling of that futurity has been the distinction, and usually the martyrdom, of a still rarer elite. Institutions, books, education, society," all go on educating individuals in the image of the past, "long after the new has come; much more when it is only coming."[84]

Mill argues that part of the task of the intellectual in the present period is to encourage the free play of alternative practices and diverse ideas. By promoting variety, free discussion, and criticism (the reformed Platonic dialectic), the intellectual contributes to an arena of effort, of struggle, and of self-development and helps limit one set of ideas while giving birth to others. The intellectual adopts a conciliatory approach to fundamental political and moral differences and encourages a wide range of activities "as the only unfailing and permanent source of improvement . . . since by it there are as many possible independent centers of improvement as there are individuals."[85]

For instance, Mill welcomes the village cooperatives initiated by Charles Fourier in France. They are an experiment in socialism that is worth promoting, protecting, and setting against the prevailing property relations in liberal societies. Here the intellectual has a particularly important task, that of cultivating and protecting alternative views: "For example, if it were necessary to choose, there would be much more need to discourage offensive attacks on infidelity than on religion." Mill's *On Liberty* shows little concern that the intellectuals themselves will use their skills to exacerbate and sharpen the conflicts they encourage. "No sober judge of human affairs will feel bound to be indignant because those who force on our notice truths which we should otherwise have overlooked, overlook some of those which we see," states Mill. "Rather, he will think that so long as popular truth is one-sided, it is more desirable than otherwise that unpopular truth should have one-sided assertors too, such being usually the most energetic and the most likely to compel reluctant attention to the fragment of wisdom which they proclaim as if it were the whole."[86]

The power to select and combine also was essential to thinkers who undertook to perform the tasks necessary for the development of new synthetic truths in democratic society. Wisdom regarding the central issues of social existence is so much a product of reconciliation and combination that, in addition to the "few minds sufficiently capacious and impartial to make the adjustment with an approach to correctness," it also requires "the rough process of a struggle between combatants fighting under hostile banners." "The moment, and the mood of mind, in which men break free from error," Mill remarked, "is not, except in natures very happily constituted, the most favourable to those mental processes which are necessary for the investigation of the truth. . . . They usually resolve that the new light which has broken in upon them shall be the sole light; and they willfully and passionately blow out the ancient lamp." Mill argues that the people who are to learn the most from experience are not so much the participants in conflict as the intellectual. As he puts it, "It is not on the impassioned partisan, it is on the calmer and more disinterested bystander, that the collision of opinions works its salutary effects." This intellectual can enjoy the collision of other people's beliefs and practices, as he himself does not take sides.[87]

The antagonisms between employers and trade unions, for example, often require "impartial arbitration." If these efforts of conciliation fail, Mill proposes new modes of ownership in which the workers join the employers in having a direct interest in the profits of the enterprise. The success of these compromises could open the door to new forms of property relations—"Industrial Partnerships" or more socialized forms of private ownership—that overcome the one-sided demands that employers and trade unions make on one another. Conflicts, in short, are the raw material for the synthetic truths that the intellectuals will put forth in the future. Consequently, "the intelligent part of the public can be made to feel its value—to see that it is good there should be differences, even though not for the better, even though, as it may appear to them, some should be for the worse."[88]

Mill's distinction between the need for *diverse opinions in society and unity among the intellectual elite* is captured nicely by his views on the main problems confronting the highest intellectuals, and his response to an invitation to join a writer's society centered on the expression of diverse views. In the *Diary*, Mill complains that too many divergent opinions surround the highest thinkers, further contributing to the diffidence and lack of fortitude that plague the English intellectual: "It requires in these times much more intellect to marshal so much greater a stock of ideas and observations. This has not yet been done, or has been done only by very few: and hence the multitude of thoughts only breeds increase of uncertainty. Those who should be the guides of the rest, see too many sides to every question. They hear so much said, or find that so much can be said about everything, that they feel no assurance of the truth of anything."[89]

Accordingly, when Mill is invited to join the Neophyte Society, whose purpose was, as Mill understood it, to bring together intellectuals of sundry opinions to exchange views and become better writers, he says no. Receiving the invitation at the same time as he is writing the first draft of *On Liberty*, which posits the value of contending opinions and ways of life in society, Mill dismisses the value of a group that is organized around expressivism. "With respect to the mere faculty of expression independent of what is to be expressed, it does not appear to me to require encouragement. There is already an abundance, not to say superabundance, of writers who are able to express in any effective manner the mischievous commonplaces which they have got to say," complains Mill. "I would gladly give any aid in my power towards improving their opinions; but I have no fear that any opinions they have will not be sufficiently well expressed; nor in any way should I be disposed to give any assistance in sharpening weapons when I do not know in what cause they will be used. For these reasons I cannot consent that my name should be added to the list of writers you send me."[90] Mill values *social* diversity and *social* dialectics, not differences and antagonisms among the intellectual elite.

Not that Mill succeeded in forging unity among the intellectual elite. While editor of the *Westminster Review* from 1834 to 1840, Mill battled to create an alliance among the philosophical radicals, romantics such as Carlyle and John Sterling, and select critics of liberalism—Sarah and John Austin and Tocqueville, among others. But this project failed because, as Mill put it, conditions for unity remained premature and, quoting John Austin, "The country did not have the men."[91] Recognizing the failure of his coalition project, Mill reconciled to the task of laying the philosophic foundation for unity among the intellectuals of the future:

> I do not find my enjoyment of speculation at all abated though I see less and less prospect of drawing together any body of persons to associate in the name & behalf of any set of fixed principles. Still, no good seed is lost: it takes root & springs up somewhere, & will help in time towards the general reconstruction of the opinions of the civilized world, for which ours is only a period of preparation, but towards which almost all the things & men of our time are working; though the *men,* for the most part, almost as unconsciously as the things. Therefore, "cast ye your bread on the waters, & ye shall find it after many days."[92]

Mill discerned that, in the context of the contemporary age of transition between old and new truths, he could not identify the specific values and practices of the subsequent period; this limited his ability to construct an alliance around a positive political program. "In England," Mill notes, "there is still too much to be undone for the question, 'What Is to Be Done,' to assume its true importance." He believed he suffered the "misfortune of having been born and doomed to live in almost the infancy of human improvement." Nonetheless, "it is as preparation" for the morality of the future "that my speculations . . . may be valuable." Not unlike Nietzsche, Mill hopes for a "posthumous existence," a period in the future when his views will be looked upon as the harbinger of new values and higher forms of existence. "The remedies for all our diseases will be discovered long after we are dead," Mill writes in the final passage of his *Diary.* "It is to be hoped that those who live in those days will look back in sympathy to their known and unknown benefactors."[93]

THE POLITICS OF LIBERTY AND WISDOM

This identification of the crucial role of the intellectuals in the formation of *Bildung* leads Mill to develop two notable political proposals in *On Representative Government.* Not surprisingly, they assign a disproportionate role to the highly educated.[94] In one proposal, Mill advocates an electoral system of proportional representation whereby voters list preferences for candidates, including contestants who are not members of citizens' local constituencies, so that the intensity of electoral support and minorities' views contributes to the seats in the national assembly. Mill argues that proportional representation will generate both liberty and wisdom. On the one hand, this system of voting will deepen the character of political liberty by the attachment it forges between voters and their representatives. The citizen now is able to identify with a national representative's specific views or character. Every elector who voted for a representative, states Mill, did so because he is the individual, in the whole list of candidates for the national assembly, "who best expresses the voter's own opinions, or because he is one of those whose abilities and character the voter most respects, and whom he most willingly trusts to think for him. The member would represent persons, not the mere bricks and mortars of the town—the voters themselves, not a few vestrymen or parish notabilities merely."[95]

On the other hand, Mill argues that proportional representation introduces wisdom into the representative assembly and the nation as a whole. That is, the primary minority group Mill aims to empower through this electoral system is "the minority of instructed minds." These distinguished individuals, who are unlikely to have taken the time to build majority support in a local constituency, would have a better chance to attain a sufficient number of votes from a national minority. "The minority of instructed minds scattered through the local constituencies," Mill writes, "would unite to return a number, proportioned to their own numbers, of the very ablest men the country contains. They would be under the strongest inducement to choose such men, since in no other mode could they make their small numerical strength tell for anything considerable." Mill aims to avoid the problem of the American electoral system identified by Tocqueville, in which "the highly cultivated members of the community, except such as them as are willing to sacrifice their own opinions and modes of judgment, and become the servile mouthpieces of their inferiors in knowledge, do not even offer themselves for Congress or the State Legislatures, so certain is it that they would have no chance of being returned."[96]

Plural voting is Mill's second proposal for establishing a disproportionate role for the highly educated in politics. Once again, Mill's two goals are liberty and wisdom (and the modern and ancient conceptions of justice). The right to vote should be based on the modern principle of fundamental human equality, including the equality of women: "But (though every one ought to have a voice) that every one should have an equal voice is a totally different proposition." Mill also embraces the ancient conception that there should be a fit between one's capacities and aptitude and one's rights and responsibilities. The quality and extent of one's right to vote should be based on one's intellectual character. Mill's position is to give more votes to those who are more mentally cultivated.[97]

Mill starts from the belief that passing a literacy test is the fundamental re-

quirement for the right to vote since suffrage presupposes the ability to deliberate and choose among public issues. To judge well, Mill continues, requires
knowledge and a sense of the moral good: "If with equal virtue, one is superior
to the other in knowledge and intelligence—or if with equal intelligence, one
excels the other in virtue—the opinion, the judgment of the higher moral or
intellectual being is worth more than the inferior; and if the institutions of the
country virtually assert that they are of the same value, they assert the thing
which is not." From this perspective, Mill proposes that the public has a general
interest in allowing the more knowledgeable and public-spirited to cast extra
votes. Discarding the traditional view that property ownership signifies political abilities, Mill argues that more votes should be given to those who have
achieved higher levels of mental development. Mill recognizes that intellectual
qualities are very difficult to identify, although he does recommend a system of
general examination. He also "proposes a hierarchy of occupations for determining how many votes each person should receive:" an order of ascension that
"moves from unskilled to skilled labor, rising to the liberal professions and from
there to successful and well-established professionals." The more learned, and
the higher the rung, the more votes one would have.[98]

Mill believes that plural voting, along with proportional representation, will
increase the chances that an instructed minority will be elected to the national
assembly. He also believes that plural voting will establish an ennobling spirit in
society. While no mode of existence that does not harm others should be out-
lawed, it is important that the cultivated intellect be accorded the highest place
among the different ways of life. The citizen should recognize that it is for his
own well-being that everyone has the right to influence government, but also
that "the better and wiser" have more influence than others. "It is important
that this conviction should be professed by the state, and embodied in the national institutions," Mill asserts. "Such things constitute the *spirit* of the institutions of a country; that portion of their influence which is least regarded by
common, and especially by English thinkers, though the institutions of every
country . . . produce more effect by their spirit than by any of their direct pro-
visions, since by it they shape their national character."[99]

The mechanisms of proportional representation and plural voting help to
incorporate the requisite portion of wisdom into the political system, believes
Mill. He charges the elected instructed minority with mitigating and counter-
ing the weaknesses endemic to representative government, which are rooted in
its popular or democratic character. As Mill argues, "It has been seen that the
dangers incident to a representative democracy are of two kinds: danger of a

low grade of intelligence in the representative body, and in the popular opinion which controls it; and dangers of class legislation on the part of the numerical majority, these all being composed of the same class."[100] Perceiving and pursuing the general interest in the representative assembly is the task of the elected intellectuals, as they stand above partial and conflicting interests in society. Higher goals than a party or sectoral outlook govern them, as their loyalty to truth and the general good is higher than their obligation to any particularistic outlook. While democratic society might not develop a classless outlook, the instructed minority must do so. Their general sense of wisdom and justice equips them to respect the general good, but it is their ability to reconcile and synthesize the competing claims of society that provides their greatest political contributions. As Mill states in describing his role to his constituents. "Believing as I do that society and political institutions are, or ought to be, in a state of progressive advance; that it is the very nature of progress to lead us to recognize as truths what we do not as yet see to be truths."[101]

The highly educated representatives would improve the intellectual quality of the assembly's deliberations, and though they would rarely have their complete proposals pass, they would elevate the moral tone in the nation by identifying the higher and lower civil practices and beliefs society is generating. Mill's goal is to "keep popular opinion within reason and justice, and to guard it from the various deteriorating influences which assail the weak side of democracy. . . . A democratic people in this way will be provided with what in any other way it would almost certainly miss—leaders of a higher grade of intellect and character itself. Modern democracy would have its occasional Pericles, and a habitual group of superior and guiding minds."[102]

Mill's preoccupation with the vices of representative government that derive from its democratic character and his insistence on the privileged role of intellectuals, who contribute wisdom to the representative assembly, undermine Nadia Urbinati's thesis that Mill's thought, properly understood, focuses exclusively on *extending* among the public forms of dialogue on a wider array of political and moral matters. In Urbinati's account, Mill's proposals for plural voting should be discounted because they reflect his inability to fully understand his own thinking. "Plural voting," she argues, "contradicted . . . the basic criterion of a free and open competition that characterized Mill's 'good' democracy. . . . It is incoherent to defend democracy as a system that supports open political competition, and then recommend a procedure that has the effect of protecting a minority from losing an open race."[103] As I discuss in chapter 7, there are weaknesses in Mill's vision of the political role of the democratic intellectual. Nonetheless, there is a consistency to Mill's position that many of his admirers and critics fail to see: he always maintained an appreciation for both the ancient and modern conceptions of justice; he consistently focuses on the problem of reconciling wisdom and liberty.

FREEDOM AS AN END

Mill's concern for self-assertion, innovative practice, and free discussion, however, is not exclusively driven by tactical considerations for an age of transition from one set of moral beliefs to another. Although Mill advocated a distinct role for an intellectual elite in the representative assembly and society, he also stated quite clearly that no elite could be trusted if it was not subjected to the controlling power of the entire people.[104] While the intellectuals reconcile and synthesize new standards of better and worse from the many, varied ways of life and beliefs, Mill insists that these substantive values of the future must be integrated with conceptions of equal rights and self-development. To attain both freedom and progress, liberal society needs to accompany the moral concern for better and worse ways of life with procedural neutrality. "I have said that it is important to give the freest scope possible to uncustomary things, in order that it may in time appear which of these are fit to be converted into customs," states Mill. But freedom of thought and action is not solely concerned with discovering "better modes of action." It also is a necessary for individuals to fully develop and flourish as human beings:

> Human beings are not like sheep; and even sheep are not indistinguishably alike. . . .
> If it were only that people have diversities of taste, that is reason enough for not attempting to shape them all after one model. . . . Such are the differences among human beings in their sources of pleasure, their susceptibilities of pain, and the operation on them of different physical and moral agencies that, unless there is a corresponding diversity in their modes of life, they neither obtain their fair share of happiness, nor grow up to the mental, moral, and aesthetic stature of which their nature is capable.[105]

Mill did not envision a future in which an identified good is propounded legally. Human beings are secure from harm at the hands of others only in proportion as they have the power of being, and are, self-protecting. Free human conduct also is necessary for us to discover and realize our distinct feelings and thoughts. Therefore, while the intellectuals and public will generate beliefs and practices that cultivate reason, will, and deeper social unity, it is crucial that general rules and a moral atmosphere be established in order that people remain confident individual decision making is being freely exercised. There is a distinction between advising a person what to do and making him do it. "Considerations to aid his judgment, exhortations to strengthen his will may be offered to him, even obtruded on him, by others," Mill argues; "but he himself is the final judge. All errors which he is likely to commit against advice and warning are far outweighed by the evil of allowing others to constrain him to what they deem his good."[106] Moreover, as the public embraces practices and modes of existence that cultivate their higher faculties, their demand for freedom will increase, rather than decrease: "Whatever invigorates the faculties, in however small a measure, creates an increased desire for their more unimpeded exercise; and a popular education is a failure if it educates a people for any state but that which it will certainly induce them to desire, and most probably to demand."[107]

In *On Liberty*, Mill justifies individual choice as an end in itself because it cultivates our higher natural capacities, because human progress should not be prevented, because it has become an integral part of human happiness, and because the post—Protestant Reformation world requires it.[108] The substantive principles of the future that are generated by the reconciliation and synthesis of contrasting outlooks and practices must not preclude freedom of action, which, in turn, will also allow new outlooks and ways of life to generate. Whatever ideas of the good life we adopt respecting the foundations of civil society, and under whatever political institutions we develop, "there is a circle around every individual being, which no government . . . ought to be permitted to overstep: there is a part of the life of every person who has come to years of discretion, within which the individuality of that person ought to reign uncontrolled either by any other individual or by the public collectively."[109] Mill warns the "highest minds" that, as they hold positions they maintain to be very important and believe opposition to them to be extremely harmful, they often feel legitimate frustration and anger. Nonetheless, these individuals must respect the modern idea of justice: "If he [one of the highest minds] neither himself does them any ill office, nor connives at its being done by others, he is not intolerant: and the forbearance, which flows from a conscientious sense of the importance to mankind of the equal freedom of all opinions, is the only tolerance which is commendable, or, to the highest moral minds, possible."[110]

Mill cautions the "teachers of mankind" that in the future the range of beliefs and values that are no longer fought over will increase. This development will bring out both the highest and lowest features of humanity. On the one hand,

Mill anticipates that this consolidation will reflect humanity's general improvement toward a consensus around which practices and beliefs are right and wrong. On the other hand, this decline of contradiction will intensify the public's general tendency to impose its specific ideas of the good upon all members of society, to reject all dissent, and to oppose all modes of existence that do not conform to the norm. "The disposition of mankind," Mill writes, "whether as rulers or as fellow-citizens, to impose their own opinions and inclinations as a rule of conduct of others, is so energetically supported by some of the best and some of the worst feelings incident to human nature, that it is hardly ever kept under restraint by anything but want of power; and as the power is not declining, but growing, unless a strong barrier of conviction can be raised against the mischief, we must expect, in the present circumstances of the world, to see it increase."[111]

It is these two concerns—the expectation of increasing unity around improved, synthetic principles of right and wrong and the recognition that intolerance toward alternative views is woven into the character of the human being—that lead Mill to insist that free discussion and self-regarding activities must not be restricted in the morality of the future. In his discussion of *On Liberty* in the *Autobiography*, Mill anticipates that free discussion will be easier to stimulate in the contemporary period. Unfettered liberty of discussion, Mill insists, "is a feature belonging to periods of transition, when old notions and feelings have been unsettled, and no new doctrines have succeeded to their ascendancy. . . . But this state of things is necessarily transitory." The greater challenge regarding free discussion will come in the future when Mill's *Bildung* has taken shape and society has consolidated around new principles of right and wrong: "It is then that the teachings of the *Liberty* will have their greatest value."[112]

In short, Mill developed two justifications for the writing of *On Liberty*. He articulated what Allan Megill calls a "Tocquevillian justification": to preserve, under the circumstances of mass homogeneity, individuality and plural paths of human development. Mill also put forth what Megill calls a "Saint-Simonian justification": to preserve liberty after a new era of deeper consensus and spiritual unity is forged. The latter concern leads Mill in *On Liberty* to remind the "teachers of mankind" that "where this advantage [antagonism over different ideas of the good] can no longer be had, I confess I should like to see [them] endeavoring to provide a substitute for it—some contrivance for making the difficulties of the question as present to the learner's consciousness as if they were pressed upon him by a dissentient champion, eager for his conversion. . . .

The Socratic dialectics, so magnificently exemplified in the dialogues of Plato, were a contrivance of this description."[113]

THE COMPLETE HUMAN NATURE

Mill depicts the good liberal society as an arena of self-assertion, tension, and self-development in which contrasting counterparts produce new political and moral truths. This vision of *Bildung* is consistent with Mill's integration of the reformed Platonic dialectic with the social dialectics of Coleridge and the German Romantics. It also is consistent with the apparently contradictory lessons—unbound freedom and engraved unifying truths—that Mill claimed he learned from the history of moral development articulated by the Saint-Simonians and Comte.

The Saint-Simonians and Comte explained that the West had been characterized by organic periods—ancient Greek and Roman polytheism, early and middle Christianity—during which positive creeds were accepted as authoritative and as a result structured political and social life. They understood that the West had been defined by critical, negative periods—the age of Greek philosophy and the Reformation, among others—during which the old authoritative opinions were criticized and overthrown but not replaced by new ones. These thinkers were explicit about their strategy of bringing the contemporary critical era, a continuation of the era launched by the Reformation, to an end and "substituting a new regime that would have structural similarities with but differ substantively from the precritical, Christian regime of the past."

Mill learned from the Saint-Simonians and Comte that history has issued periods dominated by opposing trends. In Mill's account, the heroic founders of the ancient Greek and Roman families, tribes, and races (whether mythical or not) provided deities that cultivated a courageous, innovative will toward the future.[114] In turn, the universalism of Christianity induced people to obey a general moral framework, which required them to control their impulses. Mill also agrees that contemporary times are a continuation of the critical period launched by the Reformation, an era of "loud disputes, but weak beliefs." The present "age seemed smitten with an incapacity of producing deep or strong feeling. . . . An age like this, an age without earnestness, was the natural era of compromises and half-convictions." The Saint-Simonians and Comte taught Mill a "much clearer conception than before of the peculiarities of an age of transition in opinion, and [I] ceased to mistake the moral and intellectual characteristics of such an age, for the normal characteristics of humanity."[115]

Unlike the Saint-Simonians and Comte, however, Mill maintained that the present critical period must continue and deepen, as there is not enough raw material for the development of new higher truths. "The old opinions in religion, morals, and politics," Mill writes, "are so much discredited in the more intellectual minds as to have lost the greater part of their efficacy for good, while they have still vitality enough to be an effectual obstacle to the rising up of better opinions on the same subjects." "So long as this intellectual anarchy shall endure, we may be warranted in believing that we are in a fair way to become wiser than our forefathers; but . . . we have not yet advanced beyond the unsettled state, in which the mind is, when it has recently found itself in grievous error, and has not yet satisfied itself with the truth."[116] And unlike the Saint-Simonians and Comte, he neither looks forward to nor welcomes an exclusively organic period. The contrasting moral drives of the past, Mill argues, suggest the desirability of an era that harmonizes and synthesizes the opposed forces into a third, higher era. He looks forward to an epoch that combines creative individuality and new moral and political truths. It will be a period of energy, creativity, and willfulness. It also will be characterized by new unified convictions about what is morally right and wrong. Mill summarizes:

> I looked forward, through the present age of loud disputes but generally weak convictions, to a future which shall unite the best qualities of the critical with the best qualities of the organic periods; unchecked liberty of thought, unbounded freedom of action in all modes not hurtful to others; but also convictions as to what is right and wrong, useful and pernicious, deeply engraven on the feelings by early education and general unanimity of sentiment, and so firmly grounded in reason and in the true exigencies of life, that they shall not, like all former and present creeds, religious, ethical, and political, require to be politically thrown off and replaced by others.[117]

Mill believed that Comte's concern for establishing higher types of individuals and practices and the modern liberal focus on universal equality under the law were both half right: "We hold the amount of the truth in the two [sides] to be about the same. M. Comte has got hold of half the truth, and the so-called liberal or revolutionary school possesses the other half . . . each sees what the other does not see."[118] To Mill, the conflict between an unleashed human creativity and the imperatives of general moral development is the primary contradiction generating humanity's progress and happiness. These two contrasting outlooks and practices have presented themselves as antithetical forces in various forms throughout history. And unlike Coleridge and the German Romantics, Mill does not maintain that this thesis and antithesis will invariably resolve into a synthesis. His advocacy of eccentricity aims to regenerate the conditions for a future synthesis. The envisioned creation and synthesis of contrasting counterparts do not center on the formation of a specific substantive outlook or idea of the good. They are designations of the constituent elements of a complete human nature: creative individuality and right conduct.

Chapter 7 Mill and Political Philosophy

Unlike traditional liberals of Anglo-Scottish thought who focus primarily on protecting a private sphere for human conduct, Mill believed that societies also needed to create institutions and practices that contributed to the development of the human faculties, moral education of society, and human excellence. Specific proposals to achieve these goals are a representation system that ensures a disproportionate role for the highly educated, public voting, an education system characterized by "restraining discipline," an idea of the best life, and a reflection that is generally ignored or dismissed in the secondary literature, namely, his argument for a Religion of Humanity and aesthetic culture; such a religion and culture would supplement and possibly replace Christianity in establishing human perfection as creative practices devoted to the welfare of fellow beings.[1]

These distinct emphases in Mill's political philosophy have posed a riddle that has long vexed analysts. On the one hand, Mill is a consistent advocate for the freedoms of speech, religion, women, assembly, self-government, the market, and emigration. On the other hand, Mill is well known for arguments that transcend liberal concerns about protecting the individual from state and social domination. Contemporary commentators have developed two schools of thought—traditionalist and revisionist—in response to these currents in Mill's thought. Both schools of thought paint a picture of Mill's positions that is too thin or narrow. Mill in fact left himself vulnerable to these restricted interpretations. Mill failed to heed Tocqueville's warnings regarding the character of the democratic intellectual and did not anticipate—as Nietzsche did—the difficulty of integrating ancient practices or romantic self-expression into modern culture. Mill was also too optimistic about the possibility of reconciling the different aims of liberty or free human conduct with wisdom or ideas of better and worse modes of existence.

THE TRADITIONALISTS' CONFUSED MILL

The traditional interpretation of Mill, most notably articulated by Isaiah Berlin, is that the contradictory emphases in his thinking are expressions of his eclecticism. According to this view, no coherent doctrine can be found in Mill's work. On the one hand, Mill appreciated the utilitarian outlook that one's life decisions are driven by the rational pursuit of pleasure and the avoidance of pain. At the same time, Mill is attracted both to the romantic argument that the liberated individual is spontaneous and to the Comtean view that social science is establishing a path to human progress. Facing this labyrinth of ideas in Mill's thinking, Berlin concludes that Mill's political philosophy, and modern liberalism itself, is rooted in uncertainty about whether any of these partial truths—utilitarianism, romanticism, or any one outlook—can claim the mantle of truth. Rather than envisioning new synthetic truths from competing truths, Berlin claims, Mill adopts an agnostic stance toward notions of the good. Mill will not condemn any activity as being bad as long as it does not have an ill effect on the affairs of others. Modern liberalism is based on Mill's ambivalence concerning what partial truths are right or wrong, good or bad.[2]

Berlin and the traditional interpretation provide insights into the tensions that animate Mill's thinking, identifying how Mill praises the qualities of choice, diversity, and freedom while also developing an analysis that uses the "language not of a philosophical radical, but of Burke, or Carlyle, or Chesterton."[3] The shortcoming of this interpretation is the assumption that Mill's diverse emphases are rooted in perplexity and are not a purposeful attempt to root modern individuality in a new ethical and moral context. What they miss is the possibility that, as opposed to a poorly directed eclecticism, Mill's contrasting currents of thought express complementary goals. One finds in key essays of the Mill corpus the warning that if the pursuit of pleasure is not accompanied by a developed understanding of what is good, it will lead to "miserable individuality." He defines freedom of action as the freedom to do what one enjoys, while to attain higher freedom the individual must will the desires he desires. To Mill, the opportunity to gain self-command of one's aims requires the traditional empiricist goal of limiting the determination of our actions and allowing the freedom to make choices. However, moral freedom requires that individuals have the option of self-amendment of character; and Mill argues that civil society must develop the practices and values that make possible this freedom to self-develop. The result is a version of liberalism that has a richer, fuller notion of the individual: not just as the bearer of a limited number of rights, but also as a person that can and should be cultivated in a particular direction, including the ability to amend oneself.

The traditional interpretation fails to appreciate Mill's distinct concerns. Berlin does not recognize Mill's two different conceptions of liberty and mistakenly calls him confused for assuming that the "negative goal" of warding off interference with free action is the necessary *and* sufficient condition for developing both freedom and higher types of human character.[4] Berlin is correct to disassociate Mill from a strict positive conception of liberty in which free choice becomes identified with choosing what is rational or right. But Berlin fails to identify the middle ground Mill occupies between his own positive and negative conceptions of freedom. Mill's political philosophy advocates the absence of impediments to actions that do not harm others *and* the development of distinct practices and values that encourage the individual's capacity to command one's character—if one wishes. Berlin's portrait of a hyperindividualistic Mill also ignores Mill's position that the moral conscience envisioned by Hume, Smith, and empiricism's associational psychology was not capable of generating a just moral outlook and that new synthetic truths—derived from alternative ways of life—would deepen social unity. "[Mill] took human solidarity for granted, perhaps altogether too much for granted," charges Berlin. "He did not fear the isolation of individuals or groups, the factors which make for alienation and disintegration of individuals and societies."[5] But Mill took the task of cultivating the just moral conscience and higher forms of social unity very seriously, and Mill did not pose the requirements for liberty against the conditions for moral development. "The communities in which reason has been most cultivated, and in which the idea of social duty has been most powerful," summarizes Mill, "are those which have most strongly asserted the freedom of action of the individual—the liberty of each to govern his conduct by his own feelings of duty, and by such laws as his own conscience can subscribe to."[6]

Crucial to understanding *On Liberty* is the recognition that the loss of liberty is not only based on coercion by other men. Liberty is also lost by the lack of self-development of character. England is characterized by a climate in which fewer and fewer legal restraints are placed on public conduct, but now very few people "desire liberty" and cultivate aims that "are properly their own." In previous ages, Mill continues, when liberty was understood to be self-command, "the individual was a power in himself; and if he had great talents or a high social position, he was a considerable power."[7]

But why does Mill's *On Liberty* fail to clearly demarcate these distinct philosophical conceptions of liberty? Why does he often use the term *liberty* to denote distinct views of freedom? For instance, when Mill puts forward that "the sole end for which mankind are warranted, individually or collectively, in interfering with the liberty of action of any of their number, is self-protection," he clearly is focusing on the restraints imposed by other men: "physical force in the form of legal penalties" and "the moral coercion of public opinion."[8] But when Mill says most people "do not desire liberty" he does not mean that the general public wishes to be coerced or restricted in their actions. Mill's point is that these individuals lack the goal of realizing self-command of character: "Society has now fairly got the better of individuality; and the danger which threatens human nature is not the excess, but the deficiency of personal impulses and preferences. . . . The mind itself is bowed to the yoke . . . by dint of not following their own nature they have no nature to follow: their human capacities are withered and starved: they become incapable of any strong wishes or native pleasures, and are generally without either opinions or feelings of home growth, or properly their own."[9]

Had Mill made these distinct conceptions of liberty clearer, he might have limited the confusion that continues to surround his political philosophy. More broadly, Mill's clarification of distinct conceptions of liberty would have put empiricism and classic liberalism in a better position to meet British Idealism's future challenge that it was the only outlook in England insistent that the individual recognize himself as the author of his own actions.[10] Does this failure in *On Liberty* confirm Berlin's thesis that Mill is unable to clarify and choose between different conceptions of liberty?

THE DIFFERENT MEANINGS OF LIBERTY

Mill's reasons for using single terms to convey publicly different moral meanings are given in "Of the Requisites of a Philosophical Language, and the Principles of Definition" and "On the Natural History of the Variations in the Meaning of Terms" in the *Logic*. Here, he lays out how the political philosopher promotes contrasting meanings for the same moral term to create vitality and synthesis. His analysis of language in the *Logic* exemplifies why contemporary commentators' failure to recognize Mill's appreciation for premodern and other alternative currents of thought leads to limited analyses of Mill's thought.[11]

In Mill's account, the designation of distinct conceptions of liberty under a single term contributes to a more comprehensive understanding of freedom itself. Language itself cannot be understood from a purely logical or nominalist perspective. There are too many profound historical and social determinants of language for us to claim that we can employ language as a tool while ignoring its cultural context. Watch out, Mill warns, for philosophers—such as Hobbes and Bentham—who want to tame language and make it produce uniform conceptions and thoughts; the result of such practices is that the true significance of ethical and moral terms is lost. Reformers of language want to strip language of its ambiguity and thus of its critical force. The desire for order, on the one hand, and fetish concerning logic, on the other, drives these thinkers to imagine dystopic schemes for regulating and simplifying the chaotic potential lodged in language. Mill writes, "Language loses one of its inherent and valuable properties, that of being the conservator of ancient experience; the keeper-alive of those thoughts and observations of former ages, which may be alien to the tendencies of the passing age." These thinkers want to tell us what words like *virtue* and *citizen* mean once and for all so we will stop upsetting society with arguments about them.

Such reduction of language to the decisions of philosophers, Mill insists, would blind us to the complex and diverse origins and significations of words. Nominalists and logicians recognize that many of our past views and experiences are no longer conveyed in our language: "These persons, in examining the old formulas, easily perceive that words are used in them without a meaning. . . . [T]hey naturally enough dismiss the formula, and define the name without reference to it."[12] Nominalists and logicians focus on fastening down words like *liberty, loyalty,* and *virtue* to what they signify in conventional usage and introduce the practice of employing these terms uniformly according to that connotation. The forgotten meanings of our moral terms are lost, and alternative experiences no longer contribute to challenging the prevailing norms and practices. There is no room in the modern imagination for a contrast between competing outlooks: "The ancient formulas are consequently treated as prejudices; and . . . people are no longer taught as before . . . that there is truth in them. They no longer remain in the general mind surrounded by respect, and ready at any time to suggest their original meaning. Whatever truths they contain are not only in these circumstances, rediscovered far more slowly, but, when rediscovered, the prejudice with which such novelties are regarded is now, in some degree at least, against them, instead of being on their side."[13]

We gain more than we lose, Mill continues, by opening ourselves to the competing connotations revealed by a searching historical interrogation of key ethical terms. "The history of a word," he writes, "by showing the causes which determine its use, is . . . a better guide to its employment than any definition; for definitions can only show its meaning at a particular time, or at most the series of its successive meanings, but its history may show the law by which the succession was produced." Indeed, Mill insists that we can get a lot out of paying attention to the ambiguities of language and reexcavating their original force and meaning. He proposes that philosophers discover the vital past experiences that our most important moral terms convey and put forth these meanings to challenge our contemporary understandings. The philosopher must take advantage of what Aristotle and many ancient philosophers understood, "that there are such things as ambiguities of language" and that it is delightful to discover and exploit them.[14]

To Aristotle, however, it is our natural capacity to speak, or *logos,* that leads the human animal to agree and disagree on moral terms and concepts. Errors are made and differences arise, Aristotle insists, in the discovery of what kinds of good are best to organize our lives—those means that for us constitute human happiness. Our deliberative conclusions about both means and goals are always uncertain: "For comprehension is neither about what always is and is unchanging nor about just anything that comes to be. It is about what we might be puzzled about and might deliberate about."[15]

To Mill, our contemporary ideas and practices are based on the overcoming or negation of previous experiences. As Mill maintains that the Englishman is now generally inclined to agree, history is a critical source of our differences, and the contrasting character of our moral terms is a potential source of tension and creativity. "While the formulas remain," Mill insists, "the meaning may at any time revive." Upon discovering the forgotten or unused properties of our ideas, the "philosopher announces [the truth] again to mankind, not as a discovery but as the meaning of that which they have been taught and still profess to believe." The philosopher creates an unfinished dialectic between contrasting moral experiences, forging a perpetual tension "in spiritual truths, and in spiritual doctrines of any significance."[16] In *On Liberty,* Mill uses the term *liberty* to signify two complementary, but distinct, conceptions of freedom: the limitations on the external coercion of the individual's actions by state and society; the cultivation of "well-developed human beings" who make their own decisions and desire their own desires. Mill's use of divergent conceptions of liberty in *On Liberty* does not reflect a poorly thought out eclecticism, as many of his traditionalist interpreters claim. He identifies contrasting ideas of liberty for the purpose of establishing a comprehensive account of individuality that combines self-development with the moral obligation not to harm other individuals.

THE REVISIONISTS' RESTRICTED MILL

In recent decades, revisionist literature has criticized the traditional view that Mill has no coherent philosophy. Alan Ryan, John Rees, and others focus on chapters 4 and 5 of *On Liberty,* the last chapter of *Utilitarianism,* and a few fragments from other essays, arguing that Mill has developed a liberal doctrine rooted in utilitarian ethics.[17] Mill, in Ryan's account, is fleshing out the precepts of utilitarianism in the modern context where both the law and public opinion are potential fetters to free human conduct. Elaborating the "harm principle," Ryan argues that Mill's analysis of moral conduct centers on whether the behavior of an individual impedes the actions of others: if it does, the action is immoral; if not, the action is moral. The area of law and morality is "other-regarding" and only in this area can sanctions or punishments be applied. Law and morality differ only in the types of sanctions used. Mill's thinking, Ryan argues, revolves around *how* behavior that afflicts the lives of others should be opposed.

Invoking traditional Anglo-Scottish themes, Ryan explains that "people live in society in order to protect themselves against actions aimed at harming them, so, if an action is wrong or immoral, then society must stop it. The only question is, how?" To Ryan, Mill answers that either public opinion or the law can be mobilized against such behavior depending upon which form of restraint creates a better cost/benefit ratio for society. Mill's political philosophy centers on the development of public opinion and law that establishes "general rules that aim at promoting such interpersonal goods as peace, justice, and honesty."[18] Self-regarding actions do not belong to the area of morality, and we therefore cannot apply sanctions to them. Ryan argues that since Mill advocates utilizing public opinion and the law only for curbing immoral behavior, he establishes moral space for individuals to pursue personal and aesthetic ideals and an ethical framework that allows the greatest happiness for the greatest number.

Mill, however, never refers to morally just behavior as "other-regarding conduct," as it indicates moral behavior requires transcendence of the self and its desires. In Mill's account, the just moral conscience motivates the individual to adhere to the rules of justice because of the self-respect it generates. The just individual is characterized by continence and self-control. His moral conscience informs his desires and prevents him from taking actions that in his view reflect a debased character. The idea that Mill envisioned "other-regarding conduct" as an essential component of morality overlooks Mill's challenge to Kant's conception of the moral conscience. Both recognized the moral conscience as a state of consciousness which itself creates a sense of duty. Where Mill differs from Kant is with Kant's claim that the moral conscience is based on contra-causality: choosing one course of action, while preferring another. In Mill's account, the just moral conscience creates the *desire* to do right; just acts are forms of self-fulfillment, not of self-denial.

Moreover, Mill's comprehension of ethics and morality is far more complex than that of a decision-making mode for determining whether public opinion or the law provides the best general framework for free human conduct. Mill consistently posits that the rules and mores of modern justice are a necessary, but not sufficient, condition for human happiness and developed individuality. Even at the level of preventing harm to others, Mill's moral theory is not as simple as Ryan suggests. For instance, when Mill testifies before the Royal Commission on the Contagious Disease Acts, he states that a main reason for his opposition to state-sponsored medical tests and treatment of prostitutes is its moral legitimization of a debased form of individualism: prostitution. Mill reacts angrily when asked if it would promote the happiness for the greatest number if such tests not only exist but are paid through the licensing of prostitutes and brothels, and not by taxes: "It seems to me that all the objections which exist against the Acts, exist in extreme degree against licenses, because they have still more the character of toleration of that kind of vicious indulgence, than exists under the Acts at present, or can exist in any other way."[19] In contrast to Ryan, Mill's conception of happiness is grounded in an understanding of human nature that distinguishes higher and lower pleasures, connects the development of human faculties to the overall increase of happiness, and sees such development as hinging upon reformed civil institutions, law, education, and culture.[20]

THE TAMING ROLE OF WOMEN

Ryan and the revisionists' limited view of Mill's account of ethics and morality is best exemplified by their restricted interpretation of *The Subjection of Women*. To Ryan, Mill's goal in advocating the emancipation of women is solely the legal expansion of the realm of individual freedom to the greatest possible extent.[21] But Mill's position is much more comprehensive and complex. Mill's *Subjection of Women* appropriates and revises part of Socrates' discussion in book 9 of the *Republic* on why the philosopher is happier than the tyrant to explain how a self-commanding existence is superior to a life centered on the pursuit of unbridled passions. Mill's book also considers equal rights and reciprocal relations between marital partners a necessary condition for the cultivation of a just morality, one in which an individual regards the rights of other human beings as fully worthy as one's own. Most important, Ryan and the revisionists ignore Mill's most stunning claim in *Subjection of Women:* that the emancipation of women transforms the family from being a scene of tyranny and caprice that radiates an evil influence throughout society into acting as a potential new center of innovation and value formation. Here, once again, contemporary commentators' failure to recognize Mill's penchant for adopting and modifying premodern and alternative currents of thought contributes to deficient explanations of his political philosophy.

Like Rousseau and Tocqueville, Mill believes that women who focus on domestic matters are a bulwark of the prosaic but socially necessary mores of honesty, frugality, fidelity, restraint, and humility.[22] But Mill points to harmful consequences as well: too often, the moral influence of women in the contemporary family is "encouraging to the softer virtues; discouraging to the sterner virtues."[23] On the one hand, women help tame undisciplined and wicked men, preventing them from becoming alcoholics, unemployed workers, or philanderers. On the other hand, women's focus on prosaic mental and social qualities fetters those few men who have the potential to become great innovators who serve the public good. "The wife is the auxiliary of common public opinion . . . ," Mill writes, "a dead weight, a drag, upon every aspiration of his to be better than public opinion requires him to be. It is hardly possible for one in these bonds, to attain exalted virtue."[24] Mill's *Subjection of Women* criticizes two types of subjections: the comprehensive subjection of women by men; the psychic subjection of creative types by the interpersonal relationships within the family.

Mill argues that the good produced by women's generating of the prosaic virtues that restrict bad men will be strengthened by women's attainment of equal rights. These mores do "not depend on the woman's servitude, but [are], on the contrary, diminished by the disrespect which the inferior class of men always at heart feel towards those who are subject to their power." More important, a new type of marital partnership is required to foster human creativity and excellence in modernity. Mill argues that in premodern ages men often displayed heroism—most notably, military courage—to defend the realm and differentiate themselves from other men, making themselves more attractive to women. At the same time, the "taming" role of women had contributed to chivalry, a moral ethos that cultivated gentleness, generosity, and self-abnegation among the warriors who defended the realm. Though chivalry never came close to attaining the lofty standard it established in theory, "it remains one of the most precious monuments in the moral history of our race," a remarkable attempt by a weak and disorganized sector to foster norms that the powerful willingly submit themselves to.[25]

In modern society, however, the opportunities for human creativity, individual prowess, and courage are diminished: industrial production, not military conflict, is the central feature of modern social life; mass organizations are more important than heroic actions for political and social prosperity; the private sphere predominates over the public realm. The association of men with women, Mill continues, is much closer and more complete than it ever was before. Men's lives are more domestic. Formerly, their pleasures and chosen occupations were among men and in men's company: their wives figured in only a fragment of their lives. As men spend more time in the private and domestic spheres, the moral and cultural dynamics shift. When males were primarily occupied with tasks outside the home and among others of the same gender, the domestic virtues of prudence, modesty, and honesty acted as an appropriate counterweight to the less sentimental political and military worlds.

Now, however, Mill worries that potentially creative men will ingest excessive doses of sentimentality, thus producing will-less types aversive to risk and unable to lead: "If he differs in opinion from the mass—if he sees truths which have not yet dawned upon them or if, feeling in his heart truths which they nominally recognize, he would like to act up to those truths more conscientiously than the generality of mankind—to all such thoughts and desires, marriage is the heaviest of drawbacks, unless he be so fortunate as to have a wife as much above the common level as he himself is."[26] Given that such restraining influences exist in every household, Mill asks whether it is "any wonder that people in general are kept down in the mediocrity of respectability which is becoming a marked characteristic of modern times?" By ending the subjugation of women, Mill counters, talented women will have the ability to work closely with their (equally talented) partners: defining goals that transcend prevailing norms and practices, building a relationship of complementary strengths, and becoming innovators that serve the public good.[27]

Perhaps the most important assault upon the taming role of women in morality came from the republican outlook of Periclean Athens, so it is instructive to identify Mill's agreement and disagreement with this position. The classical republican outlook revolved around a quality of manly valor, according to which virtuous citizens displayed patriotic courage by pursuing honor and fame in the *polis* and war. Courage took its character from a contrast with the idealized life of women, who toiled in silence and seclusion in the family. This republicanism centered on a "polarized opposition between male, courage, war, and *polis* on the one hand, and female, peace, passivity, and family on the other." Here manly virtue and the *polis* are clearly superior to and threatened by the household and the family, in which "everything serves and must serve the security of the life process."[28] Pericles' comments to the widows in the *Funeral Oration* captures this distinction clearly: "Your great glory is not to be inferior to what the gods have made you, and the greatest glory of a woman is to be least talked about by the men, whether they are praising you or criticizing you."[29]

Like Pericles, Mill is arguing that female domination of the household diminishes courage and innovative actions and drives talented men to be primarily concerned with the protection of family and home. Unlike Pericles, however, Mill neither aims to reconstitute the *polis* nor equates virility in war with virtue. Again contradicting Pericles, Mill does not completely reject the role women play in taming bad men. Most important, Mill argues that the emancipation of women will—in addition to expanding freedom to half of society—allow talented marital partners to become innovators that serve the public good.

Mill puts forth classical themes of friendship as he discusses these potentially new marital relations centered on human excellence.[30] While lacking Plato's poetic imagery, the energy and resolution of Mill's marital partners focused on "great objects" are similar to the philosophic *eros* and the attitude of classical friends toward each other in Plato's *Symposium*. Their longing for the good cannot be separated from their desire for one another. Mill states, "When the two persons both care for great objects, and are a help and encouragement to each other in whatever regard these, the minor matters on which their tastes may differ are not at all important to them; and there is a foundation for solid friendship, of an enduring character, more likely than anything else to make it, through the whole of life, a greater pleasure to each to give pleasure to the other, than to receive it."[31] Mill's discussion of the convergence of wills that develops among such partners, "their gradual assimilation of the tastes and characters to one another," and of the enriching of their respective natures is reminiscent of Aristotle's classic account in the *Nicomachean Ethics* of a friend as a second half, with the highest form of friendship existing in relation to the good (or virtue).[32] Mill, like the classics, also sees the best friendships existing beyond or outside the perspectives of society. They are isolated in a world of their own. Indeed, these friendships are partly defined by the self-conscious creation of a distance between themselves and others.

The manifest affinities between Mill and Plato and Aristotle regarding friendship may tend to obscure their important differences, as Mill, once again, modifies what he borrows from the ancients. Mill differs from Plato and Aristotle in that he posits that this type of friendship can be developed between men and women. He also associates this friendship with the highest form or ideal of marriage. A convergence of tastes and character, Mill argues, often happens between two friends of the same sex, who associate consistently in their fundamental aims, but it could be more prevalent within marriages, "did not the totally different bringing-up of the two sexes make it next to an impossibility to form a really well assorted union." And while Plato and Aristotle write that these highest friendships center on philosophy, Mill argues that they revolve around a broader and more socially responsible category—"great objects" that serve the public good—including the creation of "those great and luminous new ideas which form an era of thought."[33]

Mill's proposal for public voting also illustrates how Mill has a far more comprehensive and complex view of ethics and morality than that suggested by Ryan and the other revisionists. Public voting ensures that opinion will be mobilized to both preserve and induce the public good. "The universal observation of mankind has been very fallacious," states Mill in *On Representative Government*, "if the mere fact of being one of the community, and not being in a position of pronounced contrariety of interest to the public at large, is enough to insure a public duty, without either the stimulus or the restraint derived from the opinion of our fellow creatures." Like his views on the dual role of emancipated women, Mill's arguments for the structuring role of public voting centers on two key themes: shaming the weak and wicked to live up to their obligations and inducing the willful to pursue their ambitions by addressing the public good. Voters, insists Mill, have either private or public grounds for casting their ballots. Private motivations are based on a desire for money, anger, rivalry, or class and sectional interests. To prevent these motivations from entering into the spirit of the political institutions, Mill argues, they must be confronted with the opinion of the honest, public-oriented voters through the open ballot. Public voting also will require those who wish to innovate or think differently to work within the bounds of public opinion. "Nothing has so steady an influence as working under pressure," summarizes Mill. "No one will do that which he expects to be greatly blamed for, unless from a preconceived and fixed purpose of his own, which is always evidence of a thoughtful and deliberate character."[34]

Mill's position on the subjection of women and public voting reveals that his view of ethics and morality is far more multidimensional than Ryan's and the revisionists' argument that his moral concerns center on determining whether law or public opinion provides the best framework for free human conduct. And his views concerning the contributions of emancipated women and the open ballot is not an aberrant idea in his political philosophy. Mill's views on seminal topics of Western thought—empiricism's conception of moral sympathy, romanticism's idea of liberty, Plato, Christianity, to name a few—reveal him to be consistently concerned with situating freedom and choice within an account of ethics and the good for a human being. In contrast to Ryan's and the revisionists' picture of a circumscribed Mill, Mill's vision of a liberal society is made up of two parts: creative individuality and the unity of will needed to sustain society. These two values produce distinct but not contradictory emphases in his writings. Mill sees a need for liberal societies to discipline themselves through a commitment to the general welfare while still encouraging the forces of human creativity. He hopes to accomplish this double task by joining modern justice and general moral development with civil practices and values that engender individual self-mastery and the exertion of human energy.

MILL AND HIS INTERPRETERS

From the perspective of Mill's overall vision of the future, the traditionalists and revisionists interpret Mill narrowly: Mill's road to a comprehensive morality is treated as the single end or goal of his liberalism. What Mill considered an integral *part* of a morality of the future—the many circumstances in which free choice is to be permitted and the fewer instances in which it might be limited—has become Mill's *whole* political philosophy. Many analysts understand Mill as *the* advocate of negative liberty, which is generally understood as extending to all actions except those that may cause direct harm to others. Indeed, this view that Mill's single teaching is the need to expand free activity almost without limit has become an important part of our intellectual culture. In many respects, the general understanding of liberty and individuality held by the American citizen at the turn of the twenty-first century is consistent with his harm principle. Law, civil institutions, and public opinion are understood as lacking any legitimate authority to foster virtue and repress vice, to shape personal ends or notions of happiness, to define the ultimate worth or dignity of the human being.

This parsing of Mill's thought is not a surprise. Mill embraced and extended negative liberty, not only against the magistrate but "against the prevailing opinion and feeling." As Mill expressed it, "The only purpose for which power can be rightfully exercised over any member of a civilized community, against his will, is to prevent harm to others. His own good, either physical or moral, is not sufficient."[35] Mill also is partly to blame that only a part of his thought is embraced or adhered to and that his overall political philosophy is not recognized. Certainly Mill's idea of encouraging diversity has the potential to end, or at least discourage us, for fear of diminishing our choices and weakening our will to choose, to pursue avenues of inquiry that lead to the second leg of Mill's political philosophy; namely, the discovery of better and worse modes of life and wisdom.

In Mill's call for many different modes of life, we have the view that the good life for you is not the same as the good life for me; each of us can go our own path, and we should not collide over them. On this account, people become human in the fullest sense through the activity of freely creating their own way of life. "Different persons also require different conditions for their spiritual development," states Mill, "and can no more exist healthily in the same moral than all the variety of plants can in the same physical, atmosphere and climate."[36] Each person in this romantic-expressivist vision has something special to offer the world through his or her mode of existence. Either criticizing or following others may betray our respective ways of life. What public and civil life ought to honor and promote is only whatever sorts of behavior and outlook, whatever kinds of institutions and practices, liberate individuals, as choosing beings, from all unchosen constraints. Romantic-expressivism, in short, is resistant to establishing modes of existence as higher or lower. At the end of chapter 3 of *On Liberty,* Mill leaves us with the question of whether wisdom and diversity may be inherently antithetical or at least, to a degree, adversarial. Certainly almost all contemporary commentators, who generally portray Mill as the archetype theorist of negative liberty, ignore his concern for wisdom.[37]

When it comes to cultivating higher modes of life and wisdom, Mill's political philosophy faces constraints. He is determined to extend liberalism's commitment to secure the conditions of free human conduct through limiting the restrictions imposed by law and public opinion. He also adheres to the romantic-expressivist view that, as Wordsworth put it, the glory of the human soul is with infinity and therefore with "something ever more about to be." Still, as an empiricist he recognizes that self-developed ways of life are not generated spontaneously and do not arise necessarily; they are cultivated and sustained by circumstances. To actualize them, laws and civil society must develop practices and beliefs that generate developed minds and strong wills. Mill's liberalism, in short, must by definition be broadly inclusive of diversity, yet it cannot be totally indifferent to the character of its citizens. A society based on free human conduct and self-development is dependent on the human qualities that it does not spontaneously generate and sustain. These human qualities cannot be imported from the outside, for they must be immanent to the liberal way of life. Mill insists that only free moral agents can attain the highest human qualities and that it is not the role of law and public opinion to compel higher modes of existence; only free men and women can release the vital energies of life—most notably reason and the will—so long held down by customs and conventional practices. His commitment to free human conduct and self-development requires exercising restraint in regard to the steps that would contribute to the cultivation of the qualities he believes liberal societies need if they are to prosper and protect liberty itself.[38]

By turning to Aristotle's *Politics* we gain insights into Mill's dilemma. In the *Politics,* Aristotle notes that different types of regimes cultivate different types of citizens so that the characteristics of citizenry differ from one type of political order to another. Oligarchic regimes tend to produce citizens primarily concerned with wealth; democratic regime cultivates citizens with a political disposition centered on freedom and equality. Regimes, in short, curry citizens in the image of their central political principle. As Aristotle puts it, if the organization of composition is different, the compound creates a distinct mix of the same elements. What characterizes an excellent citizen derives from the primary aim of the political association. "Although citizens are dissimilar," Aristotle argues, "preservation of the partnership is their task, and the regime is [this] partnership; hence the virtue of the citizen must necessarily be with a view to the regime." As Aristotle explains it, the qualities of *citizenship* and the *best life* are not the same because the primary goals of the political association are in tension with or in opposition to the comprehensive development of the human faculties: "If, then, there are indeed several forms of regime, it is clear that it is not possible for the virtue of the excellent individual to be a single or complete virtue. That it is possible for a *citizen* to be excellent yet not possess the virtue in accordance with which he is an excellent *man,* therefore, is evident" (emphasis added).[39]

From the perspective of Aristotle's teachings, it follows that a regime grounded in Mill's harm principle will cultivate tolerant citizens with dispositions that generally shun commenting on whether this or that individual or social practice is better or worse, as long as these individuals and practices respect the rights of others. The root of the problem is that, as the primary goal of equality in freedom—the inviolable principle of Mill's liberalism—gains a foothold in the liberal citizen's character, rather than existing as the highest good among many, it slowly becomes the one and only aim or good. Further, Mill's argument that the free individual is not to rest and refer to an established standard but to move on in the ceaseless journey of new experiences limits our ability to say that one way of life is better than another. There is a vitalism intrinsic to romantic-expressivism which privileges that which lives, moves, and changes over that which establishes static or general standards.

This emphasis on movement and change limits Mill's ability to succeed in his challenge to Plato. Mill regretted that Plato could not reconcile the goals of wisdom and liberty; he charged that Plato grew frustrated by his inability to discover justice and increasingly became concerned solely with the character, disposition, and wisdom of a small elite of philosophers and legislators. Mill's problem comes from the opposite direction. His concerns for an overarching morality of justice and self-realized ways of life preclude his ability to develop the circumstances that will cultivate wisdom and higher ways of life. Although Mill wants to promote higher modes of existence, he always insists that we must respect the moral agency of others; even those we think are acting foolishly. Over time, as Nietzsche predicts, modern culture loses more and more confidence in its ability to identify higher and lower, better and worse, practices and ways of life: the modern intellectual is characterized by either the complacent observation (social science) or tepid celebration (historicism) of different values; the modern mind protects differences and celebrates ambiguity.

"Whither are we moving?" Nietzsche asks. "Away from all suns? Are we not plunging continually? Backward, sideward, forward, in all directions? Is there still any up and down?"[40]

To be sure, Mill is neither silent nor indifferent to the connection between promoting self-development and discovering new truths and better ways of life.

> It would be a great misunderstanding of this doctrine to suppose that it is one of selfish indifference which pretends that human beings have no business with each other's conduct in life, and that they should not concern themselves about the well-doing or well-being of one another, unless their own interest is involved. . . . I am the last person to undervalue the self-regarding virtues; they are only second in importance, if even second, to the social. It is equally the business of education to cultivate both. But even education works by conviction and persuasion as well as by compulsion, and it is by the former only that, when the period of education is past, the self-regarding virtues should be cultivated.[41]

For Mill, there is no contradiction between self-development, tolerance, and conflicting opinions, on the one hand, and the increasingly universal acceptance of new synthetic standards of good and bad, on the other hand. Fostering differences, criticisms, and contradictory paths did not mean for Mill that we quit discovering better and worse ways of life. The former was a necessary condition for the latter, and while it may seem from the focus of Mill commentators that Mill prefers the current of his thought that contributes to liberty and self-development to the current of his thought that focuses on wisdom and discovering the truth, in fact, Mill regards neither by itself as a likely or desirable way to develop the good society.

But Mill's leading principles—protection of all self-regarding activity, self-expression as the best life—set in motion a conceptual dynamic that all too easily induces silence about what ideas or practices are best. Indifference to questions about their cultivation result. Whether or not Mill's harm principle rejects legal enforcement of practices that cultivate rationality and fortitude, refuses to limit alternative modes of existence, or, most important, makes individual choice the touchstone of human development,[42] Mill's leading political principles shift focus away from a determinate set of excellences of character. Moral and intellectual qualities that determine the good human being somehow get lost in the dynamic. Indeed, spurred on by Mill's injunctions against judgmentalism, his successors become skeptical critics of Mill's judgment that there are higher and lower ideas and modes of existence. Tellingly, most of the contemporary literature on Mill focuses on the presentation of his harm principle, not as he himself presented it, but "reconstructed" and "improved," so that he is shown as one who would have agreed with expanding liberty of action in more and more spheres of society.[43] These commentators ignore Mill's view that both the romantics and ancients taught qualities of character that would lead to higher forms of individualism, and they eschew his position that the waning conflict between competing conceptions of liberty required the tactical embrace of eccentricity as an expression of the human good. In these analysts' eyes, Mill and liberalism are indifferent to substantive ethical concerns, apathetic to the human bonds that hold societies together, and antagonistic to human excellence.

One cannot accuse Mill of failing to see the necessity of wisdom and higher modes of existence for the development of individual happiness and a prosperous liberal society, for these he put forth with impressive clarity (notwithstanding, in most cases, their being overlooked by contemporary commentators). To be sure, it is one thing for Mill to say that people should continue to be open to what ideas and practices are better or worse, and quite another for analysts of Mill to say that these questions are irrelevant to human happiness and liberalism's well-being. Mill's political philosophy, however, was left vulnerable because, having underestimated the vulnerability of all sectors of liberal society to the actualization of the liberal spirit, he failed to provide adequate sustenance of the mental and moral qualities that are necessary for liberalism's comprehensive moral development. *On Liberty* does not fully clarify the disproportion between liberalism's need for moral and intellectual development and the means he proposes to identify the qualities it needs its citizens to possess.

THE DEMOCRATIC INTELLECTUAL

Accordingly, Mill's expectation that the "instructed minds" would develop as either statesmen willing to stand above public opinion or, in some circumstances, special elites who perceived and pursued the general interests has not been realized. One could apologize for Mill by pointing to other influential modern thinkers—both before and since—who also believed that either intellectuals or "noble minds" could be specifically cultivated as statesmen or classless leaders of society. For instance, Mill's belief that proportional representation would contribute to an enhanced political role for those individuals driven by higher considerations than party or pressure group is not fundamentally different from Alexander Hamilton's proposal that an electoral college will enable presidents to be statesmanlike figures who stand above the "vicious arts" of partisan politics. "Talents for low intrigue, and the little arts of popularity, may alone suffice to elevate a man to the first honors in a single State," notes Hamilton, "but it will require other talents, and a different kind of merit to establish him in the esteem and confidence of the whole Union. . . . It will not be too strong to say that there will be a constant probability of seeing the station filled by characters pre-eminent for ability and virtue."[44]

Mill's proposal that extra votes be given not to property owners but to those who have attained higher levels of intellectual excellence is consistent with the spirit of Thomas Jefferson, who argued for the need to diminish in democracy an "artificial aristocracy, founded on wealth and birth," while welcoming within government a "natural aristocracy" grounded in "virtue or talents." This "natural aristocracy," Jefferson goes on to say, "I consider as the most precious gift of nature, for the instruction, the trusts, the government of society. . . . May we not even say that that form of government is the best which provides the most effectually for a pure selection of these natural *aristoi* into the offices of government?"[45] Rousseau asserted in the *Social Contract* that an "elected aristocracy" was the best form of government, the administration of laws by those whose superiority was due to such conventional attributes as honesty, soundness of understanding, and experience in public affairs.[46] Hegel asserted the necessity of "executive civil servants" for the purpose of protecting "the particular rights [of the corporations], legality and the universal interest of the state."[47] Karl Mannheim, among many other twentieth-century thinkers, consistently expressed a Millian-like view that intellectuals comprise the only group that can at least temporarily ignore the private interests that modern societies engender in them and take on a detached view of the common good.[48]

However, identifying Mill's affinities with other seminal thinkers regarding modernity's need to cultivate in statesmen or elites a universal outlook or moral and intellectual excellence should not obscure his failure to assess accurately the character of the modern intellectual. Mill never offered a road map showing how this uniform outlook was to be forged among the intellectual elite. Consistent with his position that the character of speculative thought is the most decisive factor in founding and establishing social practices,[49] Mill assumes that his project to reconcile the fundamental divisions of Western political philosophy will unify the intellectuals of the future. What is required to unify the intellectuals is the right set of political principles. "If your opinions or mine are right," he writes to Sterling in a letter discussing his goal to reconcile the major divisions in political philosophy, "they will be in time adopted by the instructed classes."[50]

Indeed, there is a not very well thought out *current* of pantheism in Mill's approach to the modern intellectual. Pantheism, which is a characteristic of romanticism and later Continental thinking,[51] assumes that if historical forces are obeyed a primordial unity of subjective and objective good, which existed in Genesis or among the ancient Greeks, will be restored at a self-conscious or higher level. Pantheism emphasizes history as the midwife or transmitter between unity lost and unity gained. While individuals often play decisive roles at crucial moments in forging unity, pantheism tends to promote the belief that no one acts voluntarily and that whole peoples are being driven toward unity by grand historical forces above or outside of them. Mill does *not* assume that society is automatically moving toward unity, but he does state at times—despite his revulsion from English intellectual life—that the intellectual sector of English society is on the edge of full-scale agreement regarding the subjective and objective good.[52] "For my own part," he writes, "not believing in universal selfishness, I have no difficulty in admitting that Communism would even be practicable among the [intellectual] *elite* of mankind."[53] Here Mill's thought would have benefited from the treatment of democratic intellectuals and culture in Tocqueville's *Democracy in America*.

Tocqueville's thesis is that democracy overruns modern culture and politics.[54] His concern is that in democracies, unpopular and alternative ideas will no longer be proposed at all, as individuals of independent minds will become isolated and dispirited by the weight of public opinion. Tocqueville believes that as democratic individuals become more and more alike, the belief of general equality of the intellect insinuates itself slowly into the public outlook, and it becomes extremely difficult for the views of exceptional individuals, whatever they may be, to exercise influence over the public opinion.

The modern intellectual, Tocqueville warns, discovers that very few things elevate "him much above them [the public] and distinguishes him from them," and he "begin[s] to distrust himself when they are at war with him." Not only will the modern intellectual "doubt his strength, but he comes to doubt his right to it, and he is very near to recognizing that he is wrong when the greater number affirms it. The majority does not need to constrain him; it convinces him." Henceforth, the substantive outlook of the modern intellectual will not be fundamentally different from that of the mass individual, who, in turn, will display little concern for debating alternative ideas and social practices, as he is now focused exclusively on improving his material well-being. In the cultural realm, for instance, "the democratic social state and institutions give to all the imitative arts certain particular tendencies that are easy to point out," states Tocqueville. "They often turn them from the depiction of the soul to apply themselves to the body: and they substitute the representation of motion and sensations for that of sentiments and ideas; finally, in place of the ideal they put the real."[55] Tocqueville, in short, dismisses a vision of democracy in which intellectuals evaluate alternative experiences originated by creative individuals in civil society, contributing to people discovering the best life and having the opportunity to gain more control over their mental and moral faculties.

In Mill's generally laudatory reviews of Tocqueville's *Democracy in America* in 1836 and 1840, he explicitly rejects Tocqueville's thesis regarding the "learned class" being subsumed by democracy.[56] Mill counters that, in England, intellectuals generally embrace the idea that "the most serious danger to the future prospects of mankind is the unbalanced influence of the commercial spirit," and he puts forth that these learned minds must be cultivated as a social bulwark "for opinions and sentiments different from those of the mass." Mill insists that the intellectuals' capacity for limiting the excess of commercialism "by a contrary spirit, are at once apparent." He concludes that England has an advantage over America in that it possesses a well-articulated intellectual class and that energy must be devoted to making it better and better qualified for the important function of representing a unified impartial outlook in society.[57]

While Mill's view of modern intellectuals does not necessarily detract from his thesis that competent minorities or statesmen are necessary for liberalism to prosper (a position Tocqueville also maintains), it is now clear that the present-day intellectual is unable to fulfill this role. Indeed, the contemporary one-sided reading of Mill as a theorist who focuses exclusively on liberty of action reinforces Tocqueville's thesis that the modern intellectual turns from the soul to the body, substitutes motion for sentiments and ideas, and replaces the ideal with the real.

CONCEPTIONS OF FREEDOM

As Mill also draws from the various currents of political philosophy to reframe the modern conception of liberty, it becomes necessary to evaluate his theory from the perspective of his self-imposed task of mediating the differences between the empiricists' and romantics' conceptions of freedom. And here we find his theory of liberty to be far more coherent and consistent than his proposal that diversity and contrasting modes of existence will cultivate new synthetic truths and wisdom.

The opposite of freedom for empiricists such as Hobbes, Locke, and Hume was a specific kind of constraint, restrictions on human conduct coming from another human being or group of human beings. Human actions are necessitated, and therefore unfree, only when they are coerced, and they are coerced only by external impediments, imposed intentionally by other persons. On the traditional empiricist understanding of liberty, it does not matter much what we do so long as we agree to do it. From this perspective one is free to act, not free to will, as antecedent circumstances determining the will always exist.

In both the *Logic* and *Hamilton* Mill agrees with the empiricists' position that liberty requires free action. But based on a deeper conception of freedom, he recognizes that even a society that is free by egalitarian standards is not sufficient to provide "moral freedom" or the opportunity to choose one's way of life. Mill claims traditional empiricism's conception of circumstances is too narrow: it tends to overlook consideration of the motives that propel human activity and therefore ends up misunderstanding the circumstances affecting human conduct. More important, empiricism has failed to recognize that, when an agent comes to the realization of his own role in determining ends, the antecedent circumstances for human conduct undergo an important change. In particular, a life dominated by customs is one of servitude and weakness due to its ignorance of causes, whereas the free life is one of deliberative action, a life in which the more one reflects on the character of his experiences, the larger becomes his awareness of his power and free agency. An agent's outlook does not merely reflect but *alters* his world, so that it is the state of the individual's mind, as *part* of the empirical conditions, which enables him to be a free individual. From this more developed idea of freedom, for our actions to be genuinely free, we must will the outcome we desire. Such an understanding of freedom attempts to address the challenge raised by Rousseau, Kant, Coleridge, and the romantics concerning the origin, status, and quality of our desires. If my desires are not chosen but derive externally, then any goal I pursue as a reflection of them actually deepens my entrenchment in an external system of commands and prohibitions. Rather than being in charge of my life, I become an accomplice to my own dependence.

In both the *Logic* and *Hamilton,* however, Mill recognizes a conundrum as he attempts to reconcile the empiricist view of causation and the romantics' concern for free will. Human beings, in his account, are basically unfree in all activities in which desires can be understood as being determined *only* by causes external to the will. But as an empiricist, he holds that whatever happens is determined by antecedent events and circumstances. Mill, in short, requires external or antecedent circumstances that form individuals with a character that regards self-development and self-realization as the good. Mill is aware that the individual's self-consciousness does not exist in isolation and that the structure of the mind is socially developed through and in conflict with other minds. Where will these antecedents come from? As Mill asks in the *Logic*, "Our character is formed by us as well as for us; and how?"[58]

Mill's expressivist conception of liberty attempts to close the gap between empiricism's view of causality and the romantics' conception of the free will. The actualization of different ways of life will induce people to make choices about their own character, thus further promoting self-determined modes of existence. Freedom, instead of being the capacity to satisfy any desire that might occur, becomes the capacity to satisfy a particular desire—that of modifying or choosing one's character. In Mill's view, choice in regard to different modes of existence performs the same task as Plato's dialectic: allowing for the development of human judgment, which is the highest good of human life. The alternative modes of existence will create the circumstances that enable the desires for self-command to arise among human agents. Two things are necessary for "human development," insists Mill, "namely freedom and variety of situations."[59] Diverse modes of existence will create the antecedents needed to promote the romantic-expressivist goal of self-development within the empiricist view of causation.

Here it is instructive to situate Mill's position in relation to the dichotomies that Kant's and Hegel's negative and positive conceptions of freedom create. For Kant, the "state creates conditions of negative liberty that are instrumental to the positive freedom of the individual," but neither state nor society is capable of creating the conditions or experiences that cultivate the realization of autonomy in the most complete sense. A focus on developing the conditions for a fully self-defined existence will end up being the worst enemy of the "autonomy" it purports to aid. Therefore, the state creates a legal environment for the realization of autonomy by extending negative freedoms so that one can be self-determining through exercise of the moral law. The laws and practices of society should not *obstruct* the individual's ability to attain autonomy. They should grant him the external freedom to find internal autonomy.[60]

Hegel responds to this argument by charging Kant with confusing different stages of freedom—abstract right and subjective freedom—and argues that state and society are not mere instruments for the self-determination and positive freedom of the individual. Rather, the individual must experience a genuine identification with the universal interests of civil and political institutions, most notably the state. As individuals recognize their own minds—their own conception of subjective freedom, realized in the constitution of the state— they come to view the state and its institutions not as mere instruments of their freedom, but as expressions of it. It is only at this moment, with the natural workings of the mind—freed from myth and tradition—finally coinciding with a functioning concrete social world that one realizes the ideals Kant told us had to remain as "oughts." Only then does the individual enter the final and most complete stages of freedom.[61]

Like Hegel, Mill maintains that circumstances and experiences are crucial to shaping and realizing, not merely reducing obstacles to, the free will. Here Mill follows Tocqueville, however, and rejects proposals focusing on centralized states as potentially dangerous. Mill also rejects the claim that it is through identification with the universal that the individual becomes totally free.[62] Like Kant, Mill retains a commitment to a negative liberty that restricts what others can do to the individual by the exercise of their wills. This negative liberty is an essential condition for the freedom of the individual, but freedom itself is not *completely* realized merely because a condition for its exercise has been met. Hence, Mill advocates a romantic-expressive conception of the best life and transforms the Platonic dialectic whereby individuals defend their way of life against opponents. The goal is to form individuals with the qualities of mind and character capable of exercising choices skillfully, boldly, and autonomously. It is only through conflict and contradictory roads that one learns who and what one is and the possibility of growing as an individual. It is these learned experiences that Kant and others mistakenly identify as an innate free consciousness. Mill writes,

> Suppose that my experience of myself afforded two undeniable cases, alike in all the mental and physical antecedents, in one of which cases I acted in one way, and in the other in the direct opposite; there would then be proof by experience that I had been able to act in either one way or in the other. It is experience of this sort I learn that I can act at all, viz., by finding that an event takes place or not according as (other circumstances being the same) a volition of mine does or does not take place. But when this power of my volitions over my actions has become a familiar fact, the knowledge of it is so constantly present to my mind as to be popularly called, and habitually confounded with consciousness. And the supposed power of myself over my voli-

tions, which is termed Free will, though it cannot be a fact of consciousness, yet if true, or even believed, would similarly work itself into our inmost knowledge of ourselves, in such a manner as to be mistaken for consciousness.[63]

Mill's goal of creating options for the self-amendment of character creates more openness and moral indeterminacy than Hegel's corporate liberalism, while bridging Kant's division between *Rechtslere* and *Tugendlere:* the legal duties of justice and the moral duties of a self-determined existence.

THE PAST AND PRESENT

Thoughtful assessments of Mill's political philosophy are so rare in contemporary political theory because most commentators on Mill do not analyze him as a comprehensive thinker within the central currents of Western political philosophy. *On Liberty* and *Utilitarianism* are largely read independently of Mill's other writings and are connected to seminal writings in philosophy and political theory only "within a thin historical narrative informed by the progressive refinement of epistemological issues and the grounds of moral and political obligation."[64]

Emblematic of this problem, most contemporary interpretations of Mill's thinking suppress the continuities linking Mill's views to previous political philosophy. Mill clearly upholds modern goals such as choice, equality, and the conquering of human suffering. But he also addresses classical concerns of political philosophy—reason and faith, philosophy and poetry, liberty and virtue, self-interest and morality, particular and general goods. Nevertheless, there has been no attempt to explain comprehensively and systematically Mill's appropriation of classical and premodern thinking in constructing his liberal political philosophy.[65] For instance, Mill's analysis of what lessons should be taken from Plato's dialogues allowed him to deepen his arguments about the advantages and disadvantages of different types of moral outlooks. But Mill commentators' excessively narrow approach to both Mill and Plato leads them to ignore Mill's writings on Plato. Similarly, Mill writes in his *Diary,* "Religion, of one sort or another, has been at once the spring and regulator of energetic action, chiefly because religion has hitherto supplied the Philosophy of Life, or the only one which differed from a mere theory of self-indulgence."[66] Nonetheless, almost all contemporary analysts of Mill ignore his views on religion.[67]

This lacuna in the study of Mill suggests that the outlook toward liberalism held by many contemporary analysts inhibits the study of liberalism's foundational principles. All recognize that liberalism's highest goals, whether that of the self-interested, disengaged, self-expressive, or rationally motivated individual, are a radical break from the focus of ancient philosophy and medieval faith on the virtues required to live in conformity with a transcendent order. But this understanding of liberalism's new aims often contributes to overlooking how premodern and diverse currents of thought either contribute to or buttress the modern project.[68] For instance, analysts like Berlin and Ryan detach modern thinking from previous political philosophy, in the process discarding the founding assumptions of liberalism and losing the views of seminal thinkers such as Mill on the ethics and mores of liberalism. Mill scholarship fails to initiate discussions about whether the Anglo-Scottish Enlightenment failed to break sufficiently with Christianity, or whether the United Kingdom and the Continent faced different forms of one-sided moral development, or whether both romantic and ancient outlooks stood in opposition to an English liberalism that did not take responsibility for human development, or whether it is possible to reconcile empiricism's causality and romanticism's free will. Rather, the debate on Mill in contemporary political theory centers on a traditional interpretation of a simplified, ambivalent Mill unable to reconcile conflicting views, or a revisionist portrayal of a coherent prosaic Mill. Given these interpretations, it is not surprising that in recent decades liberalism has become synonymous with indifference to substantive moral concerns, hostility to human bonds that hold societies together, and antagonism to human excellence.

Mill tells us in *The Subjection of Women* that it has become more difficult to create new values in the modern era and that we have inherited a complex intellectual heritage. Unlike previous ages, he argues, potential founders confront new conditions. As civilization has developed, philosophical, political, and scientific thinking has become structured. "Nearly all the thoughts which can be reached by mere strength of original faculties," Mill writes, "have long since been arrived at; and, originality, in any high sense of the word, is now ever scarcely attained but by minds which have undergone elaborate discipline, and are deeply versed in the results of previous thinking." By knowing the past, one begins to understand both what contributes to one's own thinking and the good and bad, advantages and disadvantages, of previous thoughts and experiences. The past, Mill believes, is a crucial comparative heuristic: if we have nothing to compare the present to because we have forgotten everything in the past, on what grounds can we hope to criticize or improve upon the world as we find it? Consequently, "every fresh stone in the edifice has now to be placed on the top of so many others, that a long process of climbing, and of carrying up materials, has to be gone through by whoever aspires to take a share in the present stage of the work."[69] As contemporary interpreters of Mill restrict their analysis of his thinking to what they find to be original and beyond the past, they identify him as a founder of a modern liberalism that is far more narrow and one-dimensional than Mill's own political philosophy.

Notes

INTRODUCTION

1. John Stuart Mill, "Mill to John Sterling," October 20–22, 1831, *Collected Works of John Stuart Mill* (hereafter, *CW*), 32 vols., ed. J. M. Robson (Toronto: University of Toronto Press, 1963–91), 12: 77.

2. John Stuart Mill, *The System of Logic Rationative and Deductive* (hereafter, *Logic*), *CW,* 7: cxi (Preface to all editions).

3. The schism between the ancients and moderns is identified by Leo Strauss, *Natural Right and History* (Chicago: University of Chicago Press, 1953); C. B. Macpherson, *The Political Theory of Individualism* (London: Oxford University Press, 1962); Alasdair MacIntyre, *Whose Justice? Which Rationality?* (Notre Dame: University of Notre Dame Press, 1988). The contrasting outlook of modern British and German thought is analyzed by Charles Taylor, *Hegel* (Cambridge: Cambridge University Press, 1975). Also see, Ian Hunter, *Rival Enlightenments: Civil and Metaphysical Philosophy in Early Modern Germany* (Cambridge: Cambridge University Press, 2001); *The Enlightenment in National Context,* ed. Roy Porter and Mikulas Teich (Cambridge: Cambridge University Press, 1981).

4. John Skorupski puts forth a similar position when he states that the predominant nineteenth-century ideas of liberty "partly came from a conscious reaction [of the German Romantics] to Kant's autonomy-obsession and partly from a direct recovery of Greek ideas of self-development. Both influences, for

example, were active in shaping Mill's ethical thought. . . . [His] liberal idea was a romantic-hellenic idea of free self-development in every aspect of one's human power." "The Ethical Content of Liberal Law," in *Ethical Explorations* (Oxford: Oxford University Press, 1999), 224–25.

5. Louis Hartz, *The Liberal Tradition in America* (New York: Harcourt, 1955); Strauss, *Natural Right and History;* Macpherson, *The Political Theory of Individualism;* MacIntyre, *Whose Justice? Which Rationality?*

6. Taylor, *Hegel,* 5–50.

7. Nathan Tarcov, *Locke's Education for Liberty* (Chicago: University of Chicago Press, 1984); Nancy Rosenblum, *Another Liberalism: Romanticism and the Reconstruction of Liberal Thought* (Cambridge: Harvard University Press, 1987); Stephen Holmes, *Passions and Constraints: On the Theory of Liberal Democracy* (Chicago: University of Chicago Press, 1995); Peter Berkowitz, *Virtue and the Making of Modern Liberalism* (Princeton: Princeton University Press, 1998); Eldon Eisenach, ed., *Mill and the Moral Character of Liberalism* (University Park: Penn State University Press, 1998); Charles Griswold, Jr., *Adam Smith and the Virtues of Enlightenment* (Cambridge: Cambridge University Press, 1999).

8. For distinct positions on the overlapping traditions in American political thought, see Thomas Pangle, *The Spirit of Modern Republicanism* (Chicago: University of Chicago Press, 1988); Stephen Macedo, *Liberal Virtues: Citizenship, Virtue, and Community in Liberal Constitutionalism* (Oxford: Oxford University Press, 1990); Rogers Smith, *Civic Ideals: Conflicting Visions of Citizenship in U.S. History* (New Haven: Yale University Press, 1997). Also see, Vickie Sullivan, *Machiavelli, Hobbes, and the Formation of a Liberal Republicanism in England* (Cambridge: Cambridge University Press, 2004).

9. For a thoughtful assessment of the relation between modern and premodern thought, see Charles Taylor, *Sources of the Self: The Making of Modern Identity* (Cambridge: Cambridge University Press, 1989), 7–103.

10. Representative examples are Isaiah Berlin, "John Stuart Mill and the Ends of Life," in *Four Essays on Liberty* (Oxford: Oxford University Press, 1969), 173–206; C. L. Ten, *Mill on Liberty* (Oxford: Clarendon Press, 1989); Fred Berger, *Happiness, Justice, and Freedom: The Moral and Political Philosophy of John Stuart Mill* (Berkeley: University of California Press, 1984); Joel Feinberg, *Harm to Others: Moral Limits to Criminal Law,* vol. 1 (Oxford: Oxford University Press, 1984); John Rees, *John Stuart Mill's On Liberty* (Oxford: Oxford University Press, 1985); Alan Ryan, "John Stuart Mill and the Art of Living," in *J. S. Mill, "On Liberty" in Focus,* ed. John Gray and G. W. Smith (New York: Routledge, 1991), 9–17; Owen Fiss, "A Freedom both Personal and Political," Richard Posner, "*On Liberty:* A Revaluation," Jean Bethke Elshtain, "Liberty and the Problem of Authority," in *On Liberty—John Stuart Mill,* ed. David Bromwich and George Kateb (New Haven: Yale University Press, 2003), 179–96, 197–207, 208–23, respectively.

11. For other critiques that contemporary commentators interpret Mill too narrowly, see Eldon Eisenach, Introduction, *Mill and the Moral Character of Liberalism,* 1–5; Joseph Hamburger, *John Stuart Mill on Liberty and Control* (Princeton: Princeton University Press, 1999), xi–xviii, 1–9; Jeremy Waldron, "Mill on Culture and Society," in *On Liberty—John Stuart Mill,* 224–45.

12. Hamburger, *John Stuart Mill on Liberty and Control,* 86–107, emphasizes Mill's concern

with Christianity; Alan Ryan, *J. S. Mill* (London: Routledge, 1974), 125–33, identifies public opinion as Mill's primary target for criticism.

13. On reconstituted republicanism, Michael Sandel, *Democracy's Discontent* (Oxford: Oxford University Press, 1998); a good example of a revised critical theory is William E. Connolly, *Identity/Difference: Democratic Negotiations of Political Paradox* (Ithaca: Cornell University Press, 1991); for a new outlook based on human excellence, Laurence Lampert, *Leo Strauss and Nietzsche* (Chicago: University of Chicago Press, 1996).

14. Mill's position that empiricism had failed to develop associational psychology beyond the egoistic precepts of Locke, as well as his determination to reconcile with the romantics so that "the partisans. . . . of Locke and Kant may meet and join hands," contributed to his unwillingness to identify himself as an empiricist. Nonetheless, Mill consistently identified himself as a reformer of the "School of Experience," rather than as a member of the "School of Intuition," so I will generally identify him as an empiricist. See Mill, *Logic, CW,* 7: 14; "Coleridge," *CW,* 10: 125–31. Also see, R. P. Anschutz, *The Philosophy of J. S. Mill* (Westport, Conn.: Greenwood Press, 1953), 61–77.

15. I will be distinguishing the expressivist and moral idealist currents within romanticism throughout this book. For discussions of their relations within romanticism, Taylor, *Sources of the Self: The Making of Modern Identity,* 355–91. Also see, Lilian Furst, *Romanticism in Perspective: A Comparative Study of Aspects of the Romantic Movements in England, France, and Germany* (London: Macmillan, 1969), 13–26; M. H. Abrams, *Naturalism and Supernaturalism: Tradition and Revolution in Romantic Literature* (New York: Norton, 1971), 199–225. For a dissenting view that expressivism and moral idealism should not be identified as parts of a larger romantic outlook, Arthur O. Lovejoy, "On the Discrimination of Romanticisms," in *Essays on the History of Ideas* (Baltimore: Johns Hopkins University Press, 1948), 228–53.

16. Friedrich Nietzsche, *The Will to Power,* trans. Walter Kaufmann and R. J. Hollingdale (New York: Vintage, 1968), scts. 51, 53: 32, 33; *Beyond Good and Evil,* trans. Walter Kaufmann (New York: Vintage, 1966), sct. 224: 151–53.

17. Alexis de Tocqueville, *Democracy in America,* 2 vols., ed. and trans. Harvey Mansfield and Delba Winthrop (Chicago: University of Chicago Press, 2000), vol. 2, pt. 1: 403–78.

18. Berlin, "John Stuart Mill and the Ends of Life," 181, 185–91; Ryan, "John Stuart Mill and the Art of Living."

19. Taylor, *Hegel;* Paul Franco, *Hegel's Philosophy of Freedom* (New Haven: Yale University Press, 1999); Allan Wood, *Hegel's Ethical Thought* (Cambridge: Cambridge University Press, 1990); Steven B. Smith, *Hegel's Critique of Liberalism: Rights in Context* (Chicago: University of Chicago Press, 1989).

CHAPTER 1. THE MODERNS AND PLATO

1. Representative examples are J. Peter Euben, *Corrupting Youth* (Princeton: Princeton University Press, 1997); Gerald Mara, *Socrates' Discursive Democracy* (Albany: SUNY Press, 1997); Charles Kahn, *Plato and the Socratic Dialogue* (Cambridge: Cambridge University Press, 1996). Leo Strauss, Hans-Georg Gadamer, and Jacob Klein opposed the postwar totalitarian Plato and developed key themes of the new "literary" readings of

Plato—Socratic irony, the dramatic context of individual dialogues, contradictory teachings, among others—but their midcentury writings remained on the margins of Plato scholarship. Also see, Patrick Deneen, "Chasing Plato," *Political Theory* 28 (2000): 412–24; Charles Griswold, "E Pluribus Unum? On the Platonic Corpus," *Ancient Philosophy* 21 (1999): 420–44.

2. John Stuart Mill, *Autobiography* and "Early Draft," *CW,* 1: 25; 1: 49, respectively.

3. Berlin, "John Stuart Mill and the Ends of Life," 196; Ryan, *J. S. Mill,* 130.

4. Mill's interest in the writings of Plato has been noted but never fully elaborated by Dennis Thompson, *John Stuart Mill and Representative Government* (Princeton: Princeton University Press, 1976), 91, 113; and Maria Morales, *Perfect Equality: John Stuart Mill on Well-Constituted Communities* (Lanham: Rowman and Littlefield, 1996), 118, 127–28, 149. T. H. Irwin has a thoughtful commentary on the influence of Plato's thought and the lives of the Athenians on Mill's political philosophy in "Mill and the Classical World," in *The Cambridge Companion to Mill,* ed. John Skorupski (Cambridge: Cambridge University Press, 1998), 423–64. Also see, Berkowitz, *Virtue and the Making of Modern Liberalism,* 139–40, 151, 154.

5. John Stuart Mill, *Diary,* March 30, 1854, *CW,* 27: 665; "Mill to Harriet Taylor," January 29, 1854, *CW,* 14: 141–45; "Mill to Harriet Taylor," February 7, 1854, *CW,* 14: 151–53.

6. John Stuart Mill, "Grote's Plato," *CW,* 11: 377–440; "Mill to George Grote," November 26, 1865, *CW,* 16: 1120–21.

7. All nine translated dialogues with commentaries are published in Mill, *CW,* 11: 39–174.

8. F. E. Sparshott, "Introduction," in *CW,* 11: xix. Also see, Nadia Urbinati, *Mill On Democracy: From the Athenian Polis to Representative Government* (Chicago: University of Chicago Press, 2002), 138–46.

9. John Stuart Mill, "Translation and Commentary on *Protagoras,*" *CW,* 11: 41; "Mill to Thomas Carlyle," October 5, 1833, *CW,* 12: 181; Friedrich Schleiermacher, *Dialectic, or the Art of Doing Philosophy,* trans. Terrence Tice (Atlanta: Scholars Press, 1996); "On the Worth of Socrates as a Philosopher," trans. Connop Thirlwall in *A Life of Socrates,* ed. Gustav Friedrich Wiggers (London: Taylor and Walton, 1840), cxxix–clv.

10. *Schleiermacher's Introductions to the Dialogues of Plato,* trans. William Dobson (New York: Arno, 1973), 134–35, 169–71, 184–85, 188.

11. *Schleiermacher's Introductions to the Dialogues of Plato,* 6–7; *Christmas Eve: Dialogue on the Incarnation,* trans. Terrence Tice (Richmond: John Knox Press, 1967). Mill's rebuttal of all these positions is discussed and analyzed in chapters 2 and 3.

12. As quoted in E. N. Tigerstedt, *Interpreting Plato* (Stockholm: Almqvist and Wilskell, 1977), 7.

13. John Stuart Mill, *On Liberty, CW,* 18: 243. Also see, Dana Villa, *Socratic Citizenship* (Princeton: Princeton University Press, 2001), 59–124.

14. John Stuart Mill, *Utilitarianism, CW,* 10: 205.

15. John Stuart Mill, "The Utility of Religion," *CW,* 10: 404.

16. *Autobiography, CW,* 1: 8–18.

17. John Stuart Mill, "De Tocqueville on Democracy in America (II)," *CW,* 18: 195.

18. John Stuart Mill, "Inaugural Address Delivered to the University of St. Andrews," *CW,* 21: 219.

19. "Mill to Herbert Spencer," February 9, 1867, *CW,* 16: 1237. For criticisms of Mill's emphasis on the ancients in higher education, Thomas Huxley, *Science and Education* (New York: Collier, 1902): 183–84; Alexander Bain, *John Stuart Mill: A Criticism with Personal Recollections* (London: Longmans, 1882), 126.

20. Bain, *John Stuart Mill,* 94. On Mill's role in the mid-Victorian debate on Plato and ancient Greece, Richard Jenkyns, *The Victorians and Ancient Greece* (Cambridge: Harvard University Press, 1980); Frank Turner, *Greek Heritage in Victorian Britain* (New Haven: Yale University Press, 1981).

21. For general accounts of the period, E. M. Butler, *The Tyranny of Greece Over Germany* (Cambridge: Cambridge University Press, 1935); Henry Hatfield, *Aesthetic Paganism in German Literature* (Cambridge: Harvard University Press, 1964); M. H. Abrams, *Natural Supernaturalism: Tradition and Revolution in Romantic Literature;* Jenkyns, *The Victorians and Ancient Greece;* Turner, *Greek Heritage in Victorian Britain.* Catherine Zuckert analyzes how theorizing on Plato contributed to postmodern thought in *Postmodern Platos* (Chicago: University of Chicago Press, 1996).

22. See M. H. Abrams, *The Mirror and the Lamp: Romantic Theory and the Critical Tradition* (Oxford: Oxford University Press, 1953); Furst, *Romanticism in Perspective.*

23. Friedrich Nietzsche, "Socrates," in *The Pre-Platonic Philosophers,* trans. Greg Whitlock (Urbana: University of Illinois Press, 1995), 142–50; *The Twilight of the Idols,* trans. R. J. Hollingdale (New York: Penguin, 1990), 44.

24. As Mill puts it, "The chief fruit" of a yearlong stay in France in his late youth "was a strong and permanent interest in Continental liberalism, of which I ever afterwards kept myself *au courant,* as much as of English politics." *Autobiography, CW,* 1: 63.

25. Mill, *On Liberty, CW,* 18: 253, 255–56; *Autobiography, CW,* 1: 169, 171; "Bentham," *CW,* 10: 78–79; "Inaugural Address," 220–32, 250–55.

26. John Skorupski, *John Stuart Mill* (London: Routledge, 1989), xi–xii. Walter Bagehot, "The Late Mr. Mill," *Economist,* May 17, 1871, 589: "The great merit of Mr. Mill . . . was the merit of intellectual combination." F. A. Hayek, Introduction, *The Spirit of the Age,* by John Stuart Mill (Chicago: University of Chicago Press, 1942), vii. Mill's thought is rewarding to study "because of his rare capacity of absorbing new ideas . . . [making] . . . him a kind of focus in which most of the significant changes of thought of his time combined."

27. *The Republic of Plato,* trans. Allan Bloom (New York: Basic, 1968), scts. 608c–621d: 292–303.

28. Works that identify the role of Hellenism generally and Plato specifically in the British Romantic outlook are Jenkyns, *The Victorians and Ancient Greece;* Turner, *Greek Heritage in Victorian Britain; Platonism and the English Imagination,* ed. Anna Baldwin and Sarah Hutton (Cambridge: Cambridge University Press, 1994).

29. For accounts of relations between German and British Romantics, F. W. Stokoe, *German Influence in the English Romantic Period* (Cambridge: Cambridge University Press, 1926); Rosemary Ashton, *The German Idea: Four English Writers and the Reception of German Thought* (Cambridge: Cambridge University Press, 1980); Abrams, *Mirror and Lamp; Natural Supernaturalism;* Furst, *Romanticism in Perspective.*

30. Friedrich Schiller, *On the Aesthetic Education of Man,* trans. Elizabeth Wilkinson and

L. A. Willoughby (Oxford: Clarendon, 1967), 21. Also see, Johann Gottfried Herder, "Do We Still Have the Fatherland of the Ancients?" in *Another Philosophy of History and Selected Political Writings,* trans. and ed. Ionnis Evrigenis and Daniel Pellerin (Indianapolis: Hackett, 2004), 109–17. For accounts of the German Romantics' general approach to history, Hatfield, *Aesthetic Paganism,* 45–61; Abrams, *Naturalism and Supernaturalism,* 197–252.

31. Schiller, *On the Aesthetic Education of Man,* 22; Frederich Holderlin, "Hyperion, Or the Hermit in Greece," trans. Scwarz in *Hyperion and Selected Poems,* ed. Eric L. Santer (New York: Continuum, 1990), 3–4. Also see, F. M. Barnard, *Herder's Social and Political Thought* (Oxford: Oxford University Press, 1965), 72–87.

32. Friedrich Meinecke, *Historism: The Rise of a New Historical Outlook,* trans. J. E. Anderson (London: Routledge, 1972), 38, 249, 301–03, 315, 344–45, 371, 377–78, 492–93, 510.

33. J. G. Herder, "On Recent German Literature: First Collection of Fragments," in *Selected Early Works,* ed. Ernest A. Menze and Karl Menges, trans. Ernest A. Menze and Michael Palma (University Park: Penn State University Press, 1991), 125.

34. F. W. J. Schelling, *Of Human Freedom,* trans. James Gutmann (Chicago: Open Court, 1936), 35; *Idealism and the Endgame of Theory,* trans. Thomas Pfou (Albany: State University of New York Press, 1994), 114–17.

35. Abrams, *Naturalism and Supernaturalism,* 197–324; Furst, *Romanticism in Perspective,* 136–69.

36. Plato, *Meno,* in *Plato in Twelve Volumes,* trans. W. R. M. Lamb (Cambridge: Harvard University Press, 1990), vol. 2, scts. 84a-c: 314; William Wordsworth, "Ode: Intimations of Immortality from Recollections of Early Childhood," in *Poetical Works,* ed. Ernest de Selincourt (Oxford: Oxford University Press, 1974), 234–35. Also see, A. W. Price, "Wordsworth's 'Ode on the Intimations of Immortality,'" in *Platonism and the English Imagination,* 217–28; Abrams, *Naturalism and Supernaturalism,* 136.

37. Wordsworth, "Preface and Appendix to the *Lyrical Ballads,*" 70, 73, 80, 84, 90–91. Also, Abrams, *Mirror and the Lamp,* 100–103

38. Samuel T. Coleridge, *Biographia Literaria,* in *The Collected Works of Samuel Taylor Coleridge* (hereafter, *CW*), 16 vols., ed. Kathleen Coburn (Princeton: Princeton University Press, 1983), vol. 7, pt. 2: 15–16.

39. Samuel T. Coleridge, *On the Constitution of Church and State, CW,* 10: 13.

40. Samuel T. Coleridge, *Statesman's Manual,* Appendix C, *CW,* 6: 62–65; *On the Constitution of Church and State, CW,* 10: 55. Also see, Keith Cunliffe, "Recollection and Recovery: Coleridge's Platonism," in *Platonism and the English Imagination,* 207–16.

41. Percy Shelley, "Refutation of Deism" and "In Defence of Poetry" in *The Complete Works of Percy Bysshe Shelley,* 10 vols., ed. Roger Ingpen and Walter E. Peck (London: Longmanns, 1926–30), 6:23–60; 7:109–42, respectively. "Shelley to Thomas Jefferson Hogg," October 22, 1821, *The Letters of Percy Bysshe Shelley,* 2 vols., ed. Frederick Lafayette Jones (Oxford: Oxford University Press, 1964), 24. Also see, Jennifer Wallace, *Shelley and Greece: Rethinking Romantic Hellenism* (London: Macmillan, 1997), 141–45.

42. Shelley, "In Defence of Poetry," 135, 137.

43. *The Republic of Plato,* scts. 608c–621d: 292–303.

44. Percy Shelley, *Adonais* in *The Complete Works of Shelley,* 2, st. 52: 40.

45. G. W. F. Hegel, *Phenomenology of Spirit,* trans. A. V. Miller (Oxford: Clarendon, 1977), pars. 464–76: 8, 92; The *Philosophy of History,* trans. J. Sirbee (New York: Colonial Press, 1900), 241–65. Also see, Judith Shklar, "Hegel's 'Phenomenology:" An Elegy for *Hellas,*" in *Hegel's Political Philosophy,* ed. Z. A. Pelczynski (Cambridge: Cambridge University Press, 1971), 71–94; M. J. Inwood, "Hegel, Plato, and Greek '*Sittlichkeit,*" in *The State and Civil Society,* ed. Z. A. Pelczynski (Cambridge: Cambridge University Press, 1984), 40–54.

46. G. W. F. Hegel, *Philosophy of Right,* trans. T. M. Knox (Oxford: Oxford University Press, 1952), Preface, pars. 138, 274 A, 279: 8, 92, 286–87, 181–84; *Lectures on the History of Philosophy,* 3 vols., trans. E. S. Haldane and F. F. Simson (Lincoln: University of Nebraska, 1995), 1: 350–424.

47. Hegel, *Philosophy of Right,* par. 138: 92; *Philosophy of History,* 267–71; *Lectures on History of Philosophy,* 1: 384–447. Also, Franco, *Hegel's Philosophy of Freedom,* 103–14.

48. Hegel, *Philosophy of Right,* Preface, pars. 46, 184A, 185, 206, 258, 262A: 10, 42–43, 267, 123–24, 132–33, 156–59, 280; *Lectures on the History of Philosophy,* 1: 24–48, 90–116; 2: 49–70.

49. Hegel, *Lectures on the History of Philosophy,* 3:220–52, 293–313, 423–79.

50. For a summary of this scholarship, Tigerstedt, *Interpreting Plato,* 9–62.

51. Nicolas Capaldi discusses in *John Stuart Mill: A Biography* (Cambridge: Cambridge University Press, 2004), 144–45, the unappreciated point that Mill and Hegel address many similar themes in their political philosophies. "The similarity between Mill and Hegel was the result of the indirect influence of their reading the same sources in German and French Romanticism and also the influence on Mill of friends like Sterling. . . . The congruence is not so remarkable once we realize that both were attempting to make sense of the same new world of liberal culture, that both had begun with a rejection of the Enlightenment project, that both had seen the importance of coming to terms with Kant, and that both had recognized the need for a more historicized position."

52. George Grote, *Plato, and the Other Companions of Socrates,* new ed., 4 vols. (London: John Murray, 1888).

53. Turner, *The Greek Heritage in Victorian Britain,* 383–401.

54. For excellent discussions on the role of Socratic skepticism in the classical world, Julia Annas, "Plato the Skeptic," and Christopher Shields, "Socrates among the Skeptics," in *The Socratic Movement,* ed. Vander Waerdt (Ithaca: Cornell University Press, 1994), 309–40, 341–66, respectively.

55. Grote, *Plato, and the other Companions of Socrates,* 4: 127–29. While James Mill, Grote, and John Mill made important claims on Plato, the nineteenth-century empiricists made fewer claims than either the Romantics or Hegelians to Plato's legacy. Bentham, for instance, was particularly hostile. He wrote that "while Xenophon was writing history, and Euclid giving instruction in geometry, Socrates and Plato were talking nonsense under the pretence of teaching wisdom and morality. This wisdom of theirs, insofar as it had a meaning, consisted in denying the existence of matter made known to everybody by experience." Thomas (Lord) Macaulay was more ambivalent. "Assuredly," he wrote, "if the tree which Socrates planted and Plato watered is to be judged by its flowers and leaves, it is the noblest of trees." Nonetheless, Plato and the ancients focused

too much attention on cultivating the highest type of human character, while leaving individuals with lesser qualities to their own fates. Plato's goal was to perfect a few men, while the modern philosopher—most notably, Bacon—lengthened life and extinguished diseases. Plato's aim was noble, but Bacon's goal was realizable. See Jeremy Bentham, *Deontology and A Table of Springs of Action,* ed. Amnon Goldworth (Oxford: Clarendon, 1983), 135–36; Thomas Macauley, "Lord Bacon," in *Critical, Historical, and Miscellaneous Essays,* 6 vols. in 3 bks. (Boston: Houghton, Mifflin, 1880), vol. 3, bk. 2: 439–40.

56. Grote, *Plato, and the Other Companions of Socrates,* 4: 37, 123.

57. Ibid., 1: 301–39; 4: 95–132.

58. Ibid., 1: 342.

CHAPTER 2. LIBERTY AND THE JUST MORAL CONSCIENCE

1. "Grote's Plato," *CW,* 11: 415.

2. *Plato's Statesman,* trans. and ed. Seth Bernadete (Chicago: University of Chicago Press, 1984), scts. 292e–311c: 45–67.

3. "Translation and Commentary on the *Protagoras,*" *CW,* 11: 40–41.

4. "Grote's Plato," *CW,* 11: 412–15.

5. Ibid., 11: 382; "Mill to George Grote," November 26, 1865, *CW,* 16: 1120–21. Also see, "Mill to Fonblanque," January 30, 1838, *CW,* 13: 370: "What is the meaning of your insisting upon identifying me with Grote . . . or the rest? Do you in your conscience think that my opinions are at all like theirs? Have you forgotten, what I am sure you once knew, that my opinion of their philosophy is and has for years been *more* unfavourable by far than your own? and that my radicalism is of a school the most remote from theirs, at all points, which exists. *They* knew this as long ago as 1829, since which time the variance has been growing wider and wider." For Grote's reservations regarding Mill's thinking, Bain, *John Stuart Mill,* 82–83. The very different analyses of Mill's engagement with the ancients by Arlene Saxonhouse and Nadia Urbinati are weakened by their common assumption that Mill embraced Grote's positions on the classics. Arlene Saxonhouse, *Athenian Democracy: Modern Mythmakers and Ancient Theorists* (Notre Dame: University of Notre Dame Press, 1996), 18–22; Urbinati, *Mill on Democracy,* 14–18, 34, 36, 45–46, 60, 61–63, 143, 145, 152–53. For a thoughtful discussion on how Mill's and Grote's distinct views on the ancients and Plato are linked to broader philosophic and political differences, Irwin, "Mill and the Classical World," 431–39, 448–52.

6. "Translation and Comments on *Protagoras,*" *CW,* 11: 61; "Grote's Plato," *CW,* 11: 417–21.

7. *Utilitarianism, CW,* 10: 205. For the critique that Mill enlists Socrates as a utilitarian, Ryan, *J. S. Mill,* 110–11; Hamburger, *Mill on Liberty and Control,* 134.

8. "Grote's Plato," *CW,* 11: 417–21.

9. Thomas Hobbes, *Leviathan,* ed. Edwin Curley (Indianapolis: Hackett, 1994), pt. 1, chs. 1, 3, 5, 9: 6–7, 12–15, 22–27, 49; John Locke, *An Essay on Human Understanding,* ed. Peter Nidditch (Oxford: Oxford University Press, 1975), bk. 2, chs. 22–23: 288–317.

10. "Comments on James Mill's *Analysis of the Human Mind,*" *CW,* 31: 239. For Mill's most comprehensive statements on "mental chemistry" and the limitations of empiricism's as-

sociational psychology, *Logic, CW,* 8: 668–97, 842–43, 849–60; *Hamilton, CW,* 9: 177–210, 286–301, 430–70; "Coleridge," *CW,* 10: 125–131; "Bain's Psychology," *CW,* 11: 339–74. For an excellent, comprehensive analysis of this feature of Mill's political philosophy, Fred Wilson, *Psychological Analysis and the Philosophy of John Stuart Mill* (Toronto: University of Toronto Press, 1990); "Mill on Psychology and the Moral Sciences," in *The Cambridge Companion to Mill,* 203–54. Also see, Skorupski, *John Stuart Mill,* 259–82; Capaldi, *John Stuart Mill,* 43–44, 175–77, 309–12, 318–22.

11. *Logic, CW,* 8: 668–97, 842–43, 849–60; *Hamilton, CW,* 9: 125–49, 301–48; "On Bain's Psychology," *CW,* 11: 339–74; *On Liberty, CW,* 18: 229–30, 247–50.

12. Coleridge, *Biographia Literaria, CW,* 7, vol. 1: 124.

13. Paul Franco, *The Political Philosophy of Michael Oakeshott* (New Haven: Yale University Press, 1990), 18; G. W. F. Hegel, *The Phenomenology of Spirit,* trans. Miller (Oxford: Clarendon, 1977), 21; Coleridge, *Biographia Literaria, CW,* 7, vol. 1: 82–128; *Logic, CW,* 13: 239–61.

14. "Bain's Psychology," *CW:* 11: 345. Abrams, *Mirror and Lamp,* 169, notes that when Coleridge contrasts how the Imagination recreates its elements to the aggregative powers of the Mechanical Fancy, he "applies terms borrowed from those physical and chemical unions most remote, in their intimacy, from the conjunction of impenetrable discretes in what he called 'the brick and mortar' thinking of the mechanical philosophy. Thus, imagination is a 'synthetic,' a 'permeative,' and a 'blending, fusing, power.'"

15. *Hamilton, CW,* 9: 257; "Comments on James Mill's *Analysis of the Human Mind,*" *CW,* 31: 115.

16. "Bain's Psychology," *CW,* 11: 345; *Hamilton, CW,* 9: 181–82, 184. Also see, Andy Hamilton, "Mill, Phenomenalism, and the Self," in *The Cambridge Companion to Mill,* 139–75.

17. Furst, *Romanticism in Perspective,* 140–47; Abrams, *Mirror and Lamp,* 180–82.

18. William Wordsworth, "Preface of 1815," in *Wordsworth's Literary Criticisms,* 183–86. Also, Abrams, *Mirror and the Lamp,* 181.

19. "Bain's Psychology," *CW,* 11: 345; "Coleridge," *CW,* 10: 129–30. *Coleridge's Shakespearean Criticism,* 2: 170–71. See Skorupski's position that Mill stretches "naturalism"—the view that we are natural beings in a natural world—as far as he can to adopt the idealists' position that consciousness shapes reality in *John Stuart Mill,* 249–50; "Introduction: The Fortunes of Liberal Naturalism," 6–16. For an alternative argument that Mill broke from empiricism and embraced idealism, see Capaldi, *John Stuart Mill,* 314–20. While I agree with Skorupski on this question, I hasten to add that some of Mill's closest contemporaries pointed out an idealist current in his thought. See Herbert Spencer, "On Moral Character," *John Stuart Mill: His Life and Work, Twelve Sketches,* ed. Herbert Spencer et. al. (Boston: Osgod, 1873), 46–51; Bain, *John Stuart Mill,* 121. Furthermore, while the future British idealists initially criticized Mill's moral psychology, some would grow to appreciate Mill's role in initiating the movement from empiricism to idealism in England. See Bernard Bosanquet, *Logic,* 2 vols., 2nd ed. (Oxford: Oxford University Press, 1911), 1: vi; Sandra Den Otter, *British Idealism and Social Explanation: A Study in Late Victorian Thought* (Oxford: Clarendon, 1996), 55–64.

20. *Logic, CW,* 8: 677.

21. *Utilitarianism, CW,* 10: 230–31; *Autobiography, CW,* 1: 142–43, 165–67.

22. "Inaugural Address," *CW,* 21: 247; "Translation and Comments of the *Gorgias,*" *CW:* 11, 149. Aristotle makes the same point in the *Nicomachean Ethics,* trans. Terence Irwin (Indianapolis: Hackett, 1985), 1179b5–10: 291–92: "Now if arguments were sufficient by themselves to make people decent, the rewards they would command would justifiably have been many and large, as Theoginis says, and rightly bestowed. In fact, arguments seem to have enough influence to encourage and stimulate the civilized ones among the young people, and perhaps to make virtue take possession of a well-born character that truly loves what is fine; but they seem unable to stimulate the many towards being fine and good."

23. "Grote's Plato," *CW,* 11: 385, 406–16.

24. "Bentham," *CW,* 10: 90.

25. Mill argues that Descartes is the founder of this view of universals that Hegel attributes to Plato. *Logic, CW,* 8: 751–52.

26. "Inaugural Address," *CW,* 21: 229–30.

27. *Utilitarianism, CW,* 10: 249.

28. "Grote's Plato," *CW,* 11: 415; *Hamilton, CW,* 9: 46. Mill's position should be distinguished from that of Leo Strauss, who maintains that Plato used poetry to protect philosophy itself. For Strauss's (and Nietzsche's) position on the relation between philosophy and poetry in Plato, see Robert Devigne, "Plato, Nietzsche and Strauss," *Political Science Reviewer* 26 (1997): 397–434.

29. "Grote's Plato," *CW,* 11: 382–83; *Autobiography, CW,* 1: 25; "Translation and Commentary on *Parmenides,*" *CW,* 11: 222–39.

30. "Grote's Plato," *CW,* 11: 398–99, 411, 413.

31. Ibid., 415–17.

32. *Utilitarianism, CW,* 10: 219.

33. Capaldi, *John Stuart Mill,* 262: "[Mill] has made the 'right' part of the good."

34. Adam Smith, *The Theory of Moral Sentiments* (Indianapolis: Liberty Classics, 1976), pt. 1, sct. 1: 47–73; pt. 2, sct. 1: 135–53. Also see, Griswold, *Adam Smith and the Virtues of Enlightenment,* 113–46; Joseph Cropsey, *Polity and Economy* (Chicago: University of Chicago Press, 1956), 1–65.

35. Smith, *Theory of Moral Sentiments,* pt. 3, chs. 2–3, scts : 113–56; pt. 3, ch. 1: 112. Here we can clearly see the basis for Rousseau's charge—which would influence Mill—that modernity brings the division in man's soul between *amour de soi* and *amour-propre* to the breaking point. J. J. Rousseau, "Discourse on Inequality," *The Basic Political Writings,* trans. Donald A. Crese (Indianapolis: Hackett, 1987), 63, 67–68, 77–81.

36. "Comments on James Mill's *Analysis of the Human Mind, CW,* 33: 220, 231–42; "Bain's Psychology," *CW,* 11: 362–64.

37. *Hamilton, CW,* 9: 177–78.

38. Immanuel Kant, *Critique of Pure Reason,* ed. Norman Kemp Smith (New York: St. Martin's, 1965), 415–22; *Groundwork of the Metaphysics of Morals* in *Practical Philosophy,* trans. and ed. Mary Gregor (Cambridge: Cambridge University Press, 1996), 52–53.

39. *Logic, CW,* 8: 859.

40. Michael Sandel, *Liberalism and the Limits of Justice* (Cambridge: Cambridge University Press, 1982).

41. *The Subjection of Women (hereafter, SOW), CW,* 21: 265–66. For an interesting discussion of the critique that Kant assumes too much, rather than too little, Bernie Yack, "The Problem with Kantian Liberalism," in *Kant and Political Philosophy: The Contemporary Legacy,* ed. Ronald Beiner and William James Booth (New Haven: Yale University Press, 1993), 224–44.

42. *Utilitarianism, CW,* 10: 219.

43. "Coleridge," *CW,* 10: 131.

44. "Bain's Psychology," *CW,* 11: 351. Also, Wilson, *Psychological Analysis and the Philosophy of John Stuart Mill,* 129–30.

45. Rousseau, *Discourse on Inequality,* 77–80; Karl Marx, "On the Jewish Question," in *The Marx-Engels Reader,* ed. Robert C. Tucker (New York: Norton, 1978), 26–52.

46. *SOW, CW,* 21: 272–73, 275.

47. Ibid., 325.

48. Ibid., 287–90, 331–33, 338.

49. Ibid., 21: 295.

50. For the position that Mill's *SOW* is exclusively concerned with extending rights and individualism, Catharine MacKinnon, *Toward a Feminist Theory of the State* (Cambridge: Harvard University Press, 1989), 7, 42–43; Zillah Eisenstein, *The Radical Future of Liberal Feminism* (Boston: Northeastern University Press, 1986), 132–33; Gail Tulloch, *Mill and Sexual Equality* (Hertfordshire, UK: Harvester Wheatsheaf, 1989).

51. *SOW,* 21: 295. Mary Wollstonecraft had made a similar point—civility in the family was a school for the virtue of toleration among citizens—in the *Vindication of the Rights of Women* (New York: Prometheus Books, 1996), 32: "If you wish to make good citizens, you must first exercise the affections of a son and brother . . . for public affections as well as public virtues, must ever grow out of private character. . . . Few, I believe, have had much affection for mankind, who did not first love their parents, their brothers, sisters. . . . The exercise of youthful sympathies forms the moral temperature; and it is the recollection of those first affections and pursuits that gives life to those that are afterward more under the direction of reason." For discussions that Mill's *SOW* is concerned with the cultivation of higher forms of sociality and a just moral outlook, Mary Lyndon Shanley, "Marital Slavery and Friendship: John Stuart Mill's *Subjection of Women,*" *Political Theory* 9 (1981): 229–47; Morales, *Perfect Equality;* Nadia Urbinati, "John Stuart Mill on Androgyny and Ideal Marriage," *Political Theory* 19 (1991): 626–48.

52. *On Liberty, CW,* 18: 266; *SOW, CW,* 21: 294–95; *Utilitarianism, CW,* 10: 247–51.

53. Hugo Grotius, *On the Law of War and Peace,* trans. Kelsey (New York: Bobbs-Merrill, 1925), pt. 1, ch. 1, scts. 4–8: 35–37; Samuel Pufendorf, *The Law of Nature and Nations,* trans. C. H. Oldfather and W. A. Oldfather (Oxford: Clarendon, 1934), bk. 1, ch. 1, sct. 19: 18–20; bk. 1, ch. 7, scts. 7–9: 118–20.

54. Smith, *Theory of Moral Sentiments,* bk. 2, sct. 2, ch. 3: 86; David Hume, *A Treatise of Human Nature,* ed. L. A. Selby and P. H. Nidditch (Oxford: Oxford University Press, 1975), bk. 3, pt. 2, scts. 2, 5–6: 491, 522–30. For analysis of the relation between the natural law jurists and Anglo-Scottish thought, Knud Haakonssen, *Natural Law and Moral Philosophy: From Grotius to the Scottish Enlightenment* (Cambridge: Cambridge University Press, 1996).

55. *Utilitarianism, CW,* 10: 246–47.

56. Grotius, *On the Law of War and Peace,* sct. 44; John Locke, *Essay Concerning Human Understanding,* ed. Peter Nidditch (Oxford: Oxford University Press, 1975), bk. 2, ch. 28, sct. 14: 358; Hume, *Treatise of Human Nature,* bk. 3, pt. 2, sct. 2: 489–91, 497–500; Smith, *Theory of Moral Sentiments,* bk. 2, pt. 3, ch. 4: 289.

57. *Considerations on Representative Government, CW,* 19: 388; *SOW, CW,* 21: 335.

58. *On Liberty, CW,* 18: 310; *Considerations on Representative Government, CW,* 19: 383–98.

59. *Utilitarianism, CW,* 10: 228.

60. *Considerations on Representative Government, CW,* 19: 376.

61. *Hamilton, CW,* 9: 464–65.

62. Immanuel Kant, *Religion Within the Limits of Reason,* trans. Theodore M. Greene and Hoyt H. Hudson (San Francisco: Harper, 1960), 173–74; *Lectures on Ethics,* trans. Louis Infield (New York: Harper, 1963), 130–133; Howard Caygill, *A Kant Dictionary* (Oxford: Blackwell, 1995), 125.

63. *Utilitarianism, CW,* 10: 249–50.

64. *Hamilton, CW,* 9: 453.

65. Richard Wollheim points out that Mill never used the phrase "other-regarding" conduct in "John Stuart Mill and Isaiah Berlin: The Ends of Life and the Preliminaries of Morality," in *The Idea of Freedom: Essays in Honor of Isaiah Berlin,* ed. Alan Ryan (Oxford: Oxford University Press, 1979), 268. The emphasis on "other-regarding" conduct in Mill's thought is pivotal to a revisionist interpretation of Mill developed by Alan Ryan, John Rees, and others, who argue that Mill's political philosophy centers on preventing harm to others. Alan Ryan, "John Stuart Mill and the Art of Living"; John Rees, *John Stuart Mill's On Liberty.*

66. *Hamilton, CW,* 9: 452–53. Sharon Krause describes similar motivations in her depiction of the honorable individual in *Liberalism with Honor* (Cambridge: Cambridge University Press, 2002), 2–7.

67. J. J. Rousseau, *The Confessions,* in *The Collected Works of Rousseau,* vol. 5, ed. and trans. Christopher Kelly (Hanover, N.H.: University Press of New England, 1995), ch. 9: 404–05; *The Social Contract,* bk. 1, ch. 8: 150–51; Arthur Melzer, *On the Natural Goodness of Man: On the System of Rousseau's Thought* (Chicago: University of Chicago Press, 1990), 132–35.

68. Kant, *Critique of Pure Reason,* xii.

69. Immanuel Kant, *Critique of Practical Reason,* in *Practical Philosophy,* 166–67. Griswold, *Adam Smith and the Virtues of Enlightenment,* 313–14, discusses Kant's challenge to Anglo-Scottish thinking around these points; although Griswold mistakenly argues that nature plays no role in Mill's conception of morality. Also see, Julia Annas, *The Morality of Happiness* (Oxford: Oxford University Press, 1993), 137–41.

70. *Utilitarianism, CW,* 10: 230; Skorupski, *John Stuart Mill,* 14, 35.

71. Aristotle, *Nicomachean Ethics,* scts. 1103a25; 1106b35–1107a25: 33–34, 44–46. For a thoughtful discussion on the affinities between Aristotle's and Mill's conceptions of human nature, see Frederick Appel, "Natural Affinities? The Concept of Nature in J. S. Mill and Nietzsche," Paper presented at the Annual Meeting of the American Political Science Association, San Francisco, Calif., August 1996.

72. "Nature," *CW,* 10: 379–80, 397. Also see, Russell Muirhead, *Just Work* (Cambridge: Harvard University Press, 2004), 126: "Mill's discussion of such virtues as courage and truthfulness shows that he believes, much like Aristotle, that virtue often consists in developing habits—through training and under the guidance of reason—that counter the tendency of instinct. Virtue is not simply a convention but reflects an understanding of what human nature makes tempting and what, through decision and reason, it makes possible. Virtue, as Mill discusses it, can be conceived as unnatural only if we read reason out of human nature and render human nature and animal nature the same."

73. "Nature," *CW,* 10: 394–95, 396.

74. Holmes, *Passions and Constraints: On the Theory of Liberal Democracy,* 179–201; Julia Annas, "Mill and the Subjection of Women," *Philosophy* 52 (1977): 179–94.

75. Nietzsche's view of nature parallels Mill's position in three important ways. First, Nietzsche criticizes the assertion that nature itself embodies a normative ought or standard: "(I)t [Nature] is neither perfect nor beautiful, nor noble, nor does it wish to become any of these things. None of our aesthetic and moral judgments apply to it. Nor does it have any instinct for self-preservation or any other instinct. Let us beware of saying that there arc laws in nature. There are only necessities: there is nobody who commands; nobody who obeys; nobody who trespasses." Next, Nietzsche rejects Kant's position that humanity has the capacity to raise itself beyond or above nature: "When one speaks of *humanity,* thc idea is fundamental that this is something which separates and distinguishes man from nature. In reality, however, there is no such separation: "natural" qualities and those truly "human" are inseparably grown together. Man, in his highest and noblest qualities, is wholly nature and embodies its uncanny character." Finally, Nietzsche argues that ethics and moralities enable man to realize his highest natural capacities: "But the curious fact is that all there is or has been on earth of freedom, subtlety, boldness, dance, and masterly sureness, whether in thought itself or in government, or in rhetoric and persuasion, in the arts just as in ethics, has developed only owing to the 'tyranny of such capricious laws'; and in all seriousness, the probability is by no means small that precisely this is "nature" and "natural." Friedrich Nietzschc, *The Gay Science,* trans. Walter Kaufmann (New York: Vintage, 1974), sct. 109: 167–69; "Homer's Contest," in *The Portable Nietzsche,* trans. Walter Kaufmann (New York: Viking, 1978), 32; *Beyond Good and Evil,* sct. 188: 100. Also see Appel, "Natural Affinities? The Concept of Nature in J. S. Mill and Nietzsche;" Skorupski, "Introduction: The Fortunes of Liberal Naturalism." For analysis of continuities and differences in Mill and Nietzsche, see chapter 6.

76. The classic statement on virtue-centered ethics is Aristotle, *Nicomachean Ethics.*

77. For analyses that distinguish virtue-centered ethics and rule-governing moralities, Krause, *Liberalism with Honor;* Charles Larmore, *The Morals of Modernity* (Cambridge: Cambridge University Press, 1996); Onora O'Neill, "Duties and Virtue," in *Royal Institute of Philosophy Supplement: 35,* ed. A. Phillips Griffiths (Cambridge: Cambridge University Press, 1993), 107–22; Michael Davis, "Civic Virtue, Corruption, and the Structure of Moral Theories," in *Ethical Theory: Character and Virtue,* ed. Peter French, Theodore Uehling, Jr., Howard Wettstein (South Bend: University of Notre Dame Press, 1988), 352–67; J. B. Schneewind, "The Misfortunes of Virtue" (Cambridge: Cambridge University Press, 1998).

78. "Bentham," *CW,* 10: 98.
79. George Kateb, "A Reading of *On Liberty,*" in *On Liberty—John Stuart Mill,* 30.
80. *SOW, CW,* 21: 331–33; "Inaugural Address," *CW,* 21: 252–57; *Autobiography, CW,* 1: 241; "Bentham," *CW,* 10: 95–100; "Coleridge," *CW,* 10: 133–36; *Principles of Political Economy* (hereafter, *Political Economy), CW,* 3: 752–57; "Civilization," *CW,* 18: 130–32; *On Liberty, CW,* 18: 267–75.
81. *Utilitarianism, CW,* 10: 259. Even in those rare cases in which violating the rules of justice is permissible, such as breaking the law to save a life, Mill refuses to sanction injustice: "In such cases, as we do not call anything justice which is not a virtue, we usually say, not that justice must give way to some other moral principle, but that what is just in ordinary cases is, by reason of that other principle, not just in the particular case."
82. Aristotle distinguishes the excellent individual and the good citizen in *The Politics,* trans. Carnes Lord (Chicago: University of Chicago Press, 1984), 1276bl5–1276bl25: 89–91. Here I agree with William Galston's point that Mill "retained a . . . conception of virtue as an intrinsic good" and that "the practice of virtue, so understood, would also be supportive of the liberal polity." But I disagree with his position that Mill believed that "the good human being and the good citizen are identical." Mill's awareness of the distinction between these different types plays a crucial role in his political philosophy. Galston, *Liberal Purposes: Goods, Virtues, and Diversity in the Liberal State,* 218. For related discussions on the moral dilemmas that derive from liberalism's willingness to uphold the individual's right to practice "miserable individuality," see Jeremy Waldron, "A Right to do Wrong," in *Liberal Rights* (Cambridge: Cambridge University Press, 1993), 63–87; R. M. Hare, *The Language of Morals* (Oxford: Clarendon, 1961), 150–62; *Freedom and Reason* (Oxford: Clarendon, 1963), 157–85.
83. *SOW, CW,* 21: 329. Mill adds that the one notable exception to this protection of the weak being raised above the cultivation of the strong is the conjugal relation.
84. John Rawls and others miss this tension that animates Mill's thought. They insist that Mill raises the goal of autonomy above all other considerations and would not allow outlooks and ways of life that are not centered on self-development to endure. John Rawls, *Political Liberalism* (New York: Columbia University Press, 1993), 199–200; Stephen Macedo, "Liberal Civic Education and Religious Fundamentalism: The Case of God v. John Rawls," *Ethics* (1995):368–96; Larmore, *Morals of Modernity,* 128; William Galston, *Liberal Pluralism* (Cambridge: Cambridge University Press, 2002), 21–23.
85. "Inaugural Address," *CW,* 21: 253; *SOW, CW,* 21: 313.
86. "Mill to John Austin," April 13, 1847, *CW,* 13: 712; "Mill to John Lalor," July 3, 1852, *CW,* 14: 93; "Mill to Gustave d'Eichthal," May 15, 1829, *CW,* 12: 32. Mill argues that on the Continent, especially France, the moral problem comes from the opposite direction. In "France, Germany, and the Continent generally" there are many individuals who have a love of country, of virtue, of great accomplishments, but in exerting energy to realize these and other desires, the Continental individual is willing to inflict harm on other people, a practice that the morally just English eschew. "It is of no use to debate which of these states of mind is the best, or rather the least bad. It is quite possible to cultivate the conscience and the sentiments [love of virtue, nation, and great deeds] too." "Inaugural Address," *CW,* 21: 252–53; *SOW, CW,* 21: 313.

87. *Autobiography, CW,* 1: 259; *Political Economy, CW,* 3: 754.
88. "Civilization," *CW,* 18: 131; *Diary,* January 17, 1854, *CW* 27: 644; "Comparison of French and English Intellectuals," *CW,* 23: 444. For further discussion of Mill's evaluation of the English, see Edward Alexander, *Mathew Arnold and John Stuart Mill* (New York: Columbia University Press, 1965), 192–231; Hamburger, *Mill on Liberty and Control,* 33–34, 161–64, 223–24.
89. *Political Economy, CW,* 3: 754.
90. "De Tocqueville on Democracy in America (II)," *CW,* 18: 200.
91. "Civilization," *CW,* 18: 132; "The Negro Question," *CW,* 21: 94.
92. "Coleridge," *CW,* 10: 123; "Bentham," *CW,* 10: 107; *Political Economy, CW,* 3: 757. In a related argument, Capaldi distinguishes "civilization": equality under the law, private property, limited government; which induces material progress, and "liberal culture": those practices and values that cultivate the individual's mental and moral faculties. In Capaldi's account, Mill believed liberal culture is necessary to prevent the corruption of civilization: "The future of civilization depends upon the masses' exercising their power in such a responsible way that we shall continue to enjoy the benefits of civilization. Mill did not believe that this would happen on its own. Civilization would not endure unless the masses came to understand and appreciate the moral foundations of liberal culture." I would add that Mill also believed that the promotion of self-developed individuals would generate debates about higher and lower modes of existence, new synthesis, and higher levels of social unity. To Mill, "civilization" and "culture" were necessary to avoid corruption *and* generate progress. Capaldi, *John Stuart Mill,* 138, 148–56. Also see, Edward Alexander, "The Principles of Permanence and Progression in the Thought of J. S. Mill," in *James and John Stuart Mill/Papers of the Centenary Conference,* ed. J. M. Robson and Michael Laine (Toronto: University of Toronto Press, 1976), 126–42; Bernard Semmel, *John Stuart Mill and the Pursuit of Virtue* (New Haven: Yale University Press, 1984), 114–19; J. W. Burrow, "Autonomy and Self-realization: From Independence to Individuality," in *Whigs and Liberals: Continuity and Character in English Political Thought* (Oxford: Clarendon, 1998), 77–100; Alan Kahan, *Aristocratic Liberalism: The Social and Political Thought of Jacob Burkhardt, John Stuart Mill, and Alexis de Tocqueville* (Oxford: Oxford University Press, 1992), 41–57.
93. "The Negro Question," *CW,* 21: 91. Also see, "De Tocqueville on Democracy in America (I)," *CW,* 18: 74–78; "De Tocqueville on Democracy in America (II)," *CW,* 18: 196–200; *SOW, CW,* 21: 328–29, 331–33; "Inaugural Address," *CW,* 21: 252–57; *Autobiography, CW,* 1: 259; "Bentham," *CW,* 10: 95–100; "Coleridge," *CW,* 10: 133–36; *On Liberty, CW,* 18: 253–55; 267–75.

CHAPTER 3. THE CULTIVATION OF THE INDIVIDUAL AND SOCIETY

1. *Considerations on Representative Government, CW,* 19: 459.
2. Hobbes, *Leviathan,* pt. 1, ch. 5: 22–27; pt. 2, ch. 17: 106–10.
3. Locke, *An Essay Concerning Human Understanding,* bk. 2, ch. 21, sct. 42: 274–75.
4. J. B. Schneewind, *The Invention of Autonomy* (Cambridge: Cambridge University Press, 1998), 299; Locke, *An Essay Concerning Human Understanding,* bk. 2, ch. 21, sct. 37: 254–55.

5. John Locke, *Two Treatises on Government,* ed. Peter Laslett (Cambridge: Cambridge University Press, 1966), bk. 2, sct. 77: 336–37.

6. C. A. Helvétius, *De l'Homme,* in *Oeuvres Complètes,* 10 vols., ed. Jean François Saint-Lambert (Paris: Hildensheim, 1969), 7: 231–33, 270–80. Jeremy Bentham and James Mill developed very similar views of democracy's exclusive ability to establish the proper relation between self and general interests. Jeremy Bentham, *The Constitutional Code,* in *Collected Works of Jeremy Bentham,* 11 vols., ed. John Browning Bowring (New York: Russell, 1962), 9: 94–145; James Mill, "Essay on Government," in *Utilitarian Logic and Politics,* ed. Jack Lively and John Rees (Oxford: Oxford University Press, 1978), 55–95. For John Mill's critique of this view on establishing the proper relation between particular and general interests, "Bentham," *CW,* 10: 105–09; "Coleridge," *CW,* 10: 150–55. For a thoughtful discussion of Mill's relationship to Helvétius's thought, see, G. W. Smith, "Freedom and Virtue in Politics: Some Aspects of Character, Circumstances, and Utility from Helvetius to J. S. Mill," *Utilitas* 1 (May 1989): 112–34.

7. Hobbes, *Leviathan,* pt. 2, ch. 21: 134–46; David Hume, *A Treatise of Human Nature,* bk. 2, pt. 3, scts. 1–3: 399–417. For a general survey of this position on the will in political philosophy, Arthur Schopenhauer, *Prize Essay on the Freedom of the Will,* trans. Eric Payne (Cambridge: Cambridge University Press, 1999), ch. 4: 58–80.

8. Thomas Hobbes, "Of Liberty and Necessity: A Treatise," in *English Works,* 11 vols., ed. William Molesworth (London: Longmans, 1839–44), 4: 240; *Leviathan,* pt. 1, ch. 5: 22–27; ch. 14: 79–89.

9. Hume, *A Treatise of Human Nature,* bk. 2, pt. 3, sct. 1: 399.

10. Ibid., bk. 1, pt. 3, sct. 14: 171 ; *Enquiries Concerning Human Understanding,* ed. L. A. Selby-Bigge (Oxford: Oxford University Press, 1975), sct. 8: 95. For an examination of how Hobbes and Hume developed this position in opposition to the idea of an autonomous will, Stephen Carwell, *The British Moralists and the Internal "Ought"* (Cambridge: Cambridge University Press, 1995).

11. Franco, *Hegel's Philosophy of Freedom,* 3. Jean-Jacques Rousseau, "Discourse on the Origins of Inequality," 67–68, 80–88; Kant, *The Groundwork of the Metaphysics of Morals,* 49–60.

12. Rousseau, "Discourse on Inequality," 45.

13. Rousseau, *The Social Contract,* 150; *Émile, or On Education,* trans. Allan Bloom (New York: Basic Books, 1979), bk. 5: 444–45.

14. Jean-Jacques Rousseau, *The Reveries of the Solitary Walker,* trans. Charles Butterworth (Indianapolis: Hackett, 1992), 1.

15. Kant, *Groundwork of the Metaphysics of Morals,* 72–73, 75–79; Kant, *Critique of Practical Reason,* in *Practical Philosophy,* trans. and ed. Mary Gregor (Cambridge: Cambridge University Press, 1996), 162–66. For further discussion on the relation between Rousseau's and Kant's thought, Patrick Riley, *Will and Political Legitimacy: A Critical Exposition of Social Contract Theory in Hobbes, Locke, Rousseau, Kant, and Hegel* (Cambridge: Harvard University Press, 1982), 96–162; Richard Velkley, *Freedom and the End of Reason: On the Moral Foundation of Kant's Critical Philosophy* (Chicago: University of Chicago Press, 1989).

16. In *Hamilton* (published in 1865) Mill notes that the unstated goal in his discussion of the

free will in the *Logic* (published in 1844) was to develop an alternative conception of freedom to that of Kant. See John Stuart Mill, *Hamilton, CW:* 9: 467–68. For Mill's comments on the direct connection between the *Logic* and *Hamilton,* see "Mill to Bain," December 1861, *CW,* 15: 752; "Mill to Bain," January, 7, 1863, *CW,* 15: 815–18. For an
assessment of how Mill came to an understanding of Kant and Kantianism, John Skorupski, *John Stuart Mill*, 5–12: "The antagonism between naturalism and various forms
of post-Kantian idealism became the central philosophical debate of the nineteenth century. It is the constant background of Mill's philosophical writings." For Mill's general
engagement with romanticism, Capaldi, *John Stuart Mill;* Anschutz, *The Philosophy of
J. S. Mill,* 61–77; Semmel, *John Stuart Mill and the Pursuit of Virtue,* 165–73; Abrams,
Mirror and Lamp, 23–25, 102–04, 311–35.

17. John Stuart Mill, *Logic, CW,* 8: 836. Mill found it necessary in *Hamilton* to defend this
statement in the *Logic* that "everyone's instinctive consciousness" rejected determinism
because this comment intimated some type of a priori instinct or contracausal source of
freedom. "When I applied the words feeling and consciousness to this acquired knowledge," Mill states, "I did not use those terms in their strictly psychological meaning,
there being no necessity for doing so in that place; but, agreeably to popular usage, extended them to (what there is no appropriate scientific name for) the whole of our familiar and intimate knowledge concerning ourselves." *Hamilton, CW:* 9: 450; Semmel,
Mill and the Pursuit of Virtue, 19–53, and Capaldi, *John Stuart Mill,* 179–80, provide
general background on the debate in nineteenth-century English philosophic and religious circles on the relation between determinism and free will.

18. *Autobiography, CW,* 1: 175–77; "Comments on James Mill's *Analysis of the Human
Mind,*" *CW,* 31: 138–40. Also see, Robert Cummings, "Mill's History of His Ideas," *Journal of the History of Ideas* 25 (1964): 235–36; Eldon Eisenach, "Self-Reform as Political Reform in the Writings of John Stuart Mill," *Utilitas* 1 (1990): 242–58; Capaldi, *John Stuart
Mill,* 232–41.

19. *Hamilton, CW* 9: 467.

20. Mill, *Autobiography, CW* 1: 177; *Diary,* March 3, 1854, *CW,* 26: 658–59. Mill considered
this reformulation of liberty and necessity the most important contribution of the *Logic.*
See "Mill to Robert Fox," February 14, 1843, *CW,* 13: 569; "Mill to Alexis de Tocqueville,"
November 3, 1843, *CW,* 13: 612. Mill's goal of reconciling empiricism and idealism and his
statement that the human mind is part of the circumstances that shape human conduct
is remarkably similar to Marx's statement in 1845 (one year after Mill's *Logic* was published) on the need to overcome the division between "materialism" and "idealism":
"The chief defect of all hitherto existing materialism . . . is that the thing, reality, sensu-
ousness, is conceived only as an object of *contemplation,* but not as *human sensuous activity, practice,* not subjectively. Hence it happened that the *active* side, in contradistinc-
tion to materialism, was developed by idealism—but only abstractly, since, of course,
idealism does not know real, sensuous activity as such. . . . The materialist doctrine that
men are products of circumstances and upbringing, and that, therefore, changed men
are products of other circumstances, and changed upbringing, forgets that it is men who
change circumstances and that it is essential to educate the educator himself." Karl
Marx, "Theses on Feuerbach," in *The Marx-Engels Reader,* 1: 143; 3: 144.

21. Bernard Williams, *Moral Luck* (Cambridge: Cambridge University Press, 1981), 101–13; Robert Pippin, "Ethical Reasons and Kantian Rejoinders," in *Idealism as Modernism* (Cambridge: Cambridge University Press, 1997), 97, n. 10.

22. *Logic, CW,* 8: 836–43; *Hamilton, CW,* 9: 437–69. For thought-provoking discussions that Mill developed conceptions of liberty to reconcile the conflict between empiricism and romanticism, see Richard Friedman, "A New Exploration of Mill's *On Liberty,*" in Eisenach, ed., *Mill and the Moral Character of Liberalism,* 273–300; G. W. Smith, "The Logic of J. S. Mill on Freedom," *Political Studies* 28 (1980): 238–52; J. W. Burrow, "Autonomy and Self-realization: From Independence to Individuality," in *Whigs and Liberals: Continuity and Change in English Liberal Thought* (Oxford: Clarendon Press, 1998). Also see, "Tocqueville to Mill," October 27, 1843, in Alexis de Tocqueville, *Oeuvres Complètes,* ed. Mayer (Paris: Gallimard, (1951–) 2: 345. Tocqueville praises Mill's differentiation between "necessity . . . and *irresistibleness,* fatalism . . . as a ray of light." Mill is "opening a neutral terrain upon which the two opposed schools, or at least thoughtful men from the two schools, would easily be able to meet and to understand each other" (my translation). As argued by Capaldi in *John Stuart Mill,* 185–86, where he explains that the success of the *Logic* was rooted in the fact that members of both the empiricist and romantic traditions felt vindicated by it.

23. *Logic, CW,* 8: 840–41; Smith, "The Logic of J. S. Mill on Freedom," 241. Skorupski associates Mill's concept of "moral freedom" too closely with the realization of, not the opportunity for, a self-amended life in *John Stuart Mill,* 351.

24. John Gray, *Mill on Liberty: A Defense* (London: Routledge, 1986), 55; Wendy Donner, *The Liberal Self: John Stuart Mill's Moral and Political Philosophy* (Ithaca: Cornell University Press, 1991), 181; Urbinati, *Mill on Democracy,* 173. Also see Capaldi's helpful distinction between Mill's conceptions of "liberty" and "freedom" in *John Stuart Mill,* 249–54.

25. Rawls, *Political Liberalism,* 199–200; Larmore, *The Morals of Modernity,* 128; Galston, *Liberal Pluralism,* 21–23.

26. *Hamilton, CW,* 9: 450.

27. Kant, *Groundwork for the Metaphysics of Morals,* 69–71, 81–83.

28. Kant, *Critique of Practical Reason,* 189–90. Also see, Henry Allison, "Morality and Freedom: Kant's Reciprocity Thesis," *Philosophical Review* 95 (1986): 395–424; Christine Korsgaard, "Morality as Freedom," in *Kant's Practical Philosophy Reconsidered,* ed. Yirmiyahu Yovel (Dordrecht: Kluwer, 1989), 23–48.

29. Here I differ with two thoughtful commentators on Mill—John Skorupski and Nicholas Capaldi—who, while noting the important affinity between Kant's and Mill's view of autonomy, overlook their differences in regard to the character of the ideals that motivate this form of freedom. Skorupski, *John Stuart Mill,* 253; Capaldi, *John Stuart Mill,* 140.

30. Contemporary reflections of this dichotomy in political theory can be found in rational choice theory, which emphasizes the role of self-interest in decision making, and in the myriad schools—civic republicanism, Rawlsians, communitarians—that emphasize the decisive role of universal obligations. Krause critically examines this dichotomy throughout *Liberalism with Honor.*

31. *Considerations on Representative Government, CW,* 19: 444; *Utilitarianism, CW,* 10: 210, 212–1; "Remarks on Bentham's Philosophy," *CW,* 10: 12, 15; *Sedgwick's Discourse, CW,* 10: 56.

32. Waldron, "Mill on Culture and Society," 228. Also see, Muirhead, *Just Work,* 117–18.

33. Mill, *On Liberty, CW,* 18: 301–05.

34. *Considerations on Representative Government, CW,* 19: 444–45.

35. John Stuart Mill, "Reform of the Civil Service," *CW,* 18: 209; "Notes on the Newspapers," *CW,* 6: 227, 289; *Utilitarianism, CW,* 10: 215.

36. *On Liberty, CW,* 18: 261, 301–04; *Considerations on Representative Government, CW,* 19: 470.

37. Marcus Tullius Cicero, *De Finibus Bonorum et Malorum,* trans. H. Rackham (New York: Putnam, 1931), bk. 5, sct. 9: 419.

38. Aristotle, *Nicomachean Ethics.*

39. *Diary,* February 6, 1854, *CW,* 26: 651. For a related discussion, Krause, *Liberalism with Honor,* 5–7.

40. Antony Thorlby, "Liberty and Self-development: Goethe and John Stuart Mill," *Neo-Helicon* 1 (1973): 343. Also see, Kateb, "A Reading of *On Liberty*," 33: "The highest value of such individuality resides in . . . the sheer fact that he or she has attained fullness of realization or creative originality, or has shown resoluteness in a plan of life deliberately carried out; in sum, a person has reached full humanity, which is the highest end."

41. *Utilitarianism, CW,* 10: 215; *Autobiography, CW,* 1: 145.

42. *Utilitarianism, CW,* 10: 209–19; *On Liberty, CW,* 18: 261. Wilhelm von Humboldt, *The Limits of State Action,* ed. J. W. Burrow (Indianapolis: Liberty Fund, 1993), 10.

43. *On Liberty, CW,* 18: 270.

44. For a thoughtful discussion of these different teleological approaches, see William Galston, "What Is Living and What Is Dead in Kant's Practical Philosophy," in *Kant and Political Philosophy: The Contemporary Legacy,* 215–16. Also see, Krause, *Liberalism with Honor,* 6–7, 38.

45. "Bentham," *CW,* 10: 95; *Logic, CW,* 8: 841–41; *Autobiography, CW,* 1: 175–77.

46. See Furst's analysis of core themes of romanticism in *Romanticism in Perspective,* 15.

47. *Autobiography, CW,* 1: 147; "Bentham," *CW,* 10: 98–100; "Coleridge," *CW,* 10: 129–32; "Inaugural Address," 224-33, 253–57; *On Liberty, CW,* 18: 222, 252–57. Also see, Muirhead, *Just Work,* 116: "Mill's idea of 'individuality' weaves together the romantic value of authenticity, or the revealing of what is definitive, unrepeatable, and ingenious about a specific person, and a more ancient perfectionist emphasis on development, or the cultivation of the qualitatively higher powers residing in human nature."

48. "Bentham," *CW,* 10: 95–96.

49. Maria Morales and Nadia Urbinati identify Mill's debt to Plato in *SOW.* Morales, *Perfect Equality,* 127–28; Urbinati, "J. S. Mill on Androgyny and Ideal Marriage," 637. Dennis Thompson notes the influence of Plato in Mill's discussion of higher and lower pleasures in *Utilitarianism* in *John Stuart Mill and Representative Government,* 58–60. In a related discussion, Geraint Williams identifies how the ancients inform Mill's conception of happiness in "The Greek Origins of J. S. Mill Happiness," *Utilitas* 8 (1996): 5–15.

50. *The Republic of Plato,* scts. 571a–592b: 251–75.

51. *SOW, CW,* 21: 289.

52. Ibid., 279–80, 283–89, 295–96, 325–29.

53. Ibid., 334–36.

54. *Utilitarianism, CW,* 10: 211–12.

55. Ibid.

56. Ibid., 211, 213. Mill makes the same point in the *Diary* (March 23, 1954), *CW,* 27: 663: "There is needed a . . . philosophical estimate of happiness. Quality as well as quantity of happiness is to be considered; less of a higher kind is preferable to more of a lower. The test of quality is preference given by those who are acquainted with both. Socrates would rather choose to be Socrates dissatisfied than to be a pig satisfied. The pig probably would not, but then the pig knows only one side of the question: Socrates knows both." As Isaiah Berlin suggests, Mill's qualification of distinct kinds of happiness undermined the utilitarian method of Bentham and his father, as it abandoned the premises that provided simple rules for political and moral calculus: identifying happiness as measurable units; reducing political and moral questions to gross assessments of pleasure and pain. Berlin, "John Stuart Mill and the Ends of Life," 181.

57. "Grote's Plato," *CW,* 11: 410–12.

58. *Autobiography, CW,* 1: 25.

59. *On Liberty, CW,* 18: 231–32, 242–43; "Inaugural Address," *CW,* 21: 229–30.

60. John Stuart Mill, "Grote's History of Greece II," *CW,* 11: 310; *On Liberty, CW,* 18: 250–51; "Grote's Plato," *CW,* 11: 404.

61. "Grote's Plato," *CW,* 11: 414.

62. *On Liberty, CW,* 18: 246–47.

63. Ibid., 18: 36 244–46. Villa explains how Mill aims to introduce the dialectic into the center of society in *Socratic Citizenship,* 80–90.

64. "Nature," *CW,* 10: 372.

65. "Grote's Plato," *CW,* 11: 410.

66. Ibid., 403.

67. *On Liberty, CW,* 18: 251–52.

68. "Grote's Plato," *CW,* 11: 401, 404–05, 413.

69. *On Liberty, CW,* 18: 244; "Grote's Plato," *CW,* 11: 403–05.

70. "Grote's Plato," *CW,* 11: 411; *Logic, CW,* 8: 842; *Hamilton, CW,* 9: 853; *Utilitarianism, CW,* 10: 215–16.

71. *On Liberty, CW,* 18: 231; "Grote's Plato," *CW,* 11: 403–05.

72. "Grote's Plato," *CW,* 11: 405; *On Liberty, CW,* 18: 251–52.

73. "Grote's Plato," *CW,* 11: 402–403.

74. *The Republic of Plato,* scts. 484a–492a, 163–72.

75. "Grote's History of Greece," *CW,* 11: 314, 316; "Grote's Plato," *CW,* 11: 405, 409.

76. *Auguste Comte and Positivism, CW,* 10: 325; *Autobiography* (Early Draft), *CW,* 1: 244, 246; *On Liberty, CW,* 18: 262–63.

77. *On Liberty, CW,* 18: 227, 247–48, 268.

78. *Diary,* January 13, 1854, *CW,* 27: 642.

79. John Morley, "Mr. Mill's Autobiography," *Fortnightly Review* 21 (1874): 5. Waldron, "Mill on Culture and Society," 229: "The basis of Mill's case for liberty is not at all a com-

placent faith in the marketplace of ideas; it is a worry—a surprisingly resonant worry for us—that the public forum has already been corrupted by an atmosphere in which attention spans are cut short and no one will risk taking any idea seriously, as something worth bringing thoughtfully into critical relation with the truth. . . . It was not enough for the state to withdraw from the fray. Unless society changed its complexion, the phenomena of mass timidity and collective mediocrity would ensure that nothing but the blandest platitudes were manufactured in the lukewarm ambience of the contemporary marketplace." Also see, Walter Houghton, *The Victorian Frame of Mind* (New Haven: Yale University Press, 1957), 1–23, 218–42, and John Burrow, "Autonomy and Self-realization," "Balance and Diversity," in *Whigs and Liberals*, 77–100, 101–24, respectively, for further analysis of the despair felt by Mill and other Victorian intellectuals over the timid character of the English mind.

80. *Autobiography* (Early Draft), *CW*, 1: 244; "Duveyrier's Political Views of French Affairs," *CW*, 20: 300; *Diary*, February 18, 1854, *CW*, 26: 655. Also see, J. M. Robson, *The Improvement of Mankind: The Social and Political Thought of John Stuart Mill* (Toronto: University of Toronto Press, 1968), 118–59; Hamburger, *Mill on Liberty and Control*, 19–41. This shift in Mill's thinking parallels the change that occurred in Wordsworth, Coleridge, and other British Romantics' views when their hopes regarding the French Revolution were dashed, and they turned to the task of changing men's minds rather than their circumstances. Abrams, *Naturalism and Supernaturalism*, 336–48.

81. *Considerations on Representative Government, CW*, 19: 381–82; "Mill to Edward Herford," January 22, 1850, *CW*, 14: 45; "Mill to Comte," October 23, 1842, *CW*, 13: 552–53 (my translation). For other analyses that emphasize the moral character of Mill's thought, Eisenach, ed., *Mill and the Moral Character of Liberalism;* Hamburger, *Mill on Liberty and Control;* H. S. Jones "John Stuart Mill as Moralist," *Journal of the History of Ideas* 53 (1992): 287–308; Stefan Collini, "The Idea of Character: Private Habits and Public Virtues" and "Their Master's Voice: John Stuart Mill as Public Moralist," in *Public Moralists: Political Thought and Intellectual Life in Britain, 1850–1930* (Oxford: Oxford University Press, 1991), 91–118, 121–69, respectively.

82. *On Liberty, CW*, 18: 252–56.

83. Plato, *Timaeus*, in *Readings in Ancient Greek Philosophy: From Thales to Aristotle*, ed. S. Marc Cohen, Patricia Curd, and C. D. C. Reeve (Indianapolis: Hackett, 2000), scts. 35a–36b: 330–31; *Plato's Sophist: Part II of The Being and the Beautiful*, trans. and ed. Seth Benardete (Chicago: University of Chicago Press, 1986), scts. 255d–260b: 51–57.

84. "Grote's Plato," *CW*, 11: 381, 411; *On Liberty, CW*, 18: 253.

85. Samuel Coleridge, *Anima Poetae, CW*, 14: 124, 142–43. For general background on Coleridge's dialectical outlook and his relation to German Romanticism, Abrams, *Mirror and Lamp*, 170–75, 356–58, and *Naturalism and Supernaturalism*, 266–68, 360–66; "Coleridge and the Romantic Vision of the World," in *Coleridge's Variety*, ed. Beer (London: Macmillan, 1974), 103–15. Mill maintained that Coleridge was not an original thinker: Coleridge's contribution to English philosophy centered on his importing German Romanticism from the Continent. "Coleridge," *CW*, 10: 119–30. For Coleridge's assessment of his debt to German philosophy, *Biographia Literaria, CW*, 7: vol. 1, 152–67.

86. "Coleridge," *CW*, 18: 122–23; *On Liberty*, 18: 252. Capaldi explains the central role of syn-

thesis in Mill's understanding of philosophy, although he underestimates the role it also plays in Mill's vision of social development. Capaldi, *John Stuart Mill,* 25, 53–54, 143.

87. Samuel T. Coleridge, *Hints Toward the Formation of a More Comprehensive Theory of Life,* ed. Seth B. Watson (Philadelphia: Lea and Blanchard, 1848), 63. Furst, *Romanticism in Perspective,* 78–82, 324–25, discusses how, in the German Romantics' understanding, the synthesizing feature of their dialectical outlook distinguished their dialectics from those of the ancients.

88. *On Liberty, CW,* 18: 253–57.

89. Samuel T. Coleridge, "Essays on the Principles of Method," *CW,* 4, n. 1: 480; *Biographia Literaria, CW,* 7, vol. 2: 16–17; *Religious Musings,* in *The Complete Poetical Works,* 2 vols., ed. E. H. Coleridge (Oxford: Oxford University Press, 1912), 1: 108–25; *On the Constitution of the Church and State, CW,* 10: 16.

90. *Diary,* April 11, 1854, *CW,* 27: 667.

91. *Liberty, CW,* 18: 257; "De Tocqueville on Democracy in America (II)," *CW,* 18: 198; *Considerations on Representative Government, CW,* 19: 274–75. Ben Knights, *The Idea of the Clerisy in the Nineteenth Century* (Cambridge: Cambridge University Press, 1978), 37–71, 140–77.

92. Bentham," *CW,* 10: 78, 93–94; "Coleridge," *CW,* 10: 119–25; *Logic, CW,* 7: cxi; *Political Economy, CW,* 2: 4.

93. Coleridge," *CW,* 10: 122–24.

94. On Genius," *CW,* 1: 333; *Autobiography, CW,* 1: 169; "Bentham," 91; Alexander, *Matthew Arnold and John Stuart Mill,* 9. In the *Diary,* February 28, 1854, *CW,* 27: 657, Mill identifies the greatest thinkers as individuals who attempted to understand the whole, but whose "value is the value of some of their fragments": "Aristotle, Bacon, Hobbes, Locke, Hartley, Hume, Reid, Stewart, Brown, Descartes, Leibnitz, Spinoza, Kant, Condillac, Montesquieu, Adam Smith, Ricardo, Bentham . . . and Plato." Mill continues that Berkeley and Rousseau are the only great thinkers of moral philosophy and "the psychological department of thought" who were explicitly oppositionists or partial thinkers.

95. Duveyrier's Political Views of French Affairs," *CW,* 20: 306–07.

96. Bentham," *CW,* 10: 107–09; "Coleridge," *CW,* 10: 122–24; *Considerations on Representative Government, CW,* 19: 459–60; *On Liberty, CW,* 18: 274–75.

97. Barnard, *Herder's Social and Political Thought,* 144–45; von Humboldt, *Limits of State Action,* 16–37.

98. Smith, *Hegel's Critique of Liberalism,* 175. For further discussion of *Bildung,* Taylor, *Hegel,* 3–50; Barnard, *Herder's Social and Political Thought,* 85–108; Abrams, *Naturalism and Supernaturalism,* 187–95; W. H. Bruford, *The German Tradition of Self-Cultivation: 'Bildung' from Humboldt to Thomas Mann* (Cambridge: Cambridge University Press, 1975). For analyses of how the concept of *Bildung* influenced Victorian intellectuals, Ashton, *The German Idea;* Houghton, *The Victorian Frame of Mind,* 285–91. Capaldi identifies the central role of *Bildung* in Mill's thought but emphasizes the current of *Bildung* centered on self-discovery. He rarely mentions those aspects of *Bildung* centered on hierarchy and a unifying culture. Capaldi, *John Stuart Mill,* 287–92. Also see, Thorlby, "Liberty and Self-development: Goethe and John Stuart Mill."

99. *Considerations on Representative Government, CW,* 19: 459; *On Liberty, CW,* 18: 253–54; "Bentham," *CW,* 10: 107–09.

100. Waldron, "Mill and the Value of Moral Distress," 120–21. Here I agree with Waldron's challenge to many Mill commentators; namely, that Mill values moral distress among the public around contending *opinions* concerning better and worse ways of life, and that Mill did not consider hurt moral feelings that derive from clashing opinions a violation of the harm principle. Indeed, Mill advocates the clash of contentious values and moral distress because both cultivate the faculties of reason and will and are indispensable for moral progress in society. For a review of the readings of Mill that argue moral distress falls within the scope of Mill's view of harm, C. L. Ten, *Mill on Liberty,* 24–44. Also see, Ted Honderich, "*On Liberty* and Morality-Dependent Harm," *Political Studies* 30 (1982): 504–22.

101. *Considerations on Representative Government, CW,* 19: 459–66; *On Liberty, CW,* 18: 252–57.

102. *Diary,* January 18, 1854, *CW,* 27: 644; *On Liberty, CW,* 18: 257, 275.

103. For Mill's most comprehensive statements on Athens and Sparta, "Grote's History of Greece (I)," *CW,* 11:273–304; "Grote's History of Greece (II)," *CW,* 11: 309–37; "On Genius," *CW,* 1: 329–39; "Guizot's Essay and Lectures on History," *CW,* 20: 260–94.

104. Thucydides, *History of the Peloponnesian War,* trans. Rex Warner (New York: Penguin, 1954), 1: 73–77. I alter Warner's translation slightly at times to make it more literal.

105. "Guizot's Essays and Lectures on History," *CW,* 20: 269.

106. "Grote's History of Greece (II)," *CW,* 11: 313–14.

107. Ibid.

108. Hannah Arendt, "Thinking and Moral Considerations," *Social Research* 51 (1984): 27.

109. "Grote's History of Greece (II)," *CW,* 11: 314–21.

110. "On Genius," *CW,* 1: 336; "Grote's History of Greece (I)," *CW,* 11: 273.

111. *Logic, CW,* 8: 942.

112. "Grote's History of Greece II," *CW,* 11: 316, 327. Also see, *On Liberty, CW,* 18: 263–66.

113. John Stuart Mill, "Two Publications on Plato," *CW,* 11: 241.

114. Krause identifies similar advantages and disadvantages with honor in *Liberalism with Honor,* 127.

115. Urbinati, *Mill on Democracy,* 3–7; "Grote's History of Greece (II)," *CW,* 11: 314, 316; *Logic, CW,* 8: 942; "Guizot's Essays and Lectures on History," *CW,* 20: 273–74.

116. "Grote's History of Greece (II)," *CW,* 11: 331–37.

117. "Grote's History of Greece (I)," *CW,* 11: 299–305.

118. "The Utility of Religion," *CW,* 10: 407–10; "Nature," *CW,* 10: 393–94.

119. "Guizot's Essays and Lectures on History," *CW,* 20: 269.

120. *Logic, CW,* 8: 842–43; *Utilitarianism, CW,* 10: 234–39.

121. Wilson, *Psychological Analysis and the Philosophy of John Stuart Mill,* 98.

122. *Logic, CW,* 8: 850, 854. Wilson, *Psychological Analysis and the Philosophy of John Stuart Mill,* 84–99.

123. Maurice Mandelbaum, *History, Man, and Reason* (Baltimore: Johns Hopkins University Press, 1971), 195. Also see Skorupski, *John Stuart Mill,* 254–69.

124. "Bentham," *CW,* 10: 95–96; "Coleridge," *CW,* 10: 125. In failing to recognize how hu-

manity consistently develop forms of consciousness that lead to variegated aims, Mill makes the paradoxical point that empiricism had been "abstract and metaphysical," while German transcendentalism had been "concrete and historical." For further discussion of this point, Anschutz, *The Philosophy of J. S. Mill*, 60–77.

125. *Utilitarianism, CW,* 10: 238; *Logic, CW,* 8: 842–43, 849–60; Alexander, *Matthew Arnold and John Stuart Mill*, 207. Janice Carlisle, *John Stuart Mill and the Writing of Character* (Athens: University of Georgia Press, 1991).

126. Kant, *Groundwork of the Metaphysics of Morals*, 55.

127. *Logic, CW,* 8: 842; *Utilitarianism, CW,* 10: 238. Rousseau also argues that humanity's capacity to will contributes to both base and noble human conduct. See Rousseau, "Discourse on Inequality," 45; *The Social Contract,* bk. 1, ch. 8, 150–51. For further discussion of Mill's and Kant's similarities and differences in regard to the will, Skorupski, *John Stuart Mill*, 354–59. For a related discussion on how conceptions of honor have both continuities and differences with Kant's categorical imperative, Krause, *Liberalism with Honor*, 82.

128. "Grote's History of Greece (I)," *CW:* 11, 299–305; "Grote's History of Greece (II)," *CW:* 11: 314–21; *On Liberty, CW,* 18: 263–66.

129. Alan Ryan, *John Stuart Mill* (London: Pantheon, 1970), 87–101; Martin Hollis, "J. S. Mill's Political Philosophy of Mind," *Philosophy* 47 (1972): 334–47.

130. *Utilitarianism, CW,* 10: 313; *Logic, CW,* 8: 842–43. Mill's account of rationality and fortitude here contains echoes of Wordsworth's discussion of reason and repetition, especially in Wordsworth's reference to the notion that both of these qualities are linked to the Poet's gaining command of his art. See William Wordsworth in "Preface and Appendix to *Lyrical Ballads,*" 72: "For all good poetry is the spontaneous overflow of feelings: but though this be true, Poems to which any of value can be attached, were never produced on any variety of subjects but by a man, who being possessed of more than the usual organic sensibility, had also thought long and deeply. For our continued influxes of feelings are modified and directed by our thoughts, which are indeed representative of our feelings; and, as by contemplating the relation of these general representatives to each other we discover what is really important to men, so, by the repetition and continuance of this act, our feelings will be connected with important subjects."

131. Capaldi, *John Stuart Mill*, 276: "External mastery is a means to self-discovery and internal mastery or autonomy."

132. *On Liberty, CW,* 18: 262–63.

CHAPTER 4. *ON LIBERTY:* OVERCOMING ONE-SIDED MORAL DEVELOPMENT

1. *SOW, CW,* 21: 313; "Inaugural Address," *CW,* 21: 253; *Autobiography, CW,* 1: 59, 61, 63; "Chapters on Socialism," *CW,* 5: 737–38.

2. Hamburger, *John Stuart Mill On Liberty and Control*, 86–107.

3. Ryan, *J. S. Mill*, 125–33.

4. *On Liberty, CW,* 18: 217.

5. Ibid., 217–18.

6. Ibid., 218–20.

7. Ibid.

8. Rousseau, "Discourse on Inequality," 67–68.

9. *On Liberty, CW,* 18: 253; "Coleridge," *CW,* 10: 123.

10. Rousseau, *The Social Contract,* bk. 1, ch. 7: 150–51.

11. "August Comte and Positivism," *CW,* 10: 299; "Coleridge," *CW,* 10: 123; *On Liberty, CW,* 18: 22–27. Also see, Thompson, *John Stuart Mill and Representative Government,* 43–50; Richard Dagger, *Civic Virtues: Rights, Citizenship and Republican Liberalism* (Oxford: Oxford University Press, 1997), 101–04; Villa, *Socratic Citizenship,* 109–11; Skorupski, *John Stuart Mill,* 46.

12. *Logic, CW,* 8: 840.

13. For Mill's own assessment of Tocqueville's influence on his thinking, *Autobiography, CW,* 1: 199–201. For an exchange of letters between Mill and Tocqueville that capture key differences between them, "Tocqueville to Mill, March 18, 1841," in Tocqueville, *Oeurves Complètes,* 6: 337–38; "Mill to Tocqueville," August 9, 1842, *CW,* 13: 535–37. Also see, H. O. Pappe, "Mill and Tocqueville," *Journal of the History of Ideas* 25 (April 1964): 217–38. For Wordsworth and Coleridge on the value of approaching customs in new and unfamiliar ways, William Wordsworth, *The Prelude,* in *Wordsworth's Poetical Works,* ed. Thomas Hutchinson, rev. ed., Ernest de Selincourt (Oxford: Oxford University Press, 1974), bk. 1: 497–98; bk. 2: 506; bk. 6: 529; Coleridge, *Biographia Literaria, CW,* 7, pt. 2: 142–59.

14. "Mill to Theodore Gomperz," October 5, 1857, *CW,* 15: 539; "Mill to Pasquale Villari," March 9, 1858, *CW,* 15: 550; "Mill to Arnold Ruge," March 2, 1859, *CW,* 15: 598.

15. T. H. Green, *Liberal Legislation and Freedom of Contract: A Contract,* in *T. H. Green: Lectures on the Principles of Political Obligation and Other Writings,* ed. Paul Harris and John Morrow (Cambridge: Cambridge University Press, 1986), 194–212; Isaiah Berlin, "Two Concepts of Liberty," in *Four Essays on Liberty,* 118–72.

16. *On Liberty, CW,* 18: 223. Mill adds that, in the absence of a clearly defined conception of liberty, he does not always agree with those who wish to make the law more silent so as to place less external restraints on conduct: "One side is at present as often wrong as the other; the interference of government is, with about equal frequency, improperly invoked and improperly condemned."

17. *Autobiography, CW,* 1: 61.

18. *On Liberty, CW,* 18: 220–21.

19. Ibid., 222; "Auguste Comte and Positivism," *CW,* 10: 322. Also see, *Autobiography, CW,* 1: 45, where Mill explains that as a child he learned "to take the strongest interest in the Reformation as the greatest and decisive contest against priestly tyranny and for liberty of thought."

20. *On Liberty, CW,* 18: 222. Hamburger, *John Stuart Mill On Liberty and Control,* 89–91, has an informative discussion of Mill's opposition to the current of intolerance he found in the thinking of Locke, Blackstone, and Milton.

21. *On Liberty, CW,* 18: 274; Locke, *Two Treatises on Government,* 2, sct. 27: 305–06. Also see, Friedman, "A New Exploration of Mill's Essay on Liberty," 292.

22. *On Liberty, CW,* 18: 228–29.

23. Baruch Spinoza, *Ethics,* trans. and ed. G. H. R. Parkinson (Oxford: Oxford University

Press, 2000), pt. 3, prop. 59: 211; John Locke, *A Letter on Toleration*, trans. J. W. Gough, ed. Raymond Klibansky (Oxford: Clarendon, 1968), 65–69.

24. *On Liberty, CW,* 18: 231, 235–37. For a related discussion on Mill's view that the public has a general tendency to impose its specific ideas of the good upon all members of society, to reject all dissent, and to oppose all modes of existence that do not conform to the norm, Villa, *Socratic Citizenship,* 59–124. For a contrasting position, which argues that Mill's political philosophy is grounded in the belief that individuals lack a tendency toward norm conformity and have an agonistic temperament, Urbinati, *Mill on Democracy,* 125.

25. *On Liberty,* 18: 237–39. Waldron contrasts Locke's and Mill's views on persecution in "Locke, Toleration, and Persecution," in *Liberal Rights,* 88–114.

26. *On Liberty, CW,* 18: 240–43.

27. Ibid., 231–32. Isaiah Berlin revises Mill when he argues that choice, not cultivated judgment, is the highest human quality: "For [Mill] man differs from animals primarily neither as the possessor of reason, nor as inventor of tools and methods, but as a being capable of choice, one who is most himself in choosing and not being chosen for." See Berlin, "John Stuart Mill and the Ends of Life," 178.

28. *On Liberty, CW,* 18: 232.

29. Ibid., 235–36. Mill also discusses Marcus Aurelius's repression of Christianity, but his purpose in doing so is to identify a lost opportunity: the reconciliation of the ancient ethos of perfecting the individual with the Christian/modern conception of universal obligation. Also see, Alexander, *Matthew Arnold and John Stuart Mill,* 246.

30. *On Liberty, CW,* 18: 241–42.

31. Stefan Collini's term for a section of British political intellectuals writers who, from the mid-Victorian era to the decade after World War I, sought to articulate a new moral outlook for modern Britain. Collini, *Public Moralists: Political Thought and Intellectual Life in Britain, 1850–1930.*

32. *On Liberty, CW,* 18: 241, 242, 243.

33. Hamburger, *John Stuart Mill On Liberty and Control,* 95; Shirley Robin Letwin, *The Pursuit of Certainty* (Cambridge: Cambridge University Press, 1965); Maurice Cowling, *Mill and Liberalism* (Cambridge: Cambridge University Press, 1963).

34. Niccolò Machiavelli, *Discourses on Livy,* trans. Harvey Mansfield and Nathan Tarcov (Chicago: University of Chicago, 1999), bk. 2, ch. 2: 129–33.

35. Rousseau, "Discourse on Inequality," *Émile, or On Education.* Also see, Melzer, *On the Natural Goodness of Man,* 17.

36. *On Liberty, CW,* 18: 241–42.

37. Ibid., 248–49.

38. Ibid., 255.

39. Ibid.

40. Ibid., 254–57.

41. Ibid., 222, 255.

42. Ibid., 255.

43. Ibid., 255–56.

44. Ibid., 256.

45. Ibid., 253, 256–57.

46. Mill, *SOW, CW,* 21: 295.

47. "Mill to Harriet Mill," January 21, 1855, *CW,* 14: 303; "The Utility of Religion," *CW,* 10: 422.

48. *On Liberty, CW,* 18: 236–37. For an informative discussion of Mill's views of Marcus Aurelius, Alexander, *Matthew Arnold and John Stuart Mill,* 246–52.

49. *On Liberty, CW,* 18: 257. Also, Alexander, *Matthew Arnold and John Stuart Mill,* 36.

50. "Auguste Comte and Positivism," *CW,* 10: 270.

51. "The Utility of Religion," *CW,* 10: 419; "August Comte and Positivism," *CW,* 10: 272–78; "Grote's History of Greece (I)," 274–81.

52. "Auguste Comte and Positivism," *CW,* 10: 275–76.

53. Ibid., 276; "Grote's History of Greece (I)," *CW,* 11: 286–87.

54. *On Liberty, CW,* 18: 236–37.

55. "Auguste Comte and Positivism," *CW,* 10: 276–77.

56. "Mill to Thomas Dyke Acland," December 1, 1868, *CW,* 16: 1500.

57. "Utility of Religion," *CW,* 10: 425. Also see, Houghton, *The Victorian Frame of Mind,* 127.

58. "Nature," *CW,* 11: 383.

59. "Coleridge," *CW,* 10: 145.

60. *On Liberty, CW,* 18: 242–43.

61. "Nature," *CW,* 11: 383.

62. Ibid., 10: 383.

63. "Coleridge," *CW,* 10: 144–45.

64. *On Liberty, CW,* 18: 222.

65. Ibid., 248; *Autobiography, CW,* 1: 45.

66. Locke, *An Essay Concerning Human Understanding,* bk. 1, ch. 3, sct. 9: 70–72; David Hume, "Idea of a Perfect Commonwealth," in *Essays: Moral, Political, and Literary,* ed. Eugene Miller (Indianapolis: Liberty, 1987), 514–15.

67. "Civilization," *CW,* 18: 131–32.

68. "Coleridge," *CW,* 10: 142.

69. *On Liberty, CW,* 18: 303.

70. "Coleridge," *CW,* 10: 143.

71. "Corporation and Church Property," *CW,* 4: 199; *Autobiography, CW,* 1: 191: "I urged [in an essay in the *Jurist* in 1833] strenuously the importance of having a provision for education, not dependent on the mere demand of the market, that is, on the discernment of average parents, but calculated to establish and keep up a higher standard of instruction than is likely to be spontaneously demanded by the buyers of the market." This opinion has "been confirmed and strengthened by the whole course of my subsequent reflections." Also, Alexander, *Matthew Arnold and John Stuart Mill,* 222–24.

72. "Spirit of the Age (I)," *CW,* 22: 228; "The Utility of Religion," *CW,* 10: 425.

73. *Autobiography, CW,* 1: 247

74. "Utility of Religion," *CW,* 10: 422–28; *On Liberty, CW,* 18: 252–57.

75. Hobbes, *Leviathan,* pt. 4, chs. 44–47: 411–88; Melzer, *On the Natural Goodness of Man,* 144.

76. Baruch Spinoza, *Theological-Political Treatise* (Gebhardt Edition), trans. Samuel Shirley, ed. Seymour Feldman (Indianapolis: Hackett, 2001), ch. 14: 153, 156.

77. Rousseau, *Social Contract,* 226–27; *Émile,* 266–313. For general background on the Enlightenment's reformed and natural religion, Amos Funkenstein, *Theology and the Scientific Imagination: From the Middle Ages to the Seventeenth Century,* (Princeton: Princeton University Press, 1986); Richard Tuck, *Natural Rights Theories* (Cambridge: Cambridge University Press, 1979), and "The 'Modern' Theory of Natural Law," in *The Languages of Political Theory in Early-Modern Europe,* ed. Anthony Padgen (Cambridge: Cambridge University Press, 1987), 99–119; Knud Haakonssen, *Natural Law and Moral Philosophy: From Grotius to the Scottish Enlightenment,* (Cambridge: Cambridge University Press, 1996); Steven B. Smith, *Spinoza, Liberalism, and the Question of Jewish Identity* (New Haven: Yale University Press, 1997).

78. Schneewind, *The Invention of Autonomy,* 169. Samuel Pufendorf, *On the Duty of Man and Citizen,* trans. Michael Silverthorne, ed. James Tully (Cambridge: Cambridge University Press, 1991), bk. 1, ch. 3: 37; Hugo Grotius, *Law of War and Peace in Three Books,* trans. Francis W. Kelsey (New York: Bobbs-Merrill, 1925); Locke, *Two Treatises of Government,* 1, sct. 58: 200.

79. Pufendorf, *On the Duty of Man and Citizen,* bk. 1, ch. 3: 36.

80. Abrams, *Naturalism and Supernaturalism,* 192–95; Hunter, *Rival Enlightenments,* 353–76; Taylor, *Sources of the Self,* 368–90; Henning Graf Reventlow, *The Authority of the Bible and The Rise of the Modern World,* trans. John Bowden (London: First Fortress Press, 1985).

81. Among the British (and American) publics there also were movements back to religious orthodoxy, which kept the religious debate in the United Kingdom within the confines of Theism. For essays that examine the different stresses and strains confronting Victorian Christianity see, *Victorian Faith in Crisis,* ed. Helmstadter and Lightman (Stanford: Stanford University Press, 1990). Also see, Taylor, *Sources of the Self,* 401–10; James Crimmins, "Religion, Utility, and Politics: Bentham versus Paley," in *Religion, Secularization, and Political Thought: Thomas Hobbes to J. S. Mill,* ed. James Crimmins (London: Routledge, 1990). Even the exceptions to the general tendency to keep debate within the parameters of Theism attacked natural religion indirectly: Hume spoke out through Philo in a fictitous dialogue; Grote composed Bentham's book critiquing Theism, based upon Bentham's unpublished writings and through the use of a pseudonym. David Hume, *Dialogues on Natural Religion,* in *Dialogues and the Natural History of Religion,* ed. J. C. A. Gaskin (Oxford: Oxford University Press, 1993); Jeremy Bentham [Philip Beauchamp, pseud.], *Analysis of the Influence of Natural Religion on the Temporal Happiness of Mankind* (Oxford: Clarendon, 1956).

82. Smith, *Theory of Moral Sentiments,* pt. 2, sct. 1, ch. 5n10: 77n10; Locke, *Essay on Human Understanding,* bk. 1, ch. 3, sct. 6: 68–69; bk. 2, ch. 28, sct. 7: 352; *Two Treatises of Government,* 2, ch. 2, scts. 6–7: 288–90; William Paley, *Considerations on the Theory of Religion* (London: Rodwell and Martin, 1820), 19–24. In much of the Anglo-Scottish Enlightenment, self-preservation and happiness were reserved for the most part to the dissenting Protestant sects, as Catholics and atheists continued to be seen as sources of civil strife. Locke, *Letter on Toleration,* 133–35.

83. Pufendorf, *On the Duty of Man and Citizen,* bk. 1, ch. 4: 43.

84. John Locke, *The Reasonableness of Christianity,* ed. I. T. Ramsey (Stanford: Stanford University Press, 1958), sct. 245: 70.

85. Adam Smith, *An Inquiry into the Nature and Causes of the Wealth of Nations,* 2 vols., ed. R. H. Campbell and A. S. Skinner (Indianapolis: Liberty Press, 1976), vol. 2, bk. 5, pt. 3, ch. 1: 314–15; Locke, *Letter Concerning Toleration,* 47, 65, 67. Also see, Voltaire, *Philosophical Letters,* trans. Ernest Dilworth (New York: Macmillan, 1961), 22–27; Smith, *Spinoza, Liberalism and the Question of Jewish Identity,* 171.

86. Thomas Hobbes, *De Cive,* in *Man and Citizen,* ed. Barnard Gert (Garden City, N.Y.: Doubleday, 1972), Preface: 97–98; Spinoza, *Theological-Political Treatise,* ch. 19: 218.

87. Smith, *Spinoza, Liberalism, and the Question of Jewish Identity,* 131–34, 152–56.

88. David Hume, *The History of England* (Indianapolis: Liberty, 1983), vol. 4, ch. 38: 3–15.

89. See John Figgis, "Non-Resistance and the Theory of Sovereignty," "Erastus and Erastianism," in Figgis, *The Divine Right of Kings* (Cambridge: Cambridge University Press, 1934), 219–55, 267–316, respectively; Robert Devigne, *Recasting Conservatism: Oakeshott, Strauss, and the Response to Postmodernism* (New Haven: Yale University Press, 1994), 99–100.

90. *Autobiography, CW,* 1: 73.

91. This point—that Mill's thought centers on forging a moral synthesis for the future—is developed by Alexander, *Matthew Arnold and John Stuart Mill,* 34–73.

92. "Auguste Comte and Positivism," *CW,* 10: 361.

93. *Diary,* February 25, 1854, *CW,* 27: 657; *Autobiography, CW,* 1; 47: "The world would be astonished if it knew how great a proportion of its brightest ornaments—of those most distinguished even in popular estimation for wisdom and virtue—are complete skeptics on religion; many of them refraining from avowal, less from personal considerations, than from a conscientious, though now in my opinion a most mistaken apprehension lest speaking out what would tend to weaken existing beliefs, and by consequences (as they suppose) existing restraints, they should do harm instead of good."

CHAPTER 5. REFORMING REFORMED RELIGION

1. "Mill to Walter Coulson," November 22, 1850, *CW,* 14: 53. Mill presents this same point more delicately and obscurely in *On Liberty, CW,* 18: 254–55: "The Gospel always refers to a pre-existing morality and confines its precepts to the particulars in which that morality was to be corrected or superseded by a wider and higher, expressing itself, moreover, in terms most general, often impossible to be interpreted literally, and possessing rather the impressiveness of poetry or eloquence than the precision of legislation. To extract from a body of ethical doctrine has never been possible without eking it out from The Old Testament, that is, from a system elaborate indeed, but in many respects barbarous, and intended only for a barbarous people."

2. Joseph Hamburger makes a comprehensive case for this interpretation in *John Stuart Mill on Liberty and Control,* 55–85.

3. *Autobiography, CW,* 1: 45.

4. Houghton, *The Victorian Frame of Mind,* 54–89; David Berman, *A History of Atheism in Britain: From Hobbes to Russell* (London: Croom Helm, 1988); Hamburger, *John Stuart Mill on Liberty and Control,* 55–85.

5. Howard E. Gruber, *Darwin on Man: A Psychological Study of Scientific Certainty* (Chi-

cago: University of Chicago Press, 1981), 36–44; Hamburger, *John Stuart Mill on Liberty and Control,* 69–71.

6. Arthur and Elenor Sidgwick, *Henry Sidgwick: A Memoir* (London: Macmillan, 1906), 357.

7. "The Utility of Religion," *CW,* 10: 414–17.

8. Collini, "Their Master's Voice: John Stuart Mill as Public Moralist," 121.

9. For the position that Mill was generally courageous but timid in regard to debating his religious views, Hamburger, *John Stuart Mill on Liberty and Control,* 91–95.

10. "Dureyrier's Political Views of French Affairs," *CW,* 20: 313.

11. James Fitzjames Stephen, "The Laws of England as to the Expressions of Religious Opinions," *Contemporary Review* 25 (February 1875): 459–60, 471.

12. James Martineau, "John Stuart Mill," in *Essays, Reviews and Addresses,* 4 vols. (London: Longmans, 1890–91), 3: 534–35. In a letter to Bain, Mill expressed admiration for this piece by Martineau: "It [a review of *On Liberty*] seems to be by Martineau and I am obliged to him for it, since it is favourable to the utmost extent consistent with the writer's opinions and decidedly tends to increase rather than diminish the influence which he says is already so great. I really had no idea of being so influential a person as my critics tell me I am. But being thought to have influence is the surest way of obtaining it really." "Mill to Alexander Bain," October 15, 1859, *CW,* 15: 640.

13. John Morley, *Critical Miscellanies,* 4 vols. (London: Macmillan, 1898–1908), 3: 421. As Mill put it, "In writing to persuade the English, one must tell them only of the next step they have to take, keeping back all mention of any subsequent step. Whatever we may have to propose, we must contract our reasoning into the most confined limits; we must place the expediency of the particular measure upon the narrowest grounds on which it can rest; and endeavour to let out no more of general truth, than exactly as much as is absolutely indispensable to make out our particular conclusion." See "Comparison of the Tendencies of French and English Intellect," *CW,* 23: 445–46. Also see Anschultz, *The Philosophy of J. S. Mill,* 62: "Hence the charges, so frequently brought against Mill by his contemporaries, of unfair dealing in philosophical controversy. As war is sometimes said to be an extension of policy, so philosophy for Mill was an extension of politics. If then, he sometimes failed to declare his whole mind on some speculative question, he was merely practicing in philosophy the usual and necessary reticence of the politician."

14. "Mill to Auguste Comte," December 15, 1842, *CW,* 13: 559–63. The translations of Mill's letters to Comte, which were written in French, are my own.

15. "Mill to Auguste Comte," April 3, 1844, *CW,* 13: 624–26; "Mill to Auguste Comte," January 27, 1845, *CW,* 13: 655–57; "Mill to Auguste Comte," July 8, 1845, *CW,* 13: 670–72.

16. Harriet Martineau, *Autobiography,* 2 vols., ed. Maria Weston Chapman (London: Longmans, 1877), 1: 2–4; 2: 31–38. Also see, Berman, *History of Atheism in Britain,* 112–35.

17. Bain, *John Stuart Mill, A Criticism: With Personal Recollections,* 103. See Krause's discussion of Lincoln on slavery, *Liberalism with Honor,* 143.

18. "Mill to Alexander Bain," November 14, 1859, *CW,* 15: 645–46; "Mill to Alexander Bain," August 6, 1859, *CW,* 15: 631. Also see, "Mill to Arthur Greene," December 16, 1861, *CW,* 15: 754: "I am far from thinking that it would be a benefit for mankind in general, if without any other change in them, they could be made disbelievers in all religion." For

an illuminating discussion on how Mill contributed to a more liberal Christianity in his lifetime, Eldon Eisenach, "Mill and Liberal Christianity," in Eisenach, ed., *Mill and the Moral Character of Liberalism,* 192–229.

19. For analysis of Mill's writings on religion, Robert Devigne, "J. S. Mill on Liberty and Religion: An Unfinished Dialectic," and Allan D. Megill, "J. S. Mill's Religion of Humanity and the Second Justification for the Writing of *On Liberty,*" in Eisenach, ed., *Mill and the Moral Character of Liberalism,* 231–56, 301–16, respectively; Karl Britton, "John Stuart Mill on Christianity," in *James and John Stuart Mill/Papers of the Centenary Conference,* 118–46.

20. "On the Utility of Religion," *CW* 10: 404.

21. Ibid., 410–11.

22. Ibid., 417.

23. Ibid., 419. Britton, "John Stuart Mill on Christianity," 22–23.

24. "The Utility of Religion," *CW,* 10: 420.

25. Ibid., 420–22.

26. Ibid., 422. The main surprise in this list is Marcus Aurelius, who is criticized in *On Liberty* for suppressing Christianity. But Mill's criticism of Aurelius is subtle and he believes that Aurelius is one of the few ancients who understood the need to combine the classical ethos of cultivating the individual with a modern outlook of obedience to universal moral law.

27. "The Utility of Religion," *CW,* 10: 428–29.

28. Ibid., 422. In the *Autobiography,* Mill refers to his youthful Benthamism as a religion: "It gave unity to my conceptions of things. I now had opinions; a creed, a doctrine, a philosophy; in one among the best senses of the word, a religion; the inculcation and diffusion of which could be made the principal outward purpose of a life. And I had a grand conception laid before me of changes to be effected in the condition of mankind through that doctrine." *Autobiography, CW,* 1: 69.

29. "The Utility of Religion," *CW,* 10: 426–27.

30. Ibid., 422–23.

31. "Theism," *CW,* 10: 487–88; "The Utility of Religion," *CW,* 10: 422, 424; "Mill to Arthur Greene," December 16, 1861, *CW,* 15: 754. Also see, *On Liberty, CW,* 18: 255–57.

32. Coleridge, *Statesman's Manual,* Appendix C, *CW,* 6: 62–65; Shelley, *Adonais, CW,* 2, st. 52: 404.

33. *On Liberty, CW,* 18: 260–69; *SOW, CW,* 21: 299–322.

34. "Grote's Plato," *CW,* 11: 415–16; "Translation and Commentary on the *Gorgias,*" *CW,* 11: 149–50. Allan Bloom also argues that Plato sought to develop a conception of the heroic; although Bloom contends that Plato, *contra* Homer, created a standard of the highest human type that centered on understanding, not creating, truth. Bloom, "Interpretive Essay," in *The Republic of Plato,* 354.

35. Mathew Arnold, *On the Study of Celtic Literature and On Translating Homer* (New York: Macmillan, 1924), 168. Also see Hallam Tennyson, *Alfred Lord Tennyson: A Memoir by His Son,* 4 vols. (London: Macmillan, 1893), 2: 337–49.

36. For further discussion of "the grand style" of the mid-Victorian romantics, see Houghton, *The Victorian Frame of Mind,* 307–25. For analysis of mid-Victorian intellectuals' as-

sessment of England's spiritual crisis, Turner, "The Victorian Crisis of Faith and the Faith that was Lost," and Moore, "Theodicy and Society: The Crisis of the Intelligentsia," in Helmstadter and Lightman, eds., *Victorian Faith in Crisis,* 9–38, 153–86, respectively; Maurice Cowling, *Religion and Public Doctrine in Modern England,* 2 vols. (Cambridge: Cambridge University Press, 1985), 2: 103–81.

37. Hegel, *Philosophy of Right,* Preface, pars. 46, 184A, 185, 206, 258, 262A: 10, 42–43, 267, 123–24, 132–33, 156–59, 280.

38. Hegel, *Lectures on the History of Philosophy,* 2. Also see, Nietzsche, *Beyond Good and Evil,* Preface, 1–3.

39. "The Utility of Religion," *CW,* 10: 425.

40. *Plato's Statesman,* 272b–275b: 21–25.

41. *Autobiography, CW,* 1: 43; "Inaugural Address," *CW,* 21: 256; "The Utility of Religion," *CW,* 10: 425.

42. Friedrich Nietzsche, *On the Advantage and Disadvantage of History for Life,* trans. Peter Preuss (Indianapolis: Hackett, 1990), 14–19.

43. "Inaugural Address," *CW,* 21: 254–57. Also see *Diary,* January 24, 1854, *CW,* 27: 646: "The imagination at the same time being fed from youth with representations of all noble things felt and acted heretofore, and with ideal conceptions of still greater to come: there is no worthy office of a religion which this system of cultivation does not seem adequate to fulfill."

44. "Ware's Letters from Palmyra," *CW,* 1: 459–60. Also see, Alexander, *Matthew Arnold and John Stuart Mill,* 152–91.

45. Kant, "Toward Perpetual Peace," sct. 369: 338; *Groundwork of the Metaphysics of Morals,* sct. 394: 50; *The Metaphysics of Morals* in *Practical Philosophy,* sct. 445: 565.

46. "Inaugural Address," *CW,* 21: 254–57: "On these subjects, the mode of thinking and feeling of other countries [is] not only not intelligible, but not credible, to an average Englishman. To find Art . . . holding . . . an important place among the agents of civilization and among the elements of the worth of humanity . . . amaze and puzzle Englishmen, because it [is] too strange for them to be able to realize it, or, in truth, to believe it possible; and the radical difference of feeling on this matter between the British people and those of France, Germany, and the Continent generally, is one among the causes of that extraordinary inability to understand one another, which exists between England and the rest of Europe, while it does not exist to anything like the same degree between one nation of Continental Europe and another."

47. See Krause's discussion of public codes of honor in liberal societies in *Liberalism with Honor,* 2–5.

48. "Auguste Comte and Positivism," *CW,* 10: 338; *On Liberty, CW,* 18: 227; *Autobiography, CW,* 1: 219, 221. For analyses that Mill envisioned the Religion of Humanity as the general ethos of society, see Hamburger, *Mill on Liberty and Control,* 108–48; Cowling, *Mill and Liberalism;* Letwin, *The Pursuit of Certainty;* Linda Raeder, *John Stuart Mill and the Religion of Humanity* (Columbia: University of Missouri Press, 2002).

49. Francis Bacon, *The Advancement of Learning,* in *Major Works,* ed. Brian Vickers (Oxford: Oxford University Press, 1996), 215–37.

50. *Logic, CW,* 7: 388; Geoffrey Scarre, "Mill on Induction and the Scientific Method," in

Cambridge Companion to Mill, 125. Mill's essays on religion devote far less attention to analyzing whether Christian teachings reflect revealed or divine truth: "The divine message, assuming it to be such, has been authenticated by credentials so insufficient, that they fail to convince a large proportion of the strongest and most cultivated minds, and the tendency to disbelieve them appears to grow with scientific knowledge and critical discrimination." "Utility of Religion," *CW,* 10: 425; "Theism," *CW,* 10: 468–91.

51. *Logic, CW,* 7: 388–91.

52. "Theism," *CW,* 10: 446–50. For criticism of Mill's use of his inductive methods in "Theism," see Robert Carr, "The Religious Thought of John Stuart Mill: A Study in Religious Skepticism," *Journal of the History of Ideas* 23 (1992): 475–95.

53. "Theism," *CW,* 10: 482. Also see, "Mill to Arthur Greene," December 16, 1861, *CW,* 15: 754: "Like all enquiries which ascend to a time beyond credible records, and which suppose powers of the existence of which in the historical times we have no evidence, it is, and must remain, as I conceive, uncertain." For the position that Mill believed "God probably existed," Capaldi, *John Stuart Mill,* 339–50.

54. Smith identifies a similar distinction in Spinoza's investigations of God in *Spinoza, Liberalism, and the Question of Jewish Identity,* 65–71.

55. Hume, *Dialogues and Natural History of Religion; Treatise on Human Nature,* 479, 518. For an excellent discussion of this point, see Schneewind, "The Misfortunes of Virtue."

56. In the *Autobiography,* Mill explains that "my father's rejection of all that is called religious belief was not, as many might suppose, primarily a matter of logic and evidence: the grounds of it were moral, still more than intellectual." See *Autobiography, CW,* 1: 42–43. Also see, Britton, "John Stuart Mill on Christianity," 27.

57. T. H. Huxley, *Man's Place in Nature and other Anthropological Essays* (London: Macmillan, 1897); W. H. Lecky, *The Rise and Influence of the Spirit of Rationalism in Europe* (London: Longmans, 1884); Herbert Spencer, *First Principles* (New York: Bost, 1880); Benjamin Jowett, *Sermons on Doctrine and Faith,* ed. W. H. Fremantle (London: Murray, 1901). Also see, J. B. Schneewind, *Sidgwick's Ethics and Victorian Moral Philosophy* (Oxford: Clarendon, 1977), 17–21; Moore, "Theodicy and Society: The Crisis of the Intelligentsia," George Levine, "Scientific Discourse as an Alternative to Faith," and Bernard Lightman, "*Robert Elsmere* and the Agnostic Crisis of Faith," in Helmstadter and Lightman, eds., *Victorian Faith in Crises,* 153–186, 225–261, 283–313, respectively.

58. For a thoughtful discussion on the seminal importance of this debate in modern political thought, Melzer, *The Natural Goodness of Man: On the System of Rousseau's Thought,* 120–49.

59. "Nature," *CW,* 10: 385.

60. "The Utility of Religion," *CW,* 10: 425; "Nature," *CW,* 10: 393.

61. *On Liberty, CW,* 18: 255. Herein resides a key difference between Mill and Tocqueville: the role of Christianity in the morality of the future. In *Democracy in America,* Tocqueville put forth that America's reformed Christianity made vital contributions to "self-interest properly understood," the qualities of temperance, far-sightedness, and moderation that lead the democratic individual to sacrifice some immediate interests for the sake of long-term goals. Tellingly, Mill's approbatory and comprehensive reviews of *Democracy in America* do not comment on Tocqueville's analysis of Christianity. See Tocqueville, *Democracy in America,* vol. 2: pt. 2, ch. 9: 505–06; Mill, "De Tocqueville on

Democracy in America (I)," *CW,* 18: 46–90; "De Tocqueville on Democracy in America (II)," *CW,* 18: 155–204.

62. "Theism," *CW,* 10: 458.

63. *Autobiography, CW,* 1: 43.

64. "Theism," *CW,* 10: 457; "Nature," *CW,* 10: 388. Here I agree with Capaldi's argument that Mill's "Nature" and Theism" denied that nature served some type of purpose and was evidence of a benevolent creator. But unlike Capaldi, I maintain that Mill is primarily critiquing modern natural law theory, not "the classical and medieval perspective." Capaldi, *John Stuart Mill,* 347.

65. "Theism," *CW,* 10: 459.

66. "The Spirit of the Age (I)," *CW,* 22: 229.

67. *On Liberty, CW,* 18: 248.

68. "Nature," *CW,* 10: 382, 386, 393.

69. "Theism," *CW,* 10: 482–83.

70. Hobbes, *Leviathan,* ch. 2: 10; Hume, *Enquiries Concerning Human Understanding,* sct. 5, pt. 2: 47; *A Treatise of Human Nature,* bk. 1, pt. 4, sct. 7: 267–68; Adam Smith, "History of Ancient Physics," in *Essays on Philosophical Subjects,* ed. W. P. D. Wightman and J. C. Bryce (Indianapolis: Liberty Press, 1982), 113–14. Also see, Griswold, *Adam Smith and the Virtues of Enlightenment,* 336–44.

71. See F. W. J. Schelling, "Kant, Fichte, and the System of Transcendental Idealism," in *On the History of Modern Philosophy,* trans. and ed. Andrew Bowie (Cambridge: Cambridge University Press, 1994), 98–101; J. G. Fichte, *The Nature of the Scholar,* trans. William Smith (London: Chapman, 1845), 144–55. For a general survey of this subject, see D. R. Lachterman, *The Ethics of Geometry: A Genealogy of Modernity* (London: Routledge, 1989). For comparisons of British and German Romantics on the relation between the imagination and reason, see Furst, *Romanticism in Perspective,* 119–209; Abrams, *Mirror and Lamp,* 156–225.

72. *Diary,* April 11, 1854, *CW,* 27: 667.

73. Stefan Collini, Donald Winch, and John Burrow, *That Noble Science of Politics: A Study in Nineteenth-Century Intellectual History* (Cambridge: Cambridge University Press, 1983).

74. *Logic, CW,* 8: 943–52. There is a striking similarity between Mill's and Coleridge's positions on the proper relation between reason and art, as both insist that one must know nature in order to give it life and meaning. On the one hand, states Coleridge, the artist must reject the reproductive approach to art that merely copies or reflects reality. On the other hand, the artists' creativity must not stray too far from "the severe laws of the intellect." "The artist," insists Coleridge, "must first eloign himself from nature in order to return to her with full effect. Why this? Because if he were to begin with mere painful copying, he would produce masks only, not forms breathing life. He must out of his own mind create forms according to the severe laws of the intellect, in order to generate in himself that co-ordination and freedom and law, that involution of obedience in the prescript, and of the prescript in the impulse to obey, which assimilates him to nature, and enables him to understand her." Coleridge, *Biographia Literaria, CW,* 7, vol. 2: 258. For more discussion on how Coleridge had a more bounded view of art than most of his German Romantic counterparts, Furst, *Romanticism in Perspective,* 141–47. Also see,

Abrams, *Mirror and Lamp,* 55: "Of all his contemporaries, Coleridge was the most concerned with the problem of how the poetic mind acts to modify or transform the materials of sense without violating truth to nature."

75. *Logic, CW,* 8: 943, 947.

76. "Theism," *CW,* 10: 483, 484–88; "Utility of Religion," *CW,* 10: 422; "Nature," *CW,* 10: 388. Also see, "Mill to Florence Nightingale," September 23, 1860, *CW,* 15: 709, in which Mill states Nightingale's assertion of an intractable struggle on earth between good and evil "may be" right but rejects her notion that a perfect God created this conflict in order to stimulate the development of human faculties: "I tried what I could do with that hypothesis many years ago. . . . But then, a Perfect Being . . . might be expected to so form the world that the struggle against evil should be the greatest possible in extent and intensity; and unhappily our world conforms as little to this character. . . . If the Divine intention in making man was Effort towards Perfection, the divine purpose is as much frustrated as if its sole aim were human happiness. There is little of both, but the absence of both is the marked characteristic."

77. Theism," *CW,* 10: 485.

78. Kant, *Religion Within the Limits of Reason Alone,* 43, 70–71, 118–20, 146–51, 155. For a thoughtful discussion of Kant's approach to Christianity, Smith, *Spinoza, Liberalism, and the Question of Jewish Identity,* 179–85. Also, Roger Sullivan, *Immanuel Kant's Moral Theory* (Cambridge: Cambridge University Press, 1989), 142–45.

79. Hegel, *Philosophy of History,* 267–71; *Philosophy of Right,* Preface, pars. 46, 184A, 185, 206, 258, 262A: 10, 42–43, 267, 123–24, 132–33, 156–59, 280; *Lectures on the History of Philosophy,* vol. 1: 1–3.

80. Hegel, *Philosophy of History,* 344, 416–17, 496–97; *Philosophy of Right,* par. 138: 92. Franco, *Hegel's Philosophy of Freedom,* 105, 217; Pippin, "Ethical Reasons, Kantian Rejoinders,"107.

81. Hegel, *Philosophy of Right,* sct. 152: 109.

82. Ibid., scts. 182–359: 122–223; Franco, *Hegel's Philosophy of Freedom,* 216–17; Pippin, "Ethical Reasons, Kantian Rejoinders,"125. For the most comprehensive position on the continuity between Christianity and modernity, Max Weber, *The Protestant Ethic and the Spirit of Capitalism,* trans. Talcott Parsons (New York: Scribner's, 1958). Also see, Nietzsche, *Beyond Good and Evil,* sct. 202: 115–17. For a valuable critique of the position that modernity is a secular version of Christianity, Hans Blumenberg, *The Legitimacy of the Modern World,* trans. Robert M. Wallace (Cambridge: MIT Press, 1983), 3–87.

83. "Grote's History of Greece (II)," *CW,* 11: 314.

84. *On Liberty, CW,* 18: 252–53. Also see, "Spirit of the Age (I)," *CW,* 22: 234: "They [the public] usually resolve that the new light which has been broken in upon them shall be the sole light; and they willfully and passionately blow out the ancient lamp, which, though it did not show them what they now see, served very well to enlighten the objects in its immediate neighborhood. Whether men adhere to old opinions or adopt new ones, they have in general an invincible propensity to split the truth, and take half, or less than half of it; and a habit of erecting their quills and bristling up like a porcupine against any one who brings them the other half, as if he were attempting to deprive them of the portion which they have." Alexander recognizes the decisive importance of Mill's view

that a new synthesis or harmony of principles of freedom is *not* imminent in *Matthew Arnold and John Stuart Mill*, 35–36, 61–64, 126, 162, 258.

CHAPTER 6. *ON LIBERTY:* THE *SUMMUM BONUM* OF MODERN LIBERALISM

1. Judith Shklar, "The Liberalism of Fear," in *Liberalism and the Moral Life*, ed. Nancy Rosenblum (Cambridge: Harvard University Press, 1991), 23. Hobbes, *Leviathan*, ch. 45: 453–68; Locke, *An Essay Concerning Human Understanding*, bk. 1, ch. 3, scts. 4–7: 68–70; Hume, "Idea of a Perfect Commonwealth," 514–15.
2. "Grote's History of Greece (II)," *CW*, 11: 314.
3. *On Liberty, CW*, 18: 261–62.
4. Ibid., 262–63.
5. Ibid., 262–63. Coleridge uses a similar metaphor in *The Statesman's Manual, CW*, 6: 71–72.
6. *On Liberty, CW*, 18: 263–65. Also, Appel, "Natural Affinities," 14.
7. Ibid., *On Liberty, CW*, 18: 263–65.
8. Ibid., 264, 271.
9. Ibid., 265.
10. "Grote's History of Greece (II)," *CW*, 11: 318, 334; Bain, *John Stuart Mill: A Criticism: With Personal Recollections*, 154. Also see Alexander's discussion of Mill's view that Pericles represented the virtues of reason and courage in *Mathew Arnold and John Stuart Mill*, 140–42.
11. "Grote's History of Greece (II)," *CW*, 11: 331.
12. *Autobiography, CW*, 1: 11; "Puseyism," *CW*, 24: 819; Thomas M'Crie, *Life of John Knox* (Edinburgh: Blackwood, 1855).
13. John Knox, "The Debate in the General Assembly," in *On Rebellion*, ed. Roger A. Mason (Cambridge: Cambridge University Press, 1994), 182.
14. Knox, "First Blast of the Trumpets," in *On Rebellion*, 28–30.
15. *On Liberty, CW*, 18: 266.
16. Ibid.
17. Alan Ryan, "Mill in a Liberal Landscape," in *The Cambridge Companion to Mill*, 517–18.
18. *On Liberty, CW*, 18: 266.
19. Also see, *SOW, CW*, 21: 308–09: "Strong feeling is the instrument and element of strong self-control: but it requires to be cultivated in that direction. When it is, it forms not the heroes of impulse only, but also those of self-conquest. History and experience prove that the most passionate characters are the most fanatically rigid in their feelings of duty, when their passion has been trained to act in that direction." Also, see Krause's discussion of moral codes in *Liberalism with Honor*, 28–29, 174. Larmore overlooks the value Mill places on restraints that cultivate social feelings and more comprehensive outlooks in *The Morals of Modernity*, 124, when he states Mill contributes to liberalism's tendency to oppose all restraints: "Liberalism is often accused of regarding every kind of limit to liberty, even the rule of law, as in itself an unwelcome imposition, to be accepted only to prevent a greater loss of liberty. And indeed, some liberals seem to have held just this view, as when J. S. Mill declared 'all restraint, *qua* restraint, is an evil.'"
20. Aristotle, *The Politics*, sct. 1280a10: 97. To Aristotle, strict or arithmetical equality char-

acterizes only commutative justice, the justice that prevails in law courts and the marketplace, where each plaintiff or negotiator is conceived as possessing equal claims. Aristotle, *Nicomachean Ethics,* scts. 1132a–1134a30: 125–30.

21. Plato, *Phaedrus,* trans. H. N. Fowler (Cambridge: Harvard University Press, 1914), scts. 269c–272b: 69–74.

22. *The Republic of Plato,* sct. 369a–370b: 45–47.

23. Ibid., scts. 370c–372a: 47–49. For a thorough discussion of this section of the *Republic* and the ancient conception of justice more generally, see Muirhead, *Just Work,* 51–70.

24. *The Republic of Plato,* scts. 373a–417a: 49–96.

25. Niccolò Machiavelli, *The Prince,* trans. Harvey Mansfield (Chicago: University of Chicago Press, 1985), ch. 6: 44. Also see, Harvey Mansfield, *Machiavelli's Virute* (Chicago: University of Chicago Press, 1996), 24.

26. Hobbes, *De Cive,* Preface: 100–01, I-4: 114; *Leviathan,* ch. 13: 74–78. Hume rejected the idea of an original contract, but he did maintain that the good society derived from the intersection of personal interests and that heroic types were politically dangerous. See David Hume, "Of the Origin of Government," "Of Commerce," "Idea of a Perfect Commonwealth," in *Essays: Moral, Political and Literary,* 37–41, 253–67, 512–29, respectively.

27. Locke, *Essay on Human Understanding,* bk. 1, ch. 3, sct. 4: 68.

28. Ibid.; *Two Treatises of Government,* bk. 2: sct. 54: 322.

29. Hume, *Treatise on Human Nature,* pt. 2, scts. 1–6: 477–534; Smith, *Theory of Moral Sentiments,* pt. 2, sct. 2, ch. 1: 82.

30. Descartes, *Discourse on Method,* pt. 2, scts. 15–19: 8–10; pt. 6, sct. 62: 33.

31. Rousseau, *The Social Contract,* bk. 2, ch. 7: 162–65.

32. Descartes, *Discourse on Method,* pt. 3, sct. 22: 12.

33. Rousseau, *The Social Contract,* bk. 2, ch. 12: 172.

34. Ibid. Also see Ruth Grant, *Hypocrisy and Integrity: Machiavelli, Rousseau, and the Ethics of Politics* (Chicago: University of Chicago Press, 1997).

35. "Nature," *CW,* 10: 394; *On Liberty, CW,* 18: 267, 269. Nadia Urbinati notes the crucial role of founders in Mill's thinking regarding the *establishment* of regimes. But as Urbinati insists that the ancients primarily taught Mill the value of political participation and public discussion, she identifies Machiavelli as the exclusive source of Mill's views regarding founders. As she insists that Mill's political thought is primarily concerned with the composition and styles of deliberative settings, Urbinati ignores the ongoing role founding types play in Mill's political philosophy. See Urbinati, *Mill on Democracy,* 57.

36. *Logic, CW,* 8: 938.

37. *On Liberty, CW,* 18: 267.

38. *SOW, CW,* 21: 273–74. Also see, Muirhead, *Just Work,* 132: "John Stuart Mill's ethic of fulfillment suggests what 'fit' comes to mean in a liberal democratic age. No longer a correspondence between individual nature and fixed social orders or places, it is rather something we each might seek and realize."

39. *SOW, CW,* 21: 280–81.

40. Wordsworth also proposed a reconciliation between the ancients and the thought of "later ages," or human excellence and human equality. But Wordsworth envisioned this synthesis differently. While Mill reconciles the practices of individuals who perform

great or heroic deeds with the protection of freedom and equality for all, Wordsworth
called for a type of poetry that extolled heroic practices existent in everyday life. Wordsworth, "Essay, Supplementary to the Preface, 1815," 213–14.

41. *SOW, CW,* 21: 253; "Inaugural Address," *CW,* 21; 313; "Bentham," *CW,* 10: 97–100.

42. *On Liberty, CW,* 18: 272.

43. Ibid., 264–65, 267.

44. Ibid., 267–68.

45. Ibid., 268.

46. Note Mill's response to Bain's view that *On Liberty* is too concerned with cultivating an
intellectual aristocracy and does not devote enough attention to universal equality and
liberty: "The *Liberty* has produced an effect on you which it never intended to produce
if it has made you think that we ought not to attempt to convert the world. I meant
nothing of the kind, and hold that we ought to convert all that we can. We *must* be
satisfied with keeping alive the sacred fire in a few minds when we are unable to do
more—but the notion of an intellectual aristocracy of *lumières* while the rest of the
world remains in darkness fulfills none of my aspirations." "Mill to Alexander Bain," August 6, 1859, *CW,* 15: 631. For contemporary commentators' criticisms regarding Mill's
position on the relations between excellent individuals and the mass, Robert Dahl,
Democracy and Its Critics (New Haven: Yale University Press, 1989), 125; Graeme Duncan, *Marx and Mill: Two Views of Social Conflict and Harmony* (Cambridge: Cambridge
University Press, 1973), 258–60.

47. *Considerations on Representative Government, CW:* 51–53; *Utilitarianism, CW,* 10: 245.

48. "The Spirit of the Age (V)," *CW,* 22: 306; "Guizot's Essays and Lectures on History,"
CW, 20: 273; "Michelet's History of France," *CW,* 20: 242.

49. *Autobiography, CW,* 1: 173.

50. Mill never used the terms "Hellenism and Hebraism" in discussing a comprehensive
morality of the future, but his contemporaries often used this framework in evaluating
his thinking. Matthew Arnold, for instance, criticized Mill in one essay for being too Hellenic and in another essay for being too Hebraic! On the one hand, Arnold accused Mill
of a degenerate Hellenism that severed human creativity from overarching moral considerations: "From whom can we more properly derive a general name for those degra-
dations of Hellenism than from that distinguished man, who, by his intelligence and accomplishments, is in many respects so admirable and so truly Hellenic, but whom his
dislike for 'the dominant sect,' as he calls the Church of England,—the Church of England, in many aspects so beautiful, calming, and attaching,—seems to transport with
an almost feminine vehemence of irritation?" On the other hand, Arnold also accused
Mill of a degenerate Hebraism, which suffocated human creativity with moral conformity: "Culture tends always thus to deal with a men of a system . . . with men like . . .
Mr. Mill. However much it may find to admire in these personages, or in some of them,
it nevertheless remembers the text: 'Be not yet called Rabbi!' and it soon passes on from
any Rabbi." Matthew Arnold, *St. Paul and Protestantism* (Macmillan: London, 1904),
xxxvii–xxxviii; and *Culture and Anarchy,* ed. J. Dover Wilson (Cambridge: Cambridge
University Press, 1932), 68. Also see, Alexander, *Matthew Arnold and John Stuart Mill,*
27–33; Mandelbaum, *History, Man, and Reason,* 204–05.

51. Friedrich Nietzsche, *Genealogy of Morals,* trans. Walter Kaufmann (New York: Vintage, 1967), First Essay, scts. 6–10, 16–17: 31–39, 52–55. Peter Berkowitz, *Nietzsche: The Ethics of an Immoralist* (Cambridge: Harvard University Press, 1995), 67–99.

52. Nietzsche, *Genealogy of Morals,* scts. 7, 9–10: 33–34, 35–39.

53. Friedrich Nietzsche, *The Will to Power,* sct. 943: 496–97; *Genealogy of Morals,* sct. 11: 39–43; *Antichrist* in *The Portable Nietzsche,* sct. 43: 618–20; sct. 57: 643–47; *Human, All Too Human,* trans. R. J. Hollingdale (Cambridge: Cambridge University Press, 1996), Preface, sct. 6: 9. For analyses of the hierarchical current in Nietzsche's thought, see Frederick Appel, *Nietzsche Contra Democracy* (Ithaca: Cornell University Press, 1999); Bruce Detwiler, *The Politics of Aristocratic Radicalism* (Chicago: University of Chicago Press, 1990); Laurence Lampert, *Nietzsche's Teachings: An Interpretation of Thus Spoke Zarathustra* (New Haven: Yale University Press, 1986).

54. Friedrich Nietzsche, *Thus Spoke Zarathustra* in *The Portable Nietzsche,* pt. 2, sct. 7: 211–14. Also, Lampert, *Nietzsche's Teachings,* 95–100.

55. Nietzsche, *Genealogy of Morals,* Essay 2, scts. 20–21: 90–92; *The Gay Science,* scts. 125: 181–82. *Thus Spoke Zarathustra,* Prologue, sct. 5: 129. Also, Leo Strauss, "Note on the Plan of Nietzsche's *Beyond Good and Evil,*" in *Studies in Platonic Political Philosophy* (Chicago: University of Chicago Press, 1983), 176; Thomas Pangle, "The Roots of Contemporary Nihilism and Its Political Consequences According to Nietzsche," *Review of Politics* 45, no. 1 (1983): 180–201.

56. Nietzsche, *Genealogy of Morals,* Essay 3, scts. 24–27: 148–59; *Beyond Good and Evil,* scts. 207, 223–24: 126–28, 150–53.

57. Nietzsche, *Beyond Good and Evil,* sct. 223: 150.

58. Richard Rorty ignores Nietzsche's position that moderns are limited by a tamed will and heavy conscience when he proposes that Nietzsche's and Mill's ethics of creativity can be reconciled by simply ignoring the hierarchical current in Nietzsche's thought. See Richard Rorty, *Contingency, Irony, and Solidarity* (Cambridge: Cambridge University Press, 1989). For thoughtful comparisons of Mill and Nietzsche, see Apple, *Nietzsche Contra Democracy,* 162–67; Ruth Abbey, "Odd Bedfellows: Nietzsche and Mill on Marriage," *History of European Ideas* 23 (1997): 81–104; Gerald Mara and Suzanne Dovi, "Mill, Nietzsche, and the Identity of Postmodern Liberalism," *Journal of Politics* 57 (1995): 1–23.

59. *On Liberty, CW,* 18: 268–69. Kateb, "A Reading of *On Liberty,*" 28: "Mill makes democracy the new and, one day, possibly the worst enemy of individuality."

60. *On Liberty, CW,* 18: 267, 261. Here Mill is addressing an issue that Berkowitz and Terchek identify as a late modern or postmodern problem: civil institutions and practices no longer spontaneously generate virtue. Berkowitz, *Virtue and the Making of Modern Liberalism,* 173–75; Ronald Terchek, "The Fruits of Success and the Crisis of Liberalism," in *Liberals on Liberalism,* ed. Alfonso J. Damico (Totowa, N.J.: Rowman and Littlefield, 1986), 18, 31–33.

61. *On Liberty, CW,* 18: 235–36, 244–46, 251–52; *Autobiography, CW,* 1: 171; Berkowitz, *Virtue and the Making of Modern Liberalism,* 151.

62. *On Liberty, CW,* 18: 245, 253–54, 268–71.

63. Ibid., 273–74.

64. Ibid., 271, 274, 275.

65. Ibid., 269.

66. Ibid.

67. *Coleridge's Shakespearean Criticisms,* ed. Thomas Raysor (Cambridge: Harvard University Press, 1930), 262–63.

68. For discussions on the difference between an expresssivist and more classical, deliberative vision of the good life, see Abrams, *Mirror and Lamp,* 3–29; Taylor, *Sources of the Self: The Making of Modern Identity,* 368–74. Also see, Charles Taylor, *The Ethics of Authenticity* (Cambridge: Harvard University Press, 1991), 55–69.

69. *On Liberty, CW,* 18: 272.

70. Ibid., 270.

71. Ibid., 269–71, 273.

72. Ibid., 277. Gertrude Himmelfarb recognizes that Mill's conception of human excellence at the end of chapter 3 of *On Liberty* differs from the idea of developed individuality at the beginning of this chapter. But Himmelfarb ignores Mill's position that eccentricity will both cultivate individuals characterized by strong wills and developed rationality and contribute to the development of higher modes of existence. She insists that Mill's goal is a postmodern type of self that isn't given but sought after, constructed, authored, fabricated, and formed by various contingent, revisable, and malleable practices of self-creation. See Gertrude Himmelfarb, *On Liberty and Liberalism* (New York: Knopf, 1974), 57–91. For similar positions that Mill anticipates postmodern conceptions of freedom, Villa, *Socratic Citizenship,* 59–114; Bruce Baum, *Rereading Power and Freedom in J. S. Mill* (Toronto: University of Toronto Press, 2000).

73. "Auguste Comte and Positivism," *CW,* 10: 287; "Bentham," *CW,* 10: 94; "Mill to Harriet Mill," February 24, 1885, *CW,* 14: 345–46. As Muirhead, *Just Work,* 129, puts it, "For Mill the diversity worth defending is not simply difference. He cherishes the diversity that, against the dampening force of custom, reveals the exercise of distinctly human faculties striving for perfection." Also, Alexander, *Matthew Arnold and John Stuart Mill,* 256–57.

74. *On Liberty, CW,* 18: 260–61.

75. Ibid., 253.

76. Ibid., 278.

77. Jürgen Habermas, *Communication and the Evolution of Society* (Boston: Beacon Society, 1979), 1–68.

78. *On Liberty, CW,* 18: 257, 284. Also, Alexander, *Matthew Arnold and John Stuart Mill,* 130–31.

79. Ibid.; "Spirit of the Age (I)," *CW,* 22: 234–35. Urbinati ignores this point in her claim that Mill viewed dialectical conflict in society as "a communicative interaction among individuals who are disposed to understand each other. The interlocutors . . . do not simply acquire an opinion; they alter their way of thinking. In Mill's view of deliberation both characteristics, the dissenting and the transformative, are needed." Urbinati, *Mill on Democracy,* 137.

80. "Bentham," *CW,* 10: 108; *Considerations on Representative Government, CW,* 19: 459; *On Liberty, CW,* 18: 253–54.

81. Waldron, "Mill and and the Value of Moral Distress," 126. Joseph Hamburger's recogni-

tion that Mill's theory provides space for a coercive public opinion contributes to his depiction of an illiberal Mill in *Mill on Liberty and Control*, 166–202. In *John Stuart Mill*, 237–38, Alan Ryan explains that Mill accepts the role of a coercive public opinion, but Ryan does not explain how this coercion "fits" in Mill's vision of the good society.

82. *On Liberty, CW*, 18: 252, 257.

83. *Considerations on Representative Government, CW*, 19: 382; *On Liberty, CW*, 18: 252, 257; "De Tocqueville on Democracy in America (I)," *CW*, 18: 83–90; "De Tocqueville on Democracy in America (II)," *CW*, 18: 196–200.

84. *SOW, CW*, 21: 294.

85. *On Liberty, CW*, 18: 272, 260–61.

86. *Chapters on Socialism, CW*, 5: 737–38; *On Liberty, CW*, 18: 253, 258–59. The social critic Caroline Fox, who had considered herself a friend and colleague of Mill in the past, was shocked by Mill's presumption of the neutral intellectual in *On Liberty:* "I am reading that terrible book of John Mill's on Liberty, so clear, and calm, and cold: he lays it on one as a tremendous duty to get one's self well contradicted, and admit always a devil's advocate into the presence of your dearest, most sacred truths, as they are apt to grow windy and worthless without such tests, if indeed they can stand the shock of argument at all. He looks through you like a baselisk, relentless, as Fate. We knew him well at one time, and owe him very much: I fear his remorseless logic has led him far since then." As quoted in Alexander, *Mathew Arnold and John Stuart Mill*, 129.

87. *On Liberty, CW*, 18: 254, 257; "Spirit of the Age (I)," *CW*, 22: 234–35. Also see, Muirhead, *Just Work*, 130. Mill believed "most individuals see only a single side, or live by one part of this untidy conflicted truth about the most important practical questions. Yet the courage to live by a part that not many see can make the visible whole to others. Many brave individuals are needed, each living some part, if anyone is to grasp the whole. . . . Grasping the whole must be beyond the reach of most, for while we (as common bearers of human nature) share in the possession of great and various potentials the realization of which is our perfection as a species, as individuals we possess some potentials more fully than others."

88. *Thornton on Labour and Its Claims, CW*, 5: 666; *On Liberty, CW*, 18: 275. The view that diverse social practices and beliefs should be transformed for higher civic purposes is proposed by Stephen Macedo in *Diversity and Distrust*, although Macedo emphasizes the decisive role of public education, not intellectuals. For brief discussions of Mill's view of the unique role of the intellectuals in a sea of divergent opinions, see Waldron, "Mill on Culture and Society," 240–42; Hamburger, *John Stuart Mill on Liberty and Control*, 154–56; Thompson, *John Stuart Mill and Representative Government*, 79–85.

89. *Diary*, January 13, 1854, *CW*, 27: 642–43.

90. "Mill to the Secretary of the Neophyte Writers' Society," April 23, 1854, *CW*, 14: 205. Also see, "Civilization," *CW* 1: 111–12: "This is a reading age; and precisely because it is so reading an age, any book which is the result of profound meditation is perhaps less likely to be duly and profitably read than at a former period. The whole world reads too much and too quickly to read well. . . . It is difficult to know what to read, except by reading every thing; and so much of the world's business is now transacted through the press, that it is necessary to know what is printed, if we desire to know what is going on. Opin-

ion weighs with so vast a weight in the balance of events, that ideas of no value in themselves are of importance from the mere circumstance that they *are* ideas." In "A Note on the Life and Thought of John Stuart Mill," in *On Liberty—John Stuart Mill,* 13–14, David Bromwich discusses Mill's disdain for the high culture of English society.

91. *Autobiography, CW,* 1: 203–05, 221–23. Also see "Mill to Tocqueville," June 11, 1835, *CW,* 12: 256–66, in which Mill proposes that Tocqueville become a regular contributor to his journal and that they start to forge unity among select intellectuals in England and France. Also see, Capaldi, *John Stuart Mill,* 125–30; Bain, *John Stuart Mill,* 55–57. In the last years of his life, 1867–71, Mill worked behind the scenes in support of John Morley's efforts to steer the *Fortnightly Review* as an organ of unity among an emerging group of public intellectuals, including Walter Bagehot, Henry Sidgwick, T. H. Huxley, Herbert Spencer, and Anthony Trollope. See E. M. Everett, *The Party of Humanity—The Fortnightly Review, 1865–1874* (Chapel Hill: University of North Carolina Press, 1939); Collini, "Their Master's Voice: John Stuart Mill as Public Moralist," 127.

92. "Mill to Gustave d'Eichthal," September 14, 1839, *CW,* 13: 403–04. For an analysis of the sociological conditions that undercut unity among the English intellectual elite from 1840 to 1870 and generated unity among this sector from 1870 to 1900, see T. W. Heyck, *The Transformation of Intellectual Life in England* (New York: St. Martin's Press, 1982).

93. "Duveyrier's Political Views," *CW,* 20: 299; "Mill to Pasquale Villari," February 28, 1872, *CW,* 17: 1873; *Diary,* April 15, 1854, *CW,* 27: 668. For an assessment of how Mill's views "lived" posthumously from 1870 to 1945, Stefan Collini, "From Sectarian Radical to National Possession: John Stuart Mill in English Culture, 1873–1945," in *A Cultivated Mind: Essays on J. S. Mill Presented to John M. Robson,* ed. Michael Laine (Toronto: University of Toronto Press, 1991), 242–72. Also see, Nietzsche, *The Gay Science,* sct. 365: 321.

94. The connection between *On Liberty* and *Considerations on Representative Government* is discussed by Berkowitz, *Virtue and the Making of Modern Liberalism,* 134–69, and Thompson, *John Stuart Mill and Representative Government,* 77–90.

95. *Considerations on Representative Government, CW,* 19: 455.

96. Ibid., 457; Alexis de Tocqueville, *Democracy in America,* vol. 1, pt. 2, ch. 5: 187–90. Also see John Stuart Mill, "Pledges [2]," in *Examiner,* July 15, 1832, *CW,* 23: 502: "We know that the will of the people, even of the numerical majority, must in the end be supreme, for . . . it would be monstrous that any power should exist capable of permanently defying it: but in spite of that, the test of what is right in politics is not the *will* of the people, but the *good* of the people, and our object is, not to compel but to persuade the people to impose for the sake of their own good, some restraints on the immediate and unlimited exercise of their own will. One of our reasons for desiring a popular government was, that men whom the people themselves had selected for their wisdom and good affections, would have authority enough to withstand the will of people when it is wrong."

97. *Considerations on Representative Government, CW,* 19: 473. Contemporary commentators' insistence that Mill be interpreted as a liberal who is *solely* concerned with free human conduct leads to their bewilderment regarding Mill's proposal for plural voting. In addition to disagreeing with Mill's proposals, they insist that Mill's views on the dispro-

portionate influence of intellectuals reflect his own confusion. See J. H. Burns, "J. S. Mill and Democracy, 1829–61," *Political Studies* 5 (1957): 158–75, 281–94; Thompson, *John Stuart Mill on Representative Government*, 99–101; Amy Gutman, *Liberal Equality* (Cambridge: Cambridge University Press, 1980), 51–56, 187–91; Charles Beitz, *Political Equality* (Princeton: Princeton University Press, 1989), 32–46. Skorupski criticizes this type of reading of Mill in *John Stuart Mill*, 35–38.

98. *Considerations on Representative Government, CW,* 19: 473–75. Also see, Berkowitz, *Virtue and the Making of Modern Liberalsim,* 166–67.

99. *Considerations on Representative Government, CW,* 19: 478.

100. Ibid., 448.

101. "Speech to the Electors of Westminster," *CW,* 28: 23.

102. *Considerations on Representative Government, CW,* 19: 460.

103. Urbinati, *Mill on Democracy,* 94, 99, 103.

104. *Considerations on Representative Government, CW,* 19: 433; *On Liberty, CW,* 18: 267–68.

105. *On Liberty, CW,* 18: 270.

106. Ibid., 277.

107. *Considerations on Representative Government, CW,* 19: 403; *SOW, CW,* 21: 336.

108. *On Liberty, CW,* 18: 246–47, 262–63, 267–68, 269–70.

109. *Political Economy, CW,* 3: 938.

110. *Autobiography, CW,* 1: 53. Donner, *The Liberal Self,* 126–28; R. J. Halliday, *John Stuart Mill* (New York: Harper and Row, 1976), 88. "For Mill, there was no question of an elite or clerisy organized as a separate ruling group or party controlling opinion and demanding deference from the non-elite, and the influence it possessed necessarily excluded compulsion, social disapprobation, and legal imposition."

111. *On Liberty, CW,* 18: 227. For an alternative argument that social unity will be accompanied by an increase in individual ideas of the good, see Charles Larmore, *Patterns of Moral Complexity* (Cambridge: Cambridge University Press, 1987), 70–71.

112. *Autobiography, CW,* 1: 158.

113. *On Liberty, CW,* 18: 250–55. Megill, "J. S. Mill's Religion of Humanity and the Second Justification for the Writing of *On Liberty.*" Michael Oakeshott overlooks Mill's argument for liberty in both the present and future when he claims Mill advocated liberty exclusively as a means to a morality of the future. Oakeshott, *Morality and Politics in Modern Europe: The Harvard Lectures,* ed. Shirley Letwin (New Haven: Yale University Press, 1993), 78–83: "Mill's plea for diversity is methodological, not substantial: diversity must be allowed only because we cannot yet be certain about what is true and what is false. But he looks forward to a time when the uniformity of perfection will establish itself unmistakably. . . . In short, 'individuality,' 'diversity' of opinion and 'eccentricity' of behaviour are all understood by Mill as the means by which a final condition of 'truth' and 'well-being' would be established."

114. Hamburger, *On Liberty and Control,* 120. "Grote's History of Greece (I)," *CW,* 11:281–90; "Auguste Comte and Positivism," *CW,* 10: 268–78.

115. *Autobiography, CW,* 1: 173; *Autobiography* (Early Draft), *CW,* 1: 241.

116. *Autobiography* (Early Draft), *CW,* 1: 244, 246; "Spirit of the Age (I)," *CW,* 22: 233.

117. *Autobiography, CW,* 1: 173.

118. "Auguste Comte and Positivism," *CW,* 10: 313. Also see, Megill, "J. S. Mill's Religion of Humanity and the Second Justification for the Writing of *On Liberty.*"

CHAPTER 7. MILL AND POLITICAL PHILOSOPHY

1. *Considerations on Representative Government, CW,* 19: 448–81, 488–500; "Coleridge," *CW,* 10: 131–36; *On Liberty, CW,* 18: 266–68; "The Utility of Religion," *CW,* 10: 417–28; "Theism," *CW,* 10: 482–89.
2. Berlin, "J. S. Mill and the Ends of Life," 181, 185–91. Also see, James Fitzjames Stephen, *Liberty, Equality, Fraternity,* ed. R. J. White (Cambridge: Cambridge University Press, 1967); Himmelfarb, *On Liberty and Liberalism;* C. L. Ten, "Mill's Defence of Liberty," in *Traditions of Liberalism: Essays On Locke, Smith, and Mill,* ed. Haakonssen (Sydney: Centre of Independent Studies, 1988), 37–54.
3. Berlin, "J. S. Mill and the Ends of Life," 199.
4. Isaiah Berlin, "Two Concepts of Liberty," in *Four Essays on Liberty,* 128: "Mill confuses two distinct notions. One is that all coercion is, in so far as it frustrates human desires, bad as such, although it may have to be applied to prevent other, greater evils; while non-interference, which is the opposite of coercion, is good as such, although it is not the only good. This is the 'negative' conception of liberty in its classical form. The other is that men should seek to discover the truth, or to develop a certain type of character of which Mill approved—critical, original, imaginative, independent, non-conforming to the point of eccentricity, and so on—and that truth can be found, and such character can be bred, only in conditions of freedom. Both these are liberal views, but they are not identical, and the connection between them is, at best, empirical." See G. W. Smith's thoughtful critique of Berlin's assessment of Mill: "J. S. Mill on Liberty," in *Conceptions of Liberty in Political Philosophy,* ed. Z. A. Pelczynski and John Gray (New York: St. Martin's Press, 1984), 183–216.
5. Berlin, "J. S. Mill and the Ends of Life," 183.
6. *SOW, CW,* 21: 336. Waldron, "Mill on Culture and Society," 226.
7. *On Liberty, CW,* 18: 263–64, 268–69.
8. Ibid., 223.
9. Ibid., 261, 263.
10. For the British Idealists' challenge, Den Otter, *British Idealism and the Social Explanation,* 52–87; Peter Nicholson, *The Political Philosophy of British Idealism: Selected Studies* (Cambridge: Cambridge University Press, 1990); "The Reception and Early Reputation of Mill's Political Thought," in *The Cambridge Companion to Mill,* 483–90; Michael Freeden, *The New Liberalism* (Oxford: Oxford University Press, 1978). The question of the different ideas of liberty in *On Liberty* is posed in Friedman, "A New Exploration of Mill's *On Liberty,*" and Smith, "The Logic of J. S. Mill on Freedom."
11. *Logic, CW,* 8: 668–97.
12. Ibid., 680, 683.
13. Ibid., 683.
14. Ibid., 678, 687.

15. Aristotle, *Nicomachean Ethics,* sct. 1143a-6.91–92: 164.

16. *Logic, CW:* 682.

17. Ryan, "John Stuart Mill and the Art of Living"; "John Stuart Mill and the Open Society," *The Listener* 89 (1973): 633–35; Rees, *John Stuart Mill's On Liberty* (Oxford: Oxford University Press, 1985); Richard Wollheim, "John Stuart Mill and the Limits of State Action," *Social Research* 40 (1973); Berger, *Happiness, Justice, and Freedom.*

18. Ryan, "John Stuart Mill and the Art of Living," 14.

19. "The Contagious Disease Acts," *CW,* 21: 357. Also see, Richard Vernon, "Beyond the Harm Principle: Mill and Censorship," in Eisenach, ed., *Mill and the Moral Character of Liberalism,* 115–30.

20. *Logic, CW,* 8: 952: "[I] hold that the very question, what constitutes this elevation of character, is itself to be decided by a reference to happiness as the standard. The character itself should be, to the individual, a paramount end, simply because the existence of this ideal of nobleness of character, or near approach to it, in any abundance, would go further than all things else towards making human life happy; both in the comparatively humble sense, of pleasure and freedom from pain, and in the higher meaning, of rendering life, not what it now is almost universally, puerile and insignificant—but such as human beings with highly developed human faculties can care to have."

21. Ryan, *J. S. Mill,* 154–58; "Sense and Sensibility in Mill's Political Thought," in *A Cultivated Mind: Essays in Honor of John Robson,* 135–37.

22. Rousseau, *Èmile, or On Education,* 37–49; de Tocqueville, *Democracy in America,* vol. 2, pt. 3, chs. 8–12: 558–76.

23. *SOW, CW,* 21: 329.

24. Ibid., 331.

25. Ibid., 327, 331.

26. Ibid., 331.

27. Ibid., 331–33. Shanley, "Marital Slavery and Friendship: John Stuart Mill's *Subjection of Women,*" 243: "The *Subjection of Women* is not only one of liberalism's most incisive arguments for equal opportunity, but it embodies as well a belief in the importance of friendship for human development and progress." Also see, Abbey, "Odd Bedfellows: Nietzsche and Mill on Marriage."

28. Stephen Salkever, *Finding the Mean: Theory and Practice in Aristotelian Philosophy* (Princeton: Princeton University Press, 1990), 172. Hannah Arendt, "What Is Freedom?" in *Between Past and Future* (New York: Penguin, 1968), 143–71. Also see, Peter Euben, *Greek Tragedy and Political Theory* (Berkeley: University of California Press, 1986).

29. Thucydides, *History of the Peloponnesian War,* 2: 151.

30. Urbinati, "J. S. Mill on Androgyny and Marriage," 637–39.

31. *SOW, CW,* 21: 334; *Plato's "Symposium,"* trans. Seth Benardete (Chicago: University of Chicago Press, 1986), scts. 207a–212a: 37–42.

32. *SOW, CW,* 21: 334; Aristotle, *Nicomachean Ethics,* scts. 1156b5–30: 212–13.

33. *SOW, CW,* 21: 314, 334.

34. *Considerations on Representative Government,* CW, 19: 493–94.

35. *On Liberty, CW,* 18: 220, 223.

36. Ibid., 270.

37. Notable exceptions are Thompson, *John Stuart Mill and Representative Government*, 54–90; Berkowitz, *Virtue and the Making of Modern Liberalism*, 134–69.

38. This tension between liberalism and virtue is examined thoroughly in Galston, *Liberal Purposes*, and Berkowitz, *Virtue and the Making of Modern Liberalism*.

39. Aristotle, *The Politics*, scts. 1276b15–1277a20: 89–91; Berkowitz, *Virtue and the Making of Modern Liberalism*, 175.

40. Nietzsche, *The Gay Science*, sct. 125: 181; *Genealogy of Morals*, Essay 2, scts. 20–21: 90–92; Essay 3, scts. 24–27: 148–59; *Beyond Good and Evil*, scts. 207, 223–24: 126–28, 150–53.

41. *On Liberty, CW*, 18: 276–77.

42. Ibid., 262–63, 269, 284–86.

43. See Gray and Smith, eds. *J. S. Mill: On Liberty in Focus*.

44. Alexander Hamilton, James Madison, and John Jay, *The Federalist Papers* (New York: Penguin, 1961), no. 69: 414. Also see *Considerations on Representative Government, CW*, 19: 525: "When the highest dignity in the state is to be conferred by popular election once in every few years, the whole intervening time is spent in what is virtually a canvas. President, ministers, chiefs of parties, and their followers, are all electioneers: the whole community is kept intent on the mere personalities of politics, and every public question is discussed and decided with less reference to its merits than to its expected bearing on the presidential election."

45. "Thomas Jefferson to John Adams," October 28, 1813, in *The Portable Jefferson*, ed. Merrill D. Peterson (New York: Viking, 1975), 533.

46. Rousseau, *Social Contract*, bk. 3, ch. 5: 181–82.

47. Hegel, *Philosophy of Right*, sct. 289: 189–90.

48. Karl Mannheim, *Ideology and Utopia*, trans. Louis Wirth and Edward Shils (New York: Norton, 1963), 136.

49. *Logic, CW*, 18: 267.

50. "Mill to John Sterling," October 20, 1831, *CW*, 12: 77.

51. Frederick Beiser, *The Fate of Reason: German Philosophy from Kant to Fichte* (Cambridge: Harvard University Press, 1987), 43–45: "Thanks to the controversy [between Jacobi and Mendelsson in 1783], pantheism became, as Heine later put it, 'the unofficial religion of Germany.' . . . In short, to use the jargon of Schiller, Schelling, and Hegel: it is necessary to find 'unity in difference.'" Also see, Abrams, *Naturalism and Supernaturalism*, 218–78.

52. For a position that Mill did believe society was being moved by historical forces toward unity, Karl Popper, *The Poverty of Historicism* (London: Routledge, 1957).

53. *Considerations on Representative Government, CW*, 19: 405.

54. De Tocqueville, *Democracy in America*, vol. 2, pt. 1: 403–78.

55. Ibid., ch. 11: 442; vol. 2, pt. 3, ch. 21: 615.

56. "De Tocqueville on Democracy in America (I);" "De Tocqueville on Democracy in America (II)," *CW*, 18: 82–90, 194–204, respectively.

57. "De Tocqueville on Democracy in America (II)," *CW*, 18: 198.

58. *Logic, CW*, 8: 840. Also see, Skorupski, *John Stuart Mill*, 38–43.

59. *On Liberty, CW*, 18: 261.

60. Franco, *Hegel's Philosophy of Freedom,* 19; Immanuel Kant, "On the common saying: 'That may be correct in theory, but it is of no use in practice," and "Toward perpetual peace," in *Practical Philosophy,* scts. 8: 289–312: 290–309, scts. 8: 366–67: 335–36. Also see, Patrick Riley, *Kant's Political Philosophy* (Totowa, N.J.: Rowman and Littlefield, 1983).

61. Hegel, *Philosophy of Right,* pars. 29, 258, 260–61, 265, 268: 33, 155–59, 160–62, 163–64.

62. *On Liberty, CW,* 18: 305–10; *Autobiography, CW,* 1: 203. Also see, H. O. Pappe, "Mill and Tocqueville."

63. *Hamilton, CW,* 9: 450, n. 67.

64. Eisenach, Introduction, *Mill and the Moral Character of Liberalism,* 3. Also see, Waldron, "Mill on Culture and Society," 225, where he complains that Mill is treated as "forerunner of our own rather flat and formalistic debates about liberalism in twentieth-century political philosophy."

65. Burrow explains continuities and differences between Mill's thought and the critical, oppositionist outlooks of past England in "Balance and Diversity."

66. *Diary, CW,* 27: 646.

67. Among the notable exceptions are Megill, "J. S. Mill's Religion of Humanity and the Second Justification for the Writing of *On Liberty;*" Karl Britton, "John Stuart Mill on Christianity;" Eldon Eisenach, *Two Worlds of Liberalism: Religion and Politics in Hobbes, Locke, and Mill* (Chicago: University of Chicago Press, 1981).

68. For an important discussion of this subject, see Taylor, *Sources of the Self: The Making of the Modern Identity,* 3–107.

69. *SOW, CW,* 21: 315.

Bibliography

WORKS BY MILL

All references to Mill are made to the complete edition, *Collected Works of John Stuart Mill*, 33 vols. edited by J. M. Robson. Toronto: University of Toronto Press, 1963–91. The form of referencing is as follows: *CW,* 16: 1120–21.

References in this study are made to the following volumes:

1: *Autobiography and Literary Essays*
2, 3: *Principles of Political Economy*
4, 5: *Essays on Economics and Society*
6: *Essays on England, Ireland and the Empire*
7, 8: *System of Logic: Ratiocinative and Deductive*
9: *An Examination of Sir William Hamilton's Philosophy*
10: *Essays on Ethics, Religion and Society*
11: *Essays on Philosophy and the Classics*
12, 13: *Earlier Letters, 1812–1848*
14, 15, 16, 17: *Later Letters, 1848–1873*
18, 19: *Essays on Politics and Society*
20: *Essays on French History and Historians*
21: *Essays on Equality, Law and Education*
22, 23, 24: *Newspaper Writings*
26, 27: *Journals and Debating Speeches*
28: *Public and Parliamentary Speeches*
31: *Miscellaneous Writings*

OTHER WORKS

Abbey, Ruth. "Odd Bedfellows: Nietzsche and Mill on Marriage." *History of European Ideas* 23 (1997): 81–104.

Abrams, M. H. "Coleridge and the Romantic Vision of the World." In *Coleridge's Variety,* edited by John Beer, 103–15. London: Macmillan, 1974.

———. *The Mirror and the Lamp: Romantic Theory and the Critical Tradition.* Oxford: Oxford University Press, 1953.

———. *Naturalism and Supernaturalism: Tradition and Revolution in Romantic Literature.* New York: Norton, 1971.

Alexander, Edward. *Matthew Arnold and John Stuart Mill.* New York: Columbia University Press, 1965.

———. "The Principles of Permanence and Progression in the Thought of J. S. Mill." In *James and John Stuart Mill/Papers of the Centenary Conference,* edited by J. M. Robson and Michael Laine, 126–43. Toronto: University of Toronto Press, 1976.

Allison, Henry. "Morality and Freedom: Kant's Reciprocity Thesis." *Philosophical Review* 95 (1986): 395–424.

Annas, Julia. "Mill and the Subjection of Women." *Philosophy* 52 (1977): 179–94.

———. *The Morality of Happiness.* Oxford: Oxford University Press, 1993.

———. "Plato the Skeptic." In *The Socratic Movement,* edited by Paul A. Vander Waerdt, 309–40. Ithaca: Cornell University Press, 1994.

Anschutz, R. P. *The Philosophy of J. S. Mill.* Westport: Greenwood Press, 1953.

Appel, Frederick. "Natural Affinities? The Concept of Nature in J. S. Mill and Nietzsche." Paper presented at the Annual Meeting of the American Science Association. San Francisco (1996).

———. *Nietzsche Contra Democracy.* Ithaca: Cornell University Press, 1999.

Arendt, Hannah. *Between Past and Future.* New York: Penguin, 1968.

———. "Thinking and Moral Considerations." *Social Research* 51 (1984): 7–37.

———. "What Is Freedom?" In *Between Past and Future,* 143–71. New York: Penguin, 1968.

Aristotle. *Nicomachean Ethics.* Translated by Terence Irwin. Indianapolis: Hackett, 1985.

———. *The Politics.* Translated by Carnes Lord. Chicago: University of Chicago Press, 1984.

Arnold, Mathew. *Culture and Anarchy.* Edited by J. Dover Wilson. Cambridge: Cambridge University Press, 1932.

———. *On the Study of Celtic Literature and On Translating Homer.* New York: Macmillan, 1924.

———. *St. Paul and Protestantism.* London: Macmillan, 1904.

Ashton, Rosemary. *The German Idea: Four English Writers and the Reception of German Thought.* Cambridge: Cambridge University Press, 1980.

Bacon, Francis. *The Advancement of Learning.* In *Francis Bacon: Major Works,* edited by Brian Vickers, 120–299. Oxford: Oxford University Press, 1996.

Bagehot, Walter. "The Late Mr. Mill." *Economist,* May 17, 1873: 588–89.

Bain, Alexander. *John Stuart Mill: A Criticism with Personal Recollections.* London: Longmans, 1882.

Barnard, F. M. *Herder's Social and Political Thought.* Oxford: Oxford University Press, 1965.

Baum, Bruce. *Rereading Power and Freedom in J. S. Mill.* Toronto: University of Toronto Press, 2000.

Beiser, Frederick C. *The Fate of Reason: German Philosophy from Kant to Fichte.* Cambridge: Harvard University Press, 1987.

Beitz, Charles. *Political Equality.* Princeton: Princeton University Press, 1989.

Bentham, Jeremy [Philip Beauchamp, pseud.]. *Analysis of the Influence of Natural Religion on the Temporal Happiness of Mankind.* Oxford: Clarendon, 1956.

———. *Deontology and A Table of Springs of Action.* Edited by Amnon Goldworth. Oxford: Clarendon, 1983.

———. *The Constitutional Code.* In *The Collected Works of Jeremy Bentham,* edited by John Bowring. 11 vols. New York: Russell, 1962.

Berger, Fred. *Happiness, Justice, and Freedom: The Moral and Political Philosophy of John Stuart Mill.* Berkeley: University of California Press, 1984.

Berkowitz, Peter. *Nietzsche: The Ethics of an Immoralist.* Cambridge: Harvard University Press, 1995.

———. *Virtue and the Making of Modern Liberalism.* Princeton: Princeton University Press, 1998.

Berlin, Isaiah. "John Stuart Mill and the Ends of Life." In *Four Essays on Liberty,* 173–206. Oxford: Oxford University Press, 1969.

———. "Two Concepts of Liberty." In *Four Essays on Liberty,* 118–72. Oxford: Oxford University Press, 1969.

Berman, David. *A History of Atheism in Britain: From Hobbes to Russell.* London: Croom Helm, 1988.

Bloom, Alan. Interpretive Essay in *The Republic of Plato,* translated by Allan Bloom, 307–436. New York: Basic, 1968.

Blumenberg, Hans. *The Legitimacy of the Modern World.* Translated by Robert M. Wallace. Cambridge: MIT Press, 1983.

Bosanquet, Bernard, *Logic.* 2nd ed., 2 vols. Oxford: Oxford University Press, 1911.

Britton, Karl. "John Stuart Mill on Christianity." In *James and John Stuart Mill: Papers of the Centenary Conference,* edited by J. M. Robson and Michael Laine, 118–46. Toronto: University of Toronto Press, 1976.

Bromwich, David. "A Note in the Life and Thought of John Stuart Mill." In *On Liberty—John Stuart Mill,* edited by David Bromwich and George Kateb, 1–27. New Haven: Yale Universtiy Press, 2003.

Bruford, W. H. *The German Tradition of Self-Cultivation: 'Bildung' from Humboldt to Thomas Mann.* Cambridge: Cambridge University Press, 1975.

Burns, J. H. "J. S. Mill and Democracy, 1829–1861." *Political Studies* 5 (1957): 158–71, 281–94.

Burrow, J. W. "Autonomy and Self-realization: From Independence to Individuality." In *Whigs and Liberals: Continuity and Change in English Political Thought,* 77–100. Oxford: Clarendon Press, 1988.

———. "Balance and Corruption: From Roman Corruption to Chinese Stationariness." In *Whigs and Liberals: Continuity and Change in English Political Thought,* 101–24. Oxford: Clarendon Press, 1988.

Butler, E. M. *The Tyranny of Greece Over Germany.* Cambridge: Cambridge University Press, 1935.

Capaldi, Nicholas. *John Stuart Mill: A Biography.* Cambridge: Cambridge University Press, 2004.

Carlisle, Janice. *John Stuart Mill and the Writing of Character.* Athens: University of Georgia, 1991.

Carr, Robert. "The Religious Thought of John Stuart Mill: A Study in Religious Skepticism." *Journal of the History of Ideas* 23 (1992): 475–95.

Carwell, Stephen. *The British Moralists and the Internal 'Ought.'* Cambridge: Cambridge University Press, 1996.

Caygill, Howard. *A Kant Dictionary.* Oxford: Blackwell, 1995

Cicero, Marcus Tullius. *De Finibus Bonorum et Malorum.* Translated by H. Rackham. New York: Putnam, 1931.

Coleridge, Samuel T. *Anima Poetae.* In *The Collected Works of Samuel Taylor Coleridge,* edited by Kathleen Coburn. 16 vols. Princeton: Princeton University Press, 1983.

———. *Biographia Literaria.* In *The Collected Works of Samuel Taylor Coleridge,* edited by Kathleen Coburn. 16 vols. Princeton: Princeton University Press, 1983.

———. *On the Constitution of Church and State.* In *The Collected Works of Samuel Taylor Coleridge,* edited by Kathleen Coburn. 16 vols. Princeton: Princeton University Press, 1983.

———. "Essays on the Principles of Method." In *The Collected Works of Samuel Taylor Coleridge,* edited by Kathleen Coburn. 16 vols. Princeton: Princeton University Press, 1983.

———. *Hints Toward the Formation of a More Comprehensive Theory of Life.* Edited by Seth B. Watson. Philadelphia: Lea and Blanchard, 1848.

———. *Logic.* In *The Collected Works of Samuel Taylor Coleridge,* edited by Kathleen Coburn. 16 vols. Princeton: Princeton University Press, 1983.

———. *Religious Musings.* In *The Complete Poetical Works,* edited by E. H. Coleridge, 130–52. Oxford: Oxford University Press, 1912.

———. *Shakespearean Criticisms.* Edited by Thomas Raysor. Cambridge: Harvard University Press, 1930.

———. *Statesman's Manual,* Appendix C. In *The Collected Works of Samuel Taylor Coleridge,* edited by Kathleen Coburn. 16 vols. Princeton: Princeton University Press, 1983.

Collini, Stefan. "From Sectarian Radical to National Possession: John Stuart Mill in English Culture." In *A Cultivated Mind: Essays on J. S. Mill Presented to John M. Robson,* edited by Michael Laine, 242–72. Toronto: University of Toronto Press, 1991.

———. "The Idea of Character: Private Habits and Public Virtue." In *Public Moralists: Political Thought and Intellectual Life in Britain, 1850–1930,* 91–118. Oxford: Oxford University Press, 1993.

———, Donald Winch, and John Burrow. *That Noble Science of Politics: A Study in Nineteenth-Century Intellectual History.* Cambridge: Cambridge University Press, 1983.

———. "Their Master's Voice: John Stuart Mill as Public Moralist." In *Public Moralists: Political Thought and Intellectual Life in Britain, 1850–1930,* 121–69. Oxford: Oxford University Press, 1993.

Connolly, William E. *Identity/Difference: Democratic Negotiations of Political Paradox.* Ithaca: Cornell University Press, 1991.

Cowling, Maurice. *Mill and Liberalism.* Cambridge: Cambridge University Press, 1963.

————. *Religion and Public Doctine in Modern England.* 2 vols. Cambridge: Cambridge University Press, 1985.

Crimmins, James. "Religion, Utility, and Politics: Bentham versus Paley." In *Religion, Secularization, and Political Thought: Thomas Hobbes to J. S. Mill,* edited by James Crimmins, 130–52. London: Routledge, 1990.

Cropsey, Joseph. *Polity and Economy.* Chicago: University of Chicago Press, 1956.

Cummings, Robert. "Mill's History of His Ideas." *Journal of the History of Ideas* 25 (1964): 235–56.

Cunliffe, Keith. "Recollection and Recovery: Coleridge's Platonism." In *Platonism and the English Imagination,* edited by Anna Baldwin and Sarah Hutton, 207–16. Cambridge: Cambridge University Press, 1994.

Dagger, Richard. *Civic Virtues: Rights, Citizenship and Republican Liberalism.* Oxford: Oxford University Press, 1997.

Dahl, Robert. *Democracy and Its Critics.* New Haven: Yale University Press, 1989.

Davis, Michael. "Civic Virtue, Corruption, and the Structure of Moral Theories." In *Ethical Theory: Characters and Virtue,* edited by Peter French, Theodore Uehling, Jr., Howard Wettstein, 352–67. South Bend: University of Notre Dame Press, 1988.

Deneen, Patrick. "Chasing Plato." *Political Theory* 28 (2000): 412–24.

Descartes, René. *Discourse on Method.* Translated by Donald A. Cress. Indianapolis: Hackett, 1980.

Detwiler, Bruce. *The Politics of Aristocratic Radicalism.* Chicago: University of Chicago Press, 1990.

Devigne, Robert. "Mill on Liberty and Religion: An Unfinished Dialectic." In *Mill and the Moral Character of Liberalism.* edited by Eldon Eisenach, 231–56. University Park: Pennsylvania State University Press, 1998.

————. "Plato, Nietzsche and Strauss." *Political Science Reviewer* 26 (1997): 397–434.

————. *Recasting Conservatism: Oakeshott, Strauss, and the Response to Postmodernism.* New Haven: Yale University Press, 1994.

Den Otter, Sandra. *British Idealism and Social Explanation: A Study in Late Victorian Thought.* Oxford: Clarendon, 1996.

Donner, Wendy. *The Liberal Self: John Stuart Mill's Moral and Political Philosophy.* Ithaca: Cornell University Press, 1991.

Duncan, Graeme. *Marx and Mill: Two Views on Social Conflict and Harmony.* Cambridge: Cambridge University Press, 1973.

Eisenach, Eldon. Introduction, *Mill and the Moral Character of Liberalism,* edited by Eldon Eisenach, 1–12. University Park: Pennsylvania State University Press, 1998.

————. "Mill and Liberal Christianity." In *Mill and the Moral Character of Liberalism,* edited by Eldon Eisenach, 192–229. University Park: Pennsylvania State University Press, 1998.

————. "Self-Reform as Political Reform in the Writings of John Stuart Mill." *Utilitas* 1 (1990): 242–58.

————. *Two Worlds of Liberalism: Religion and Politics in Hobbes, Locke and Mill.* Chicago: University of Chicago Press, 1981.

Eisenstein, Zillah. *The Radical Future of Liberal Feminism.* Boston: Northeastern University Press, 1986.

Elshtain, Jean Bethke, "Liberty and the Problem of Authority." In *On Liberty—John Stuart Mill,* edited by David Bromwich and George Kateb, 208–33. New Haven: Yale University Press, 2003.

Euben, Peter. *Corrupting Youth.* Princeton: Princeton University Press, 1997.

———. *Greek Tragedy and Political Theory.* Berkeley: University of California Press, 1986.

Everett, E. M. *The Party of Humanity—The Fortnightly Review, 1865–1874.* Chapel Hill: University of North Carolina Press, 1939.

Feinberg, Joel. *Harm to Others: Moral Limits of Criminal Law.* 2 vols. Oxford: Oxford University Press, 1984.

Fichte, J. G. *The Nature of the Scholar.* Translated by William Smith. London: Chapman, 1845.

Figgis, John. "Erastus and Erastianism." In *The Divine Right of Kings,* 267–316. Cambridge: Cambridge University Press, 1934.

———. "Non-Resistance and the Theory of Sovereignty." In *The Divine Right of Kings,* 219–55. Cambridge: Cambridge University Press, 1934.

Fiss, Owen. "A Freedom both Personal and Political." In *On Liberty—John Stuart Mill,* edited by David Bromwich and George Kateb, 179–96. New Haven: Yale University Press, 2003.

Franco, Paul. *Hegel's Philosophy of Freedom.* New Haven: Yale University Press, 1999.

———. *The Political Philosophy of Michael Oakeshott.* New Haven: Yale University Press, 1999.

Freeden, Michael. *The New Liberalism.* Oxford: Oxford University Press, 1978.

Friedman, Richard. "A New Exploration of Mill's Essay *On Liberty.*" In *Mill and the Moral Character of Liberalism,* edited by Eldon Eisenach, 273–300. University Park: Pennsylvania State University Press, 1998. First published in *Political Studies* 14 (1966).

Funkenstein, Amos. *Theology and the Scientific Imagination: From the Middle Ages to the Seventeenth Century.* Princeton: Princeton University Press, 1986.

Furst, Lilian. *Romanticism in Perspective: A Comparative Study of Aspects of the Romantic Movements in England, France, and Germany.* London: Macmillan, 1969.

Galston, William. *Liberal Pluralism.* Cambridge: Cambridge University Press, 2002.

———. *Liberal Purposes: Goods, Virtues, and Diversity in the Liberal State.* Cambridge: Cambridge University Press, 1991.

———. "What Is Living and What Is Dead in Kant's Practical Philosophy." In *Kant and Political Philosophy: The Contemporary Legacy,* edited by Ronald Beiner and William James Booth, 207–23. New Haven: Yale University Press, 1993.

Grant, Ruth. *Hypocrisy and Integrity: Machiavelli, Rousseau, and the Ethics of Politics.* Chicago: University of Chicago Press, 1997.

Gray, John. *Mill on Liberty: A Defense.* London: Routledge, 1986.

———, and G. W. Smith. *J. S. Mill, "On Liberty" in Focus.* London: Routledge, 1991.

Green, T. H. *Liberal Legislation and Freedom of Contract: A Lecture.* In *T. H. Green: Lectures on the Principles of Political Obligation and Other Writings,* edited by Paul Harris and John Morrow, 194–212. Cambridge: Cambridge University Press, 1986.

Griswold, Charles, Jr. *Adam Smith and the Virtues of Enlightenment.* Cambridge: Cambridge University Press, 1999.

———. "E Pluribus Unum? On the Platonic Corpus." *Ancient Philosophy* 21 (1999): 420–44.

Grote, George. *Plato, and the Other Companions of Sokrates.* 4 vols. London: John Murray, 1888.

Grotius, Hugo. *The Law of War and Peace.* Books 1–3. Translated by Francis W. Kelsey. New York: Bobbs-Merrill, 1925.

Gruber, Howard E. *Darwin on Man: A Psychological Study of Scientific Certainty.* Chicago: University of Chicago Press, 1981.

Gutman, Amy. *Liberal Equality.* Cambridge: Cambridge University Press, 1980.

Haakonssen, Knud. *Natural Law and Moral Philosophy: From Grotius to the Scottish Enlightenment.* Cambridge: Cambridge University Press, 1996.

Habermas, Jürgen. *Communication and the Evolution of Society.* Boston: Beacon Society, 1979.

Halliday, R. J. *John Stuart Mill.* New York: Harper and Row, 1976.

Hamburger, Joseph. *John Stuart Mill on Liberty and Control.* Princeton: Princeton University Press, 1999.

Hamilton, Alexander, James Madison, and John Jay. *The Federalist Papers.* New York: Penguin, 1961.

Hamilton, Andy. "Mill, Phenomenalism, and the Self." In *The Cambridge Companion to Mill,* edited by John Skorupski, 139–75. Cambridge: Cambridge University Press, 1998.

Hare, R. M. *Freedom and Reason.* Oxford: Clarendon, 1963.

———. *The Language of Morals.* Oxford: Clarendon, 1961.

Hartz, Louis. *The Liberal Tradition in America.* New York: Harcourt, 1955.

Hatfield, Henry. *Aesthetic Paganism in German Literature.* Cambridge: Cambridge University Press, 1964.

Hegel, G. W. F. *Lectures on the History of Philosophy.* Translated by E. S. Haldane and F. F. Simson. 3 vols. Lincoln: University of Nebraska, 1995.

———. *The Phenomenology of Spirit.* Translated by A. V. Miller. Oxford: Clarendon, 1977.

———. *Philosophy of Right.* Translated by T. M. Knox. Oxford: Oxford University Press, 1952.

———. *The Philosophy of History.* Translated by J. Sirbee. New York: Colonial Press, 1900.

Helmstadter, Richard J., and Bernard Lightman, eds. *Victorian Faith in Crisis.* Stanford: Stanford University Press, 1990.

Helvétius, C. A. *Oeuvres Complètes.* edited by Jean-Francois Saint-Lambert. 10 vols. Paris: Hildensheim, 1969.

Herder, Johann Gottfried. "Do We Still Have the Fatherland of the Ancients?" Translated and edited by Ioannis D. Evrigenis and Daniel Pellerin, 109–17. Indianapolis: Hackett, 2004.

———. "Essay on a History of Lyrical Poetry." In *Selected Early Works.* edited by Ernest A. Menze and Karl Menges, translated by Ernest A. Menze and Michael Palma, 69–84. University Park: Pennsylvania State University Press, 1991.

———. "On Recent German Literature: First Collection of Fragments." In *Selected Early Works.* edited by Ernest A. Menze and Karl Menges, translated by Ernest A. Menze and Michael Palma, 85–165. University Park: Pennsylvania State University Press, 1991.

Heyck, T. W. *The Transformation of Intellectual Life in England.* New York: St. Martin's Press, 1982.

Himmelfarb, Gertrude. *On Liberty and Liberalism.* New York: Knopf, 1974.

Hobbes, Thomas. *De Cive.* In *Man and Citizen.* edited by Barnard Gert. Garden City, N.Y.: Doubleday, 1972.

———. *Leviathan.* Edited by Edwin Curley. Indianapolis: Hackett, 1994.

———. "Of Liberty and Necessity." In *English Works,* edited by William Molesworth. 11 vols. London: Longmans, 1839–44.

Hölderlin, Friedrich. "Hyperion, or the Hermit in Greece." Translated by Willard R. Trask. In *Hyperion and Selected Poems,* edited by Eric L. Santner, 1–133. New York: Continuum, 1990.

Hollis, Martin. "J. S. Mill's Political Philosophy of Mind." *Philosophy* 47 (1972): 334–47.

Holmes, Stephen. *Passions and Constraints: On the Theory of Liberal Democracy.* Chicago: University of Chicago Press, 1995.

Honderich, Ted. "On Liberty and Morality-Dependent Harm." *Political Studies* 30 (1982): 504–22.

Houghton, Walter. *The Victorian Frame of Mind.* New Haven: Yale University Press, 1957.

Humboldt, Wilhelm von. *The Limits of State Action.* Edited by J. W. Burrow. Indianapolis: Liberty Fund, 1993.

Hume, David. *Dialogues Concerning Natural Religion.* In *Dialogues and Natural History of Religion,* edited by J. C. A. Gaskin, 29–133. Oxford: Oxford University Press, 1993.

———. *Enquiries Concerning Human Understanding.* Edited by L. A. Selby-Bigge. Oxford: Oxford University Press, 1975.

———. *The History of England: From the Invasion of Julius Caesar to the Revolution in 1868.* 6 vols. Indianapolis: Liberty, 1983.

———. "Idea of a Perfect Commonwealth." In *Essays: Moral, Political, and Literary,* edited by Eugene Miller, 512–29. Indianapolis: Liberty, 1987.

———. "Of Commerce." In *Essays: Moral, Political, and Literary,* edited by Eugene Miller, 253–67. Indianapolis: Liberty, 1987.

———. "Of the Origin of Government." In *Essays: Moral, Political, and Literary,* edited by Eugene Miller, 37–41. Indianapolis: Liberty, 1987.

———. *A Treatise of Human Nature.* Edited by L. A. Selby-Bigge and P. H. Nidditch. Oxford: Clarendon Press, 1975.

Hunter, Ian. *Rival Enlightenments: Civil and Metaphysical Philosophy in Early Modern Germany.* Cambridge: Cambridge University Press, 2001.

Huxley, T. H. *Man's Place in Nature and Other Anthropological Essays.* London: Macmillan, 1897.

———. *Science and Education.* New York: Collier, 1902.

Inwood, M. J. "Hegel, Plato, and Greek '*Sittlichkeit.*'" In *The State and Civil Society,* edited by Z. A. Pelczynski, 40–54.Cambridge: Cambridge University Press, 1984.

Irwin, T. H. "Mill and the Classical World." In *The Cambridge Companion to Mill,* edited by John Skorupski, 423–63. Cambridge: Cambridge University Press, 1998.

Jefferson, Thomas. *The Portable Jefferson.* Edited by Merrill D. Peterson. New York: Viking, 1975.

Jenkyns, Richard. *The Victorians and Ancient Greece.* Cambridge: Harvard University Press, 1980.

Jones, H. S. "John Stuart Mill as Moralist." *Journal of the History of Ideas* 53 (1992): 287–308.

Jowett, Benjamin. *Sermons on Doctrine and Faith.* Edited by W. H. Freemantle. London: Murray, 1901.

Kahan, Alan. *Aristocratic Liberalism: The Social and Political Thought of Jacob Burkhardt, John Stuart Mill, and Alexis de Tocqueville.* Oxford: Oxford University Press, 1992.

Kahn, Charles. *Plato and the Socratic Dialogue.* Cambridge: Cambridge University Press, 1996.

Kant, Immanuel. *Critique of Practical Reason.* In *Practical Philosophy,* translated and edited by Mary Gregor, 139–271. Cambridge: Cambridge University Press, 1996.

———. *Critique of Pure Reason.* Edited by Norman Kemp Smith. New York: St. Martin's Press, 1965.

———. *The Groundwork of the Metaphysics of Morals.* In *Practical Philosophy,* translated and edited by Mary Gregor, 37–108. Cambridge: Cambridge University Press, 1996.

———. *Lectures on Ethics.* Translated by Louis Infield. New York: Harper, 1963.

———. *The Metaphysics of Morals.* In *Practical Philosophy,* translated and edited by Mary Gregor, 353–603. Cambridge: Cambridge University Press, 1996.

———. "On the common saying: 'That may be correct in theory, but it is of no use in practice.'" In *Practical Philosophy,* translated and edited by Mary Gregor, 279–309. Cambridge: Cambridge University Press, 1980.

———. *Religion Within the Limits of Reason Alone.* Translated by Theodore M. Greene and Hoyt H. Hudson. San Fransisco: Harper and Row, 1960.

———. "Toward Perpetual Peace." In *Practical Philosophy,* translated and edited by Mary Gregor, 313–51. Cambridge: Cambridge University Press, 1980.

Kateb, George. "A Reading of On Liberty." In *On Liberty—John Stuart Mill,* edited by David Bromwich and George Kateb, 28–66. New Haven: Yale University Press, 2003.

Kelly, George Armstrong. *Idealism, Politics and History: Soures of Hegelian Thought.* Cambridge: Cambridge University Press, 1969.

Knights, Ben. *The Idea of the Clerisy in the Nineteenth Century.* Cambridge: Cambridge University Press, 1978.

Knox, John. "The Debate in the General Assembly." In *On Rebellion,* edited by Roger A. Mason, 182–209. Cambridge: Cambridge University Press, 1994.

———. "The First Blast of the Trumpet." In *On Rebellion,* edited by Roger A. Mason, 3–47. Cambridge: Cambridge University Press, 1994.

Korsgaard, Christine. "Morality as Freedom." In *Kant's Practical Philosophy Reconsidered,* edited by Yirmiyahu Yovel, 123–48. Dordrecht: Kluwer, 1989.

Krause, Sharon. *Liberalism with Honor.* Cambridge: Harvard University Press, 2002.

Lachterman, D. R. *The Ethics of Geometry: A Genealogy of Modernity.* London: Routledge, 1989.

Lampert, Laurence. *Leo Strauss and Nietzsche.* Chicago: University of Chicago Press, 1996.

———. *Nietzsche's Teachings: An Interpretation of Thus Spoke Zarathustra.* New Haven: Yale University Press, 1986.

Larmore, Charles. *The Morals of Modernity.* Cambridge: Cambridge University Press, 1996.

———. *Patterns of Moral Complexity.* Cambridge: Cambridge University Press, 1987.

Lecky, W. H. *The Rise and Influence of the Spirit of Rationalism in Europe.* London: Longmans, 1884.

Letwin, Shirley. *The Pursuit of Certainty.* Cambridge: Cambridge University Press, 1965.

Levine, George. "Scientific Discourse as an Alternative to Faith." In *Victorian Faith in Crisis,* edited by Richard J. Helmstadter and Bernard Lightman, 225–61. Stanford: Stanford University Press, 1990.

Lightman, Bernard, "Robert Elsmere and the Agnostic Crisis of Faith." In *Victorian Faith in Crisis,* edited by Richard J. Helmstadter and Bernard Lightman, 283–313. Stanford: Stanford University Press, 1990.

Locke, John. *An Essay Concerning Human Understanding.* Edited by Peter Nidditch. Oxford: Oxford University Press, 1975.

———. *A Letter on Toleration.* Edited by Raymond Klibansky. Oxford: Clarendon, 1968.

———. *The Reasonableness of Christianity.* Edited by I. T. Ramsey. Stanford: Stanford University Press, 1958.

———. *Two Treatises on Government.* Edited by Peter Laslett. Cambridge: Cambridge University Press, 1966.

Lovejoy, A. O. "On the Discrimination of Romanticisms." In *Essays on the History of Ideas,* 228–53. Baltimore: Johns Hopkins University Press, 1948.

Macaulay, Thomas. "Lord Bacon." In *Critical, Historical, and Miscellaneous Essays,* vol. 3, bk. 2: 336–495. Boston: Houghton, Mifflin, 1880.

Macedo, Stephen. *Diversity and Distrust: Civic Education in a Multicultural Democracy.* Cambridge: Harvard University Press.

———. "Liberal Civic Education and Religious Fundamentalism: The Case of God v. John Rawls?" *Ethics* 105 (1995): 468–96.

———. *Liberal Virtues: Citizenship, Virtue, and Community in Liberal Constitutionalism.* Oxford: Oxford University Press, 1990.

Machiavelli, Niccolò. *Discourses on Livy.* Translated by Harvey C. Mansfield and Nathan Tarcov. Chicago: University of Chicago Press, 1999.

———. *The Prince.* Translated by Harvey C. Mansfield. Chicago: University of Chicago Press, 1985.

MacIntyre, Alasdair. *Whose Justice? Which Rationality?* Notre Dame: University of Notre Dame Press, 1988.

MacKinnon, Catharine. *Toward a Feminist Theory of the State.* Cambridge: Harvard University Press, 1989.

Macpherson, C. B. *The Political Theory of Individualism.* London: Oxford University Press, 1962.

Mandelbaum, Maurice. *History, Man and Reason.* Baltimore: Johns Hopkins University Press, 1971.

Mannheim, Karl. *Ideology and Utopia.* Translated by Louis Wirth and Edward Shils. New York: Norton, 1963.

Mansfield, Harvey. *Machiavelli's Virtue.* Chicago: University of Chicago Press.

Mara, Gerald. *Socrates' Discursive Democracy.* Albany: SUNY Press, 1997.

———, and Suzanne Dovi. "Mill, Nietzsche, and the Identity of Postmodern Liberalism." *Journal of Politics* 57 (1995): 1–23.

Martineau, Harriet. *Autobiography.* Edited by Maria Weston Chapman. 2 vols. London: Longmans, 1877.

Martineau, James. "John Stuart Mill." In *Essays, Reviews, and Addresses.* 4 vols. London: Longmans, 1890–91.

Marx, Karl. "On the Jewish Question." In *The Marx-Engels Reader,* edited by Robert C. Tucker, 26–52. New York: Norton, 1978.

———. "Theses on Feuerbach." In *The Marx-Engels Reader,* edited by Robert C. Tucker, 143–45. New York: Norton, 1978.

M'Crie, Thomas. *Life of John Knox.* Edinburgh: Blackwood, 1855.

Megill, Allan D. "J. S. Mill's Religion of Humanity and the Second Justification for the Writing of *On Liberty.*" In *Mill and the Moral Character of Liberalism,* edited by Eldon Eisenach, 301–16. University Park: Pennsylvania State University Press, 1998. First published in *Journal of Politics* 34 (1972).

Meinecke, Friedrich. *Historism: The Rise of a New Historical Order.* Translated by J. E. Anderson. London: Routledge, 1972.

Melzer, Arthur. *On the Natural Goodness of Man: On the System of Rousseau's Thought.* Chicago: University of Chicago Press, 1990.

Mill, James. "Essay on Government." In *Utilitarian Logic and Politics,* edited by Jack Lively and John Rees, 55–95. Oxford: Oxford University Press, 1978.

Moore, James. "Theodicy and Society: The Crisis of the Intelligentsia." In *Victorian Faith in Crisis,* edited by Richard J. Helmstadter and Bernard Lightman, 153–86. Stanford: Stanford University Press, 1990.

Morales, Maria. *Perfect Equality: John Stuart Mill on Well-Constituted Communities.* Lanham, Md.: Rowman and Littlefield, 1996.

Morley, John. *Critical Miscellanies.* 4 vols. London: Macmillan, 1898–1908.

———. "Mr. Mill's Autobiography." *Fortnightly Review* 21 (1874).

Muirhead, Russell. *Just Work.* Cambridge: Harvard University Press, 2004.

Nicholson, Peter. *The Political Philosophy of British Idealism: Selected Studies.* Cambridge: Cambridge University Press, 1990.

———. "The Reception and Early Reputation of Mill's Political Thought." In *The Cambridge Companion to Mill,* edited by John Skorupski, 464–96. Cambridge: Cambridge University Press, 1998.

Nietzsche, Friedrich. *Antichrist.* In *The Portable Nietzsche,* translated and edited by Walter Kaufmann, 565–656. New York: Viking Penguin, 1954.

———. *Beyond Good and Evil: Prelude to a Philosophy of the Future.* Translated by Walter Kaufmann. New York: Vintage, 1966.

———. *The Gay Science.* Translated by Walter Kaufmann. New York: Vintage, 1974.

———. *Genealogy of Morals.* Translated by Walter Kaufmann. New York: Vintage, 1967.

———. "Homer's Contest." In *The Portable Nietzsche,* translated and edited by Walter Kaufmann, 32–39. New York: Viking, 1978.

———. *Human, All too Human.* Translated by R. J. Hollingdale. Cambridge: Cambridge University Press, 1996.

———. *On the Advantages and Disadvantages of History for Life.* Translated by Peter Preuss. Indianapolis: Hackett, 1990.

———. "Socrates." In *The Pre-Platonic Philosophers,* translated and edited by Greg Whitlock, 42–50. Urbana: University of Illinois Press, 1995.

———. *Thus Spoke Zarathustra.* In *The Portable Nietzsche,* translated and edited by Walter Kaufmann, 121–442. New York: Viking, 1978.

———. *The Twilight of the Idols.* Translated by R. J. Hollingdale. New York: Penguin, 1990.

———. *The Will to Power.* Translated by Walter Kaufmann and R. J. Hollingdale. New York: Vintage, 1968.

Oakeshott, Michael. *Morality and Politics in Modern Europe: The Harvard Lectures.* Edited by Shirley Letwin. New Haven: Yale University Press, 1993.

O'Neill, Onora. "Duties and Virtue." In *Royal Institute of Philosophy Supplement: 35,* edited by A. Phillips Griffiths, 107–20. Cambridge: Cambridge University Press, 1993.

Paley, William. *Considerations on the Theory of Religion.* London: Rodwell and Martin, 1820.

Pangle, Thomas. "The Roots of Contemporary Nihilism and Its Political Consequences According to Nietzsche." *Review of Politics* 45 (1983): 45–70.

———. *The Spirit of Modern Republicanism.* Chicago: University of Chicago Press, 1988.

Pappe, H. O. "Mill and Tocqueville." *Journal of the History of Ideas* 25 (1964): 217–38.

Pippin, Robert. "Ethical Reasons, Kantian Rejoinders." In *Idealism as Modernism,* 92–128. Cambridge: Cambridge University Press, 1997.

Plato. *Meno.* In *Plato in Twelve Volumes,* translated and edited by W. R. M. Lamb. Cambridge: Harvard University Press, 1990.

———. *Phaedrus.* Translated by Alexander Nehamas and Paul Woodruff. Indianapolis: Hackett, 1995.

———. *The Republic of Plato.* Translated by Allan Bloom. New York: Basic, 1968.

———. *Plato's Sophist: Part II of the Being and the Beautiful.* Translated by Seth Benardete. Chicago: University of Chicago Press, 1986.

———. *Plato's Statesman: Part III of the Being and the Beautiful.* Translated by Seth Bernadete Chicago: University of Chicago Press, 1984.

———. *Plato's Symposium.* Translated by Seth Bernadete. Chicago: University of Chicago Press, 1986.

———. *Timaeus.* In *Readings in Ancient Greek Philosophy: From Thales to Aristotle,* edited by S. Marc Cohen, Patricia Curd, and C. D. C. Reeve. Indianapolis: Hackett, 2000.

Popper, Karl. *The Poverty of Historicism.* London: Routledge, 1957.

Porter, Roy, and Mikulas Teich, eds. *The Enlightenment in National Context.* Cambridge: Cambridge University Press, 1981.

Posner, Richard. "On Liberty: A Revaluation." In *On Liberty—John Stuart Mill,* edited by David Bromwich and George Kateb, 197–207. New Haven: Yale University Press, 2003.

Price, A. W. "Wordsworth's Ode on the Intimations of Immortality." In *Platonism and the English Imagination,* edited by Anna Baldwin and Sarah Hutton, 217–28. Cambridge: Cambridge University Press, 1994.

Pufendorf, Samuel. *The Law of Nature and Nations.* Translated by C. H. Oldfather and W. A. Oldfather. Oxford: Clarendon, 1934.

———. *On the Duty of Man and Citizen.* Translated by Michael Silverthorne, edited by James Tully. Cambridge: Cambridge University Press, 1991.

Raeder, Linda. *John Stuart Mill and the Religion of Humanity.* Columbia: University of Missouri Press, 2002.

Rawls, John. *Political Liberalism.* New York: Columbia University Press, 1993.

Rees, John. *John Stuart Mill's On Liberty.* Oxford: Oxford University Press, 1985.

Reventlow, Henning Graf. *The Authority of the Bible and the Rise of the Modern World.* Translated by John Bowden. London: First Fortress Press, 1985.

Riley, Patrick. *Kant's Political Philosophy.* Totowa, N.J.: Rowman and Littlefield, 1983.

———. *Will and Political Legitimacy: A Critical Exposition of Social Contract Theory in Hobbes, Locke, Rousseau, Kant, and Hegel.* Cambridge: Cambridge University Press, 1982.

Robson, J. M. *The Improvement of Mankind: The Social and Political Thought of John Stuart Mill.* Toronto: University of Toronto Press, 1968.

Rorty, Richard. *Contingency, Irony, and Solidarity.* Cambridge: Cambridge University Press, 1989.

Rosenblum, Nancy. *Another Liberalism: Romanticism and the Reconstruction of Liberal Thought.* Cambridge: Harvard University Press, 1987.

Rousseau, Jean-Jacques. *The Confessions.* In *The Collected Writings of Rousseau,* edited by Roger Masters and Christopher Kelly. 11 vols. to date. Hanover: University Press of New England, 1990–.

———. "Discourse on the Origins of Inequality." In *The Basic Political Writings,* translated and edited by Donald A. Cress, 45–81. Indianapolis: Hackett, 1987.

———. *Émile, or On Education.* Translated by Allan Bloom. New York: Basic Books, 1979.

———. *The Reveries of the Solitary Walker.* Translated by Charles E. Butterworth. Indianapolis: Hackett, 1992.

———. *The Social Contract.* In *The Basic Political Writings,* translated and edited by Donald A. Cress, 139–227. Indianapolis: Hackett, 1987.

Ryan, Alan. "John Stuart Mill and the Art of Living." In *J. S. Mill, "On Liberty" in Focus.* edited by John Gray and G. W. Smith, 9–17. New York: Routledge, 1991. First published in *The Listener* 74 (1965).

———. "John Stuart Mill and the Open Society." *The Listener* 89 (1973).

———. *John Stuart Mill.* London: Pantheon, 1970.

———. *J. S. Mill.* London: Routledge, 1974.

———. "Mill in a Liberal Landscape." In *The Cambridge Companion to Mill,* edited by John Skorupski, 497–540. Cambridge: Cambridge University Press, 1998.

———. "Sense and Sensibility in Mill's Political Thought." In *A Cultivated Mind: Essays on J. S. Mill Presented to John M. Robson.* edited by Michael Laine, 121–38. Toronto: University of Toronto Press, 1991.

Salkever, Stephen. *Finding the Mean: Theory and Practice in Aristotelian Political Philosophy.* Princeton: Princeton University Press, 1990.

Sandel, Michael. *Democracy's Discontent.* Oxford: Oxford University Press, 1998.

———. *Liberalism and the Limits of Justice.* Cambridge: Cambridge University Press, 1982.

Saxonhouse, Arlene. *Athenian Democracy: Modern Mythmakers and Ancient Theorists.* Notre Dame: University of Notre Dame Press, 1996.

Scarre, Geoffrey. "Mill on Induction and the Scientific Method." In *The Cambridge Com-*

panion to Mill, edited by John Skorupski, 112–38. Cambridge: Cambridge University Press, 1998.

Schelling, F. W. J. *Idealism and the Endgame of Theory.* Translated by Thomas Pfau. Albany: SUNY Press, 1994.

———. "Kant, Fichte, and the System of Transcendental Idealism." In *On the History of Modern Philosophy,* translated and edited by Andrew Bowie, 94–114. Cambridge: Cambridge University Press, 1994.

———. *Of Human Freedom.* Translated by James Gutmann. Chicago: Open Court, 1936.

Schiller, Friedrich, *On the Aesthetic Education of Man.* Translated by Elizabeth M. Wilkinson and L. A. Willoughby. Oxford: Clarendon, 1967.

Schleiermacher, Friedrich. *Christmas Eve: Dialogue on the Incarnation.* Translated by Terrence Tice. Richmond: John Knox Press, 1967.

———. *Dialectic, or the Art of Doing Philosophy.* Translated by Terrence Tice. Atlanta: Scholars Press, 1996.

———. "On the Worth of Socrates as a Philosopher." Translated by William Smith. In *A Life of Socrates.* edited by Gustav Friedrich Wiggers, cxxix–clv. London: Taylor and Walton, 1840.

———. *Schleiermacher's Introductions to the Dialogues of Plato.* Translated by William Dobson. London: Taylor and Walton, 1840.

Schneewind, J. B. *The Invention of Autonomy.* Cambridge: Cambridge University Press, 1998.

———. "The Misfortunes of Virtue." *Ethics* 101 (1990): 42–63.

———. *Sidgwick's Ethics and Victorian Moral Philosophy.* Oxford: Clarendon, 1977.

Schopenhauer, Arthur. *Prize Essay on the Freedom of the Will.* Translated by Eric Payne. Cambridge: Cambridge University Press, 1999.

Semmel, Bernard. *John Stuart Mill and the Pursuit of Virtue.* New Haven: Yale University Press, 1984.

———. "John Stuart Mill's Coleridgean Neoradicalism." In *Mill and the Moral Character of Liberalism,* edited by Eldon Eisenach, 49–76. University Park: Pennsylvania State University Press, 1998. First published in *Political Science Reviewer* 24 (1995).

Shanley, Mary Lyndon. "Marital Slavery and Friendship: John Stuart Mill's *Subjection of Women.*" *Political Theory* 9 (1981): 229–47.

Shelley, Percy. *Adonais.* In *The Complete Works of Percy Bysshe Shelley,* edited by Roger Ingpen and Walter E. Peck. 10 volumes. London: Longmans, 1926–30.

———. "In Defense of Poetry." In *The Complete Works of Percy Bysshe Shelley,* edited by Roger Ingpen and Walter E. Peck. 10 vols. London: Longmans, 1926–30.

———. *The Letters of Percy Bysshe Shelley.* Edited by Frederick L. Jones. 2 vols. Oxford: Oxford University Press, 1964.

———. "Refutation of Deism." In *The Complete Works of Percy Bysshe Shelley,* edited by Roger Ingpen and Walter E. Peck. 10 vols. London: Longmans, 1926–30.

Shields, Christopher. "Socrates Among the Skeptics." In *The Socratic Movement.* edited by Paul A. Vander Waerdt, 341–66. Ithaca: Cornell University Press, 1994.

Shklar, Judith. "Hegel's 'Phenomenology': An Elegy for *Hellas.*" In *Hegel's Political Philosophy.* edited by Z. A. Pelczynski, 71–94. Cambridge: Cambridge University Press, 1971.

———. "The Liberalism of Fear." In *Liberalism and the Moral Life,* edited by Nancy Rosenblum, 21–38. Cambridge: Harvard University Press, 1991.

Sidgwick, Arthur, and Elenor Sidgwick. *Henry Sidgwick: A Memoir.* London: Macmillan 1906.

Skorupski, John. "The Ethical Content of Liberal Law." In *Ethical Explorations,* 213–33. Oxford: Oxford University Press, 1999.

———. "Introduction: The Fortunes of Liberal Naturalism." In *The Cambridge Companion to Mill,* edited by John Skorupski, 1–34. Cambridge: Cambridge University Press, 1998.

———. *John Stuart Mill.* London: Routledge, 1989.

Smith, Adam. "History of Ancient Physics." In *Essays on Philosophical Subjects,* edited by W. P. D. Wightman and J. C. Bryce. Indianapolis: Liberty Press, 1982.

———. *An Inquiry into the Nature and Causes of the Wealth of Nations.* Edited by R. H. Campbell and A. S. Skinner. 2 vols. Indianapolis: Liberty Press, 1976.

———. *The Theory of Moral Sentiments.* Indianapolis: Liberty Classics, 1976.

Smith, G. W. "Freedom and Virtue in Politics: Some Aspects of Character, Circumstances, and Utility from Helvétius to J. S. Mill." *Utilitas* 1 (1989): 112–34.

———. "J. S. Mill on Liberty." In *Conceptions of Liberty in Political Philosophy,* edited by Z. A. Pelczynski and John Gray, 183–216. New York: St. Martin's Press, 1984.

———. "The Logic of J. S. Mill On Freedom." *Political Studies* 28 (1980): 238–52.

Smith, Rogers. *Civic Ideals: Conflicting Visions of Citizenship in U.S. History.* New Haven: Yale University Press, 1997.

Smith, Steven B. *Hegel's Critique of Liberalism: Rights in Context.* Chicago: University of Chicago Press, 1989.

———. *Spinoza, Liberalism, and the Question of Jewish Identity.* New Haven: Yale University Press, 1997.

Spencer, Herbert. *First Principles.* New York: Bost, 1880.

———. "On Moral Character." In *John Stuart Mill: His Life and Work, Twelve Sketches.* edited by Herbert Spencer et al., 46–51. Boston: Osgod and Company, 1873.

Spinoza, Baruch. *Ethics.* Translated and edited by G. H. R. Parkinson. Oxford: Oxford University Press, 2000.

———. *Theological-Political Treatise.* Translated by Samuel Shirley, edited by Seymour Feldman. Indianapolis: Hackett, 2001.

Stephen, James Fitzjames. "The Laws of England as to the Expressions of Religious Opinions." *Contemporary Review* 25 (1875): 459–71.

———. *Liberty, Equality, Fraternity.* Edited by R. J. White. Cambridge: Cambridge University Press, 1967.

Stockoe, F. W. *German Influence in the English Romantic Period.* Cambridge: Cambridge University Press, 1926.

Strauss, Leo. *Natural Right and History.* Chicago: University of Chicago, 1953.

———. "Note on the Plan of Nietzsche's *Beyond Good and Evil.* In *Stdudies in Platonic Political Philosophy.* Chicago: University of Chicago Press, 1983.

Sullivan, Roger. *Kant's Moral Theory.* Cambridge: Cambridge University Press, 1989.

Sullivan, Vickie. *Machiavelli, Hobbes, and the Formation of a Liberal Republicanism in England.* Cambridge: Cambridge University Press, 2004.

Tarcov, Nathan. *Locke's Education for Liberty.* Chicago: University of Chicago Press, 1984.

Taylor, Charles. *The Ethics of Authenticity.* Cambridge: Harvard University Press, 1991.

———. *Sources of the Self: The Making of Modern Identity.* Cambridge: Cambridge University Press, 1989.

———. *Hegel.* Cambridge: Cambridge University Press, 1975.

Ten, C. L. *Mill on Liberty.* Oxford: Clarendon Press, 1989.

———. "Mill's Defense of *On Liberty.*" In *Traditions of Liberalism: Essays on Locke, Smith, and Mill,* edited by Knud Haakonssen, 37–54. Sydney: Centre of Independent Studies, 1988.

Tennyson, Hallam. *Alfred Lord Tennyson: A Memoir by His Son.* 4 vols. London: Macmillan, 1893.

Terchek, Ronald. "The Fruits of Success and the Crisis of Liberalism." In *Liberals on Liberalism,* edited by Alfonso J. Damico, 18–33. Totowa, N.J.: Rowman and Littlefield, 1986.

Thomson, Dennis. *John Stuart Mill and Representative Government.* Princeton: Princeton University Press, 1976.

Thorlby, Antony. "Liberty and Self-Development: Goethe and John Stuart Mill." *Neo-Helicon* I (1973): 91–110.

Thucydides. *History of the Peloponnesian War.* Translated by Rex Warner. New York: Penguin Books, 1954.

Tigerstedt, E. N. *Interpreting Plato.* Stockholm: Almqvist and Wilskell, 1977.

Tocqueville, Alexis de. *Democracy in America.* Translated and edited by Harvey Mansfield and Delba Winthrop. Chicago: University of Chicago Press, 2000.

———. *Ouvres Complètes.* Edited by J. P. Mayer. 10 vols. to date. Gallimard, 1951–.

Tuck, Richard. "The 'Modern' Theory of Natural Law." In *The Languages of Political Theory in Early-Modern Europe,* edited by Anthony Padgen, 99–119. Cambridge: Cambridge University Press, 1987.

———. *Natural Rights Theories.* Cambridge: Cambridge University Press, 1979.

Tulloch, Gail. *Mill and Sexual Equality.* Hertfordshire, United Kingdom: Harvester Wheatsheaf, 1989.

Turner, Frank. *Greek Heritage in Victorian Britain.* New Haven: Yale University Press, 1981.

———. "The Victorian Crisis of Faith and the Faith that Was Lost." In *Victorian Faith in Crisis,* edited by Richard J. Helmstadter and Bernard Lightman, 9–38. Stanford: Stanford University Press, 1990.

Urbinati, Nadia. "John Stuart Mill on Androgyny and Ideal Marriage." *Political Theory* 19 (1991): 626–48.

———. *Mill on Democracy: From the Athenian Demos to Representative Government.* Chicago: University of Chicago Press, 2002.

Velkley, Richard. *Freedom and the End of Reason: On the Moral Foundation of Kant's Critical Philosophy.* Chicago: University of Chicago Press, 1989.

Vernon, Richard. "Beyond the Harm Principle: Mill and Censorship." In *Mill and the Moral Character of Liberalism,* edited by Eldon Eisenach, 115–30. University Park: Pennsylvania State University Press, 1998. First published in *Ethics* 106 (1996).

Villa, Dana. *Socratic Citizenship.* Princeton: Princeton University Press, 2001.

Voltaire. *Philosophical Letters.* Translated by Ernest Dilworth. New York: Macmillan, 1961.

Waldron, Jeremy. "Locke, Toleration, and the Rationality of Persecution." In *Liberal Rights,* 88–114. Cambridge: Cambridge University Press, 1993.

———. "Mill and the Value of Moral Distress." In *Liberal Rights,* 115–33. Cambridge: Cambridge University Press, 1993.

———. "Mill on Culture and Society." In *On Liberty—John Stuart Mill,* edited by David Bromwich and George Kateb, 224–45. New Haven: Yale University Press, 2003.

———. "A Right to Do Wrong." In *Liberal Rights,* 63–87. Cambridge: Cambridge University Press, 1993.

Wallace, Jennifer. *Shelley and Greece: Rethinking Romantic Hellenism.* London: Macmillan, 1997.

Weber, Max. *The Protestant Ethic and the Spirit of Capitalism.* Translated by Talcott Parsons. New York: Scribner's, 1958.

Williams, Bernard. *Moral Luck.* Cambridge: Cambridge University Press, 1981.

Williams, Geraint. "The Greek Origins of J. S. Mill's Happiness." *Utilitas* 8 (1996): 5–15.

Wilson, Fred. *Psychological Analysis and the Philosophy of John Stuart Mill.* Toronto: University of Toronto Press, 1990.

———. "Mill on Psychology and the Moral Sciences." In *The Cambridge Companion to Mill,* edited by John Skorupski, 203–54. Cambridge: Cambridge University Press, 1998.

Wolfe, Alan. *One Nation, After All: What Middle-Class Americans Really Think About.* New York: Penguin, 1999.

Wollheim, Richard. "John Stuart Mill and Isaiah Berlin: The Ends of Life and Preliminaries of Morality." In *The Idea of Freedom: Essays in Honor of Isaiah Berlin,* edited by Alan Ryan, 253–70. Oxford: Oxford University Press, 1979.

———. "John Stuart Mill and the Limits of State Action," *Social Research* 40 (1973): 1–30.

Wood, Allan. *Hegel's Ethical Thought.* Cambridge: Cambridge University Press, 1990.

Wordsworth, William. "Ode: Intimations of Immortality from Recollections of Early Childhood." In *Wordsworth's Poetical Works,* edited by Thomas Hutchinson, rev. ed. Ernest de Selincourt, 460–62. Oxford: Oxford University Press, 1974.

———. "Essay, Supplementary to the Preface of 1815." In *Wordsworth's Literary Criticisms,* edited by W. J. B. Owen, 192–218. London: Routledge, 1975.

———. "Preface and Appendix to the *Lyrical Ballads.*" In *Wordsworth's Literary Criticisms,* edited by W. J. B. Owen, 68–95. London: Routledge, 1975.

———. "Preface of 1815." In *Wordsworth's Literary Criticisms,* edited by W. J. B. Owen, 175–91. London: Routledge, 1975.

———. *The Prelude.* In *Wordsworth's Poetical Works,* edited by Thomas Hutchinson, rev. ed. Ernest de Selincourt, 494–588. Oxford: Oxford University Press, 1974.

Yack, Bernie. "The Problem with Kantian Liberalism." In *Kant and Political Philosophy: The Contemporary Legacy,* edited by Ronald Beiner and William James Booth, 224–44. New Haven: Yale University Press, 1993.

Zuckert, Catherine. *Postmodern Platos.* Chicago: University of Chicago Press, 1996.

Index

Adeimantus, 25, 172

Aeschylus, 19

Agis, 99

Alcibiades, 16, 80, 96–98, 164, 169–71

American civil war, 140

Anaxagoras, 123–24

Anaximander, 88

Ancients, 6, 17, 55–56, 63, 74, 95, 96, 97, 172–73, 177, 106, 217; and Descartes, 175–76; and German Romantics, 17; and Hellenism, 6, 182, 272n50; and Hobbes, 93; and Hume, 93; and Locke, 93, 174; and Mill, 2, 13–14, 38, 49, 72, 74–77, 93–94, 104, 119–22, 123–25, 145, 161–62, 177–79, 181, 188, 198, 212; and moderns, 3, 55–56, 177–78; and Nietzsche, 8, 184, 208; and Rousseau, 99, 175–76. *See also* Alcibiades, Aristotle, Athens, Plato, Sparta

Anglo-Scottish tradition, 4, 7, 15, 31–37, 41–43, 47–48, 49, 106, 207, 213, 232;

and Mill, 3, 5, 7, 45, 48–50, 106, 112–13, 122, 125–30, 142, 156–57. *See also* empiricism, Enlightenment, liberalism

Annas, Julia, 54

Apollo, 75, 191

Arendt, Hannah, 95

Aristedes, 40

Aristocracy, 58, 89, 225

Aristotle, 53–55, 74–75, 172, 212, 218, 221–22, 243n22, 270n20; and Mill, 53–55, 75, 123–24, 177, 212, 222

Arnold, Matthew, 147, and Mill, 272n50

Associational psychology, and Coleridge, 31, 33–35; and Grote, 32; and Hegel, 33; and Hobbes, 32–33; and Hume, 32; and Kant, 33; and Locke, 32, 33, 37, 41; and Mill, 31–35, 41–45, 68, 99–102; and Mill and Plato, 35–38; and Smith, 41–42; and Wordsworth, 34–35. *See also* empiricism

Athens, 27, 95–98, 101–02, 123–24, 164,